AF890920

Marta Gnyp

YOU ME AND ART

Artists in the 21st Century

SKIRA

Cover
Robert Longo
Untitled (Jules)
from the series *Men in the Cities*, 1979–1983
Charcoal and graphite on paper, 243.8 × 152.4 cm
Collection of Centre Pompidou, Paris

Design
Marcello Francone

Editorial Coordination
Eva Vanzella

Copy editor
Lorenzo Barbieri Hermitte

Layout
Barbara Galotta

First published in Italy in 2018 by
Skira editore S.p.A.
Palazzo Casati Stampa
via Torino 61
20123 Milano
Italy
www.skira.net

© 2018 GNYP GmbH, Berlin
© 2018 Skira editore, Milan
© Carl Andre, Robert Longo by SIAE 2018
© Damien Hirst and Science Ltd. All rights reserved by SIAE 2018
© Anish Kapoor. All Rights Reserved, DACS/SIAE, by SIAE 2018

All rights reserved under international copyright conventions.
No part of this book may be reproduced or utilised in any form or by any means, electronic or mechanical, including photocopying, recording, or any information storage and retrieval system, without permission in writing from the publisher.

Printed and bound in Italy.
First edition

ISBN: 978-88-572-3832-6

Distributed in USA, Canada, Central & South America by ARTBOOK | D.A.P. 75, Broad Street Suite 630, New York, NY 10004, USA.
Distributed elsewhere in the world by Thames and Hudson Ltd., 181A High Holborn, London WC1V 7QX, United Kingdom.

CONTENTS

INTRODUCTION

If I wasn't me, I guess I wouldn't be who I am
Mark Bradford

A friend of mine recently made a comment about an artist she had just met: "He doesn't look like an artist. He's so normal". She seemed a bit puzzled because he didn't fit in with her idea of an artist: bohemian, rule breaker and idealist who is "living his life to the full". I can understand her hidden disappointment. I remember reading in awe about Willem de Kooning, who in the 1940s had so little money that after a day working in his studio he had to decide whether he would eat something or smoke cigarettes.[1] I admired Lee Krasner and Jackson Pollock who had only lived to make art – even in a barn without electricity.[2] I regretted not having lived in the East Village in New York City in the 1980s as it seemed to be one big ongoing party with artists dressed like birds of paradise.[3] All for art's sake.

I still love reading these stories, but today they somehow feel like documents of the past. Obviously, there are still artists who live a bohemian life or live it from time to time, but interest in bohemia as a template for living an artistic life is gone. Today's bohemian model seems to be the territory of hipsters. Expensive jeans look like homemade, shabby artists' garments and go perfectly with excessive and not-at-all-subversive tattoos. Bohemia has become a term with a historical meaning, but it's no longer a relevant alternative for an artistic existence.

What's more, artists neither demand that people change the way they live their lives, nor do they want to be a kind of Salvation Army. Even the idea of the artist as a shaman has been tamed: Glenn Brown called it something that information passes through without having a sense of being original.[4] The overwhelming majority of artists don't want to start a revolution, nor do they want to burn down museums to start from a zero point. Even if their art sharply contrasts with what was made by previous generations, today's artists tend to speak with deep respect of the past, as will become clear in the interviews. A telling metaphor for this attitude is the imaginary gentle embrace of Michaël Borremans by Rembrandt when the Belgian artist visited Rembrandt's House in Amsterdam and looked at the master's etchings, full of admiration. Sean Scully used another seventeenth-century North European artist to make his point. In his opinion, today's artist is no longer like a traveling gypsy or an existential figure in an attic, but more like Peter Paul Rubens, a worldly and socially powerful figure.

Is there any common denominator for contemporary artists then, especially when everything can be art and when everything ever done can be redone? Or, to paraphrase Damien Hirst, is the thing today's artists have most in common the fact that they have nothing in common, and that's just fine? These and many other questions arose during my interviews with the outstanding contemporary artists that are included in this book. The interviews also provide a great material with which to analyze the changing art world and transformations in our existing art system. As artists operate in close connection with curators, collectors, and gallerists, I have given voice to a few excellent actors from these categories to make the picture more complete. François Pinault speaks about his experiences and his vision of contemporary art as a collector; Anthony d'Offay reflects on artists and the post-war art system from the perspective of a gallerist, while Demetrio Paparoni reflects on the state of contemporary art as an art historian, curator, and critic. My insider perspective as an art advisor, collector, art historian and art sociologist allow me to add a few aspects of the contemporary art world that I present at the end of this introduction.

> *Art is mediation between human beings expressed*
> *through a physical object*
> Carl Andre

Artists make art, which floats somewhere between religion, philosophy, decoration, and social mileage bonus card. Nothing new. Still, over hundreds of years of existence, art has succeeded in maintaining its strange and ungraspable character. Some things will never change: art is what artists make and in return, art is what makes artists into artists.[5] The core activity of being an artist is thus the idea of making art. All artists included in this book claim that artwork needs to have a physical presence in the world. Many artists stressed that an idea could only become true by doing something, and many would agree with Mark Grotjahn who argued that it is "one thing to say you know something mentally but it is another thing to actually know it physically".

Consequently, for most of today's artists the studio has remained the central place of their artistic existence; a place where creation meets destruction, power meets failure, where daily boredom can turn into sparks of energy beyond human understanding. The notion of (divine) inspiration has disappeared from the vocabulary of contemporary artists; instead, there is the daily struggle, hard work, and organization of labor. However, despite this mundane description of creative processes, making art continues to be somehow magical. I could condense many artists' statements about these processes into one sentence: you can't force art, you can only create a situation in which art can happen.

Artists make art, which brings us to another solid component of artistic thinking: the medium, which in most cases is no longer understood within the modernistic imperative of purity. Today's artists are aware of the history of the medium they use. This does, however, not stop them but in fact seems to encourage them to mix, borrow, and appropriate from other media and investigate the limits of their chosen medium. We are living in eclectic times with a continuation of great historical traditions going hand-in-hand with permanent border crossings of strategies and concepts.

Contemporary art seems to have produced a liberated art system, at least from the aesthetic point of view. As Demetrio Paparoni mentioned, being outside of any ideological system means that artists have enormous freedom and don't need to apply codes in order to be considered contemporary. An artistic strategy and its logic have become more relevant for each separate oeuvre than loyalty to one singular medium and its specificities. Kaari Upson has embraced all kind of media for her projects, varying between performance, installation, drawings, and sculptures. For Damien Hirst, thinking in terms of one medium alone has lost its relevancy since, in his opinion, a single approach cannot reflect our multifaceted world. Next to a variety of methodologies, delving profoundly into the characteristics of one single medium has, however, remained a serious path for an artistic career. Mary Corse has been consistently focused on painting and its relation to light. Painting in the broad sense, as an interpretation of reality seeking its way into constructed images, formed the life-long fascination for Wojciech Fangor.

The very process of making art varies from artist to artist as well. While assistants allow Robert Longo to create a distance to his work that offers him new insights into what could be done better, for Sean Scully painting using his own hand is the ultimate act of creation. Whereas Walton Ford cannot conceive of working in any other way than by himself, Damien Hirst makes no distinction between works made by his own hand and those made by assistants as, to him, the essence of artistic process is the concept and organization of various elements. Art is what artists make, but how they make it is ultimately a personal decision.

We will never be able to tell how big the percentage of luck in our success is
Adrian Ghenie

Artists make art, which means that each artwork carries personal marks made by each creator. What struck me during the conversations was the realization that the majority of the artists have built their success pursuing their highly individual interests and reacting to profoundly subjective experiences. The discovery of their own visual language seems to go via fiascos of trying to be someone else or adjusting to the expectations of others. Reading the interviews, it seems that failures were invented to bring artists back to their roots, which form a reservoir of ideas and primordial energy, however cheesy the latter might sound. William Kentridge formed his peculiar artistic method after realizing that his work was very inauthentic because he was imaging what *other people* might want. Shirin Neshat found her own visual language only after her personal and confrontation of the Iranian Revolution, Adrian Ghenie took up painting again one boring evening after a period of struggling as a gallerist.

Artists are aware of the terms and connotations they are subjected to. Interestingly enough, most of the artists don't like to be categorized into a specific movement; being forced into a box seems like a burden from which everybody wants to escape. For Carl Andre thinking of abstraction as a specific modernistic phenomenon is wrong since Neolithic sculptures were already abstract. Pat Steir humorously commented on "expressionism", saying that "if you want to express yourself, you should see a therapist". Categorizations come from the outside and while being convenient tools to classify artworks and art into the chapters of art history they are experienced as simplifications. Minimal art, Conceptual art, Light and Space, and many other names are not sufficient to cover various aspects of artistic thinking.

Artists make art that claims an extraordinary position in human existence; still art is not a desert island disconnected from other territories of our life. On the contrary, art is anchored in the here and now of where and when it happens, and therefore forms a mirror of the society at large. The artists included in this book live in capitalistic societies, work with the material and ideas related to this particular environment, and react to it. Not surprisingly, despite the official ideology of the current art system that celebrates the alleged conflict between art and commerce, artists' attitudes towards money have been changing over the last decades.

Today's artists consider participation in wealth a good option to understand how society operates and possibly to gain power. Many of them have stressed that the idea has always been to make money in order to make work, but that they could also appreciate their improving financial situation. All the interviewed artists agreed that making money has never been their primary interest but having money is not a burden either. Once the bohemian model has lost its attraction, most of the artists seem to enjoy the financial success when it comes to them. Mark Bradford believes that not art but the resources generated from art can change the lives of people and he invests money in his foundation that supports local communities in Los Angeles, especially orphans. Walton Ford compares the position of the artist to other professions where success is celebrated in financial terms and asks why artists shouldn't be paid as much as movie stars, sports figures, or industrialists. Artists are increasingly interested in participating in the center of social power that in Western societies has often been related to wealth. A great, rich artist is no longer an ideological contradiction but a feasible option.

Artists make art, whose resonance and impact is unpredictable. Interestingly enough, every artist I spoke to was surprised by her or his success and stressed the role of luck instead of their abilities. Perhaps this humble attitude towards success relates to the capriciousness of history and changeable taste that makes it impossible to foresee which art will become relevant, and when. Therefore, artists can never fully be the masters of what they produce. Robert Longo mentioned that if there is a god, he is the one who gives out luck, so the only thing artists can do is to amplify the possibility of luck happening. Artists understand that the art world and the market are very fickle and that success is not a given but something that one has to be thankful for when it comes, especially since you never know how long it will last.

Artists make art, which is embedded in the broad system of relationships, networks, and dependencies that create relevancy. Great artists have always done what their talents and ideas required them to do, at the same time, however, reacting to the possibilities of the system. Good art needs to be recognized as such by the system; at the same time artists who are aware of the system can challenge it and act out of the box to find their own path that not necessarily confirms expectations.

> *Art is living matter; by its nature, it tends to question established values and cannot be constrained*
> Demetrio Paparoni

Artists make art, which is the subject of art history and an art system that has been undergoing significant shifts recently. Thousands of Instagram accounts showing awkward paintings and tawdry photos claiming "art is my life" might be symptoms of the popularization of contemporary art. Outsider artists, self-taught artists, and folk artists have invaded the art world, some of them quite successfully. This new army of artists by declaration threatens or at least questions two fundaments of the art system: artistic education and the art historical canon, the latter being put at risk through the rewriting of art history by various other groups with their own agendas.

The education of artists has long been a problematic issue and, many artists included in the book have interesting stories to tell about their path through (or lack thereof) art academies. According to Shirin Neshat, graduating from an art academy alone doesn't make one an artist since, according to her, you need profound life experience to be able to make art that has something to say. At the same time as Neshat is ambivalent about academic education in fine arts, she is also a guest lecturer at YALE University's Photography department. Sarah Lucas didn't find her own voice while studying art; it was only once she was on her own that she began to wonder why and what she was doing. Adrian Ghenie goes so far as to consider art academy teaching is damaging to students because it has everybody "stealing from the same pool". He refers here to the art discourse that has produced quite a stale narrative. At the same time, teaching and transferring knowledge and ideas can be of great value. Sean Scully thinks of his teaching activities as an important way through which to affect people.

Regarding the artistic canon, rewriting art history is happening as we speak. Thanks to the availability and accessibility of information, strong public support for all kinds of minorities, and an intense desire to create different narratives from artists, collectors, and institutions, many neglected and overlooked artists are finding their way into art historical books. Mark Bradford pushed the conversation about abstract painting away from the historically determined white American men and highlighted other artists instead such as Jack Whitten. Right now, Mary Corse and Pat Steir are getting much attention from institutions and the market, not only thanks to their highly interesting art, as this has been there for years, but also because of the current trend to redress the neglect of great women artists in the past. The opening up of Western art to the art of the rest of the world and its acceptance of whoever wants to join has far-reaching consequences we cannot yet understand.

Visual and conceptual eclecticism of our time has certainly helped producing great art. I cannot speak about artists without making a few comments about the system in which contemporary artists operate. It seems that we are shifting into another structure that has not yet been clearly defined. The existing gallery system has been crumbling; the white cube idea is losing its attraction for the audience, proved by decreasing numbers of visitors who come to see exhibitions. It doesn't mean the end of physical spaces though: artists want to display their art in galleries, although the majority of art consumers will see these works and shows online. Social media has added to the popularity and distribution of art online, but to what extent this virtual popularity translates into success in the art market and institutional recognition is unknown. Auction houses compete with galleries, putting a lot of effort into private deals, educating buyers, representing estates, and organizing exhibitions. The well-attended art fairs don't help a great deal either as they – unintentionally – privilege the most powerful players while softly killing off the mid-sized and smaller ones. The most traditional actors of the art world, public institutions, have been forced to continue the dialogue with the past instead of leading the change. Collectors are gaining in power thanks to the art-ideological freedom they now have and the money they can spend. Wrapping up, there is a lot of fluidity in the current art system that suggests we are going through a transitional phase, which is characterized by uncertainty and hijacked by moral populism.

> *The most boring thing is to know where you are heading to*
> Danh Vo

We are living in times of moral populism that, not surprisingly, has found its way to the art system. By populism I mean a social tendency that gives the illusion of power to the masses and reduces complex issues to one-liners, promising simple solutions. I describe this current wave of populism as moral because the masses – or in this case the art audience – are set in motion by moral issues. It is not my intention to analyze this broad social crusade that was born outside the art world. Suffice it to say, this moral populism is likely connected to the rise of new media and the election of Donald Trump as president of the USA (2016). Social media have made it easier to mobilize individuals, allowing them to speak up and to organize communities of like-minded people. Trump's election ignited a women's movement that prepared the ground for the #metoo movement. In the current visibility regime and media-driven capitalism, the biggest fear of institutions and companies seems to be a mass public rejection of any kind, something they try to avoid at all costs. Mass media thrives on sensation and even serious journalism dares to publish private text messages with indecent proposals. Populism admires power as long as that power gives the masses enough entertainment.

What is specific about the moral populism in the arts? Sympathy for populism already resonated in the postmodern silent transfer of agency from the artist to the public. Art theory and artists have agreed that it is the viewer who gives the final meaning to work. That artists propose but don't impose. That work gets its significance only when exposed to an audience; and this interaction changes every time a viewer engages with the work.[6] This theoretical pleasing of the viewer has found its way into other spheres of the art world. Firstly, art criticism finds itself in deep trouble as it has lost its mandate to dictate what is quality. When everybody can be an artist, everybody can be a critic. With the death of the artistic genius came the death of the critic as someone with a sixth sense who can recognize quality using his or her intuition. The replacement of knowledge combined with intuition by knowledge related to discourse didn't help really; postmodern criticism became a form of suicide because the discourse can explain and appreciate *everything*. When everything can be claimed as good or bad, judgment is a question of authority alone. The discourse has been fighting against its own redundancy by producing even more texts full of intellectual incest that continue to speak to each other in the perfect solitude of their own artificial language, always stressing, however, that it is the viewer that counts. As a result, the tendency to entertain the viewer goes hand in hand with reinforcing the authority of the major players of the art world.

Demetrio Paparoni also commented on other issues that have made the job of an art critic more difficult: the rapidly changing and fast-growing art scene demands a lot of attention to make sense of what is happening while gaining a prominent place in the art world also involves a commitment to public relations. Much has changed in the way artists are approached. Today the relationship with the artist is increasingly mediated by galleries or by those who represent them and the logic that regulates the work is not always linked to cultural dynamics.

Entertaining the viewer has also become a solid element in institutional programs. Museums have reached out to the public, some of them by organizing selfie paradises, others by adjusting their programs to topical subjects. Don't get me wrong, there are fantastic exhibitions being made and great artists being shown. What strikes me, however, is that institutions have become very sensitive to issues that could upset the general public. A recent example that occurred during the writing of this text was the cancellation of the long-planned retrospective of Chuck Close by the National Gallery of Art in Washington because of his alleged verbal sexism without awaiting any legal proof of criminal offences. However, there are also positive sides to the moral agenda: the art world opened up and set out to celebrate forgotten women artists, as well as African American, indigenous, and gender-fluid artists. How far this urge to correct will go, remains to be seen: there are voices calling for a purging of art history, so even Picasso is being scrutinized because of his machismo, which today's public abhors. Why is this urge for purity in the arts so strong?

In 1984, art critic and philosopher Arthur Danto published his famous essay in which he stated that art has come to its end. This didn't mean that good art stopped being made but that art couldn't survive without philosophy because in front of a Brillo Box in the gallery one needed philosophy to explain that this was art. At the end of art, artists became free to make art in whatever way they wished, for any purposes they wished, or for no purposes at all.[7] Museums were no longer full of dead art that needed to be destroyed but full of artistic options that could be used as much as you like. Contemporary art could be anything, and when anything could be art the question why something is art, is philosophical.

Danto called this strategy "post-historical", not as a temporal phase, but as a strategy that can exist next to other strategies like modernism that has never ceased to exist as a strategy for some artists. This post-historical attitude resulted in several important shifts. Firstly, it turned the question of quality more than ever into a question about authority and power since the quality determination relies on context and judgment instead of specified requirements. Again, when anything could be art, the institutions and gatekeepers are the ones who decide what good art is.

Secondly, the post-historical shift replaced the purity of modernism with the eclecticism of contemporary art and a wild proliferation of arbitrariness. Today's cry for purity is to a certain extent a reaction to this artistic abundance that looks like chaos. Since purity cannot be achieved in aesthetic ways, it is claimed through ethics. Indignation can no longer be caused by a style, but by moral issues. The dogmatism of modernism has shifted from being a formal attitude, which became unattainable at a certain point, to a moral standpoint. We are celebrating eclecticism, which, not so long ago, Clement Greenberg declared to be unhealthy because it opposed the modernistic ideal of "narrowing the area of competence"[8]. This means that refusal happens today not on formal, but social grounds. The uproar during the Whitney Biennale surrounding Dana Schutz's painting *Open Casket* (2016) that portrayed Emmett Till, an African American victim of violence, or the sculpture *Scaffold* (2012) by Sam Durant that was removed by Walker Art Centre because it could offend native Americans, are proof of this attitude. These works fit in perfectly with the contemporary visual and conceptual language; their rejection by the public was caused by reasons other than formal ones.

Modernism has a history of purging of the medium that produced the eclectic and chaotic post-historical attitude. From a broader perspective, the role that philosophy has played in the post-historical period has now been replaced by morality. At the moment of writing this essay, the art system often uses morality to explain quality. Hundreds of older women artists have solo exhibitions in museums for the first time in 2018, in an attempt by the institutions to appease the public that wants to see previous sins of omission redressed, from an ethical and not an aesthetic point of view. When many artists have skills and talent, when everything is possible and everything can be appropriated, it is the morality that has taken the lead as the ordering principle. How long this tendency will last, remains to be seen; great artists continue their work in whatever matrix they have chosen, as the interviews here clearly show.

[1] Mark Stevens and Annalyn Swan, *De Kooning: An American Master* (New York: Alfred A. Knopf, 2004).
[2] Gail Levin, *Lee Krasner: A Biography* (New York: William Morrow, 2011).
[3] See, amongst other things, the interviews with Walton Ford, Robert Longo, and Shirin Neshat in this book.
[4] If not mentioned otherwise all quotes come from the interviews included in this book.
[5] This tautology and interdependency between art and the artist was pointed out by the philosopher Martin Heidegger in his essay "The Origin of the Work of Art" (1935).
[6] I discussed this subject in the book *The Shift: Art and the Rise to Power of Contemporary Collectors* (Stockholm: Art and Theory, 2015) where the relevant literature on this subject can be found.
[7] Arthur C. Danto *After the End of Art: Contemporary Art and the Pale of History* (Princeton: Princeton University Press, 1997).
[8] Clement Greenberg, *The Collected Essays on Criticism*, Volume 1, *Perceptions and Judgements, 1939-1944*, edited by John O'Brian (Chicago and London: The University of Chicago Press, 1988), p. 213.

CARL ANDRE

October 2015

Marta Gnyp: *You belong to the category of artists who have not only witnessed, but also defined, the development of Western Post-War art history. Where to start with someone who has had a career such as yours?*
Carl Andre: I was born in Quincy, Massachusetts, a very nice town made famous by revolutionaries like John Quincy, John Adams and John Hancock. Frank Stella who is from Malden, MA, told me that the only thing he envied about me is the fact that I grew up in Quincy and he grew up in Malden.

MG: *You both went to the Phillips academy in Andover.*
CA: Yes, it was there that I discovered my vocation as artist.

MG: *How did it happen?*
CA: It has to be between 1951 and '52. At Phillips academy there is a very serious museum of American art called Addison gallery of American Art: everything from early colonial paintings to Jackson Pollock's work was exhibited there. In the first year I took art as a minor, which meant two hours a week in one of their studios. I was totally immersed in art there.

MG: *What medium did you use at that time?*
CA: I can't draw and I can't paint. My handicaps have been a great advantage for me, but it wasn't until a particular moment that I realized that. I was very lucky to know people like Frank Stella and other artists who helped me understand that I was simply a sculptor.

MG: *In which way has Frank Stella influenced your way of working?*
CA: I never really had a studio. I was living and working in a tiny apartment on Mulberry Street, in the lower east side, that I shared with composer, Mark Shapiro, and photographer Hollis Frampton. The rent was $19.84 a month and there was no hot water. I used to call pretty girls and ask whether I could come over to take a shower. Frank told me that if he wasn't in his studio I could go over there to work. So I did. One day I was working there,

1
Carl Andre
Pyramid (Square Plan), 1959

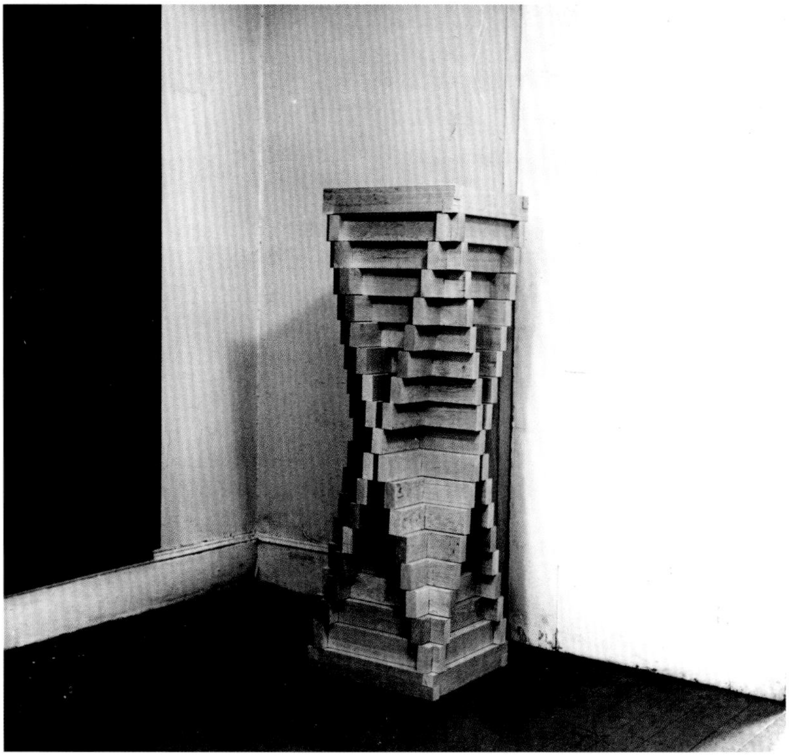

doing some sculpting, when I noticed some scraps of discarded canvases lying around. I got a couple of these patches, used paint from pots that were lying about the place and was sort of painting on them when Frank came in. He said: "Carl, if I ever catch you painting again I'm going to cut off your hands". He was dead serious. Frank was Sicilian – they say what they mean. I asked him why it is I couldn't be a good painter? He said: "because you are a good sculptor now, go and sculpt". So I did.

MG: *You had to listen to the Sicilian.*
CA: Frank was and is a truly brilliant person. He doesn't speak often but when he speaks it's gospel.

MG: *Were you always using your hands to make things?*
CA: I'm not a conceptual artist although I have an inquiring mind.

MG: *Why is it so important for you to not be categorized as a conceptual artist?*
CA: Because I don't believe that there is such a thing as Conceptual art. Art is mediation between human beings expressed through a physical object. An idea has no palpability for me. I endorse the comment made

by the French physician Joseph Guillotin: "all ideas are the same except in execution". I have desires; I don't have ideas. For me it is a physical desire to find the material and a place to work. Then I can't do anything unless I place things together and create work. I can't sit and draw a model on a piece of paper.

MG: *Do you consider yourself as a minimal artist then?*
CA: I don't mind being called that because I very much admire the work of Donald Judd, Sol LeWitt, Bob Morris and Dan Flavin, who are considered minimal artists too. We had a community of artists at Max's Kansas City, which was a bar in NY on 17th street and Park Av. The owner, Mickey Ruskin, was just in love with these artists and their work. Artists and young intellectuals went to this large restaurant with wonderful steak and lobster, an extremely lively scene and lots of beautiful girls. People talked to each other. All that doesn't exist any longer. There is no bar scene in New York anymore.

MG: *When you came to New York in 1956, a very strong art scene was the one of Abstract expressionists, who came together at the Cedar Tavern.*
CA: Yes. I met Bill de Kooning there and shook hands with Franz Kline. They were very nice and had no pretentions whatsoever. They were just as surprised by their success as anybody was.

MG: *How were these communities functioning? You spent time together and drank together; were you jointly developing your ideas about art?*
CA: The work wasn't done collectively in anyway, but good art inspires good art. When Judd, Flavin and Sol created good art, I didn't want to replicate theirs, but rather, I wanted to make art as good as theirs. This is how inspiration really works.

MG: *Were you somehow creating the ideological program of your group together?*
CA: Sol and Donald never went to these bars. Don was a family man, had a wife and children and wasn't a bar-crawler like I was. Rob Morris wasn't in these bars very often either. Bob Smithson used to go there with Nancy (Holt) – we used to have the most ferocious arguments; we could argue about anything, history, philosophy, science or poetry. People believed we were terrible enemies but this was just the way we showed each other love. It was an expression of great affection.

MG: *Was your peer group reacting to Abstract expressionism?*
CA: That's a myth that has been propagated. As far as I know, all the

people I spoke to were great admirers of de Kooning, Pollock and Kline along with other great artists of that time. But admiring someone's work doesn't mean you want to create that same work. Making art was a very private activity for me. Anyway; we were too busy picking up girls.

MG: *Who did you make the art for?*
CA: For myself.

MG: *What about your audience?*
CA: I would go back to visit my family in Massachusetts two or three times a year. I remember one night, my mother was sipping on her sherry and I was drinking my glass of wine when she said to me: "Carl, from what I hear from my friends, I understand you're rather well-known as an artist".
I said: "Yes, I can show you the reviews if you like". "If you are an artist I'd like you to make an art piece for me". So I told her that tomorrow morning I would call the gallery and have them send her the finest piece available. "Oh no you won't! Not one of those floor pieces", she cried. It seems my mother wanted me to carve her a seagull, which is a wonderful thing to do but beyond my capacity. My father, on the other hand, just thought I was playing conman. I never talked with him about my work. My parents never really accepted my art.

MG: *Did you attempt to explain it to them and others?*
CA: When people asked me what is the work about I would say: go and have a look at it. It's there; it is what it is. The only way to explain my work is to tell you the story of my life from birth to present time. It would be very boring though. A work of art is a product of a person's life – the more surprising the life, the better the work.

MG: *Are you suggesting that an artist's personality affects the quality of their work?*
CA: It's not so much the personality, that's only a part of it. The id, ego and super ego; the whole human apparatus, everything you've done, all the people you met, it's very complicated. I have a greatly deficient imagination. If I had a good, working imagination, I wouldn't need to do what I do at all. I make my works because I want to see what they look like. If I knew how they looked like I wouldn't bother making them. In the beginning, I did draw but every time I went to a gallery, or the space I was using to work, I had to rip up the stuff and start everything all over again. I realized that I shouldn't think about the work until I have the material in my hands and in the space where I was going to work.

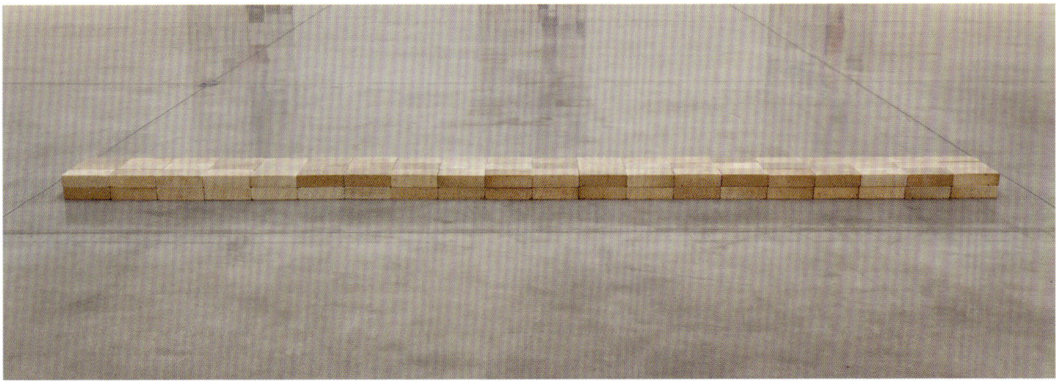

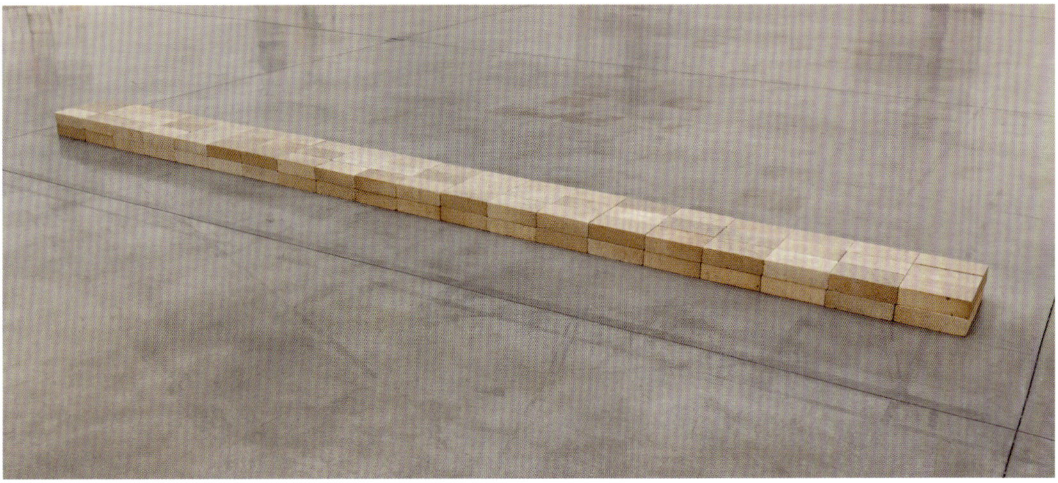

2–3
Carl Andre
Equivalent 11, New York, 1966 (destroyed) / New York, 1969 (remade)
Sand-lime brick/firebrick, 120 units, 2 high × 3 header x 20 stretcher,
6.4 × 11.4 × 22.9 cm each unit, 12.7 × 34.3 × 457.2 cm overall

MG: *Do you have control over what you're doing?*
CA: You start laying things down and you don't think anymore. A good artist is one with a task. There is no difference between the mind and the body.

MG: *Do you give instructions on how to install your work?*
CA: Not really. I want to see what you do with my work. There are configurations and descriptions, to put the work in the corner or off the wall but the parts are not numbered and nothing is precise. It takes some sensitivity and a little understanding to do it.

MG: *How radical was your work when you started your floor-pieces in the 1960s?*
CA: It wasn't radical to me but people were asking: how can you call that art? Others thought I was just trying to pull their legs. No, I was doing the best I could. People refused to believe that. People believed I was a

hoax when I said that this is what there is. There used to be a wonderful satirical comedy program on the public radio in San Francisco which was called Radio Unnamable. My art is Art Unnamable.

MG: *What about the reception of your work by critics at that time?*
CA: Some critics were very perceptive and enjoyed the work such as Eugen Goossen, Lucy Lippard and a number of others. I once ran into Clement Greenberg very late at night in an artists' bar, where he was alone and had had quite a lot to drink. There he sat: a giant of art in solitude and despair. I came to him and said: "Mr. Greenberg, I'm Carl Andre". He said: "I know who you are. By the way, please call me Clem, everybody calls me Clem". So then we had a couple of drinks – he very much liked tipping artists – he said: "I just have one thing I'd like to tell you. Stick to copper". To which I responded: "That was what my mother said". My mother collected copper bottom pans. Clem didn't like that.

MG: *Did you get a lot of angry reviews?*
CA: There is no such a thing as bad publicity; any press agent will tell you that. Your success is measured by how many lines and how much of a platform you get. It's exposure that counts.

MG: *How important, to you and your group, was the Primary Structures exhibition in 1966?*
CA: That came afterwards. The art was created before the movement got a name and received recognition. Usually, it would take some time before an artist got recognized. I knew the show was over when my art started to be taught in art schools. Kids were being told that if they want to be rich and famous they should make work like Carl Andre's. Then it becomes like a trademark. The late '50s and '60s were wonderful times. People were doing their own exciting things; there was no money in it. Money is the murderer. There was more freedom because there wasn't a market; market forces are very strong. I have never made a work of art in my life with the idea of selling it.

MG: *Did you think about becoming a trademark when you got a retrospective in the Guggenheim Museum in 1970?*
CA: To me that was the ultimate privilege. I think that the Guggenheim museum is the greatest work of art in New York. Frank Lloyd Wright was one of my heroes and to work in his space was one of the greatest gifts I ever received, especially with Diane Waldman who was the curator. A few days before the opening of the show, the director of the Museum, Tom Messer, arranged a meeting for us. In one of his private offices

he said to me, "Carl, you have to understand that I hate your work. I think your work is an insult to our museum". He said that it was only because Diane wanted the show that he agreed. Diane must have had something on Tom Messer, something like he was molesting boys, or worse (he laughs).

MG: *Why do you think he told you that?*
CA: *Messer* means "knife" in German; he wanted me to feel the twist.

MG: *How was the reception of the show?*
CA: The opening was very crowded; a lot of artists and hipsters were there. People were still asking where the art was while standing on it.

MG: *Would you agree that, between Primary Structures and your retrospective in the Guggenheim, you had become one of the dominant artists in New York?*
CA: Not really. The dominant movement was Pop art by far.

MG: *How was your relationship to Pop art?*
CA: I loathed Pop art but Andy Warhol and Roy Lichtenstein were very decent people.

MG: *They probably loathed your work.*
CA: It really wasn't an issue. Artists do what they do. You don't worry what other artists do. You may envy the fact that they sell and that they have shows. I think this is true when you're a serious artist.

MG: *Speaking of sales: many pop artists were making careers with Leo Castelli. Did he ever approach you to work with him?*
CA: Castelli was a truly great art dealer and a great gentleman. Frank Stella had an exhibition very early on with him. After he became well known, Frank arranged an appointment for me with Castelli. I don't think Leo ever said "no" to anybody. What he did say was: perhaps next year, we'll talk. He was a wonderful man. I didn't mind because I had a very good relationship with the galleries I worked with.

MG: *You were exhibiting with the Konrad Fischer gallery in Germany very early on.*
CA: My first show was in his gallery in Düsseldorf. Actually, he wanted Sol LeWitt but Sol wasn't willing to travel. I think Sol might also not have wanted to exhibit in Germany at the time because he was Jewish. This wasn't a problem for me. I was well aware of Germany's history, as well

4
Carl Andre
37th Piece of Work, 1969
exhibition view from the Guggenheim Museum, New York, 1970
Aluminum, copper, steel, magnesium, lead-zinc
216 square plates of each metal alternating by alphabetical order of chemical symbols,
1 cm × 10.9 m × 10.9 m

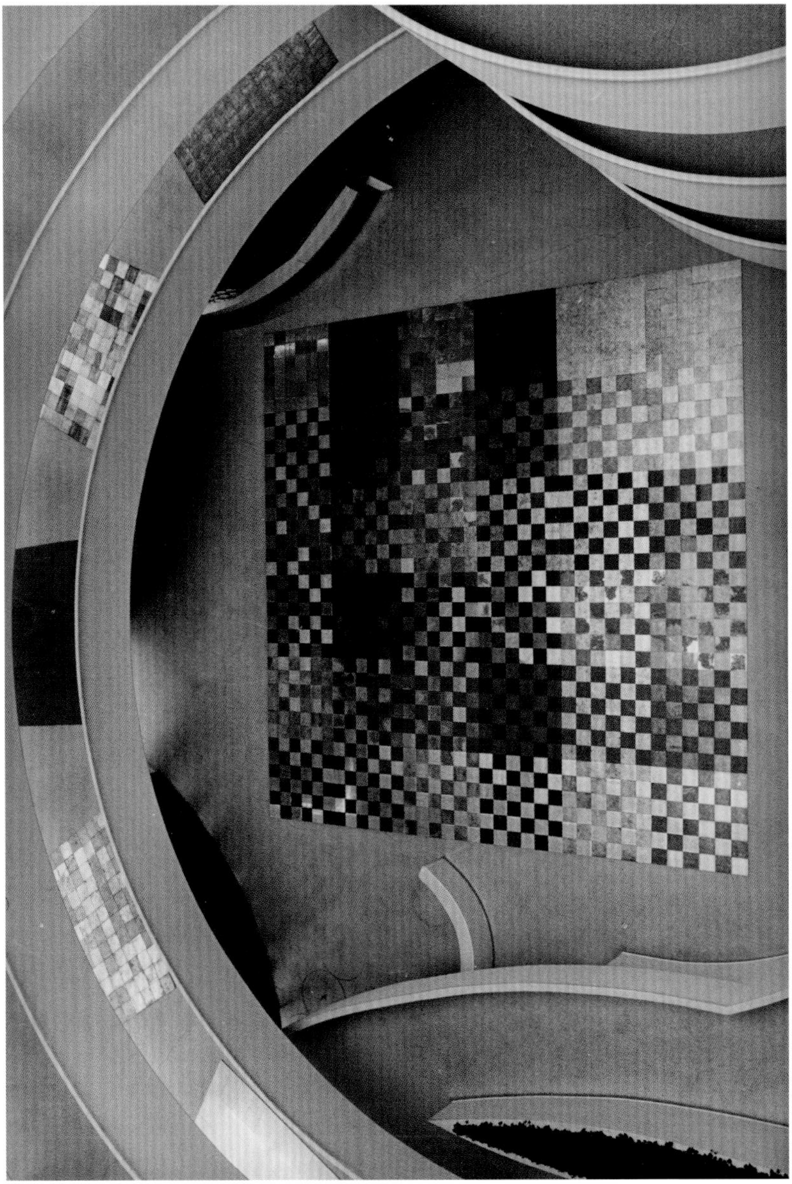

as anyone, but the people I dealt with were children during WW2. They were victims of the war as much as anybody else.

MG: *How did Konrad Fischer find you?*
CA: He read Artforum and this is how he knew about what was going on in America and that's where he saw my work. Kasper König then recommended me to him. As Konrad didn't travel, Kasper was his agent in America. When I agreed, Fischer told me, "you're not my first choice,

Carl". Everybody always told me, "you're not my first choice Carl". Well, I'm here. As we say in baseball: I'm ready to hit the ball.

MG: *What impression did Düsseldorf give you at that time?*
CA: Düsseldorf had a livelier art scene than NY at that time. Everybody knew everybody else. Joseph Beuys and the galleries of Fischer and Schmela were very active. I was very lucky to be there. If you have a choice in life between being good and being lucky – be lucky. There were a few wealthy collectors but money wasn't an issue at all.

MG: *You had to live on something though.*
CA: I sold enough of my work. I've always lived very simply. I could never drive, for example. Many things other people consider to be necessities, I have no need for me whatsoever. I never felt particularly deprived. I was just interested in having a good time.

MG: *What do you think about all the theories on Minimal art referring to the integration of the viewer within art or the lack of historical references in these works?*
CA: They are all bullshit. It's completely false. Think of Brancusi or Stonehenge. Neolithic art is all abstract. People who say that just don't know history, nor do they see the pleasure in it. Americans have a problem with pleasure.

MG: *It's not only Americans.*
CA: I only know Americans. Art made by dead people is all right with them; art by living people is suspicious. The pilgrim-founders of America were puritans, people who denied the flesh. To me, pleasure is contrary to every puritanical principle. You can spend your life indulging in pleasure. You're an artist because it's pleasurable to do so.

MG: *Do you associate your art with pleasure?*
CA: Completely!

MG: *The experience of your art is very rigorous.*
CA: Not to me. I like what Henry Moore said when he was asked how he gets his brilliant ideas for works, which were so advanced, so powerful and unique. He said: "I just continue to do, as an adult, the things I was doing when I was a child". I do that too. Kids make blocks and little kids are great artists until they learn to read.

MG: *What about the idea of development or progress in your work? In 2010 you were creating pieces that are comparable with works from the '80s and '90s.*

CA: What is worth doing is worth doing again and again and again and again; as long as it's worth doing. Worth doing means gratifying to me – if it ceases, I would do something else. Of course, nothing surprises me more than finding people who are willing to pay money for it.

MG: *A lot of money nowadays. The work I saw yesterday in your Paula Cooper gallery costed more than $700,000.*
CA: That's the resale and auction-market; it has nothing to do with me.

MG: *Do you not make any new works?*
CA: I formally announced that I've retired.
Melissa Kretschmer: Last month, we discovered two boxes of small materials that the Paula Cooper gallery had been storing for years. The gallery was always hoping Carl would come over and exhibit new pieces in the gallery. Carl keeps working with this material during the day at home. He made nineteen small pieces between late 2014 and early 2015. I come home and he shows them to me, I take measurements and photograph them. What's nice is that he doesn't have pressure from anybody.

MG: *At the moment Dia:Beacon is showing a large retrospective of your work. However, during the last twenty years, there haven't been many institutional exhibitions in the USA exhibiting your work, at least not as much as your artistic stature might require. Did the accusations of your role in the death of your third wife, the artist Ana Mendieta, partially block your institutional career in America?*
CA: It blocked me for a while. It was a huge shock and a huge tragedy.

MK: Over the years I've received emails from complete strangers asking, "how can you possible live with this man?" There was a demonstration in front of Dia's offices right after the opening of Carl's show; it was small but disturbing nevertheless.
CA: I find that the people who dislike me the most are people who have never met me.

MG: *Ana Mendieta has defined a big part of your life. You were both artists but you were making totally different art. I also heard that you two had totally different characters.*
CA: Absolutely. Ana was a fantastic artist and a fantastic human being; she was a very high-spirited personality. She was very outspoken and would tell you, or anybody, exactly what was on her mind. Some people didn't like her at all because of this. She wasn't an obnoxious person but some people were afraid of her. But we had some wonderful times together.

MG: *You came from different cultural backgrounds.*
CA: Ana descended from a very distinguished family from Cuba, on both sides. Her grandfather was a Cuban president, so they left the country because they objected to Castro. They were not supporters of Battista at all, but they didn't agree with the Castro regime; they were prominent, not among the contras, but in the non-Castro community.

MG: *Were you able to understand the nuances on Cuban relations and culture?*
CA: We travelled together to Cuba. Ana loved Cuba and everything about it. She spoke Spanish even more elegantly than how she spoke English. I liked Cuban people very much and didn't feel I was in a totalitarian country. I understood, of course, that the model of behavior was simple. If you're against the revolution you have nothing, if you accepted the revolution you were a free person, at least in the '70s.

MG: *I'm surprised you could travel there as an American.*
CA: You would go to Mexico and then you put your passport away so there was never any stamp in your passport showing that you visited Cuba. It was the era of embargo, Cuba had a lot of difficulties but they kept going because Venezuela was very sympathetic towards them and delivered a lot of oil. They flourished under restricted circumstances. Ana and I had a wonderful time in Cuba.

MG: *You still live in the same apartment in which you were living together when she died by falling down from the window. Do you have any memory of this?*
CA: No. I was asleep when it happened. All I heard was just "no, no, no"! Ana was trying to close the window. The temperature dropped by 20 degrees at night; it had been about 85 degrees and it went down to 60 in a very short time. She was very sensitive to the cold whereas I wasn't, so she got up at night without waking me up. Ana was 5 ft. tall so she had to get up on a window bench. She was trying to pull the window close and lost her balance. I heard her saying "no, no". It was terrible.

MG: *How could you put yourself together and continue working after such a tragedy?*
CA: Well, you have to go on. There are disasters in our lives but you have to move on. I had the support of friends; I found out that I had friends I didn't even know about. Of course, for the most militant feminists to this day: I'm the monster. And I will always be.
MK: People have this really weird picture of what kind of person he is. Many years ago we had a dinner with a friend who I had known for years. He called me the next day and said: oh my god, such a wonderful evening

and Carl is so different to how I imagined him! So I asked him where he got his impressions from, as this was the first time he had met him?

MG: *Melissa, you are now the fourth wife of Carl.*
MK: And the last one!

MG: *No doubt about it. Nobody speaks about the first two; were they also artists?*
CA: Rosemary Castoro was number two and Barbara Brown was number one.

MG: *Why did you always choose to marry your girlfriends?*
CA: It was a time in America when girls felt more secure if they were married.
MK: We've been together since 1995 and we finally got married in 1999. We realized that, firstly, we will always be together and secondly, that it would be easier to protect the works of art this way.
CA: There are good legal reasons to be married such as estate-matters. As husband and wife, if one dies there are no problems of inheritance because everything goes automatically and you don't pay tax.
MK: If we weren't married and something happens, everything would go to Carl's family, who would have no idea what to do with it.

MG: *How did you two meet?*
MK: When I went to NY, I exhibited in the Julian Pretto gallery. Julian was a great person; he had no money and lived under the radar, as far as the government was concerned. He had a little space on Sullivan Street, where he had two little programs going on: he displayed artists like Carl, Sol and Allan McCollum, as well as giving people like me the opportunity to have our first exhibitions. People wanted to exhibit with Julian because he had a great eye, was a very good person and was very lively company. He also always paid his artists first. The first thing he ever sold of mine, he called me and asked me to come to the gallery immediately. It was always cash. He said, "if you don't come and get it now, I might spend it". He put it in two piles and asked me to put one in my bag and one in a back pocket, in case something would happen.

MG: *You had a show together at Pretto?*
MK: We had met each other on and off but we never got to know each other until after Julian closed his gallery in 1994, because he was suffering from AIDS. Sometime after, I was putting on an exhibition in another gallery when Carl sent me a postcard inviting me for dinner. However, for four months I didn't hear anything.

5
Carl Andre
Uncarved Blocks, 1975
Red cedar (47 blocks),
30 × 30 × 90 cm each
Overall dimensions variable

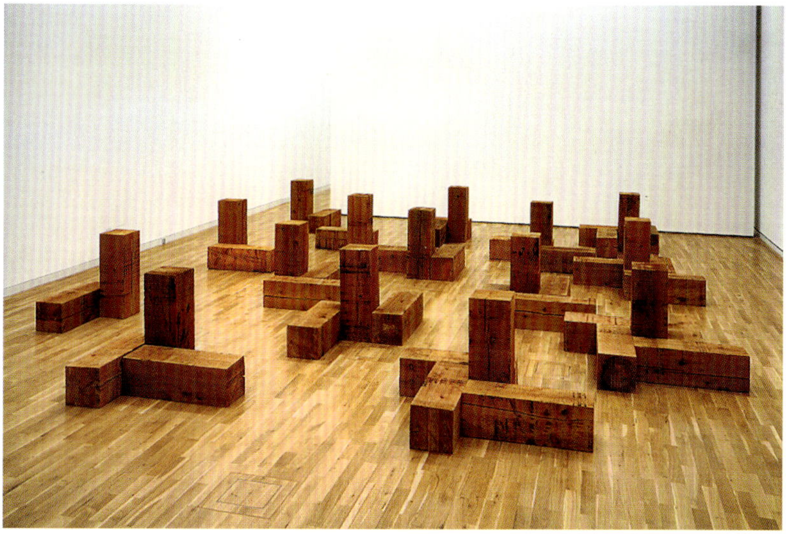

CA: I didn't know how to get in touch with her.
MK: He was leaving messages in the gallery but they wouldn't pass them on to me.
Finally, I ran into Carl during an opening in Tribeca. He invited me to dinner with friends and that's how it started.
CA: That was the best thing that happened to me in my adult life. I'm still alive because of Melissa. When we met I was more or less drinking myself to death. It is not that she said anything about my behavior at all, but here was this sober person and here I was, making a fool out of myself. If I hadn't had Melissa in my life I wouldn't have had very long left.

MG: *Looking back in retrospect, what do you think is the importance of your art?*
CA: I have no idea. It is important to me.

MG: *Why do you think your art landed in art history books?*
CA: You have to be in a right place in the right time. I wasn't the only one; there was Judd, Morris, LeWitt and Flavin. I was very much attracted to Taoism, which is a sort of Chinese philosophy; there is a thing in Taoism about the uncarved block. The uncarved block is wiser than the carved block because the uncarved block can be many things, whereas the carved block's destiny has already been determined.

MG: *Rumors have it that it was Frank Stella who pointed out the possibilities of the uncarved block to you.*
CA: I was carving in Frank's studio when Frank came in and said: "that is very good". He ran his hand down the uncarved side of the block and

said "but that's also sculpture". I took that to mean that the uncarved block could be as much sculpture as the carved one.
MK: Years later, when Carl was recalling the story, Frank started laughing. When Carl asked him whether it was true or not, he said, "You still don't understand: I wanted you to carve the other side". That's a nice story but it shows the shift in the ideology behind thinking about sculpture, that made you important for the world of art. I believe you're one of the people who changed sculpture.
CA: No, I added to it, not changed. Things change all the time. On the other hand, somebody said, "the more things change the more they remain the same", which to a certain degree is also true. There is this wonderful woman who lives in our building and who wakes me up in the morning around 10 am. She makes sure I'm up and that I function; she gets me the New York Times, she gets herself a coffee and a donut and comes back. She would sit here and talk; she's a very good friend. This morning I wanted to express my gratitude so I made a little sculpture for her. She was delighted and so was I. That, for me, is why I make art.

MICHAËL BORREMANS

July 2013

Marta Gnyp: *How do you prepare for an exhibition?*
Michaël Borremans: I always have a lot of ideas and gradually they go through a distillation-process. It starts with the concentration of thoughts. Once a month, I have a sleepless night, where I start thinking feverishly and somehow I'm a bit sharper than usual. I write down all sorts of things that would keep me busy the following month. It happens very organically. Each exhibition is a separate story, also thematically, if you can speak of themes at all.

MG: *Why wouldn't you speak of themes?*
MB: I don't work thematically. But ultimately, works from a certain period always have an element connecting them together. So, you could say that there *is* a kind of subject; for example there was a time I painted girls sleeping, or girls who seemed to be dead. That's probably a way to express something that you're subconsciously dealing with.

MG: *Have you ever tried to analyze it?*
MB: No, that's not my job. It most probably has a function somewhere. Other people do write about it. It's not interesting to me because I work very intuitively. Everything is really chaotic. I can't work structurally.

MG: *What does intuitively means to you?*
MB: Following my feelings.

MG: *I think that's such a loaded phrase.*
MB: Yes, but it indicates a kind of direction. I painted a large number of standing figures, for example. All of the sudden I thought, "I also have a large cardboard plant". I already painted it before, but, by painting it again and digesting it a bit, I realized that I wanted to paint the cardboard plant in a huge size. That doesn't come out of nowhere; it comes from a process that's continuously at work. But how exactly that works…

MG: *Do you always work like this?*
MB: Yes, I don't think I could do differently.

MG: *I've read that you started as a photographer.*
MB: I was working intensively with photography for a few years and I had even seriously thought of doing something with it, professionally.

MG: *Art photography?*
MB: Fashion photography. I studied visual arts and graphics at Saint Lucas in Ghent, followed by a few years of photography. My grandfather was a photographer. My first contact with images was in my grandfather's darkroom, as a three-year-old. Such an early experience is very profound so I developed a sincere passion for the profession of photography. Seeing the images appear in that darkroom was very magical, also due to the light. I discovered that I could do anything with this medium and, also, that I could stage things just as I liked. I honestly thought that, with a certain specialization, I could become a professional photographer. As a consequence, I only photographed women. I was very young. But there came a time when I had to make a decision, because I was also drawing. I was truly asocial at that time.

MG: *In what sense?*
MB: I lived fairly isolated. I felt like an old man when I was young. I preferably sat inside, reading books and doing my work. I didn't go out much. Until my 20th birthday I did this, but by then it was enough.

MG: *What kind of women did you photograph during that time?*
MB: They were all beautiful women, mostly friends and friends of friends.

MG: *In a studio?*
MB: No, just wherever I could. I think some of the photos are still very strong. That says something; if you still think they're good many years later. So there was some photographic potential in me, but at the same time, I was aware of the fact I had to choose. I was also involved in music back then. One day I took the decision to sell my guitars. I then understood I'm not social enough for a photographer and, on top of that, I had to travel a lot, when I hate traveling. So then I said, "I'm going to be an artist, I'm going to do something that would require as few people as possible". That was my decision.

MG: *Were you already painting at that time?*
MB: No, I was drawing a lot and wanted to develop it further. I only started painting when I was 33. That was, again, a decision which I took in one

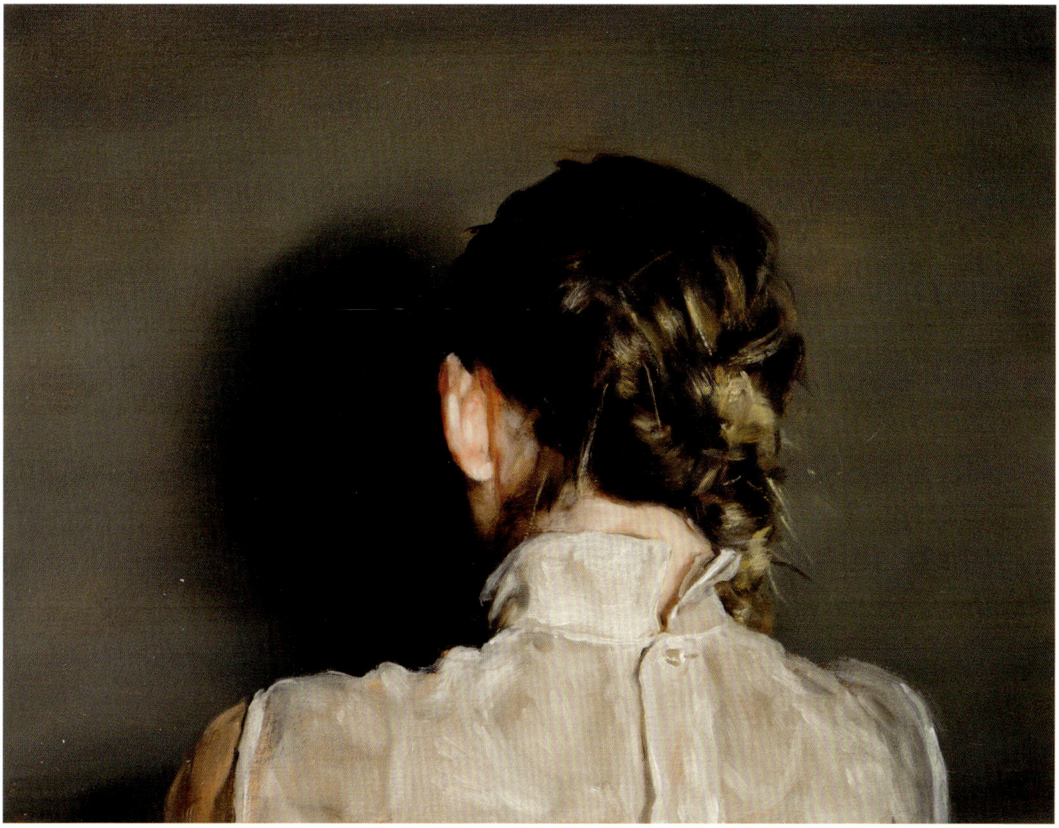

1
Michaël Borremans
The Ear, 2011
Oil on canvas, 42 × 53 cm

day; I remember where it was very well. I had just moved to Ghent and was living in a little, rented house and had a small room where I used to work in. In that room, on a beautiful sunny day, I told myself, "today I'm going to paint, I may still draw a bit, but I'm going to focus entirely on painting". I knew that a painting could have a very different impact compared to a drawing. I suddenly realized what paintings could do for me.

MG: *Were you able to use your drawing skills for painting or did it take a long time to develop new skills?*
MB: It certainly did. I was trained in using shapes, light and shadow for drawings, so these aspects were not difficult. But then you need to learn how to work with colors, with the materiality of paint and find your way in this area. That has been and is a permanent evolution for me; my earlier work was very thickly painted.

MG: *How were you making a living at that time?*
MB: I was teaching drawing at an art school, and I liked it very much. At

the same time, I knew I wasn't a real teacher; it was just a job to me. I worked as a teacher for ten long years and, at some point, I decided I'm not going to do this until my retirement, as I'd become a frustrated old man and that really was like a nightmare to me. In the mid-'90s, I quit and concentrate exclusively on painting.

MG: *Those were also the times in which painting was regularly declared dead within the art discourse.*
MB: I fully understand why. But, on the other hand, painting never really died. When I was studying, the Neue Wilden were around; there was still attention to painting, even figuration. When I began painting, my colleague, Luc Tuymans, started gaining attention for his work. I've also always followed the work of Gerhard Richter, a very interesting artist. He has also become better with age, which is a characteristic of a good artist. I noticed I could find my own language within painting.

MG: *Was the rich tradition of painting not intimidating to you?*
MB: That was exactly what was so interesting. It's a historically charged medium. I wanted to use that weight of history in my work. Like a judoka, using his own weight to enforce his strikes and thrusts, I wanted to use the historical weight of painting.

MG: *Do you seek to measure yourself with the likes of the old masters?*
MB: Not at all. It is more of a dialogue in which you participate. That's why I have all these implicit references in my work that refer to history of art. I find that interesting. If you want to do something pure and autonomous you should work with a new medium but it's impossible with painting; you can never be purely conceptual, since it is actually a romantic medium.

MG: *What is romantic about painting?*
MB: It remains an ultimately irreplaceable medium. It's like a hammer: you can replace the material of a hammer with modern technology but the function stays ever the same. Painting is highly rudimentary; it has always existed and always will. Each era has painters who reflect upon the present time and its society; they are truly interesting witnesses from the art historical point of view.

MG: *You sometimes hear voices claiming that painting doesn't fit in the 21st century.*
MB: Bullshit. Paintings are still the most reproduced images and still bring the most money.

MG: *Within the art market, we can indeed speak about the triumph of painting.*
MB: Do you know why? If there's a war you can just cut off the frame, roll up the canvas and carry it along. On top of that, modern media is totally outdated after five or ten years.

MG: *What also helps is that many paintings can be used as decoration.*
MB: A painting often has a mystical aspect to it.

MG: *When we talk about the market, how do you explain this obsession with young abstract art?*
MB: I don't follow what's happening now. What interests me personally in contemporary art is usually not painting. I admire, for example, Paul McCarthy, especially because what he does is very different from what I do. There are certainly some similarities in the content of our work, such as the way he uses clichés and interprets them. I do that too, but in a very different style.

MG: *You apply a more serene version.*
MB: I want to make beautiful paintings. Or something that seems beautiful.

MG: *When we talk about painting, we often talk about the development of this medium within modernism. Your paintings are very psychologically complex and are quite charged in the iconographic sense, as well as being full of references to art history. They're enigmatic, but formally they remain in the tradition of Velazquez or Manet; there is nothing shocking there.*
MB: That's right. Is that a problem?

MG: *No. But your success questions the view that inventions of one's own time are so important.*
MB: I strongly question technology. My email, coincidentally, is not working at the moment and I love it. I receive emails but cannot reply. I think that's a great luxury.

MG: *So making paintings with an iPhone like David Hockney is not meant for you.*
MB: Technological interventions in painting don't fascinate me. Meanwhile, I also completely abandoned the concept of reconstructing the photographic image in a painting. That's not interesting, certainly not now. I still use photography as a technical, intermediate step but it's not recognizable.

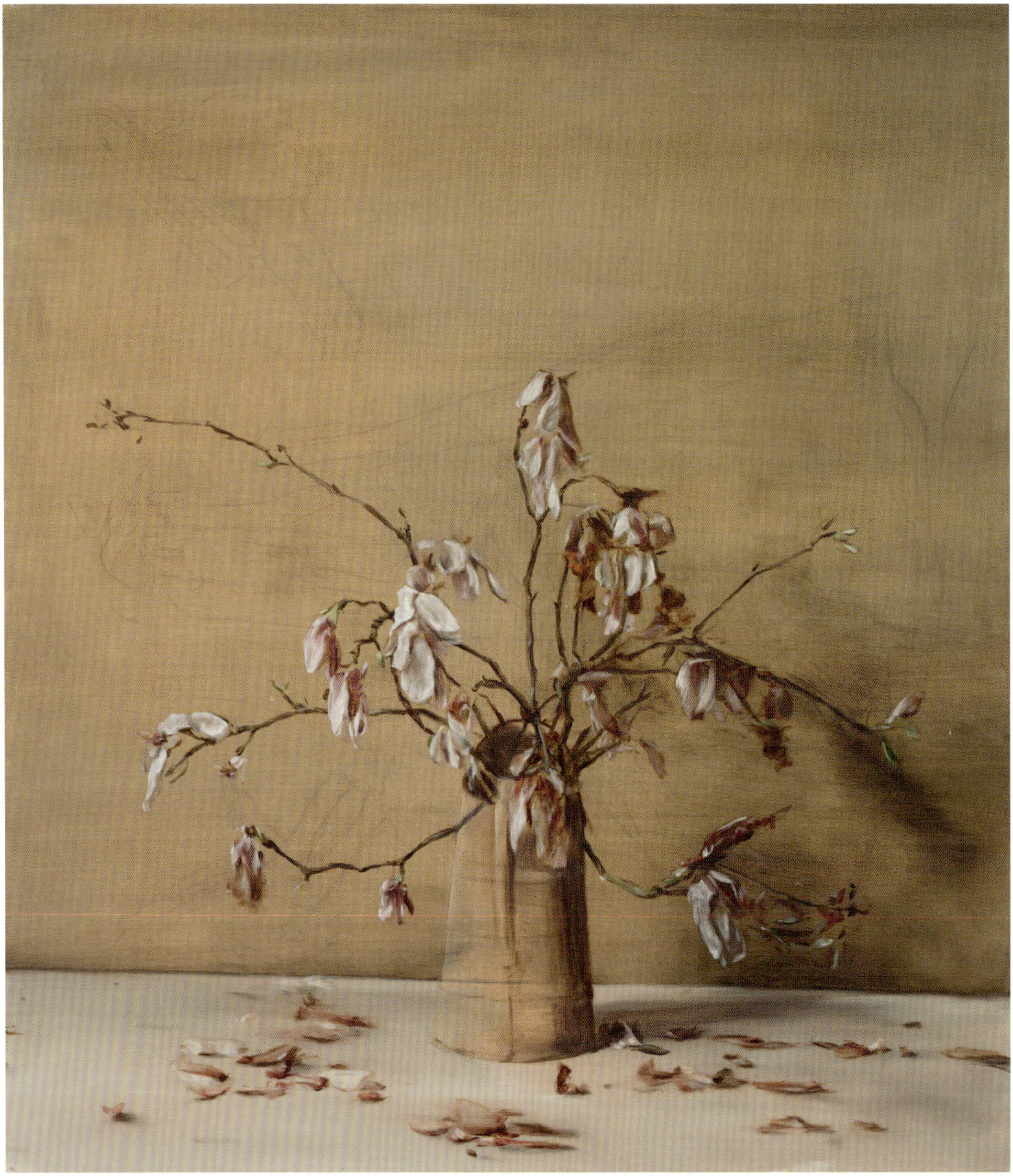

2
Michaël Borremans
Magnolias - (I), 2012
Oil on canvas, 140 × 120 cm

MG: *Knowing that your work is deeply rooted in the great tradition of painting, why do you have such a huge success?*
MB: That's for different reasons; one of the reasons I like less is that they're beautifully painted.

MG: *Why don't you like it?*
MB: I need to make my paintings "beautiful", otherwise it wouldn't work. I can feel that this is essential in order to maintain the dialogue with the tradition. I see it certainly as my responsibility but consider it interesting for myself too. However, if people only appreciate it for that, I think they misunderstood the work. Because I also want my art to have other qualities. Maybe my work just hasn't arrived at that point yet. I am very critical of what I'm doing. If I have a retrospective exhibition and I'm confronted with all my work, I often think that my work is good, but I wouldn't do it now in this manner.

MG: *Because?*
MB: Because I've evolved in my thinking about what I want to do.

MG: *A central idea remains that your work is a kind of platform to get the viewer thinking and make them an accessory to this thread of thoughts.*
MB: In this perspective it's also true that the work is as intelligent as those who look at it.

MG: *That's easy to say. You shift the responsibility to the viewer.*
MB: I'm trying to re-formulate the work each time anew; therefore, I'm experimenting. A theme that often reappears in my work is the representation, in and for itself. Therefore, I'm now going to paint a cardboard plant. I never paint at first hand. I would never paint a portrait or *en plein air*. I only paint representations of things. It is interesting to project more things into a medium than what the medium can actually bear itself. I take the viewer to another place and that has always fascinated me as an artist.

MG: *Can you give an example?*
MB: I was raised Catholic and had to go to church every Sunday, where I could look at the paintings hanging there. Not that they were very attractive, but it fascinated me that they were differently constructed spaces. A space that was a space or suggested a space despite that it was just a canvas. Thanks to this capacity a painting can evoke mysticism.

MG: *But such an experience also occurs because of the time you take looking. As a child, in church you're forced to watch a painting for an hour.*
MB: It was so boring in church…

MG: *It was always a bit repetitive. You're always in the same place in the church. Perhaps it's this repetition that caused the mystical experience.*
MB: Of which I'm now very grateful. Another thing that was crossing my mind in church was the enormous possibilities that such a space offers. You could build another floor inside, you could use this wing for this or for that, you could turn it into a studio. As early as childhood, I knew I was going to be somewhat of an artist. I've known it since I was six years old.

MG: *Your new studio is in a chapel.*
MB: It's the perfect place: 15 meters deep, 8 meters wide and 9 meters high, with windows on one side, facing north, and a large statue of the Virgin Mary.

MG: *Was it strange for your family that you wanted to become an artist?*
MB: No, they could feel it. I wasn't good at football and stuff like that. And I was always my bedroom drawing; I wasn't so social as a child. I've become much more social thanks to teaching for ten years. I've changed a lot in my social behavior; I now even dare to speak to a group of people. Before, I'd be terrified.

MG: *Did you have talent in drawing?*
MB: I had talent, but not extreme, I was not a child prodigy. When I was very young, I slept in the same room with my brother, who's seven years older, and he would scare me so much that I begged him to sleep together in his bed. I was three back then, he was a bit of a sadist. In return, I had to make drawings on his back, and he had to guess what it was. It was a game: I was allowed in his bed if I, for example, made twenty drawings on his back. I don't know whether it has influenced my artistic development, but it certainly was a remarkable period that continued for a few more years.

MG: *You wanted to be an illustrator?*
MB: I thought I understood how a drawing works and it interested me immensely. So I was convinced I was going to do something in that direction. Whatever that would be, it might have been something commercial, perhaps director of a TV series.

MG: *You decided to go to art school.*
MB: From that moment on, I liked to go school. It was awful before, I always got punished because I was drawing and was not paying attention to what was going on in class.

3
Michaël Borremans
The Visitor, 2013
Oil on canvas, 50 × 42 cm

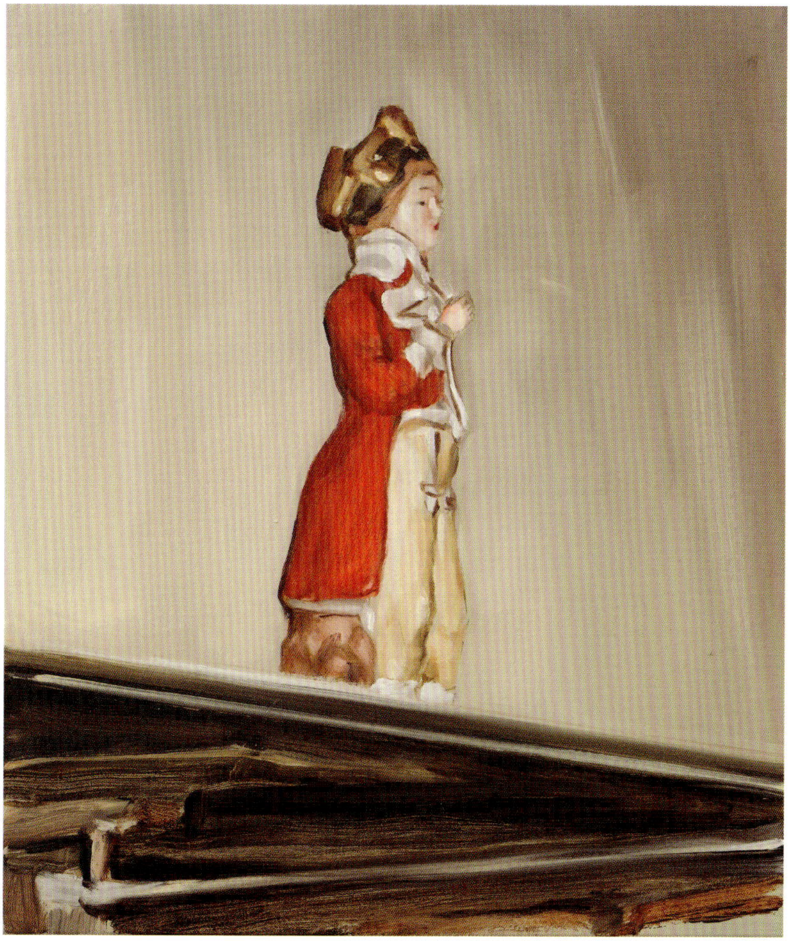

MG: *Punishment is also a theme in your work.*
MB: In Catholic schools, in the late '60s and early '70s, you got boxes on the ears and writing-punishments easily.

MG: *Did you never have enough of drawing?*
MB: No, although the success stayed away. The work from that period is still good though. I was already convinced by its quality back then, although no gallery or museum wanted to show something. I kept the work under my mattress and enjoyed my hidden treasure. I thought, "my career is not really flourishing, but it's fascinating to do this work". It was just a pity that nobody saw it because, ultimately, art is communication. I consoled myself with the thought that when I'm dead, the work will be found and appreciated. I was convinced. Success came at a time when I was no longer expecting it. That's why I could put it into perspective.

MG: *How did the success come?*
MB: I exhibited several times in small, local non-profit spaces. It usually went like this: twelve visitors would visit the show; they would say that the show was interesting but I sold nothing. I thought, this doesn't make sense. But then I heard that here in Ghent a new space for artists had been opened by some people from the Association of Friends of the Museum of Contemporary Art, in Ghent. If you, as a promising artist, showed your work there, you'd either be totally taken down or you'd be immediately noticed by a gallery owner or collector, which is what happened to Luc Tuymans, for instance. I knew I had to have an exhibition there. I put quite a lot of effort, but I ultimately succeeded and the show was a huge success. Mind you, I was 37 by then. I could've sold everything but I did the opposite. I thought, "this is my capital and I won't throw away immediately". The museum bought a painting; there was a new director at that time. Whenever a museum buys your work, everyone wants to buy a piece from you too. There was also direct interest from several galleries. I kept them all at bay because I was a little overwhelmed.

MG: *Didn't you think you should feed the market first and then continue to produce?*
MB: No. I knew these works were worth more and I wanted to keep them, too. I realized that this work was my ticket to build my career. If I'd sold all that work, I'd still have pictures of it, but that's less convincing. I played a very tactical game. I have always set high standards for myself, also in this field. I wanted a real career and not something that was half-hearted, otherwise I'd rather keep my work hidden under my mattress.

MG: *Didn't you have any doubts about your art during this time when there was no interest in your work?*
MB: Of course I did. I was always convinced that what I was doing was right, but I wasn't convinced others would like my work. I thought, either the world isn't ready for it yet or it doesn't deserve my art.

MG: *What do you think of the prices which are now being paid for your work?*
MB: Great for the owners. It doesn't keep me awake at night.

MG: *Is it a kick?*
MB: Yes, in a certain way. It's also a danger. Personally, I find contemporary art to be overrated. If you look at 19th century work, for example Courbet's, not a random name, the prices are much lower.

MG: *What went through your mind when you heard a small painting of yours was sold for more than $600,000?*
MB: Works in a gallery don't sell for such prices. I think I have sold that one work for something like 50,000. That's nice for the owner, of course. When my work entered the auction for the first time and achieved a high price, it did make me think that it's good to know why I'm painting. I have many works, which I don't sell, which I don't even show. I was never in it for the money. I'm experimenting a lot with other media: what I earn from a painting, I can invest in films and sculptures.

MG: *What is the ultimate goal of these experiments?*
MB: That it would lead to something relevant. That somewhere, in the visual culture, it would find its function. Painting has the big advantage of producing resistant images that don't easily disappear in today's iconoclastic spate.

MG: *Have you been ever afraid of losing your talent?*
MB: No. My eyes aren't as good as they were in the beginning, that's what I'm more worried about. But if I lose everything tomorrow, I would still be very grateful. Then I'd do something else, but something that would also be visual.

MG: *Are you still continuing to make films?*
MB: I have a few projects waiting, but they are very technically demanding. I think I have to go to Hollywood so to do it I would need to give one of my paintings as a gift to the producer… I'm very keen to do it though. I cannot pull the production off the ground by myself; that's too complex, and it wouldn't be good.

MG: *When is a work good?*
MB: When things happen that you can't really control.

MG: *Isn't that a cliché?*
MB: Yes, it's a *cliché*, but it's also true. What I do is one thing; what happens accidentally is precisely the element that determines whether the work is very good or just good. That's what causes the work to rise beyond the artist himself. You should just be thankful for that when it happens. But as an artist, you must be able to see it. Sometimes, something interesting happens and people don't see it.

MG: *That's interesting, I spoken with Thomas Schütte early this year and he said almost exactly the same thing. He said, "As an artist, I can only create the context in which art happens".*

MB: He's right. Same here. A very good artist, by the way, I admire his work. Some sculptures are fantastic.

MG: *So, as I understand, sculpting may be one of your next projects?*
MB: Well, yes, I did show a sculpture last year, here in Ghent – a large sculptural installation. I've been experimenting with this medium for over ten years now but I had to throw away most of those pieces. It's a painstaking process.

MG: *Is it about the human form?*
MB: It's figurative. But it is very time-consuming; I do it as a hobby since I'm not technically educated as a sculptor. But, today, the technical possibilities available are astounding. One can scan something and make it 4 meters high using each possible material that can be milled out or printed. These new things create unprecedented opportunities and I keep on thinking about it.

MG: *Are you excited about the upcoming exhibitions?*
MB: Showing new work is sensational because I always have stage fright. In September, I'm putting on an exhibition at Zeno X in Antwerp, then two in Tokyo, and next year a retrospective at Bozar in Brussels.

MG: *Is it important to you that your retrospective is held in Belgium because of your Belgian collectors?*
MB: It is good that it's in Bozar, but the collectors in Belgium are really something of the past year. It was, especially, museums and collectors in the U.S. that were purchasing my work at an early stage, less European museums. Now they do want me.

MG: *Why America so early?*
MB: I think it has to do with the fact that, by then, America, and New York in particular, had taken over the pioneering role in art. I sound like I'm generalizing now, but since the '70s and '80s Europe has only followed trends; nobody sticks their neck out; most institutions aren't there for artists very early on. To add to this, European museums have no money. It's a problem that needs to be seriously reconsidered. Apparently, Americans are willing to take the risks, and are, at that point, without complexes. My work's always been very well received in America.

MG: *How did Americans discover your work? At a fair?*
MB: Yes.

MG: *What do you think about the fact that many young artists imitate you?*
MB: They usually don't do that well. They often didn't understand any-

4
Michaël Borremans
Melon, 2017
Oil on cardboard,
24.3 × 20.9 cm

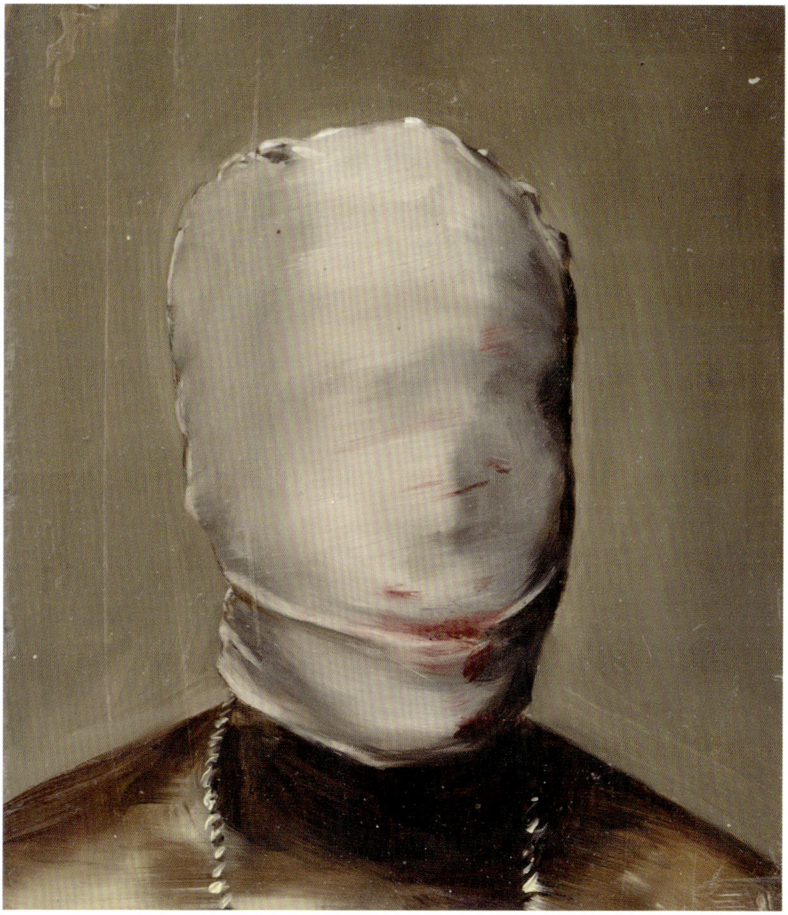

thing. Of course it is flattering to have influence but I prefer my work to inspire, rather than to be imitated or copied. What I usually see I find fairly uninspired. And I don't like being pushed into the same corner as those who imitate me. You could dedicate your entire career to a particular element I have touched on in my work and delve into that instead.

MG: *If you would think in terms of discourse and theoretical developments, development rather than progress, which place would you give your art in this framework?*
MB: It's very synthesizing, I think, in contrast to the past century where we've had a more analytical approach. And that makes it interesting. If it had an impact, that would be the important aspect.

MG: *Do you think you can pass on this synthesis as an aspect of painting to other artists?*

MB: Yes, because it can be applied in different ways, not only to painting. By the way, painting can also be horrible. I can fully understand all those curators who organize big events and exhibitions that don't include painting.

MG: *What still be a challenge for you in painting?*
MB: Take a look at Goya or Manet – try to keep it that simple. That's extremely difficult. Capturing that nuance of a specific spot exactly. It's that tiny, little difference that determines whether there's an effect or not. And you can't really approach that rationally; you're in a flow, it happens and you see it happening. Sometimes I'm lucky and that's addictive. Sometimes I look at Velazquez and, soon after, I'm talking to him.

MG: *How do you talk to him?*
MB: The way something is painterly solved, the way suggestions are evoked: it seems technical, and partially it is technical, but the rest is very intuitive. Recognizing this in someone else's work is very pleasant – moments of touching emotions, being so close to other artists. I had such a weird experience: years ago I visited Rembrandt House in Amsterdam. I was very much engaged with etching; I copied and studied much of his work. In Rembrandt House, you could see several of his etchings but most of them were reprints. However, there were a number of prints done by Rembrandt himself. Because he could paint so well, he made those etchings into paintings; he brought magic into it. I noticed that and I suddenly felt his arm around me, that warmth and heard him saying, "At least you understand me". I was fifteen or sixteen. I imagined it, but after this embrace, I thought, we're of the same kind, and yes, that's encouraging.

MG: *Didn't you think, "I'm crazy?"*
MB: No, it was profound, I know it was imagination, but it seemed so real.

MG: *So you were admitted to the greats very early on.*
MB: I thought I might have a chance, if Rembrandt accepted me.

MARK BRADFORD

November 2013

Marta Gnyp: *There is this amazing story about you working in mother's hair salon as a teenager. It must be quite important for you because it's pretty much the first information you get once you open your website. What did you do there?*
Mark Bradford: I was a hairdresser, my mom was a hairdresser; it was a family business.

MG: *Were you also interested in fashion?*
MB: It was in the '80s and I think I was more interested in club-life and disco. I didn't go to university, and if you didn't go to university you to the streets.

MG: *You had no interest in art, no interest in social issues and politics. How did art get your attention?*
MB: Well, I was engaged in a particular sort of outsider culture, with all these freaks, which my friends and I were, and then I thought what do I want to do with my life? I knew I didn't want to work in a hair salon. That was my mother's dream. I didn't realize it at the time, but people I knew were performance artists of all kinds. We would make costumes and dance routines, but there was no name for it in the '80s, not in the black community at least. So I thought, "well, the only things I seem to be interested in are creative things". And that naturally led me to go to an art school.

MG: *So what you called "freak" would be called a performance artist today?*
MB: Maybe... We were just young and enjoying life. It was the '80s, AIDS was everywhere, so we all thought we were going to die anyway.

MG: *Did this omnipresence of AIDS influence your lifestyle?*
MB: I think so; it was very Caligula. Well, you grow up, as a child you wonder what kind of life you could have and what world you could inherit. And then, you turn eighteen and you want to take risks and you want to

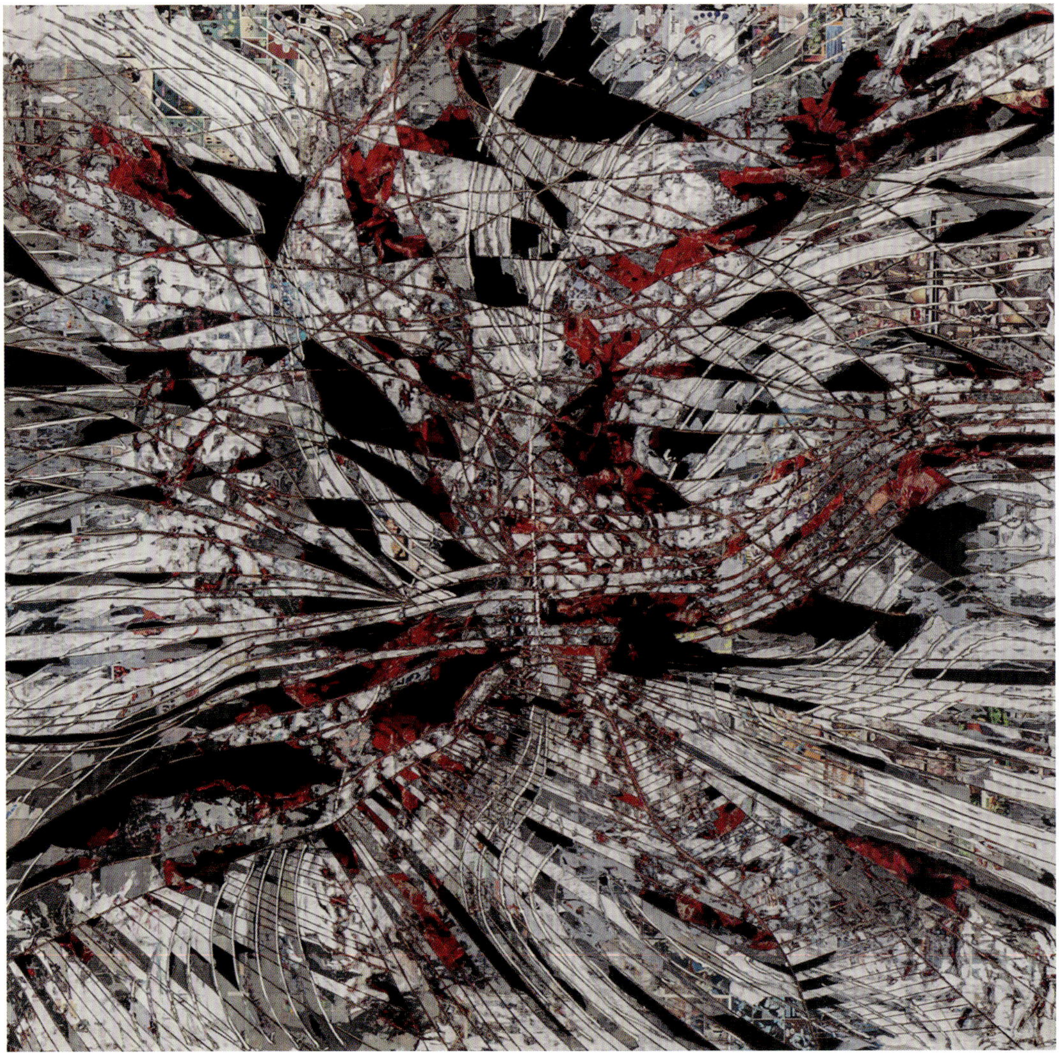

1
Mark Bradford
I heard you got arrested today, 2018
Mixed media on canvas, 304.8 × 304.8 cm

take drugs. You want to do what every other generation has done. And suddenly this new disease takes that away. And you deal with being young and old at the same time. You're dancing with a friend who has a diaper on because he has diarrhea and it won't stop. It's both. And you're eighteen or nineteen and can't process so much death. My way was to throw myself into this kind of mentality, which was what the doctors were saying, everything dies, and it's just a matter of time.

MG: *I assume there was also social disapproval of the lifestyle that presumably led to AIDS?*
MB: It was very much that "the bad people got this disease". The people

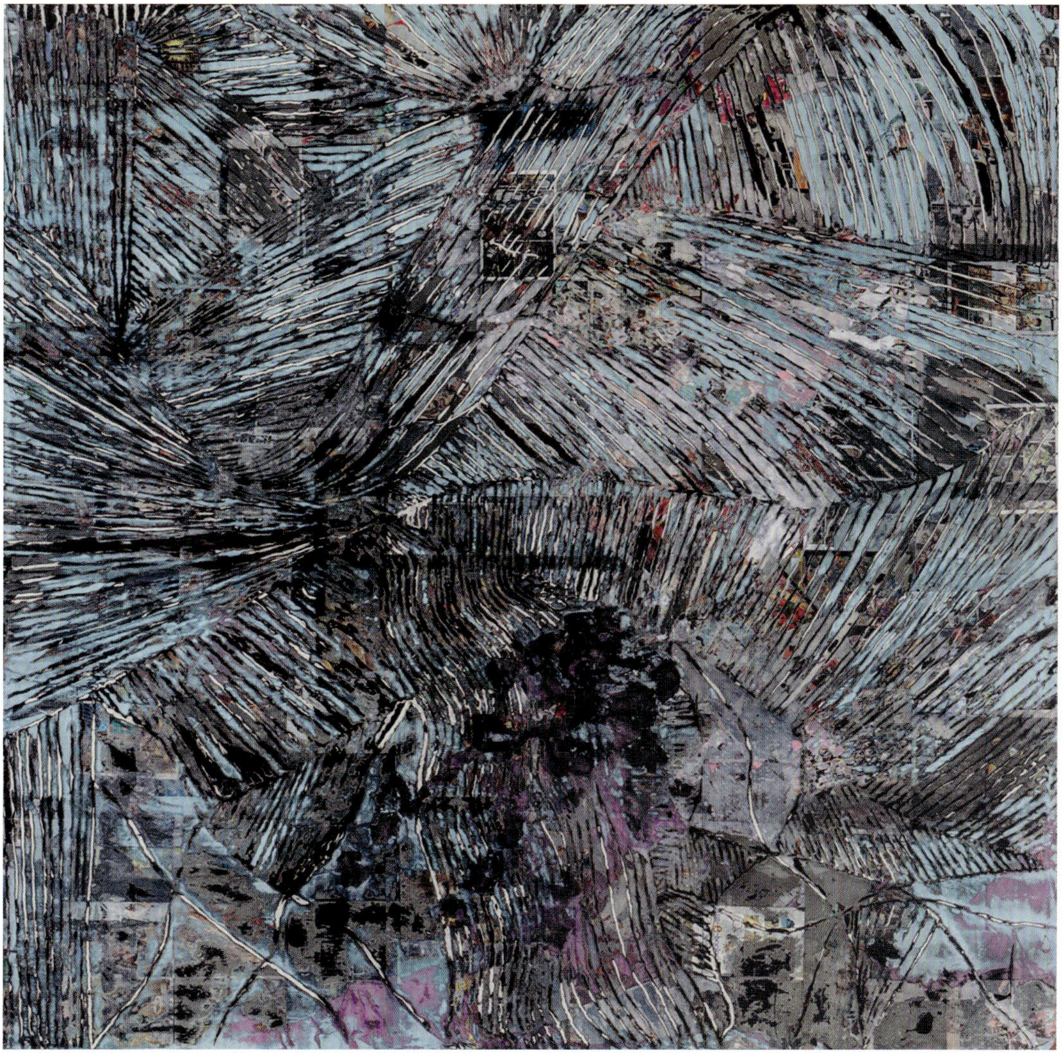

2
Mark Bradford
Moody Blues for Jack Whitten, 2018
Mixed media on canvas, 243.8 × 243.8 cm

who were bad people, who were fringe people, gay people, people who didn't care about the rules. So I thought, well, that would be me. So I think it just became a very expressive time for me, as death was always there. In the nineties, it started to become more political and the government finally started to acknowledge it, but in the eighties there was none of that.

MG: *Would you say that the '80s formed you? Not least because of the confrontation with death and excess?*
MB: Absolutely. The '90s were cool. I went to CalArts, (California Institute of Art), where I discovered reading and learning about ideas. Foucault was an eye-opener to me; I started to discover ideas.

MG: *You started art school at CalArts relatively late, it was only 1991. When did you decide you needed this kind of education?*
MB: Well, a girl needs to know when to get off the bar stool, you know. You can't spend your whole life in clubs.

MG: *What made you decide to go to school?*
MB: In the '80s, I was 100 percent convinced that everybody would die...I was one of the first hundred people that were invited for an experiment to take an AIDS test, when they first developed one. At the beginning they didn't even have a test. They took us to this military bunker, it was crazy. There were no real writing about the mechanisms of AIDS; how saliva or sweat could work... it was more like hysteria and propaganda. And all I saw were people dying. I was seventeen and I absolutely believed we would all die. So after I lived through it I went to school. I think the social part of my work comes from the times before I went to art school. Abstraction gives me room to develop my own ideas around certain issues.

MG: *And then, during the nineties, with some help of the French post-structuralists, you managed to conceptualize your thoughts and ideas about social relationships.*
MB: Firstly, I had lived it and after, I sort of found theoretical support for what I'd already done. I did it backwards. I lived and then went to school.

MG: *Is this the reason the social aspect is so important in your work?*
MB: For me I see the social aspect as having to do with the body and it has to do with the ideas of the times that we live in and engage with. For me that is as important as the art world and the ideas that circulate in the art world. I feel that it's neither this nor that; I just never choose one side. I engage so much with the politics of my time and certain social, cultural and racial ideas. I couldn't raise it when I went to school, back then it was almost impossible.

MG: *You also stress the social aspect as being the opposite to the tradition of the sublime painting. You seem to be totally against reading or looking at your art through metaphysics.*
MB: Oh absolutely, I don't know what I'd be channeling or where it would be coming from. My work is very much grounded in the times I grew up in and in the ideas that I I'm thinking about. That's why I use paper, because it's a container for information, it has a memory, it's an unforgiving material and it has to do with labor, and again, the performance of the body is very important to me. I find that American abstraction, especially the expressiveness of the New York school, has totally different

motives. For me, being black, should I say I am channeling this kind of native American narrative or that I am channeling this kind of dark and wild person? If you turn it around, if I'm black, what could I channel? It completely falls apart, the white side of my sublime, or my unconscious white; it doesn't work.

MG: *You don't want to be associated with the white abstract narrative at all?*
MB: I wanted to engage that narrative. Abstraction historically belonged to certain people, white males most of the time. But I want to push that open a little more. I don't think anything exclusively belongs to someone.

MG: *From the formal perspective, your work lends itself perfectly to be placed in the traditions of Abstract expressionism. It's probably unavoidable that art history would put you in this tradition.*
MB: And that's great. I have absolutely no problem with that. Because I think it expands the tradition of who can participate in that tradition and who can't participate in the tradition. I think it adds another layer to it.

MG: *You stress the social aspect of your work and the communal aspect: do you think your art can have a role in the community? Do you think your art can change something?*
MB: In the community where I live, I don't know if art can change anything. I never think of it that way. But I know that the resources from art can. I have a foundation I work with, that I started here, near my studio. And I wouldn't be able to do that if I hadn't the career that I had.

MG: *What kind of foundation is it?*
MB: It's called *Art & Practice* and it basically connects art with orphans. We use contemporary ideas to create an educational platform for foster kids, so they can work in the exhibition-space, work in the library, and we developed a program for them.

MG: *Why did you choose to work with those kids?*
MB: I have a long history with foster kids. It's something I have always been interested in. It's about them being outsiders, just because of the way they were born, outside of tradition because now they don't have parents. I am just trying to create a kind of conversation and dialogue between the arts and the service side of the community. It's been very successful. It's great. We've been talking about the social side of my work and the sort of art side of my work and I wanted to create a physical manifestation of those two ideas.

MG: *The social effect of your work is therefore created more by using the money you earned with your art and putting it into social projects related to art than by engaging in theoretical discourse. At the same time, by doing what you do, you defy some art-historical notions of abstraction.*
MB: Exactly. From the art history point of view, popping the can of abstraction open is a thing I wanted to engage in. There are a number of African-American painters or abstract painters who were erased out of the history books and who are now being re-thought and being placed back in history like Jack Whitten. The same thing applies to women, where were they? When you read about Abstract expressionism, there are only a very few women mentioned. I think history should always be remapped, re-questioned and rewritten. I don't think that it should be this static thing.

MG: *You said that the kids are kind of outsiders. Have you felt being kind of an outsider?*
MB: I never felt I was an outsider, I felt totally fine. I felt that in many areas in school I was coined an outsider, I was attacked, "this one is the strange kid", and I was not participating in the center of power. And the sense of having to sort of navigate when you don't play by the rules so much, that's something that I was very familiar with, very early on. Yes I was worried, yes I had hard days, but I always thought that I was more free. My mother raised me that way.

MG: *Do you confront people with their judgments?*
MB: I love to make people aware of things other than the main conversation of those who are politically correct and whose behavior is correct. You can compare it to someone who has five puppies but only has enough room for four; the last one gets left out. I love to throw light on that one. Because of the struggle that person has to do in order to make it, alone and with little support from society or the neighborhood in which he or she grew up in, or the schools they went to. My story is the one of the little puppy that you drop in the dessert and it comes back. It relates to foster kids, because they had very difficult lives and lived in very difficult situations, their lives are filled with a lot of sexual abuse, replacement. I think it's healthy for us to look at it and ask how we can bring it into the conversation? My mother was a foster kid so I grew up with this idea.

MG: *People in your area probably look at you as some kind of a miracle.*
MB: I don't think they look at me as a miracle. Nothing has changed; they still think I'm strange. My career is just as much a mystery to me as to them... I never think about it... I've been on my own so long and had to figure out so many things, I'm kind of a one man show.

3
Mark Bradford
Bird of Paradise (detail), 2018
Mixed media on canvas, 213.4 × 274.3 cm

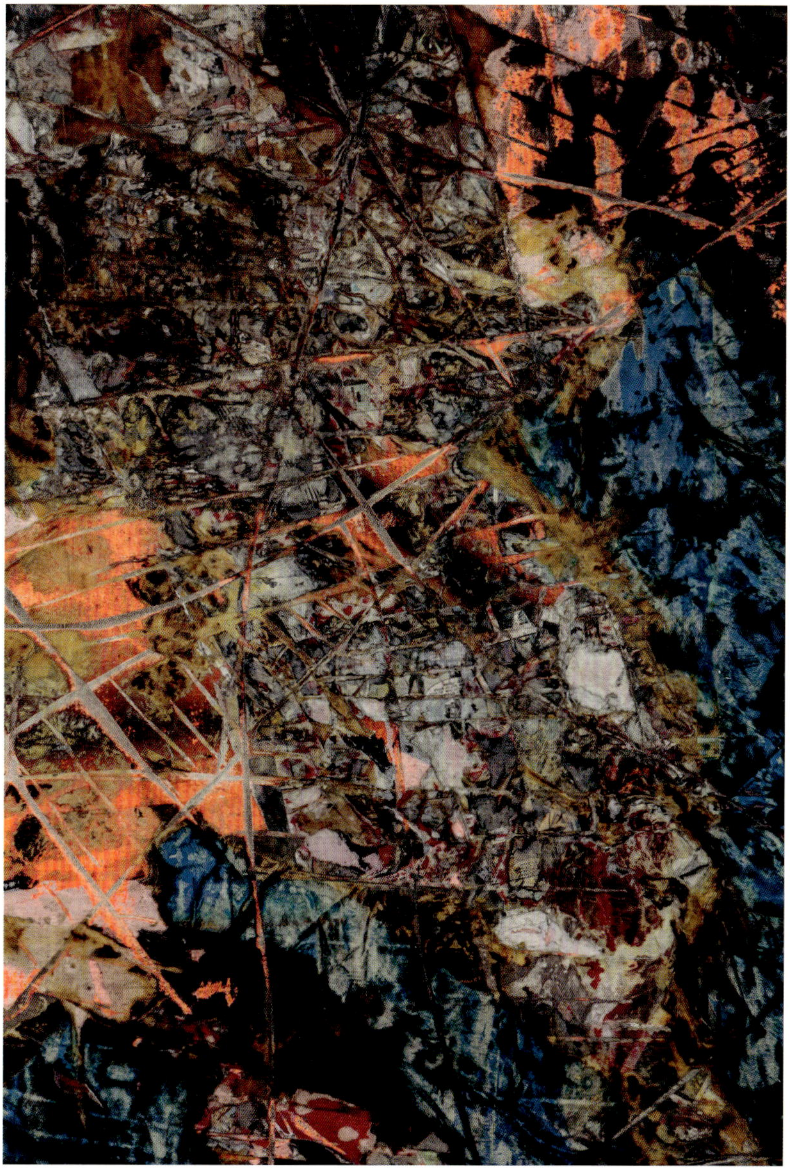

MG: *How does this success feel to you? When did you feel that it was coming to you, this kind of excessive success?*
MB: I won the Whitney Biennale prize in 2007. And I was very surprised, I thought oh… that's interesting. To say that I don't really think about it isn't a hundred percent true. I'll tell you how I think about it: when I was fifteen, I was a super strange little guy, doing whatever I was doing that day, and then I really grew up a lot in one summer, I am over two meters in height: very, very tall. I was super shy and kind of awkward, in my own little world at that age. But then I became a super standout kind of boy,

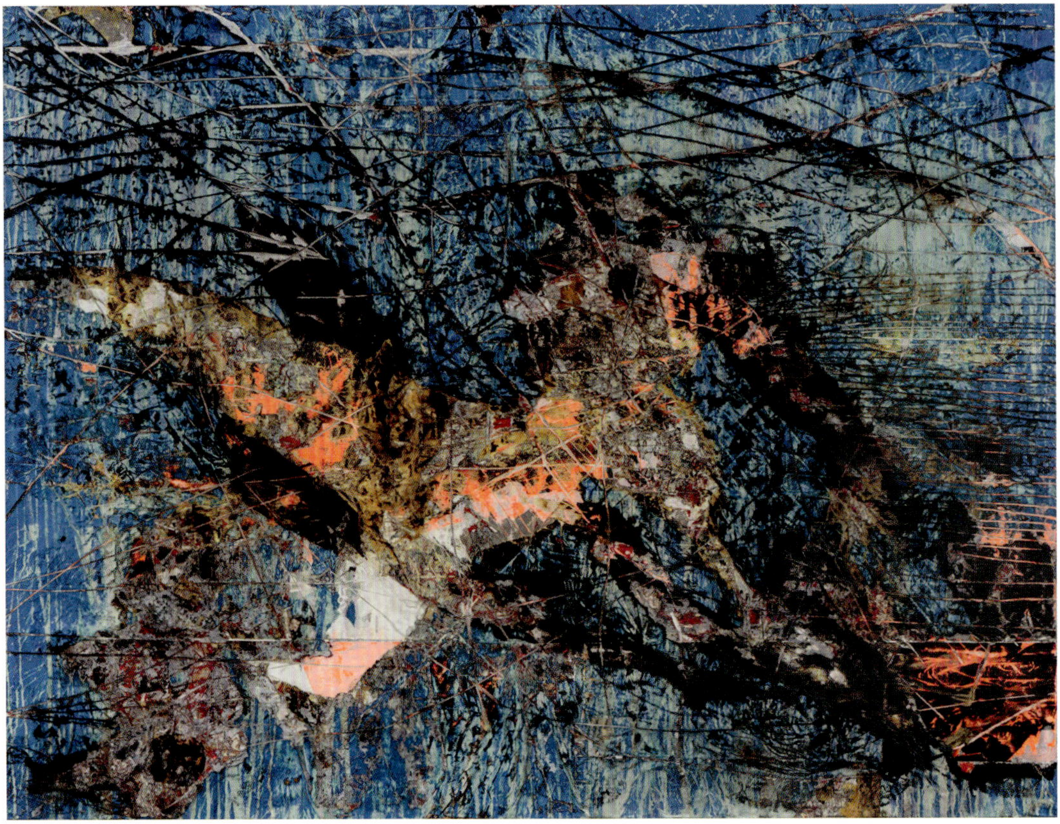

4
Mark Bradford
Bird of Paradise, 2018
Mixed media on canvas,
213.4 × 274.3 cm

physically. And I remember how much I disliked it, how much I disliked the attention, because they were like, "oh you should be a basketball player", and I was saying: no, I want to do this, I'm interested in this, so it became a split between two things: what other people wanted me to be, and what I wanted to be. And this is what it feels like now, having success. I'm just going to ignore it. If I look like a basketball player for the rest of my life that's fine but I'm not going to be one. And that's what fame is for me: oh Mark now you're famous, you should do this, or you should do that. I do what I want. I've been doing this so long that I'm in control of my own subjectivity.

MG: *So what is it that you want to do?*
MB: I'm doing this foundation and I want to do some interesting projects in Europe.

MG: *Artistic projects?*
MB: Yes. I like to do large-scale sculptures. I want to do something really interesting in the Middle East, I haven't decided what yet. I want to make my own tiles, make my own… I'm very curious.

MG: *Do you work with assistants?*
MB: I have a family I work with. I've known them since they were little boys, with no artistic background. I have one assistant with an art-background, for technical stuff. But the Lopez family helps me, I've trained them up, they don't know that I'm famous. They couldn't care less, which is perfect, I'm just Mark.

MG: *You became known for incorporating existing materials from around your neighborhood. Do you still do it? Walking through the streets in search of materials to take back to your studio?*
MB: No, I walk around a lot and look at billboards but the material I use now isn't coming from the streets, I didn't want it to become some kind of "Mark" urban myth that becomes attractive. I use paper, period. I don't just use urban material.

MG: *And where does your interest in cartography come from?*
MB: I've always been super interested in exploring; I wanted to be an explorer and an archeologist. I traveled a lot, I traveled through Europe in the '80s, and I went everywhere. I love civilizations and the marks that they leave behind. I love visiting ruins; when you dig down there's another culture underneath it, and another culture underneath that. I've always been attracted to this kind of cultural memory. I like digging up memories. I've always liked cities and urban myths. My favorite thing is to walk down the street, any street, in Berlin, in the middle of the night though, always in the middle of the night. And I never like to walk inside anywhere.

MG: *But you don't see a lot in the middle of the night.*
MB: You do, you see little things. I like when things are closed up and I like the outside of buildings, I don't like the interior of homes. I never have the desire to go in. In a city like Amsterdam, for example, I walk along the canals but I never like to look inside at what's behind those big windows. I love industrial areas. I have always liked public places where people have private conversations. I've never liked private homes.

MG: *That's interesting. I just saw your painting in Centre Pompidou, and it was so full of light. I can't imagine you preferring a city in the night because I associate your paintings with light.*
MB: Isn't that funny? It's very difficult to differentiate color at night. I like that; when I'm in the studio working really deeply with colors, I'm trying to see the difference between a black and a black, it's very hard when you're using paper, so the way shadows hit a very dark building at

night feels very much the way pieces of paper respond to each other. It's very hard to have translucency, to have depths, to have movement. It's easy to do it in the daytime, but, really, to have paper look like it's paint, you have to see it in the dark. Strange.

MG: *Does your success in the art-market influence your work? I can imagine that there's a famous waiting list for your work.*
MB: What am I supposed to do with that? There's nothing I can do with that information, it's not going to influence what I do in the studio, one way or another. You have to have good art dealers whom you trust.

MG: *How do you feel when you see your painting at an auction?*
MB: I hate it, who wouldn't? It's like a love-letter you wrote to somebody being on the auction block, it's so personal and so private. I don't mind that people sell my work. You do what you need to do but I hate how public an auction. I wish the seller did it through the gallery. And that's mainly the way it has been done, just, through galleries; this is respect towards the work and the relationship. I always find it a bit funny, the auction house respects the person that is selling it, but the artist is on the block, we have no privacy. So selling at auction always makes me really uncomfortable; not because they're selling the work, but because it's so public.

MG: *So do you have any conflict with the collectors who are selling your work in this way?*
MB: No, I don't have any problems… it's just uncomfortable. Works of art are like relationships; they're super private. We black people have a saying – putting your business on the street. Nobody wants to have their business out on the street. Like when you're having a bad time in a relationship, not everyone needs to know. And that's how it feels like; you flip through the catalogue and there you are.

MG: *Do you have personal contact with the collectors?*
MB: Not too many but I do know some. Over the years, you get to know a few.

MG: *When you speak with collectors, do you feel they treat you like a trophy because you're producing these great works of art? Do you not think there's a possibility of having a normal relationship with the buyers of your work?*
MB: I think the possibility of having a normal relationship is there because I treat everybody the same. I really do. As a rule, I don't accept hierarchy in the art world. I come from a service background. I worked in my

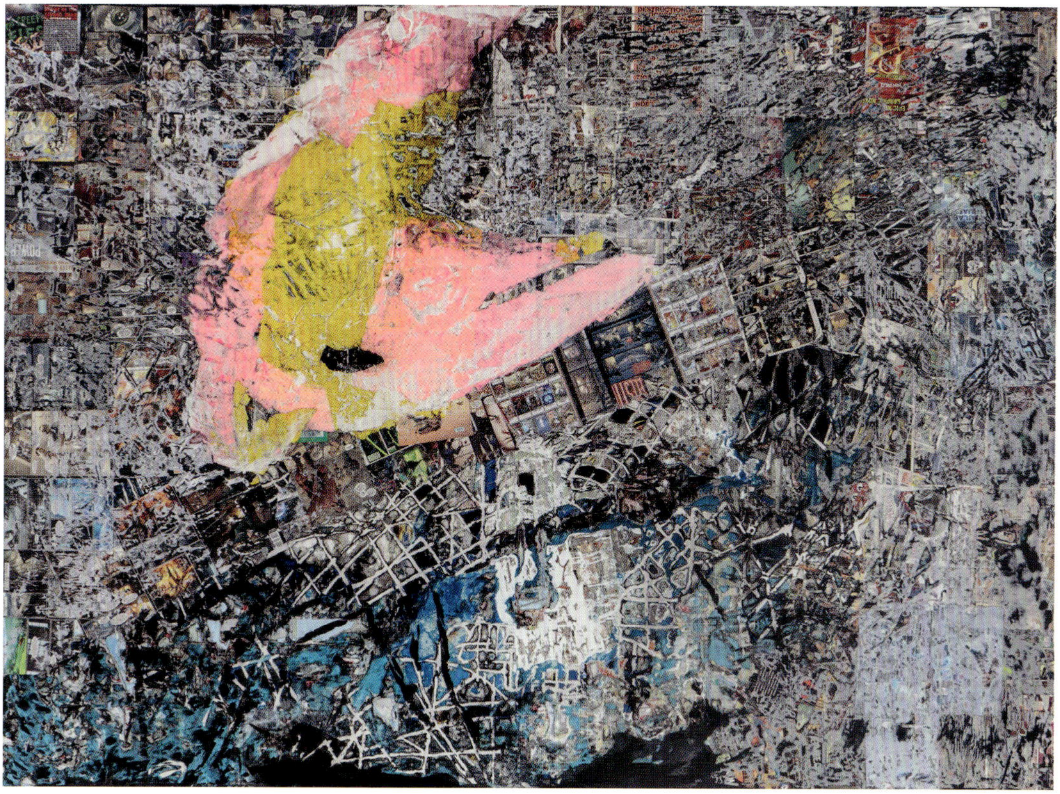

5
Mark Bradford
Rocket, 2018
Mixed media on canvas, 182.9 × 243.8 cm

mom's hairdressing salon when I was eleven, I was the little boy that sat you down under the hairdryer and went to the store to buy you a soda. So I am very used to sort of treating people kindly and respectfully, all people, so I think I've carried this part with me. If someone whispers in my ear that this person is this or that, I don't care. If they're an asshole, they are an asshole; if they're decent, they are decent. It's much easier to just treat everybody decently.

MG: *Do you think the fact that you are tall, African-American and gay help create a kind of myth around who you are, which also contributes to your success as an artist?*
MB: I don't know. I'm sure I'm made up of all those parts. So if I wasn't me, I guess I wouldn't be who I am.

MG: *You have been living in Los Angeles your whole life more or less. How is Los Angeles now? Is it becoming a more artistic city?*
MB: I like it because the paintings dry pretty quickly. I can pull my paintings out into the sun and they dry really fast, it's true.

MG: *That's the mystery of LA.*
MB: It takes forever to dry in other parts of the world. I think it's the last frontier. LA has the history of no history. No matter how serious the city wants to take itself, it's really young. The city is so young that it can't help to be just a little bit tacky, just a little bit vulgar. Which I kind of like. I think there's a lot of space in LA. You can live here in your studio and be completely isolated and do your work, or you can go out and see people. It doesn't have a center, a real center. It's almost like one big abstract painting.

MG: *Is the abstract quality of LA what connects the city to your art?*
MB: My mother always showed me things to draw, and I would always draw abstract, even at school, when drawing a pony, the pony was always abstract. I never got this figurative moment. LA is, in a way, like my paintings: people would stand in front of my painting and they'd say: I think this is Cairo and I see a face there. And I would look and say, I don't see any of that. So I think that's kind of LA, people always try to find the face, the fork and the pony. But they're not there, there is no center, and you just have to be okay with that.

GLENN BROWN

March 2016

Marta Gnyp: *The first painting on your website dates back to 1988 and looks completely different to what you are doing now. What did you think about painting at that time?*
Glenn Brown: In the late 1980s, neo-expressionist painting, represented by artists like Julian Schnabel, A.R. Penck or Georg Baselitz was very fashionable. At the same time though, there was the other school of painters, like Sigmar Polke and Gerhard Richter, who were addressing the ideas of photography as well as printed image, and who I considered to be much more profound in dealing with painting than the artists that were throwing paint around. It seemed to me to be very difficult to make relevant, figurative painting that didn't acknowledge photography.

MG: *You studied at Goldsmiths in London alongside artists who later became known as the YBA [Young British Artists]. During that time, painting was not considered very relevant…*
GB: I started my Masters in 1990 at Goldsmiths. London still seemed to be a backwater – New York and Cologne were the major art cities. The notion in the air was that painting was dead or at least unimportant. Certainly at Goldsmiths, video, photography and installation were what seemed relevant. But maybe that's because painting was not looked at in the way I wanted to look at it. I've always wanted to look at things or thoughts that are neglected or overlooked.

MG: *Did you always want to be an artist?*
GB: The first course I attended was a so-called foundation course, which was a one-year study of design, painting, sculpture or photography – if you're sure what to do you have a year to find out. I did a lot of life drawing at that time, which in a way was antiquated. I thoroughly enjoyed being in a class filled with all these plaster casts and realized then that I didn't want to do anything else in my life.

MG: *I'm thinking about your 1991 painting,* The Day the World Turned Auerbach. *This early painting has, what I'd call, your main, signature characteristics. Was seeing Auerbach a moment of revelation for you?*

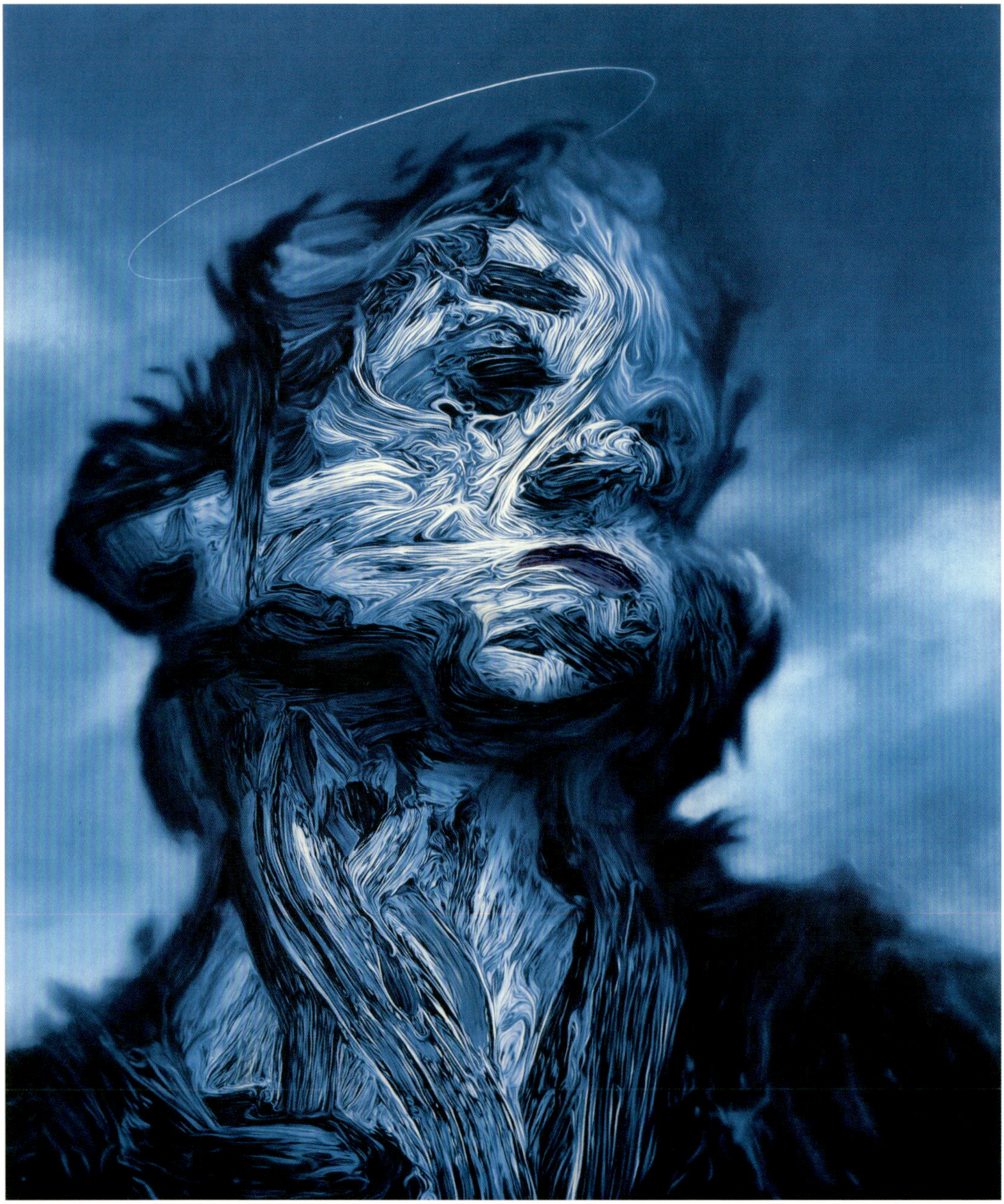

1
Glenn Brown
Shallow Deaths, 2000
Oil on panel, 70 × 57.5 cm

GB: Soon after I started at Goldsmiths, I was grouped up with three other students on a course, as we were all doing ridiculously similar work, using photography in terms of painting, comparable to Gerhard Richter's work. The head of the course, artist Gerard Hemsworth, asked us, "Why do you paint? Why do you not simply take photographs? You are far more interested in the mediated image". My way of answering these questions was to stop painting for a while and do something else. I thought, "What can I paint instead of photographs?" Richter's work was a model that became more like a shackle. I was chained down by his sense of painting. As a painter he uses paint but he doesn't deal with painting in a traditional way, he doesn't deal with composition of color or form. And then, I discovered: I will paint *paint*. This is the most stupid and obvious answer, conceptually, but it was the right one at the time. Looking around the person who was using the thickest paint layers in painting was Franz Auerbach.

MG: *So, choosing Auerbach was a conceptual decision and not an emotional one.*
GB: It was a very conceptual decision. I used to make painting based on photographs of the moon surface, which were flat surfaces with undulations. Since a painting is fundamentally a flat surface with undulations of paint on it, it was very easy for me to step over from the moon paintings into painting paint. It fitted into the conceptual model.

MG: *You mentioned several times that post-structuralism is a very important concept which relates to your work...*
GB: At that time, French philosophy was very important at Goldsmiths. It was very exciting to think about art in terms of a language: to break visual codes down and try to understand what you're doing through philosophy rather than making nice paintings. While structuralism suggested that there was one language, post-structuralism suggested there are many languages which are conjoined. Art is just another language you need to understand to be able to communicate.

MG: *Derrida proposed that texts refer to themselves, not to the reality that the texts attempt to describe. Did you think in the same way about paintings? That paintings actually communicate with other paintings, but not with the outside world?*
GB: In some sense, exactly the opposite. Painting was tied to film, theater, photography and all the other possible languages that were connected to each other. That's why Deleuze and Guattari became so important to me because they came up with their idea of the *rhizome*; a structure in which everything is connected.

MG: *If you think about painting as a language that you need to learn in order to understand, this means that painting – in relation to your case – is not easy to read.*
GB: Nobody can really understand all of the languages all at the same time. You can bring your knowledge of other languages into the painting, such as architecture, photography and tools that interchange with other disciplines. My audience doesn't necessarily need the knowledge of painting to enjoy them, although my paintings reference European art history very strongly.

MG: *So you don't mind if a viewer sees your works without understanding the historical art references? That they appreciate them mostly in terms of beauty and decoration?*
GB: I would like my work to be beautiful and decorative. Both are complicated terms that can be very challenging. Fashion is certainly very good at claiming the idea of what beauty is. If contemporary fashion designers were doing things that had to do solely with pleasure, symmetry and perfection, it just wouldn't work. The contemporary audience wants imperfection; they want purposefully awkward things because they make you think.

MG: *Do you think about the viewer when making a painting?*
GB: Absolutely. I have a lot of pieces in my studio because I'm working on all of them at the same time. I'm very good at starting a painting but not very good at finishing it. My friends – artists and non-artists – look at the work when I'm making it and criticize it, ("You could make this blue; you could change this; you made this decision that doesn't seem right..."). I listen to what they say and I change the work accordingly or not. This process is very important to me. I've never made a painting just by myself.

MG: *Why not?*
GB: Two heads are better than one. You could fall into bad habits or take easy routes; it's always good to have as many views on something as possible. You don't need to listen to it, but you should know it.

MG: *This attitude relates to your ideas about originality.*
GB: I think that originality is impossible to achieve. As I said, we need a language in order to communicate, which means that the structure needs to be borrowed, otherwise it means nothing. In order to be an artist and to be understood, you have to borrow from other artists or cultures; you have to take the ideas and put them together, placing your work in relation

2
Glenn Brown
Drawing 16 (after Van Noordt), 2017
Indian ink and acrylic paint on film, frame, 32.1 × 22.6 cm

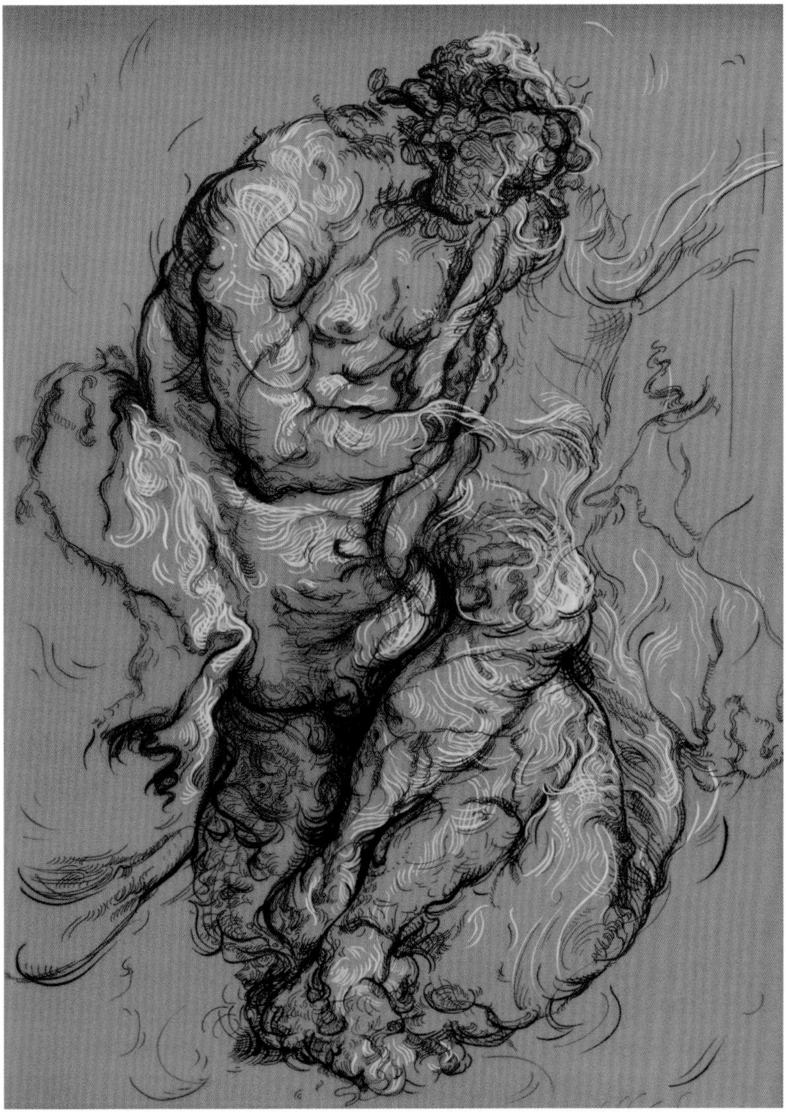

to what has happened before you. I can't be totally original otherwise I make totally irrelevant work.

MG: *I do understand how relevant this concept is for your work but I'm very curious whether, deep inside, you do or don't consider yourself to be a brilliant and original individual.*
GB: I don't think about myself as a genius. It would be meaningless because that involves lifting yourself outside the framework and environment you are in, which is so important. Artists I talk to, people I have conversations with, they all change the way I think. I *do* honestly believe that I'm part of a structure.

MG: *One of your paintings that plays around with Rembrandt's work carries the title* Joseph Beuys. *Beuys considered himself a shaman; he wanted to heal the world and was a very charismatic person. Why did you want to engage with him?*
GB: I think the word shaman is very important here: Shaman is a conduit; it's something that information passes through. Shamans don't have a sense of being original but present ideas to society in a different way, which my painting *Joseph Beuys* does as well. It's a son of Rembrandt in a fanciful costume – you might not even be able to tell whether it is a boy or a girl. It has a green face that looks very peculiar. In many ways, it's the opposite of how Joseph Beuys wanted to present himself. In my version, he's not the serious intellectual going off to heal the world, but a shabby, spoilt, child with gold earrings on. Maybe that's what was going on all the time in Beuys's art; maybe that's the real him and all the rest is who he pretended to be.

MG: *The title is essential to understand the work.*
GB: Many of the titles I use present an idea contrary to what is actually happening in the painting. They are there to make you challenge your notion of what a painting is. So many of my paintings are upside down – again to challenge you – to make you look at something completely afresh as if you've never seen it before.

MG: *For your paintings, you very often use works of Old Masters. I was wondering whether it's a kind of* aemulatio, *the Renaissance idea of competing with the other masters to show that you're better.*
GB: I don't believe the world is getting better; I don't believe art is getting better either. I just think it's changing. I'm not trying to reproduce better versions of Auerbach or Rembrandt. I'm just trying to make something that is different and relevant today in the 21st century in the view of what I think of the world; again, being a conduit in order to put together ideas in a new way, which are not necessary new ideas to begin with.

MG: *Have you never enjoyed the fact that you're doing something better?*
GB: I want to do my work as well as I possibly can. I may be competitive with my peers but I don't claim to be able to create paintings like Rubens, Goya or Titian did.

MG: *Although you use existing images as the basis for your paintings, you need to pick among billions that are available. How do you choose, especially taking into account that you make so few paintings?*
GB: I read a lot of books, I go to museums, I see as many works as I can in different formats, I search on the Internet. Certain images stand out

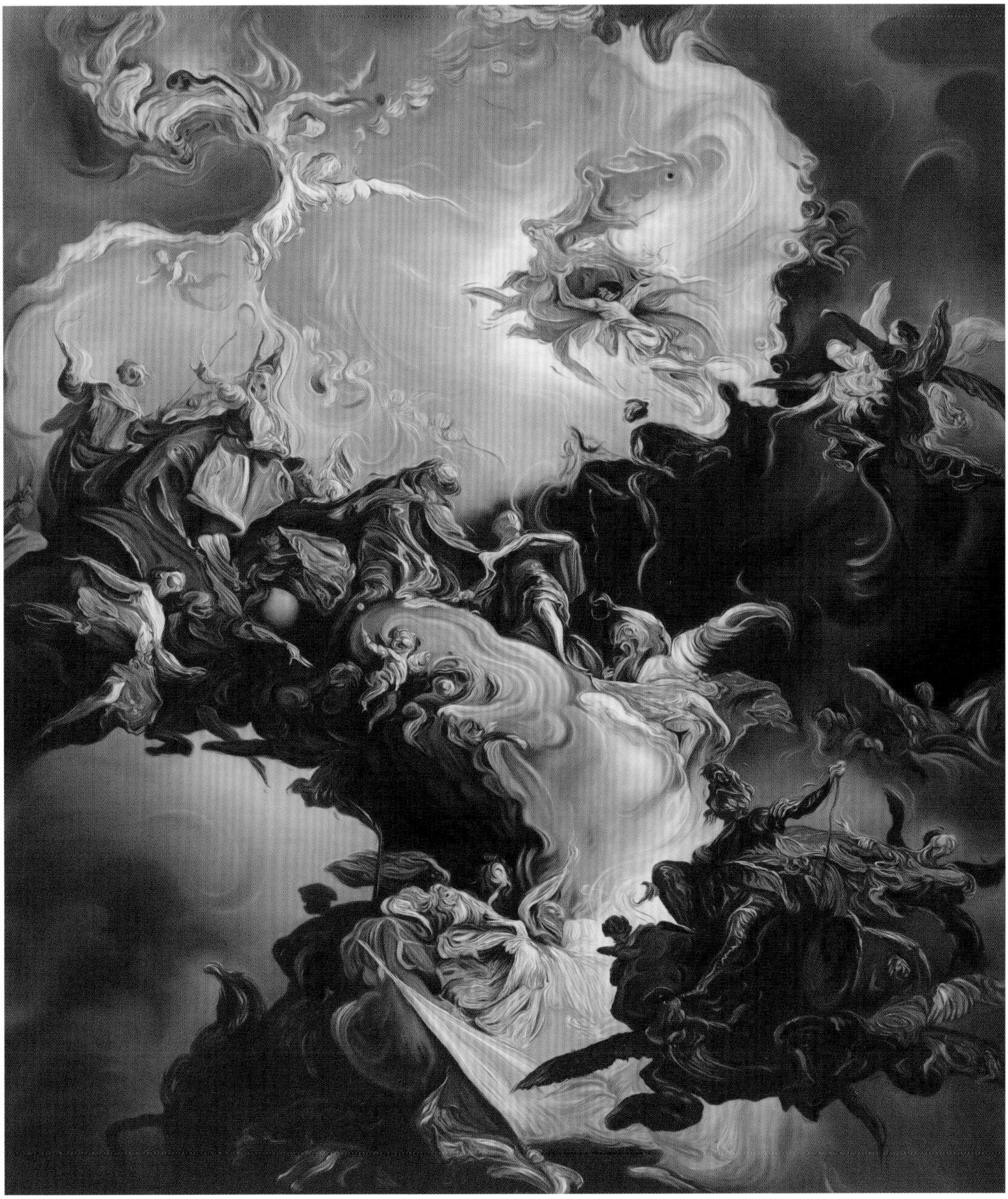

3
Glenn Brown
Let's Make Love and Listen to Death from Above, 2017
Oil on panel,
231 × 192 × 2.8 cm

so I'll take notes about them. The digestion period from taking notes to starting to paint can be one or two years but then I know the images have relevance. What surprises me is that I often have an idea for a painting and search for a particular image that fits into my concept. For example, I know I want to paint a big, blue painting so I try to find a subject matter that fits with a big, blue painting. I also like that many museums, like the Metropolitan Museum of Art in New York and the Rijksmuseum in Amsterdam, have digitalized all their images now, so I can get wonderful high-res images of virtually all works from their collection.

MG: *The majority of your audience sees your works for the first time, and maybe the only time, on the Internet. This means they'll never notice what you do with the paint and never experience your concept of painting – which looks like a very thick impasto but, in reality, is very flat. Does that bother you?*
GB: It does bother me. Sometimes people come to me and say, "I like your paintings, it's so nice that somebody can make a gestural painting in this age". So I say that they've missed the point. I do make objects that have to be seen in the flesh. I love the technology of painting: it's so precise; the color is very defined: no printing or computer screen could ever reproduce this. Every other medium seems so poor in comparison to painting and the beauty it can have. I like it so much.

MG: *The irreproducible quality of painting guarantees its future...*
GB: Well, 3D-printing might come along and change everything, but not for the time being.

MG: *Why has painting become more accessible in our time?*
GB: It's been very interesting for me to see how contemporary art in London has changed so massively in my lifetime. It's been fantastic to watch the public appear from nowhere and fill museums like the Tate Modern or the Serpentine Gallery. The audience of contemporary art has quadrupled in the past twenty years, which I think is great. Previously, museums were often the boring places where academics went and that didn't really have any impact on contemporary culture at all. That's changed. We seem to be living in a wonderful time for art.

MG: *The popularity of contemporary art can be credited to more entertaining programs in museums and also to the explosion of the art market in the last fifteen years. People have very different reasons to enter the art world. What is the main reason for you entering the art world?*
GB: I make paintings, drawings and sculptures for people to see. If nobody saw them I'm not sure that I would like to make them. I want to comment

on art history and major issues such as what does it mean to be a human being, how do we think about life and death, what is beauty. I want my comments to be relevant and to affect the audience; I want their feedback. Some people might see my work as extremely ugly, others might think it is extremely beautiful. Sometimes it looks very modern, sometimes very old-fashioned. Making works that have opposites in them creates a certain dynamic. I make paintings that have many details in them so people will come, look very closely and then step back again. You are animating somebody by moving him around and making him think.

MG: *Art as medium to make people think...*
GB: If you're left with many questions after looking at art, that's what counts for me. It's like seeing a film and worrying about what could happen to the main character later on. The illusion becomes mixed in with reality but it changes your perception of reality and how you relate to the world. That's what a good exhibition does: you enjoy looking at the work but you then walk outside and start seeing elements of it somewhere else.

MG: *Let's speak about the current artist-model. You've been criticizing the "macho model" by making the painter's gesture look fake and by questioning the idea of originality. What do you think about the current popularity of the macho painters who are in vogue? Don't you think that art is a territory that loves divine inspiration and grows from the soil of myths?*
GB: I kind of like those big macho gestures too. I fall for them as much as anybody else does: you can attack them and compliment them at the same time. When I make what appear to be big gestures, which take weeks to paint, I get pleasure out of it and the audience understands this sensibility in my work as well. Georg Baselitz started doing remakes of his own paintings: he cut, put and remixed them together and actually criticized his own sense of self. Such paintings can be ironic, gestural and romantic, all at the same time. Julian Schnabel is very good at this; you are never quite sure what he means, whether a work is meant to be romantic or ironic.

MG: *Another concept used by you is appropriation...*
GB: In terms of appropriation, the artist that influenced me the most was Sherrie Levine. She was the one that first made me realize how wonderful it was to see a piece of work and not quite know what you're looking at – a photograph or a photograph of a photograph. It was a conceptual notion which was bewilderingly fantastic.

4
Glenn Brown
They Slipped the Surly Bonds of Earth and Touched the Face of God, 2017
Oil on panel,
128.5 × 82.5 × 2.2 cm

MG: *Subsequently, you've been mixing the idea of high and low art. You used images of Salvador Dalí, covers from science-fiction books and titles of pop songs. Do you believe that the division between high and low can be lifted?*
GB: Will you put Dalí in the high or low art category? I'm not quite sure. There's nothing better than listening to a piece of pop music and then realizing how profound the lyrics are and how complex the philosophical ideas behind it are. Similarly, an awful lot of what is considered high art is actually poor and simplistic in what it represents. I think people will always claim that something is more important than something else.

MG: *Your art is visually appealing and conceptually demanding. It this a recipe for high art?*
GB: I think there are lots of recipes and a lot of museums have different ideas about what high art is. Lots of artists present supposedly rigorous sociopolitical notions but, under closer inspection, they may be on the level of an eight-year-old. Conceptual art can be guilty of being simplistic.

MG: *How important are museums in detecting good art?*
GB: I think museums are wonderful places: they can challenge, educate and entertain all at the same time. I think art should be entertaining. A lot of museums probably have a pretty good take on how the audience is and how to challenge them. Tate did a wonderful job in challenging the whole role of art, although they tend to think of performance and video as being more interesting than painting at the moment. They're probably right.

MG: *From the institution to the market, your paintings have become very difficult to acquire and very expensive to buy.*
GB: It partially reflects the fact that I produce very few paintings. I would like to make more of them but I can't make them any quicker because I don't want to produce works I'm not proud of. It takes hundreds of work hours to make a painting, figure out whether it is working or not, repaint some areas, change them… It's a huge waste of time, but in the end, it's the only way I can create something. The painting is almost a by-product of a complex creative process. People are paying a lot of money for them, which wouldn't be the case if I created forty paintings a year. In an ideal world, I wouldn't sell any of them but keep them and lend them to people – so that people could show them.

MG: *Do you keep any for yourself?*
GB: I do because I can lend them to exhibitions. Many of my paintings have spent most of their time on loan to different places in the world,

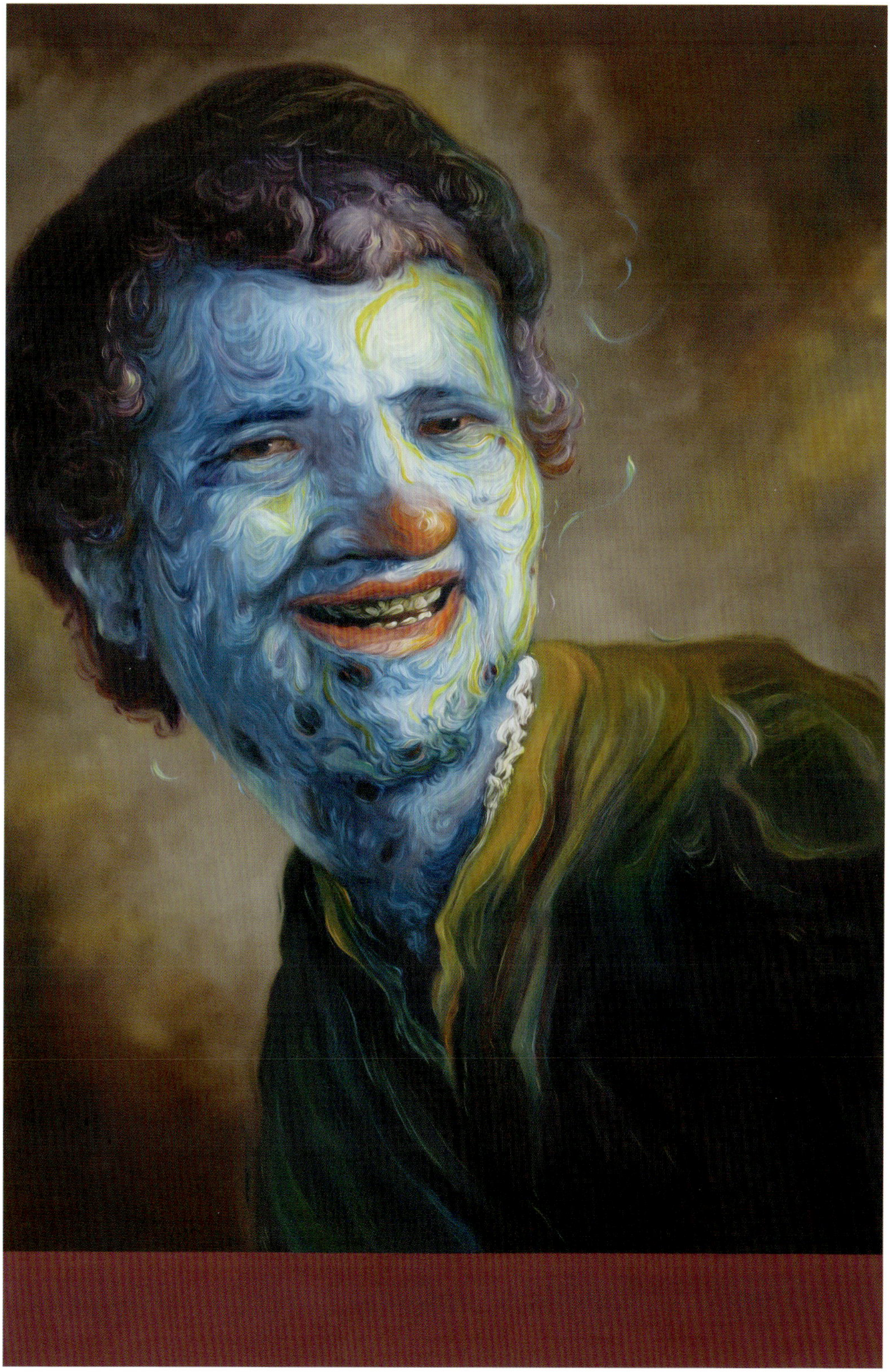

being displayed and viewed. I want them to be seen by as many people as possible.

MG: *Are you surprised by your success?*
GB: Of course. I've been very lucky. The art world is very fickle and the art market is equally fickle – you can be celebrated, one moment, and then be considered the most old-fashioned artist, the next. You never know how long it lasts.

MG: *You're turning fifty this year. Do you consider yourself a middle-aged person now? It must be a strange idea.*
GB: Very much so. It gives you a very different view of life. When I'm comparing myself with artists from the past, I think that, maybe, my best years are in the past. It's very interesting to see that a lot of artists made wonderful works in their twenties and in their thirties, but by the time they were forty their work became rather dull and boring. There aren't so many artists that produce their best work at fifty.

MG: *Does it scare you?*
GB: I enjoy being older. When I was younger the world was full of problems and I was full of agonies about whether I was good enough. The older you get the more you realize problems aren't so important and you learn to enjoy life more. You have more experience in life. As an artist, I've seen thousands of paintings; I enjoyed thousands of things. When you see something good, you really know it's good; there is no case of maybe. The hit I get from seeing something fantastic is far deeper and more complex now than when I was in my twenties or thirties.

MG: *Are you also wiser?*
GB: Hopefully.

MG: *Can you give me an example?*
GB: When I see my work from the past and I see the work I make now, I make fewer mistakes, I know how to solve problems. I know how to present myself in a way that is coherent and more meaningful than I did years ago.

MG: *What about your private life? This is a subject you try to avoid all the time. Is that deliberate?*
GB: For fifteen years I didn't allow anybody to take a photograph of me because I didn't want anybody to know what I looked like. I considered it irrelevant. This was a time when artists like Damien Hirst and Grayson

Perry used their public persona as a vital element of their work. I thought there must be a different way because it seemed to be a bit too easy, in the end. I wanted to do the complete opposite.

MG: *Did you attend your openings?*
GB: I did, but if somebody asked, "May I take a photograph of you?" I would say, "I would rather you didn't", which was sometimes funny. Anyway, now I decided to allow photographs because I'm nearly fifty (laughs). There's an English author called Julie Burchill, who writes for The Times as a cultural journalist. For about twenty years, the photograph that started her columns was one that was taken when she was eighteen. It was very funny when I actually met her for the first time because she was not what I expected her to look or sound like. She developed a state of mind where she said it doesn't matter any more, and you're able to relax after a while. You can play and finish the game, you don't need to carry on to the bitter end.

MG: *The lack of information about your private life used to be a part of your concept of being an artist in the public space.*
GB: Yes. I like to be a conduit of art to pass through, the conduit to art history. I like the mystic idea of being invisible, to some extent.

MG: *What about religion? Religion is very present in your work, at least the religious sensibility. Are you a religious person?*
GB: I'm an atheist so for me it's a concept, but a really important one. I wouldn't say that I'm a spiritual person; I'm fascinated by why people find spiritual realms so important and why people need organized religions as controlling mechanisms in their life. It intrigues me that people fall into these tricks so easily. I think religions are like fairytales; they are very interesting and you learn a lot from them but don't take them as the absolute truth, because they are just fairytales written by people who tried to help or control the world.

MG: *How do you see your work in the future? Do you expect big changes?*
GB: About a year and half ago I started drawing really seriously, which I'd never done before. In the past I was telling others that drawing is very important, that it's the skeleton of painting and the structure holding everything together, but I wouldn't do it myself. In the last two years, my work has changed enormously; drawing carried me away.

MG: *You stopped painting.*
GB: I did. I wanted a new challenge and my challenge was to make drawings. I'm very dogmatic when I decide something.

MG: *Don't you miss making paintings?*
GB: Not at the moment. I'm still too fascinated by black and white and line. It is all about the line at the moment and I can't multitask. I'm sure I'll go back to using color because I love the sensation of what color can do. Maybe the drawings will gradually turn into paintings...

MARY CORSE

February 2018

Marta Gnyp: *You must be extremely busy at the moment! As we speak, you're preparing two important institutional exhibitions, one at Dia:Beacon opening in May and your survey at the Whitney Museum in New York opening in June.*
Mary Corse: Yes, actually there are three exhibitions. Another reason I'm so busy is that I also have a show in London, in May. The months leading up to a show can be quite intense for an artist.

MG: *Are you creating new works for them?*
MC: Yes. That's why I have a good excuse to spend a lot of time painting. I paint, paint, and paint. I like painting. You'd think I'd be sick of it by now, but it's still very freeing.

MG: *The Whitney survey attempts to show the development of your whole* oeuvre. *What about Dia:Beacon. Will they focus on a specific part of your work?*
MC: The Whitney exhibition starts with early work and it runs up to the present. The Dia:Beacon exhibition mostly focuses on early work, with one recent painting. They will have the first light paintings and an early electric light piece. There's a good balance between the shows, and you get what I was focused on then, and how one idea led to the next.

MG: *Are you very productive? Do you paint quickly, or is it a complicated creative process?*
MC: Well, my works are very detailed so it takes a lot of time to make them.

MG: *Why is the process so important to you?*
MC: Well, painting gives me a deeper connection. As soon as a paint brush is in my hand and I'm painting, it becomes a different conversation to that of our daily thoughts and judgments. The concern about what's going on in the world disappears and it all turns into a different dialogue, a conversation with abstraction.

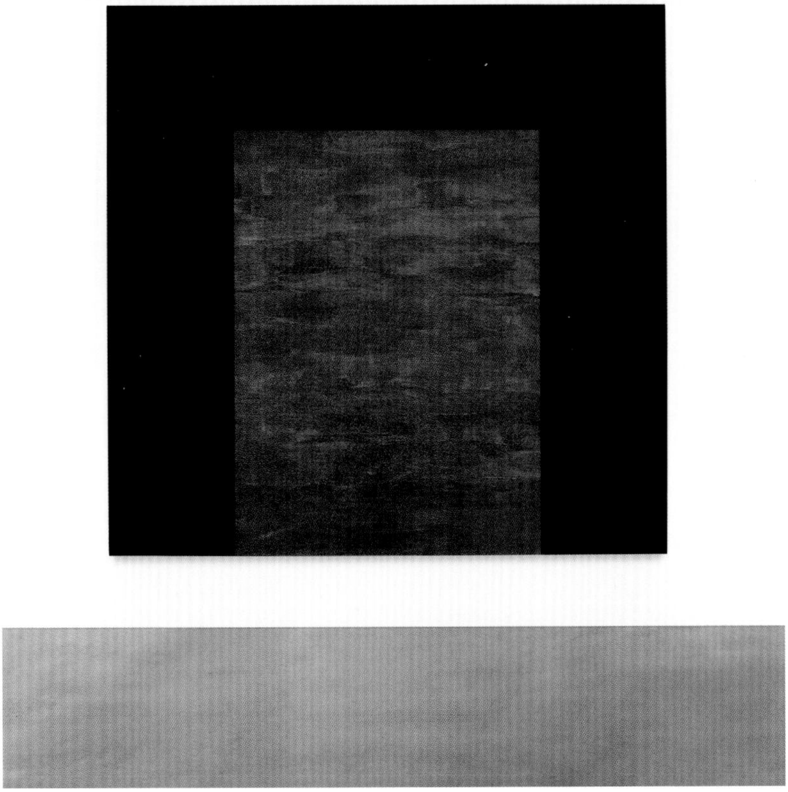

1
Mary Corse
Untitled (Black Light Arch Series), 1992
Glass microspheres in acrylic on canvas, 243.8 × 243.8 cm

MG: *What does this conversation with abstraction offer you?*
MC: I find it very exciting and satisfying to my psyche. The act of painting has the ability to truly transcend the moment and put you in a different sphere. Obviously, it does that for me. I consider that sanity in the midst of searching for meaning. We need meaning, which is consciousness. And I find it, there, in painting. I find a place of infinite dialogue instead of finite thinking.

MG: *Did you have this deep relationship with painting from the very start? I read that you were exposed to culture, in a broad sense, already in your childhood. You started classical piano lessons at the age of five, followed by jazz and ballet. Was visual art a part of your education as well?*
MC: I started painting early and I've always used it as a place I could go to. As a nine-year-old I was drawing the human figure realistically. Then, in the seventh, eighth, and ninth grade I had a fantastic instructor at

2
Mary Corse
Untitled (Electric Light),
1968 / 2017
Argon, Plexiglas, high frequency generator, light tubes, monofilament, 121.9 × 121.9 × 15.2 cm light box; 243.8 × 137.2 × 20.3 cm transformer cabinet

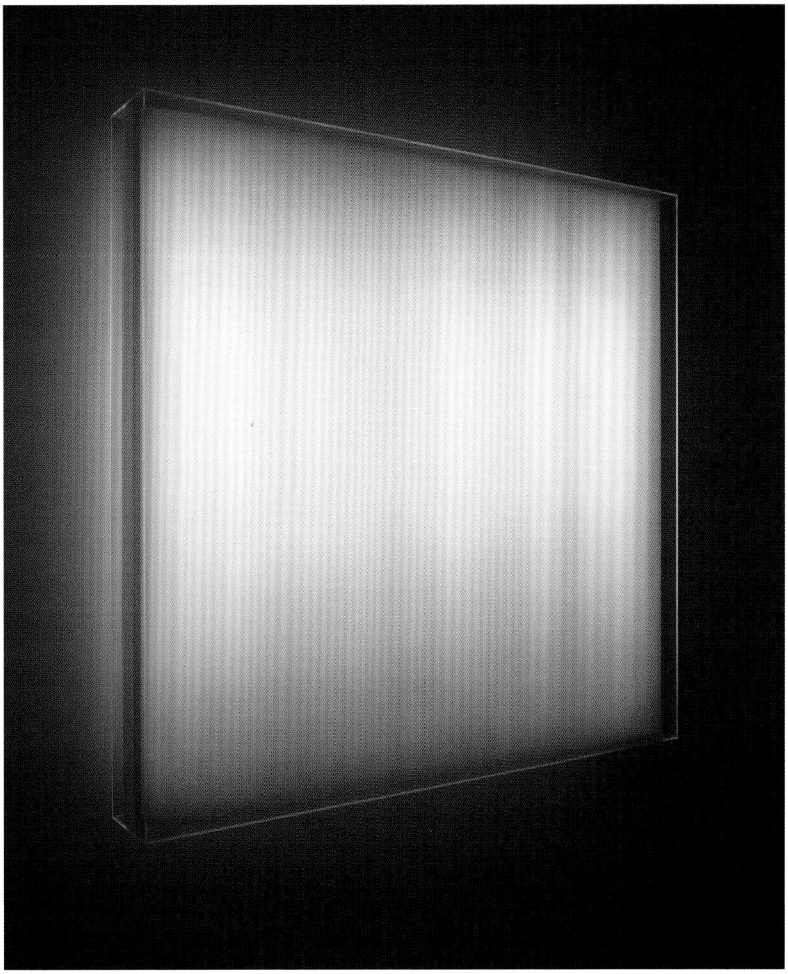

the school I attended in Berkeley. Her lessons gave me a kick-start into Abstract Expressionism.

MG: *Have you always been interested in abstraction? Figurative painting never really engaged you much?*
MC: I'm interested in abstraction but I'm actually sort of a realist. I'm interested in creating a painting that makes you feel some kind of truth about our human condition and where we are on the planet. We live in abstraction. You don't see the other side of the moon. You don't see the room on the other side of the wall. But they're still there. And that's why abstraction has interested me from an early age. It's about the truth. I want truth to be in the painting, along with other things like ambiguity, space and time. Time is an important part of my work. That's why I make them so wide – so that it takes time to walk across them.

MG: *The process seems to be as important to you as the final result.*
MC: Oh yes. I like making things. I like doing things and making things happen. I like discovering things and researching. In the '70s, I was designing this really big earth-kiln to make an 8 ft ceramic tile. All the kiln builders told me, "Oh, it'll never work". But I kept going until I found something that did. The same thing happened when I made my wireless electric light pieces in the late '60s – the ones with the generator hidden in the wall. I was building my own generators for those. [chuckles] I love the process.

MG: *The act of creation...*
MC: I love to use my hands to make things. Out of what? Out of abstract forces. You try to make something that has meaning out there, where things appear meaningless or questionable.

MG: *Let's go back to your fascination with abstraction. When you were getting your MFA in the mid-1960s, Abstract Expressionism was kind of dying out.*
MC: Well, I actually started with Abstract Expressionism when I was about twelve at private grade school. This was in the mid-1950s when Abstract Expressionism was very strong. Jackson Pollock was still painting. By the '60s, I was moving away from it.

MG: *I read that, in 1964, you made this abstract blue and red painting that became very important to you because you involved abstraction with light.*
MC: Yes, I was starting to go down my own path. It's funny, it's like the paintings tell me what to do. You have to be able to have that abstract conversation. The paintings would say, "Oh, I need this", "a little bit here", "a little bit there". After studying Josef Albers, Hans Hofman, and mostly Willem de Kooning for a few years, the paintings started telling me other things. I started making my own, and the first one of these was the red and blue painting. The most interesting thing about this particular painting to me was the flash of light between the red and the blue. Through the painting, I saw how opposites can work and that certainly made me see light in painting for the first time. Next, I used silver flakes and colors in my paintings and then, when I started painting with white, that was really about light too. The white turned into light.

MG: *Has this reduction process required extreme discipline? You had to concentrate on a very limited color-palette.*
MC: When it comes to making paintings I always think of it as a passion. No, you don't have to be disciplined to go minimal. It feels great to get rid of things, to get rid of your ego and your hang-ups. I used to sand the

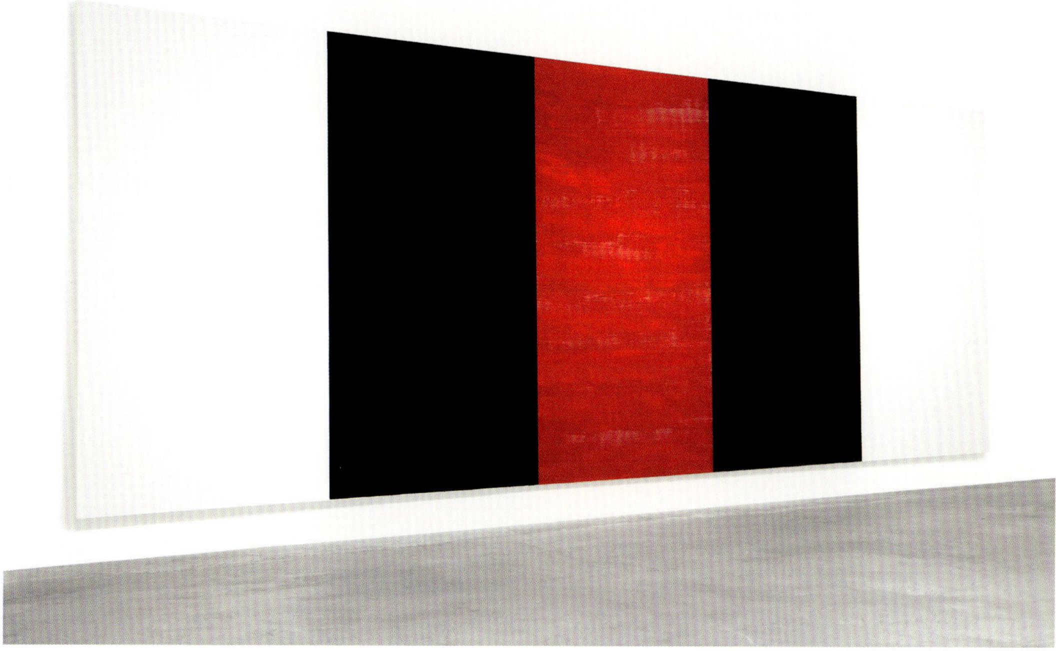

3
Mary Corse
Untitled (White, Black, Red), 2001
Glass microspheres in acrylic on canvas, 243.8 × 609.6 cm

brushstroke out because I wanted to get rid of subjectivity. I didn't want any artist-ego, nor any signature.

MG: *This phase didn't last very long, though, and you went back to subjectivity. There* is *a brushstroke in your paintings.*
MC: There is, yes. I put the brushstroke back into the painting in the late '60s. I was very young when I made those first flat, white paintings, twenty-two or twenty-three. Then, I went from white into the white light and from there to the wireless flat electric light boxes. In order to build the bigger, high-frequency wireless ones I had to get the materials from *Edmund Scientific*, and they wouldn't sell the parts to you unless you'd passed a certain test, so I had to go and learn about physics. When I was there, I got interested in quantum physics, and that triggered some kind of an amalgamation in my brain that kept changing and changing. I'm still fascinated by it, realizing what a perceptual reality we are living in. Before physics, I was looking for a truth out there, an objective truth. Afterwards, I understood that perception creates reality so I put subjectivity, the brushstroke, back in my paintings.

MG: *Searching for the truth sounds like a philosophical goal.*
MC: Well, for me, that's what art is for. We're not going to search for a

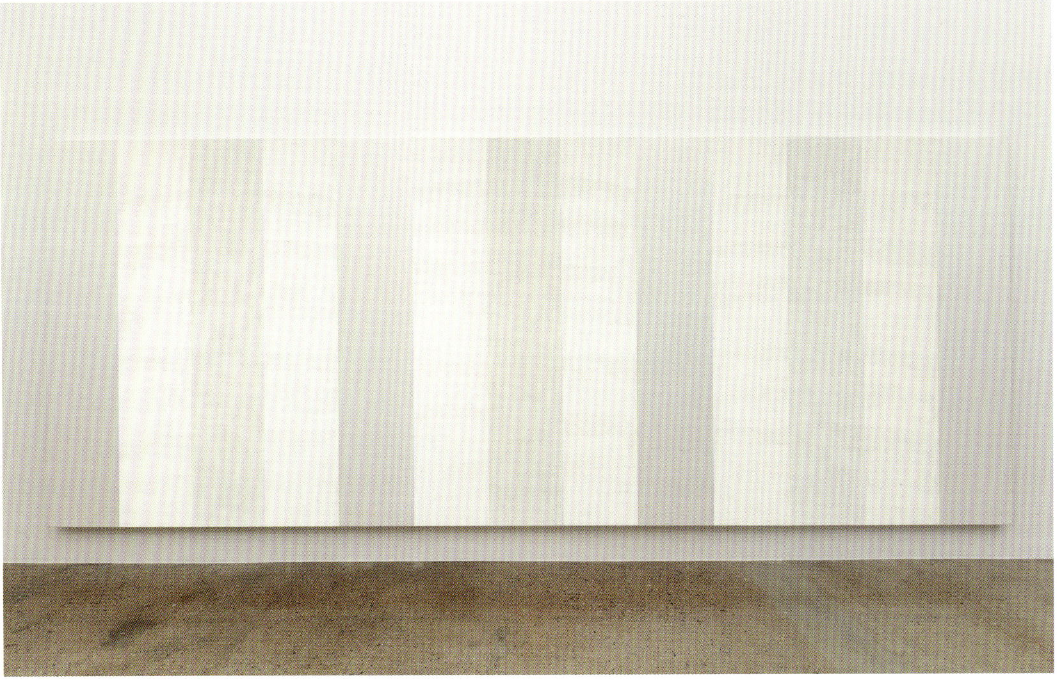

4
Mary Corse
Untitled (White Multiband, Horizontal Strokes), 2003
Glass microspheres in acrylic on canvas, 243.8 × 609.6 cm

lie. The idea is to get rid of delusion or experience the feeling of truth. What else is art about?

MG: *On the one hand you're searching for the hardly-graspable truth, on the other you are fascinated by physics based on concrete facts, which therefore limits what can be known.*
MC: Physics has become metaphysics – facts are not so concrete. I always said, artists and physicists are the opposite sides of the brain – put them together sometimes. It's part of our human state to have both kinds of thinking. We have logic and thinking, which in my opinion don't go as far because they're finite. They're the past. To me, the other side, intuition without thought, is where art comes from.

MG: *You use very unconventional materials, glass microspheres, to paint. Did you discover these microspheres in an intuitive way?*
MC: Well, after I had made those Plexiglas light pieces in the '60s, I wanted to find a way of putting light in paintings. Painting, to me, has never been about the paint, but what the painting can make you feel. When I realized just how much perception was a part of reality, I wanted this factor to be in my paintings. I wanted to have the brushstroke but also wanted to retain the light. So, I went around trying to find out how

I could insert light in the painting. I would try different materials, such as Murano paint, stuff that glows in the dark, and all kinds of different things. And then I noticed the paint on highways. I was driving down the road when the white dividing line lit up and I thought, "Oh, let's try that". What I like about this material is that it changes with your perception. It's not reflective – reflective is one-two. A microsphere is a prism – one-two-three; it creates a triangle between the surface, the viewer and the light source. So, as you move, the painting changes. Therefore it puts the painting – let's say the art – into your perception rather than on the wall.

MG: *Is that not slightly contradictory? You just said that art is within the perception of the viewer, but at the same time the painting is still an autonomous object.*
MC: Well, I used to think that, but not any longer. I don't think of the painting as an object that's out there now. Perception is what happens inside you. Art is when you wake up to the truth of our human condition.

MG: *The way I understand it, painting is something that has a life of its own.*
MC: Well, that's part of the painting's life. It talks to you *and* it's in your perception. I think it's the question of our times, even though I think that I'm the only person asking it. [chuckles] Now that we've realized perception creates reality, we can do whatever we want to do. We want to go to the moon, we go to the moon. Whatever you dream up, you try. Perception can create reality. But the question is: *How* subjective is the universe? What is that, how much is out there, how invisible is matter, *really*? We live in such a mystery. The reason I like both physics and art is that they're methods of inner-searching, or ways of learning and experiencing the human condition in this questionable reality we live our lives in.

MG: *Do you think art has the ability to make something that is normally invisible visible?*
MC: I do. It's invisible until you make it visible. [chuckles] But art can talk about invisible things. That's why I'm not really interested in making a picture of something "out there". You want to make something that comes about from "in here".

MG: *Is your career, or to put it differently, your life as an artist, exactly what you wanted to do originally?*
MC: I never thought of my life as an artist in terms of a career, for one thing. We didn't think of art as a career. I think that idea just popped up

twenty or thirty years ago. No, I painted because that's what I love to do. It's satisfying to see a painting I like. I never thought of it as a career, so I never chose it as a career.

MG: *Still, are you enjoying what's happening to you now? The international recognition you're receiving, with different museums queuing to exhibit your work?*
MC: Oh, yes. I feel very lucky that I have something I love to do and it's being appreciated. Things are moving forward.

MG: *You've often been associated with the* Light and Space *movement, which, as I've understood it, you don't consider to be entirely correct?*
MC: Well, for one thing, it should be light, space and time. It's a big question. My art is more about the inner environment.

MG: *We were talking about you as an artist. Have you ever considered yourself a female artist?*
MC: I never thought of art as a gender thing.

MG: *You must have been quite special, making generators and doing things that were maybe, at that time, not so usual for women.*
MC: I never thought about that. There must have been other women who were figuring out how to do it themselves. I've always felt very feminine and I think I'm very feminine. There's no factor that would have prevent me from creating what I wanted, or anyone else. I was a single mom who raised two kids. At that time, how many female artists were doing that?!

MG: *Which was probably not so easy.*
MC: It wasn't easy. But what was I going to do, *not* raise my sons? Give up painting? [chuckles] Neither of the two were going to happen. My work survived during the toughest years thanks to Richard Bellamy, and eventually things changed. Now I'm painting more than ever before.

ANTHONY D'OFFAY

March 2016

Marta Gnyp: *How did you start your gallery?*
Anthony d'Offay: I started dealing in books when I was seventeen. When I was twenty-one, I got a small sum of money as compensation after an accident. I was able to buy a very interesting poetry library and became so fascinated by its books that I produced a catalogue, which was a big success. When you're studying at university and you manage to do something successful outside your area of study, that tells you which direction you should move in. I became a full-time dealer in rare books and drawings. I moved to London at the age of twenty-three, and opened a tiny gallery when I was twenty-five.

MG: *I read that it was very successful from the start. Why?*
AdO: I think because we were producing very good exhibitions. I put together exhibitions such as *The Influence of Whistler on English Painting*; *The English Friends of Paul Gauguin*; *Dream and Fantasy in Victorian Painting*. But when we made an exhibition of drawings by Hokusai, we got great reviews for the first time.

MG: *Where did you get the drawings?*
AdO: I worked on it intensely for two to three years. I believe in proper research. I worked with Jack Hillier, a great friend, who had written the standard monograph on Hokusai. It was a very exciting thing to do. There was a show at the Stedelijk Museum in Amsterdam, in 1951, with drawings by Rembrandt, Van Gogh and Hokusai, three of the greatest draftsmen of all time. It is rather difficult to do a selling show of Rembrandt or Van Gogh so I wanted to see what we could do with Hokusai. It was a beautiful exhibition. People came from Japan to buy works.

MG: *So you became a specialist in Japanese art at the age of twenty-eight?*
AdO: We did an exhibition entitled *Actors and Courtesans, The Japanese Print 1770–1800*, displaying very rare prints. I remember a collector who flew from Japan to see the show. Then, in a very non-European way, he said,

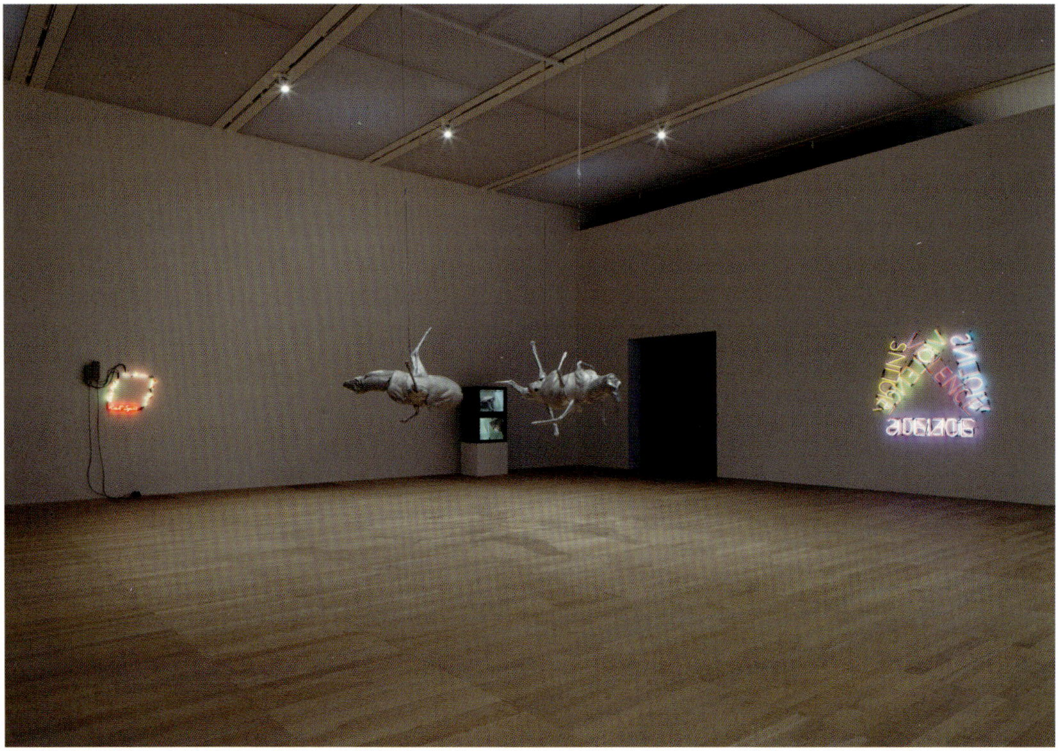

1
Installation view of *ARTIST ROOMS: Bruce Nauman*, Tate Modern, 2009

"I need time with you", so we sat down for three hours and talked. Then he stood up, bowed, and said, "It is an honor to buy these prints from you". A wonderful idea, trusting the dealer rather than the work of art.

MG: *Were you building your reputation?*
AdO: As time went on I felt we should try to open a big contemporary gallery.

MG: *Why did you want to switch when you were doing so well?*
AdO: Because London needed it. I was friends with several artists. I started representing Lucian Freud in 1970. Through him, I also made friends with Francis Bacon, who I saw often. I was beginning to realize it was my duty to try to bring the best artists in the world to London.

MG: *How did you find Beuys?*
AdO: He had a big show in Rotterdam with drawings belonging to his friend Heiner Bastian. I went to the show and met Beuys for the first time.

MG: *Why do you think Beuys was such an important artist?*
AdO: If you think of the history of modern art, we had Abstract Expres-

sionism, then we had Pop art, followed by Minimal art and then Conceptual art. Then, in 1981, *The New Spirit in Painting* exhibition in London pointed everyone in a new direction. But Beuys's retrospective at the Guggenheim, in 1979, was the real moment of change. It categorically told New York that there was more in the world than just American art.

MG: *How did Beuys convey this message?*
AdO: Through a 1977 sculpture called *Tallow* – 22 tons of fat brought into the museum by removing one of Frank Lloyd Wright's iconic windows. His sculptures of fat and felt had something shamanistic about them and were often connected to performance. Beuys had a very profound concern for young peoples' education and the development of their creativity. He strongly believed that we have a real obligation to empower each other. Beuys was also one of the initiators of the Green Party. He had an unforgettable presence; you were very self-conscious when he was in the room. I remember Richard Hamilton telling me he had an exhibition opening somewhere in Germany, and it was a big success. Then Beuys, who was his friend, arrived. Hamilton said to me, "God, I wish he hadn't come". All the cameras, all the attention turned to Beuys.

MG: *How come he was so charismatic? Was he manipulating people?*
AdO: He was like Andy Warhol; both of them were almost killed. Both of them had a near-death experience: Beuys when his plane crashed, Warhol when he was shot. If you die and you come back from the dead, you very often change as a person.

MG: *Do you believe Beuys's story about the plane crash and his being saved by the Tatars?*
AdO: If you didn't believe it you could ask him to take his hat off and look at the scars on his head. It wasn't a comfortable sight. If you fall on your head from an airplane in Crimea, you're lucky if some Tatars pick you up and nurse you back to life.

MG: *And after he recovered he felt he had a mission in the world.*
AdO: A lot of his ideas had to do with healing: he dreamed of healing the world. Think of *PLIGHT*, [a big installation by Beuys first exhibited in the gallery in 1985 and now owned by the Centre Pompidou]. The word "plight" means three things: a promise, as in "I plight my troth"; a plight is also a difficult situation; thirdly, there's the French word, *plier* – to fold, just as the felt in the installation was folded. However, the promise was the most important aspect. The sculpture had to do with the healing of the gallery, which had been suffering from noisy building work.

Beuys saw it as a muffling sculpture. As a visitor you were immediately taken aback at the silence, the smell of felt, hearing your heart beating, listening to your body.

MG: *Would you say Beuys was the most charismatic artist you worked with?*
AdO: All artists are unique and extraordinary, you only have to think of Freud, Beuys and Andy Warhol. They were all so different, so brilliant, and so strange that you could truly say there was nobody like them.

MG: *All three of them lived their lives through art.*
AdO: They considered art as the most important activity for changing the world.

MG: *How did it work in daily life?*
AdO: Beuys said to people: everybody is an artist, meaning everybody has to develop the creativity of an artist.

MG: *On the other hand, his charismatic appearance made people think differently, that they could never be like him.*
AdO: When he went to the openings of his exhibitions, he'd would always immediately talk to the shyest, youngest person in the room. He was trying to make the world a better place, especially the world recovering from the Second World War. I could understand it because I was born in 1940 and I remember the war. I remember the bombs falling, I remember looking at a German airplane which had crashed at the end of our street.

MG: *How did you experience the war?*
AdO: For a young child, the sound of sirens – warning for a bombing raid – was very exciting. I didn't feel fear, but a big adventure. We all ran to the air-raid shelters which were at the bottom of the garden. We sat there, made a cup of tea in a concrete box, and listened to airplanes bombing until it was over. Immediately after the war, my father became a surgeon in the British Army on the Rhine. I expect he was putting people back together after air-raids or people who had houses collapsing on them. I noticed, however, that the war had a very good effect on my parents. When my father came back home for weekends, my parents were extremely loving to each other and to us. I thought the war was wonderful.

MG: *What about the idea of Germany as the enemy?*
AdO: We had prisoner-of-war camp within walking distance of our house. Through barbed wire I could see rather unhappy looking men on the

other side. At the end of the war all the reckoning with Germany started: the Holocaust, war criminals, Eichmann and all those things. It deeply affected Baselitz, Kiefer, Richter and Polke. They all felt the experience they lived through strongly and always felt influenced by it. Being German affected all of them, but none more than Beuys. He actually took part in the war.

MG: *Did Beuys speak about his experience with you?*
AdO: He was a POW of the Coldstream Guards Regiment. So, once, I said to him that I assumed everybody had looked after him very properly. He said: "They were fantastic. Really wonderful. There was only one problem". When I asked what that was he replied, "No food. I used to have a pair of scissors, and cut grass with the scissors and try to cook it; not so much fun". I don't think he would ever have said anything about it if I hadn't asked him. Nobody was tortured, nobody was shot, they were just not given any food, only just enough to survive.

MG: *Did the war play a part for other artists as well?*
AdO: I remember Lucian Freud telling me he had had great fun going around Berlin painting swastikas on the walls. Lucian was always a bad boy. If you made a rule, he was going to break it as quickly as he could.

MG: *Did this attitude get him into trouble?*
AdO: When he was taken on by the Acquavella Gallery in New York, he had racing debts of £2.8 million. But he then said to me: "You know what's more exciting than winning? Losing. Because then you need to mobilize your energy and be creative".

MG: *Beuys wasn't afraid of getting into trouble either.*
AdO: Beuys was dismissed from the Düsseldorf Academy because he wanted to allow all students that wanted to come to his classes. You can imagine how annoying it was for the art school and for other professors. Then he said, "After World War One there was a young German who wanted to join the art college in Munich but was refused. If Hitler had been accepted by professors like me, the history of the twentieth century would be somewhat different". Beuys really knew how to reach the heart.

MG: *How was the relationship between Richter and Beuys?*
AdO: Lord Snowdon took a very beautiful photograph of Beuys's face with some felt fibers from the *PLIGHT* installation stuck to his hat. Years later, I was in the Richter-studio and saw this same image framed. I told him that I didn't know he was close to Beuys and cared so much. Richter

said an incredibly interesting thing: "No, I had to be careful, because you could start to believe his theories, change your mind and become a follower of Beuys. I didn't want to change where I was going. I had to always keep a distance". That speaks very much about the power of Beuys and his personal presence. People, in some sense, men, women, young and old, fell in love with him. Kiefer came closest to knowing him well.

MG: *What about Beuys and Warhol? Warhol's idea about art was completely different.*
AdO: They both saw each other's great power but knew that that power was completely different from their own. They were slightly amused by each other, but were also aware that the other was the real deal, a great artist. They respected each other.

MG: *What did you think about Warhol's fascination with commerce and "business art"?*
AdO: Warhol liked to say things in a provocative way. He always wanted to give the worst possible answers and say the worst possible things. Normally, we do the opposite. People hated it when he started painting money but it kept Andy amused. He liked to watch how people reacted. When we wanted to do an exhibition in London with him and I asked him what he'd like to show, he answered: "Whatever you want. You tell me and I'll do it". No other artist in history would say that.

MG: *Was he testing you?*
AdO: He was trying to make me come up with a good idea. I suggested a self-portrait and that was what we did. I thought that it was very important that he got a show with good reviews because, around 1980, he wasn't popular with art critics; everybody hated those guns, knives, and dollar signs. I wanted people to say that here is the great artist at the height of his power.

MG: *Did you achieve it?*
AdO: Yes. We sold many from this exhibition to museums immediately, including a large self portrait with camouflage. The idea "you tell me, I'll do it" was an extraordinary one.

MG: *Around this time, you also started working with Kiefer.*
AdO: Our first show with him was in 1982/83. We were already working with Beuys, who was extremely important to him. Kiefer said the time that he spent alone with Beuys in Düsseldorf was the most important in his life. Thus Kiefer and I had something very strong in common: we both ad-

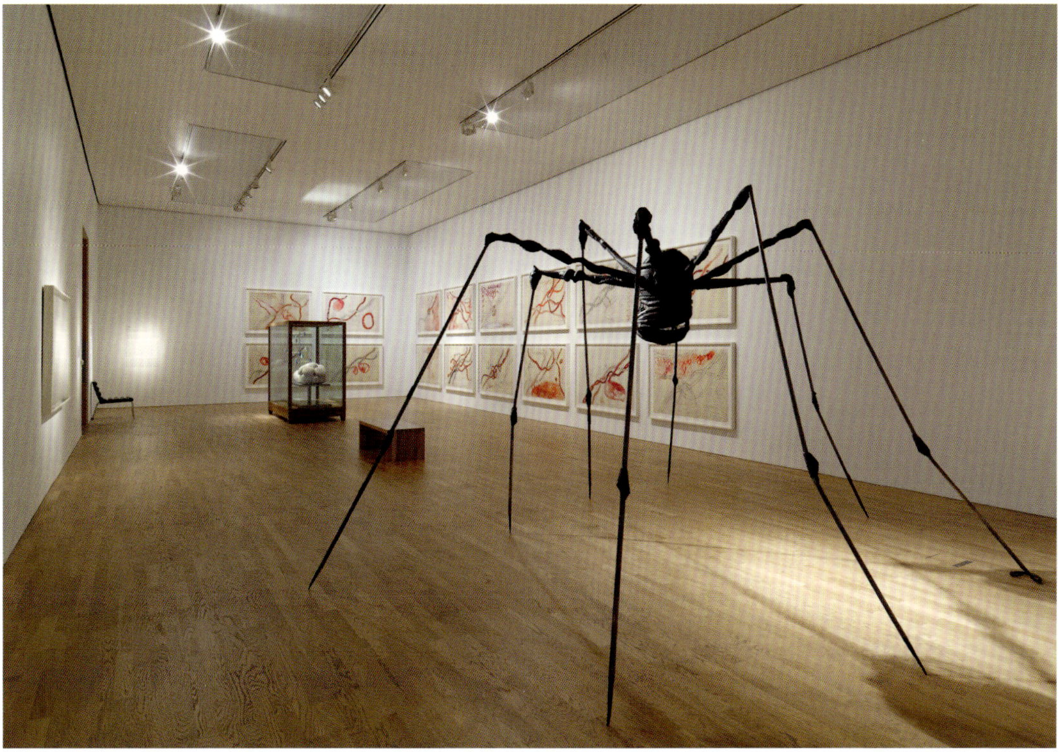

2
Installation view of *ARTIST ROOMS: Louise Bourgeois*, Middlesbrough, Mima, 2014

mired Beuys. When we did the exhibition, Anselm was delighted because works of art went into museums. He has always been very conscious of the importance of museums. He's also an extraordinarily generous person; he donated great works to *ARTIST ROOMS*.

MG: *Kiefer seems to be gaining momentum now. His importance and place in art history seem to not only be generally accepted, but also growing. Was it not difficult for him in the past to be in the shadow of other artists, like Richter, for example?*
AdO: I don't think Kiefer has ever been in the shadows. Richter was rightly recognized as one of the greatest painters of the 20th century and his prices doubled, tripled, quadrupled, whatever it was. Taste changes all the time; artists' reputations and the relevance of their work change all the time. It's a very interesting phenomenon. Another example is Bruce Nauman, who has suddenly appeared as a giant of the 20th century; not just a very interesting or extraordinary artist, but a modern master.

MG: *Do you have an explanation for these sudden changes in taste?*
AdO: Part of it is politics, what happens in the world and how people feel. For example, Louise Bourgeois has, with time, become a great 20th

century figure. She was able to do things that no man had ever attempted, like giant spiders and cells. Her ideas were liberating and beyond male thinking.

MG: *You mean we needed to go through the 1980s, and the shift in thinking about gender and identity, to be able to recognize her greatness?*
AdO: That's right. And then you need great exhibitions. Frances Morris did a magnificent job in curating the retrospective of Bourgeois in the Tate Modern, in 2007. I saw works there that I'd never seen before, which I found incredibly moving. That was the first time I appreciated what a genius Louise Bourgeois really was. It was then that we met the wonderful Jerry Gorovoy, who looked after her during the last twenty years of her life, working with her every day, calming her down, cheering her up, making sure the bronzes arrived, and that everything was done properly.

MG: *Do you think in terms of male and female when looking at art?*
AdO: What I really care about is that artists like Louise gave confidence to many women. This empowerment seems to be very important. Think what a different world it would be if half of the world's leaders were women. Couldn't we do with some women in North Korea, with some women in the Middle East or in Russia?

MG: *You never represented Louise in your gallery.*
AdO: I'm told that she wanted us to represent her, but at that time we were representing thirty of the world's greatest artists. It's always very difficult to take on more artists. However, we now have quite a lot of women in our *ARTIST ROOMS*: Agnes Martin, Vija Celmins, Ellen Gallagher, Jenny Holzer, Diane Arbus, Louise Bourgeois, Phyllida Barlow and Francesca Woodman.

MG: *Have you observed the relationship between the artists and their public?*
AdO: In a way, there are two sorts of artists: the artists that want powerful, rich, and important people to see their work, and the other sort of artists, who want the public to see their work.

MG: *So who would be in the first category?*
AdO: [laughs] You know how to answer that question.

MG: *I would love to hear it from you.*
AdO: I think artists have a special relationship to money and power. Making works of art is a sort of generosity in itself. That is to say creating can

be a painful process for many artists. Giving birth, with all its problems, is exhausting: you give away a part of yourself, it's often painful and can take a long time. And then comes the question of how you'll present the work to the world.

MG: *One needs courage to be a great artist. During the 1990s, painting went out of fashion and was declared dead. How was it for your artists, many of whom were painters, to go through this period?*
AdO: They were all great artists and great painters. Kiefer, with whom we organized a show in 1992, said this about Koons: "I don't like his work but I think it's a great idea to do this exhibition". What he meant was that he understood this as art from the present, from this time. You can have seven years basking in the light of success and then things suddenly change in the world of art. That doesn't mean an artist stops being an artist but rather that he or she very often has to spend fifteen years being that same artist and waiting... Like Kiefer, who has waited years for his great retrospective, happening now at Centre Pompidou.

MG: *Do you think they had a difficult time?*
AdO: Absolutely. You have to paint, when everybody is looking at the YBAs and Koons.

MG: *What was Koons' strength?*
AdO: To put it simply, he sees the good in everything. He picked up "banality" where Warhol left off. He gave people what they wanted in the same way that Warhol did. We started working with Jeff Koons shortly after his *Banality* exhibition in 1988. During our 1992 show, we published the Jeff Koons Handbook and sold over 50,000 copies in a year. His works and statements were something nobody had ever heard before [opens the book and reads]: "In the Large Vase of Flowers, there are 140 flowers. They're very sexual and fertile, and at the same time there are 140 assholes there". How about that?

MG: *What did you think about the YBAs?*
AdO: We were proud to show Ron Mueck and Rachel Whiteread. We did a lot to place Rachel's work in museums. Damien, who worked for us, painting walls and installing sculptures when he was a student, is today well represented in *ARTIST ROOMS*.

MG: *Many important players in the art world once worked with you. Why was it so interesting for them?*
AdO: They could earn a bit of money and spend time with Twombly, War-

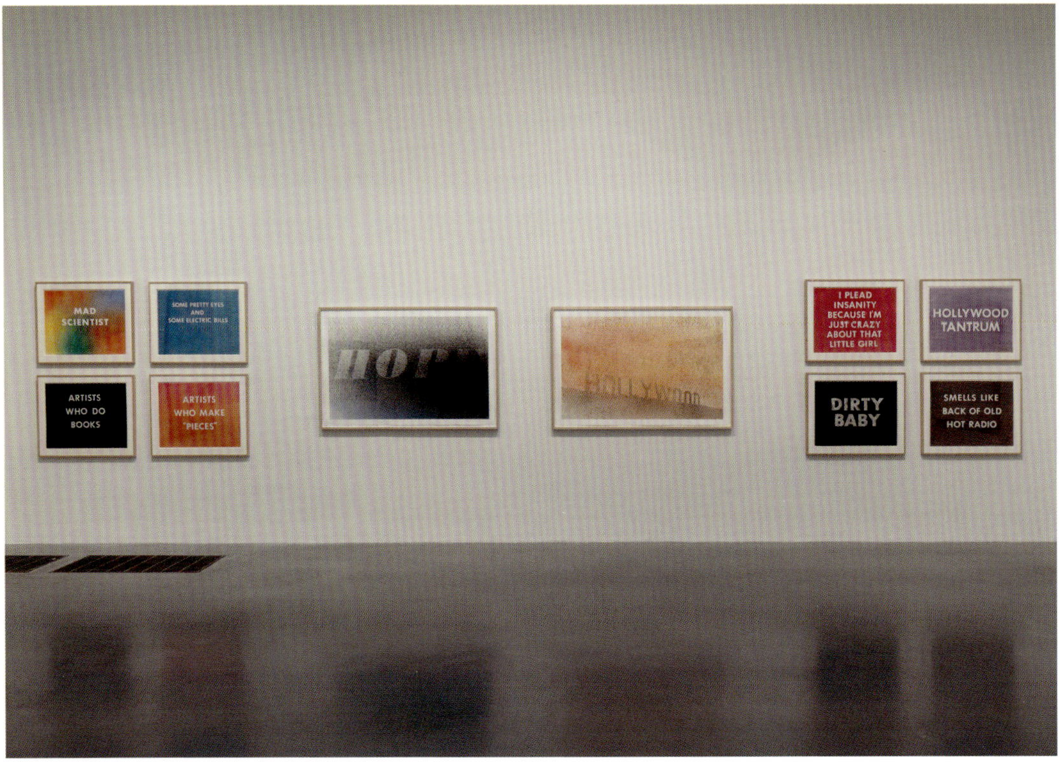

3
Installation view of *ARTIST ROOMS: Edward Ruscha*

hol, or Koons. We were very much a team. We had a lot of meetings and I didn't allow anybody to attend who didn't come up with ideas. I wanted everyone to be creative. I was over fifty and wanted to hear what people in their twenties had to say. Sadie Coles, Gavin Brown, Matthew Marks and Lorcan O'Neill all worked in the gallery. The Metropolitan Museum of Art in New York kindly invited me some years ago to give the *Stieglitz* lecture. The director, Tom Campbell, very kindly introduced me, by telling the audience that his very first job was as an intern with us in the early'80s.

MG: *Did you go and visit collectors?*
AdO: For me, artists and museums were of essential importance. For collectors, I had an excellent sales team. You can't do everything yourself. I traveled a lot. I'd go to New York, Los Angeles, Sydney, Tokyo and then back to London. If you visit Australian museums you'll find masterpieces (made) by artists we represented.

MG: *Your strategy was to go to countries that weren't completely included in the Western art network.*
AdO: It seemed to me that we were providing a service, which kept us in touch with the rest of the world. I was asked to organize the German

part of the Sydney Biennale one year; we focused on Beuys, Polke, Richter and Kiefer. In Australia, they have wonderful museums and they are very happy to collaborate.

MG: *This is a slightly different approach to, Leo Castelli, for example, who seemed to be giving collectors a lot of attention.*
AdO: Castelli was a great friend and it was an honor to work with him. He had a very special approach to communication. I remember one occasion in which we were sitting in his office in New York and he said, "Jasper Johns hasn't had a show in London yet. By the way, he's coming for coffee in ten minutes". And then, the show was fixed.

MG: *If you were to start a gallery today, would it be possible to do it in the same way?*
AdO: Impossible. I don't think the gallery we had could exist in the world of today. The idea of you spending all your time trying to sell pieces to museums is probably completely outdated. In 2001, the last year of our gallery, 55 percent of our sales went to museums, which would be unthinkable today. Museums are slow-payers. The idea of separate countries is gone – today everything is international. We had a mission: to have a great gallery, to get people to come to London and see contemporary art, together with changing people's feelings about what they saw. All the young artists grew up seeing the exhibitions we produced. They realized that they were witnessing art history.

MG: *Do you think the omnipresence of fairs has changed a lot?*
AdO: In the old days, artists didn't want to be at fairs. What's also very strange is that, in the old days, you could barely get in through the front door at the openings of exhibitions, now nobody comes any more. Collectors are all waiting for *Frieze*, *Basel* and other fairs.

MG: *You had excellent contact with museums, what about auction houses? Were you supporting artists when there was a piece on auction?*
AdO: Yes, we bought pieces at auctions if it seemed like a good thing to do.

MG: *Have you been following works, that came from your gallery, at auctions?*
AdO: Of course. The most expensive contemporary piece we sold was *the Balloon Dog* by Jeff Koons for $57 million, to Peter Brant.

MG: *Was it Peter Brant who bought it from you?*
AdO: He also has Koons' *Puppy* in a field in Connecticut. It would be very

nice if he gave it to the Met. Peter Brant could do something wonderful for the city of New York. The A/P of Jeff Koons' *Puppy*, which we sold to the Guggenheim in Bilbao, is a national treasure!

MG: *You are very much in favor of cooperating with public museums and donating works.*
AdO: Public institutions have always been of great importance to me. When you think, for example, of Berlin and Hamburger Bahnhof – the Marx Collection is a great treasure and, god willing, it'll stay in Berlin. Marx has masterpieces by Warhol, Twombly, Lichtenstein and Beuys, which are of the greatest importance to Germany and belong in that country. The same is true about the UK. Very often, we have great museums but they don't have the necessary acquisition funds. How is the Tate going to make great exhibitions without gifts? With *ARTIST ROOMS*, we were trying to think about what's important for this country.

MG: *What about private museums?*
AdO: Private museums can greatly add to the world's cultural landscape. It was a tragedy for France and for Paris that François Pinault decided to set up his museum in Venice instead of the Île Seguin in Paris, as he had originally planned. It would have been so good for the Centre Pompidou to have another big institution for contemporary art in Paris. I remember the moment I read about it when I was in New York – I burst into tears. I think it would have changed Paris in a very positive and exciting new way.

MG: *Do you think that competition between museums works positively?*
AdO: Look at the New York museums: there is a lot of competition between the Metropolitan, the Guggenheim, the Whitney, the MoMA, the New Museum – a lot of cooperation as well, but it's competition that keeps everybody on their toes.

WOJCIECH FANGOR

March 2014

Marta Gnyp: *We cannot discuss your life and art without talking about the turbulent 20th century. Let's start from the very beginning: when did you discover that you wanted to be an artist?*
Wojciech Fangor: I was already drawing as a child, as all children do. My mother collected my drawings, so I was able to look at them later on, as an adult. I discovered that I was already using perspective at the age of 3. It was remarkable. My mother told me about a drawing contest for children, which was being held in Warsaw in the '20s. Since she was convinced I had great talent, she sent my drawings there but they were all rejected as they said a child couldn't have made them.

MG: *Did you later join an art academy?*
WF: When I was nine years old, I went to France for several months with my mother, who loved art. There I got a box with oil paint, canvasses and an easel. I loved the smell of the oil paint and was desperate to paint. After our return, my mother showed my work to Professor Tadeusz Pruszkowski from the Warsaw Academy of Art, who agreed to take me on. It didn't last long, however, because soon the Second World War broke out.

MG: *What did you do when the war started?*
WF: On September 6, 1939 all men able to carry weapons were called to leave Warsaw and sign up for military service. My father, who couldn't drive himself, asked me to escape with him. So I drove him to the Romanian border. Many people were waiting there to watch how the situation would develop, including many members of the government. On September 17, the Soviet Army invaded Poland in the east so we drove even further south, to Bucharest and later to Budapest. There, I went to the French consulate and asked them to draft me into the French army, but since I was only sixteen at the time, they rejected me for being too young for military service. So I went back to Poland.

MG: *With your father?*
WF: Alone. Actually I ran away from him when he was having dinner with

someone. I got on a train and somehow reached Warsaw and Klarysew, a little village where my mother and sister lived and where I could paint in my own studio.

MG: *How could you think about painting in such a situation?*
WF: Art was extremely important to me, even in this situation. Of course, I realized there was a war. But, at first, the terror was directed towards the Jews. Then, when the underground Polish Home Army initiated attacks on Germans, they also started using brutal violence against Poles. For each German killed, they'd kill a hundred Poles. But in Klarysew, where I was mostly living, nothing was happening.

MG: *Did you continue your artistic education?*
WF: I applied to Pruszkowski to give me private lessons once a week. Pruszkowski was a true personality. A France-oriented erudite, he had an excellent knowledge of French literature and also encouraged me to read it; he played the violin, sang and was extremely popular with women. He built a castle in the south of Poland, set up the guild of St Lucas for painters and was very enthusiastic about me.

MG: *Sounds like an inspiring teacher?*
WF: It only lasted a year and a half. The Germans were looking to arrest someone who was living in his apartment building. They asked the concierge to give them a list of all the people living in the building who had an academic title, such as doctor or professor. Since Pruszkowski was a professor at the Academy, he stood out on the list. The Germans took them all and shot them dead.

MG: *How did you live, surrounded by such terror?*
WF: I would follow all the news, official and illegal, and was waiting for the end of the war. It came in 1944. My young cousin, who was a member of the Underground Home Army, told me that an uprising was to take place in a few days. The Germans were already withdrawing; the Russian front was closing in on Warsaw. I asked my cousin whether they had coordinated the uprising with the Russians. He was upset, saying, "We don't talk with the Russians". I told him I'd be leaving Warsaw and asked him to come with me. He refused. I left and he was killed on the first day of the uprising. They jumped, with a few revolvers, onto the rows of German machine guns.

MG: *Where did you go?*
WF: To Rabka, a small town in southern Poland, perched on beautiful

1
Wojciech Fangor
Chopin, 1949
Oil on canvas, 170 × 120 cm

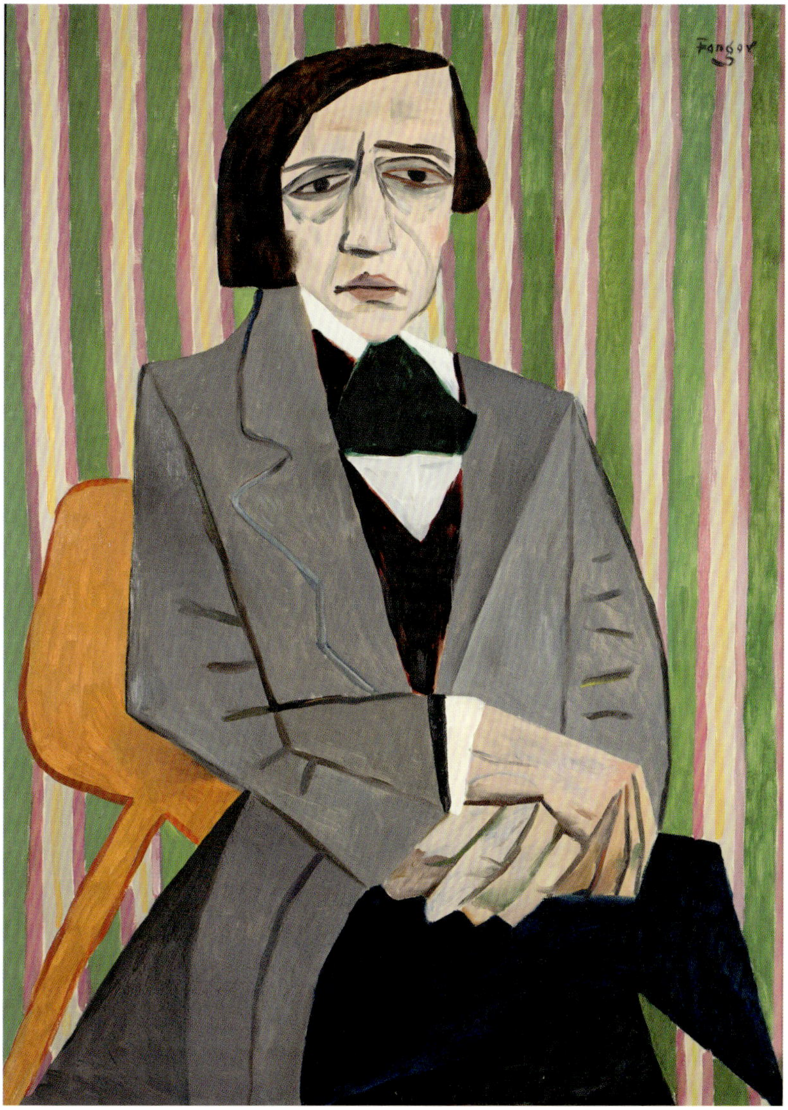

mountains. The Germans were using the pre-war sanatoria as field hospitals. A few days after my arrival, the Germans surrounded the town and took all men and women to dig trenches against tanks. We would dig trenches from 6 a.m. to 6 p.m. After a month, my girlfriend and I managed to escape.

MG: *Were you aware the war was coming to its end?*
WF: Yes. It was clear that the Germans were leaving, but at the same time the front was still there. I applied for a job at one of the hospitals to have an official document and become legal. I got the work, disposing garbage

2
Wojciech Fangor
B 106, 1966
Oil on canvas, 71.5 × 71.5 cm

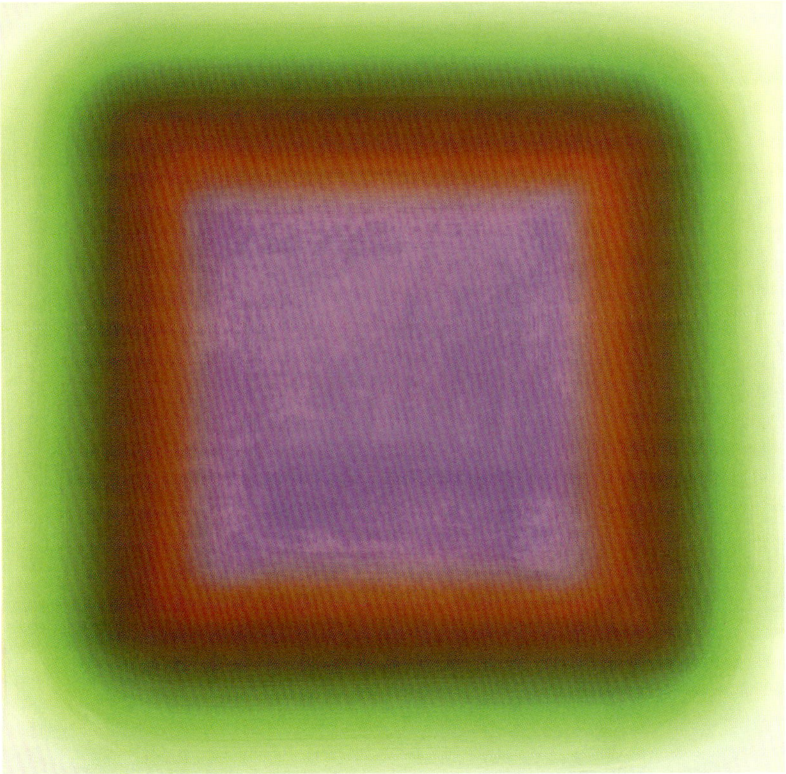

for a hospital, which wasn't the nicest job you could imagine. Another task was to strip dead soldiers of their clothes, as they buried them naked, all in a wooden case. I don't know why.

MG: *How could you keep going with this happening?*
WF: I was lucky. One day, a German officer, who was supervising us, told me, "I can see that you don't like what you are doing". I confirmed. He asked me what my profession was so I told him I was a painter. He said, "We need a painter". So I was given a cellar as a studio and was painting inventory numbers and the name of the hospital on boxes and furniture. I was very happy because I had my own place and, moreover, it was warm.

MG: *'Till the Russians arrived?*
WF: I was surprised. The Germans had helmets, knapsacks, uniforms, gas masks and machine guns. You could see they were soldiers. The Russians were like sparrows. Shabby coats, a piece of rope instead of a belt, bullets in their pockets, basic guns. I thought, "who are the Germans running away from?" I was summoned to join the army but, luckily, the doctor who was checking on me, exempted me from the front, I don't know why.

MG: *You were lucky.*
WF: I had a lot of luck during the war. I decided to return to Warsaw, which didn't exist any longer but Klarysow did. When I arrived there, I earned my living driving people around in a German truck. I was also painting landscapes and portraits. 1948 was a breakthrough-year for me. I was educated in the academic tradition. Pruszkowski was fascinated by 17th century Dutch painting and Felicjan Kowarski, who became my tutor after the death of Pruszkowski and admired romantic painting, like Delacroix, in combination with the Byzantine tradition. Both of them were very classically-oriented. In 1947 I coincidentally got my hands on a certain book in French. It was Vincent van Gogh's letters to his brother, Theo. I was fascinated. Van Gogh said museums are worth nothing and that an artist needs to work with what is today. Neither Pruszkowki nor Kowarski mentioned van Gogh or any other avant-garde artists, sporadical impressionists. Van Gogh wrote, so suggestively, about his experiences and thoughts, that I got on my bicycle and went to paint *en plein air* and in my way. He woke me up. I made about a hundred paintings during that time. It was a very important moment.

MG: *Because you left academia behind you?*
WF: Yes. I already possessed the technical skills, including drawing, but it involved a different approach to the role of color and form. If was not about the representation of reality, but an interpretation of reality, and the shifting of reality into the construction of images. A painting is something other than the appearance of reality, although there are connections between them.

MG: *Van Gogh helped you discover yourself?*
WF: Yes. More through his words than through his paintings, though. When I look at reproductions of works by someone else I always have this feeling telling me: this is *not* mine. But I can identify with someone else's emotions through words.

MG: *It was also a time of political change in Poland.*
WF: Because of the war, the German terror, and the Russian victory, I started reading newspapers and journals and got involved in the discussions of art and Marxism. I bought myself *Marx's Capital* and *The History of the Russian Revolution*. I read *The Communist Manifesto*, which is very poetic and suggestive. I became an enthusiast, privately, because I was living in a village. I later took to visiting Warsaw. The Café Lajkonik became a meeting place for artists, architects, and journalists. There I met people like Henryk Tomaszewski, who later became one of Poland's most

important graphic artists as well as Zamecznik, the architects. I got into contact with my social-artistic side.

MG: *Did they accept what you did, artistically?*
WF: My modernistic paintings were problematic. My landscapes, my portraits of Chopin, or even of Lenin, were not understood. In 1948, I had an exhibition in the Club of Young Artists and Scientists, but I didn't get much of a positive response. What made the situation even more complicated, than my artistic approach, was the problem with my father.

MG: *What happened to your father?*
WF: He got arrested in 1948. Before the war, my father was a wealthy industrialist. After the war, the young socialistic regime had allowed private initiatives if the number of employees was to be limited to fifty people. My father set up a company trading in scrap nonferrous metals. He collected and sent it to a foundry for melting. Sometimes, however, there were also half-products between the scrap and he sold them to other factories. He was making more money, but on the other hand the factories were receiving products, which they needed, and he saved these products from being used wrongly. He was denounced and accused of economic sabotage and causing losses to the state. The state organized a show trial in Katowice, in which 5,000 workers were forced to attend. The military tribunal sentenced him to death.

MG: *A nightmare.*
WF: Neither my father nor I treated this seriously, at first. It was a show trial to intimidate the bourgeoisie. But they put him in the death cell. My mother found a famous lawyer whose friend was chief of the presidential office. He simply put forth a document in which the death penalty was changed to a life sentence, which was among other documents that the president, Bierut at that time, also signed.

MG: *A life sentence in a Polish jail at that time doesn't sound very promising either.*
WF: At least he was alive. He was in jail and I was making a socialist career. I painted a work that became very popular: *Korean Mother.*

MG: *Were you truly ideologically motivated when you painted it?*
WF: Totally. At that time, anti-war propaganda was very strong. Many believed America wanted a war with the Soviet Union. When the Korean War started, the danger that the Cold War would turn hot was real. I wanted peace, so I wanted to contribute to this process.

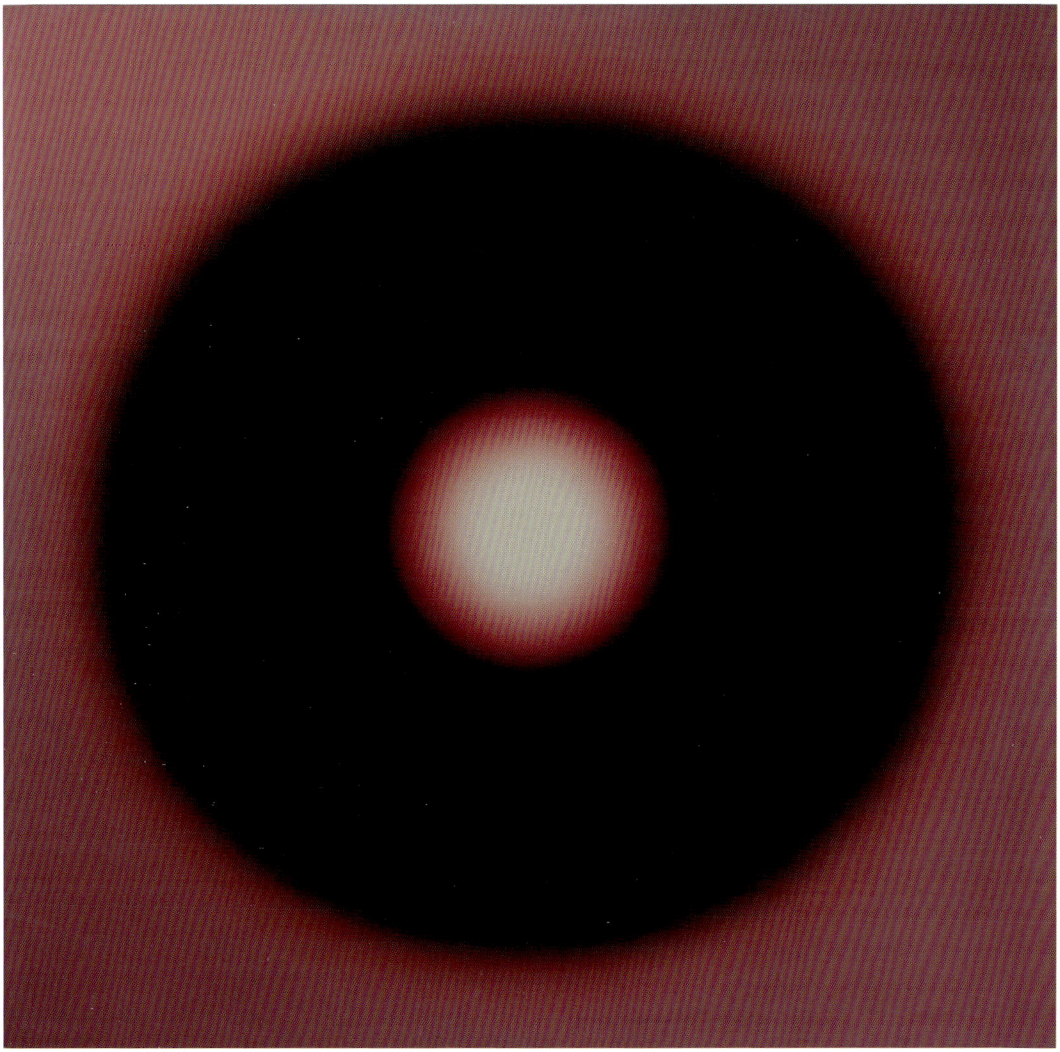

3
Wojciech Fangor
M 62, 1966
Oil on canvas, 168 × 168 cm

MG: *Didn't you have an inner conflict by pursuing a socialist career while your father was so badly treated by the very same system?*
WF: This was very complicated because I was always fighting with my father. I didn't like him. I felt uneasy in his presence. He was an outstanding businessman and saw me as his heir. He expected me to be good at school, especially with regard to economics and bookkeeping. But I didn't have any predisposition for it, nor did I like it. To my father, being a painter was like being an alcoholic. But our conflict started much earlier. He was the son of an officer; he was an officer himself and raised his children in a militaristic way. So when he was put in jail I had mixed feelings: on the one hand, I was happy that I was no longer exposed to him, on the other, I was fully aware of the injustice done to him.

MG: *How did you cope with this situation?*
WF: When I became a well-known social-realist artist I got acquainted with the Vice Minister of Culture who liked to spend his time with artists. He was friendly with Prime Minister, Cyrankiewicz. Through him I got to see Cyrankiewicz and asked him to set my father free. One week later they opened the door of the cell and let him go on convalescent leave.

MG: *Was your father grateful to you?*
WF: He had changed and become softer. It was only after his time in jail that we started to address each other informally. He still had a lot of energy and wanted to work but he didn't have any civil rights. In 1958, he asked for a revision of the 1948 sentence, when the political thaw made it possible. The High Court changed the sabotage accusation into a criminal case, which gave him his civil rights back but the state didn't need to return the confiscated assets and land. Later, when Poland became a democratic country, this revision was precisely the reason why my family couldn't get anything back. The sabotage against the state was seen as a communist affair, which could be undone, but a criminal case could not.

MG: *At that time, you also got involved in making posters.*
WF: I started making posters because I needed money. Nobody was buying paintings. Sometimes the Ministry did but not on a regular basis. I worked as a lecturer at the Art Academy for an income and insurance, so I could use the poster-work to make some extra money.

MG: *The Polish Poster School has become a name in the world. How did it start?*
WF: The idea came from the director of film propaganda at the Center of Film Distribution. She was importing films from the whole world. There was no need whatsoever to advertize for these films since there were only ten cinemas in Warsaw and there were always long queues to get in there. Still, she invited a few artists, such as Henryk Tomaszewski and myself, to help her design posters and choose other artists. I've never studied graphics but thanks to modernist techniques I knew I could do it.

MG: *You lived outside Poland for a long time.*
WF: The first time I traveled abroad was in 1956, when my father left jail. Only then was I allowed to move away from Poland. I went to Brussels when an exhibition of young Polish art was organized. We were discovered during the Youth Festival in 1955, when left-wing youth came to Warsaw en masse from all over the world. I also had a sister in Vienna who had married an Austrian before the war. She was able to arrange an

invitation to Austria and guarantee financial security for me there, which was necessary to get a passport and $5 for travel. I was investigating the possibility of staying there but I came back.

MG: *You wanted to emigrate because of the political system?*
WF: Yes. From 1954 onwards, I knew that the system was a utopia, a beautiful ideology, which produced the opposite in reality. The economic situation was absurd. I wanted to leave for the USA, which had always attracted me. Immediately after the war, I visited the American embassy in Warsaw and asked for emigration documents. I heard there was a waiting list – there was a quota for 6,000 Poles per year – and that if I apply they would be able to respond to my request in ten years.

MG: *Did you have contact with foreign artists or institutions?*
WF: In 1958, I exhibited my paintings in a show called *The Study of Space*, which was the world's first environment. After this exhibition, the director of the Stedelijk Museum in Amsterdam, Willem Sandberg, came to visit me and invited me to do a similar project in Amsterdam. The gallery owner, Beatrice Perry from Washington, came and was thrilled by my abstract works, wanting me to display them in the USA.

MG: *When did you start to make abstractions?*
WF: In 1957. Nobody understood nor liked my abstractions; the majority of the Academy didn't consider it to be art.

MG: *Where did your ideas on abstraction originate from?*
WF: Firstly, there was a universal crisis of figuration. This was in the air all over the world. Secondly, I was personally connected to architects. Even in my realism there was always a solid construction and the architects could sense it. If they wanted to work with an artist, they thought of me. I did a project with Jerzy Soltan, the architect. With Stanislaw Zamecznik, I discussed space. They thought that I had spatial intuition, which isn't functional.

MG: *How did you treat space then?*
WF: (Using) space as a material to construct independent art and not only as a material to build functional architecture. Three-dimensional space as a material to express emotions and a worldview, just like the paint on a two-dimensional surface does. I later discovered that my paintings with diffused edges of color and shape create a spatial illusion, which is not directed to the inside of the surface (like perspective), but extends in the opposite direction toward the outside of the surface, into the real

4
Wojciech Fangor
SM 19, 1975
Oil on canvas, 212 × 145 cm

space between the painter and the viewer. A new kind of spatial illusion. This discovery might have originated from my interest in astronomy and my fascination with optical instruments, with the effects of shifting the image in or out of focus. But it took some time to find the rational theory behind this phenomenon. All important discoveries originate from unconscious intuition.

MG: *Did you have contact with abstract expressionists in the USA?*
WF: None. The first time I saw a Rothko was in 1962. I was surprised that he was painting in such a similar way. I liked him very much. At that time, there were two camps: abstract expressionists and Pop art. I had contact with Anuszkiewicz, Richard Artschwager, Stanczak. Josef Albers visited my show in 1967 at Chalette Gallery in New York and said, "*chapeau bas*!" He was very positive about me. He invited me to his house in New England. He was as rational and constructed in his paintings as he was childish in his personal life. He pointed to the blue sky and clouds and said to me: "They have the same value but differ in color, the same as in my paintings". He was maybe forty years older than me but treated me as his equal.

MG: *Was it relevant for the Americans that you were a Polish artist?*
WF: Sure. In 1956, Poland was very popular in the USA because Americans treat culture in a political way. If something happens somewhere that they consider politically correct, they tend to reward that country's culture. Thanks to the anti-communist movement in Poland, in 1956, Polish art was given a chance in the USA.

MG: *How did you like living in America?*
WF: It depends. I got a job as professor in the art department of the Fairleigh Dickinson University in New Jersey, about 50 kilometers north of Manhattan. Very well kept buildings, beautiful parks, I found myself a great studio situated in the attic of what used to be a theater in the 19th century. I hired students to help me and employed them in the carpentry workshop. I worked with large canvasses. I painted many circles and waves at the time.

MG: *Did you have collectors who were buying your works?*
WF: Gallery Chalette in New York represented me. The gallery was set up by the Polish biochemist, Lejwa, who was caught in the USA when the war broke out in Poland and stayed. Together with his wife, who had the ambition and looks of Helena Rubinstein, they started the gallery which represented artists such as Victor Vasarely. I visited the gallery for the first

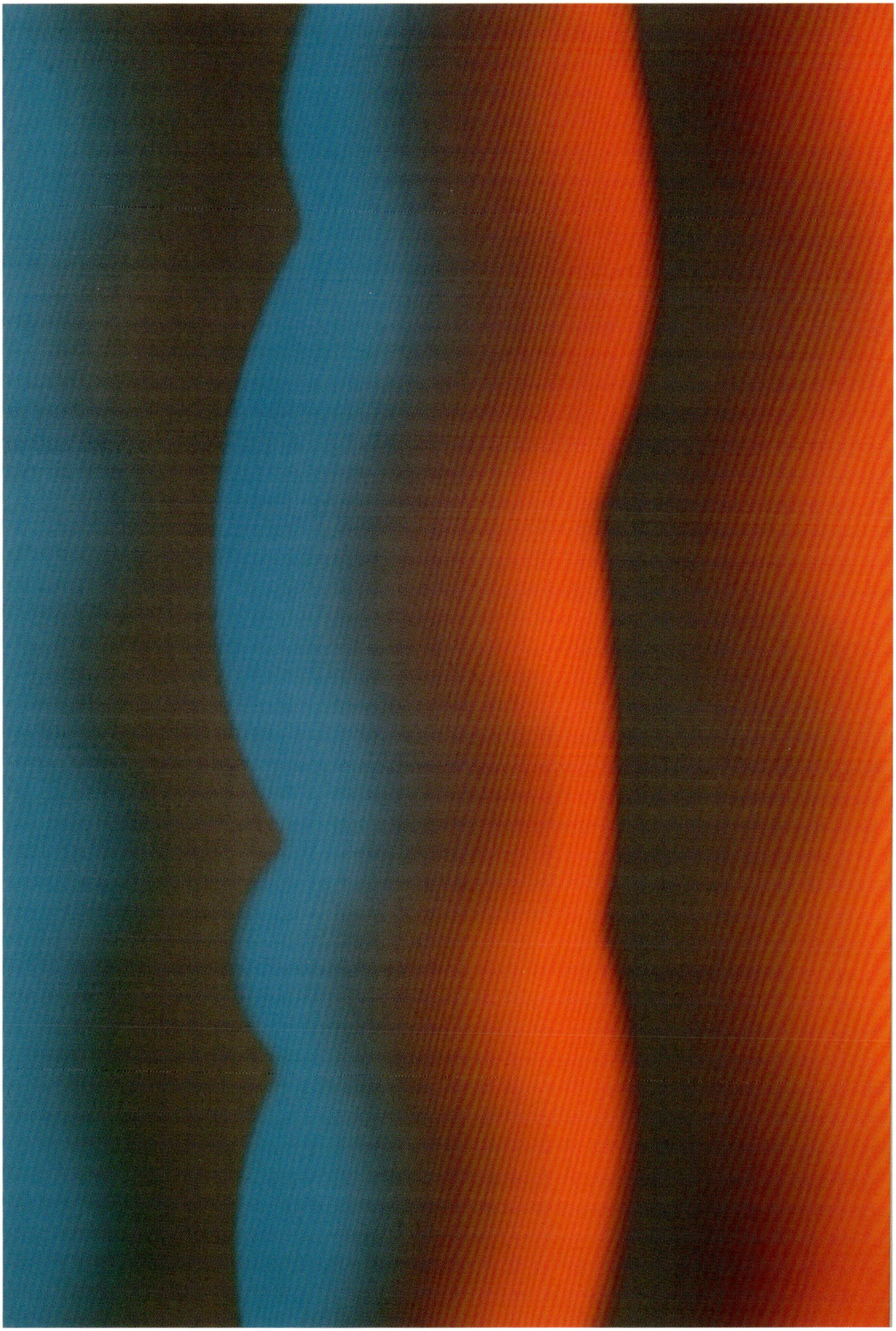

time in 1962 and showed Lejwa a few photos of my work. We had lunch together but Lejwa told me, "What you make is unsellable". Three years later, Vasarely's son, Yvral, who saw my work during a symposium at the university, brought him to me. Lejwa saw my abstract circles, grabbed my hand, and asked me to immediately join his gallery.

MG: *Were you happy with the gallery?*
WF: He was selling a lot. The price was about $1,500 per piece, of which I was getting half. I could live well thanks to my art; he may have sold more than a hundred artworks in the period between 1966 and 1973. He also helped organize my solo show at the Guggenheim Museum in 1970. It still makes a big impression in Poland because I am the only Polish artist so far to have a solo exhibition there. For the American public, the exhibition was too late to generate enough attention. Op Art was en vogue in 1965, not in 1970.

MG: *You mean the exhibition went unnoticed?*
WF: Before the exhibition started, I got a big article in The New York Times. The important art critic, Canaday, wrote an enthusiastic article about my art, although I think it was more a part of the conflict between Op Art and Abstract Expressionism as proposed by the art critic Greenberg.

MG: *Did you ever meet Greenberg?*
WF: In 1962, during a private dinner. Greenberg said, "What you're doing is interesting, it connects with our young American painting school, but you should paint on raw canvasses. "A painting is not a lollypop". I tried to explain my idea about space to him but he was totally uninterested. Canaday found Greenberg very dogmatic and wrote a whole page about me and my great art in order to provoke him.

MG: *Why did you finally decide to go back to Poland?*
WF: A French communist who dreamed about living in the USSR emigrated there but came back to Paris within a month. His French comrades asked him, "Why did you return?" He answered, "Because they let me out". I decided to go back because Poland let me in.

MG: *Was America not the country you dreamed of?*
WF: In the '80s, my artistic career had come to an end. I went on pension from the university – by the way, I've never enjoyed teaching. You cannot teach art, you can only teach technical skills. There are very good art teachers, but they're not good artists – if you give too much of yourself to students, you create by teaching. I have never liked schools, never at-

tended an art academy; never liked to be a part of an organization. Even when I was fascinated with Marxism, I was never a party member. I moved 150 kilometers north into a beautiful small village with a great view over the mountains, sixty hectares of land with wonderful lakes. In winter, the snow was sometimes three meters high and the temperature: minus thirty degrees Celsius. I had to clear the snow myself and, at a certain point in time, it became too much. I decided to move to a better place and chose Santa Fe in New Mexico, 300 sunny days a year. My wife and I loaded a big truck, and together with our four cats, we moved southward.

MG: *And did you find what you were looking for?*
WF: The nature was amazing, the architecture beautiful: a combination of Spain, the Baroque and Indian. I found a very good house to work in. But it was a cultural desert. Or, if it had at least been a desert it would have been better; it was a pseudo-culture for tourists. Fake Indian artifacts. I was painting landscapes, still life pieces and my surroundings, but nobody was interested in what I was doing. When democracy came about in Poland, returning became an option.

MG: *Had you stayed in touch with the Polish art scene?*
WF: Some people visited me. I thought if I could buy an old monument and reconstruct it, make a studio there, then I could live in Poland. Indeed, I made a career in Poland towards the end of my life. There's been a lot of interest in my work.

MG: *How do you explain this huge amount of interest?*
WF: People understood that art can be a good investment. Five rich collectors bought my works and sold them to another five rich people and doubled their investment. Obviously, I'm not getting anything from the price increase.

MG: *I can imagine that it gives you a good feeling that your works have become worth a lot.*
WF: Pity that this came when I was ninety and not when I was forty. I was also thinking about a private museum, but because of the nonchalance of Polish institutions, this idea didn't materialize. I did get a very good retrospective in the National Museum in Krakow and Warsaw.

MG: *Do you enjoy your position now?*
WF: I still paint. I need to sit, however, because my spine doesn't work. I paint what I like to paint. Maybe my current ideas will get a cultural or formal meaning later on.

WALTON FORD

March 2018

Marta Gnyp: *I recently saw your beautiful work that has a sad, dying wombat playing the main role. Why a wombat?*
Walton Ford: I do a lot of reading to get inspiration for my work. I have realized over the years that what I'm most interested in are things you can probably classify as cultural history of animals – particularly wild animals – and their interaction with human beings. Domestic animals have a sort of mutual partnership with us that has developed in an evolutionary sense: dogs came to our camps, picked up scraps, and then they started to actually enjoy our company. The same can be said for almost every domestic animal. But we can't make every animal domestic. We can tame individual animals, but we can't domesticate entire species, like a tiger. Every tiger cub is born wild, wanting to get away from people.

MG: *So, you're interested in how these wild animals have interacted with humans throughout history, and what this teaches us humans about ourselves.*
WF: Exactly. I research and find strange stories. One of them was that of Gabriel Rossetti, the Pre-Raphaelite painter who lived in Cheyne Walk in London. He kept an extensive menagerie, but was a drug-addicted lunatic artist – in a very bohemian and contemporary way – like a crazy rock star of his era. He wasn't not capable of understanding the responsibility of taking care of animals, but was obsessed with wombats, and as soon as he could get one he got one. This wombat came and lived with this crazy bohemian community in Cheyne Walk and, of course, didn't last long. I found his correspondence about the death of this wombat. Rossetti did a self-portrait of himself weeping over the wombat and wrote a poem about his death. He called the wombat an invalid when it was sick and so *The Invalid* became the title of my painting. I gave the wombat a particularly pre-Raphaelite treatment, including his pose and dramatic death on a piece of architectural scenery.

MG: *You can see the wombat thinking "why did it happen to me?"*
WF: I sometimes paint from the animal's point of view, and other times

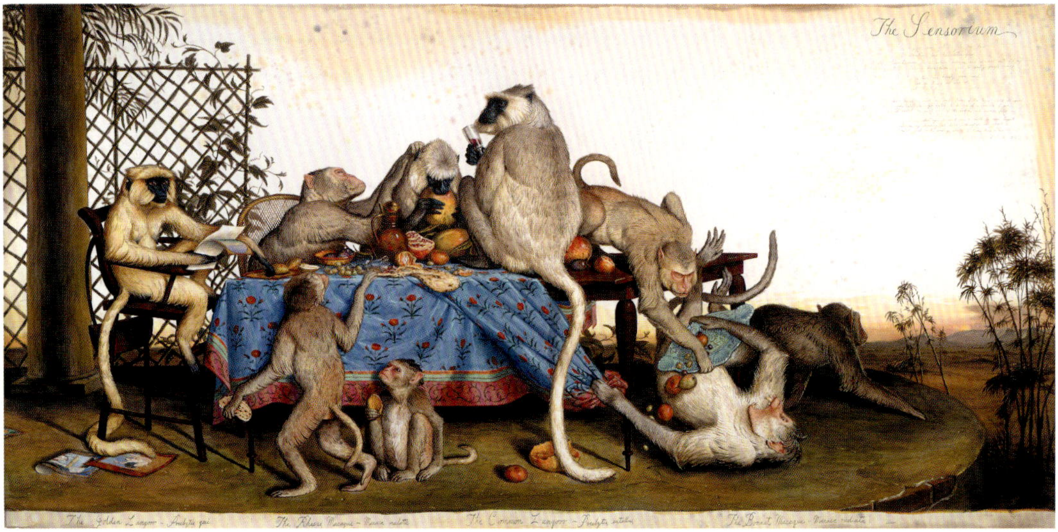

1
Walton Ford
The Sensorium, 2003
Watercolor, gouache, ink and pencil on paper, 152.4 × 302.3 cm

from the human's. In this case, I combined the two. I wanted to make the suffering of the wombat palpable, so you could feel how unfortunate it is to be trapped by a group of 19th century opium-addicted, self-absorbed artists. At the same time, you can also feel the romantic spin that somebody like Rossetti would put on it.

MG: *How did you become interested in themes about wild animals versus humans?*
WF: I was a child from the American suburbs. I would fantasize about the wilderness and I'd watch films like King Kong, projecting myself into the story. My personal fantasy world that I built up in my head had to do with being in wild places.

MG: *Why did you have this strong urge to escape into this fantasy-wilderness?*
WF: Mostly, I would climb a tree to get away from my father who was a bit of a bully. This tree was the only wilderness I could find in the suburban setting. When you're on top of a very large, old tree, nobody can find you. The birds would fly by, and you could sit there for hours. When I started this work, these childhood memories resonated in a personal way.

MG: *How did you start? Did you have a clear concept for your work?*
WF: No. I made fake 19th century natural history paintings and I didn't think they would matter to anybody. I slowly worked on this project, which now resonates outside of my own personal experience.

MG: *Do you think one condition for good art is that it must come from a profound personal experience?*
WF: I believe, if you try to make issue-based art, it can become very preachy and insufferable. When you're trying to be didactic or self-important about your message, it usually restricts your ability to reach people. I'm lucky this work came from a very personal place, and whether it was interesting to the rest of the world or not was irrelevant to me.

MG: *In the meantime, our relationship to nature has become a big issue.*
WF: Yeah, look at what we are doing to the planet and all the animals that we share it with. It does become interesting to explore our relationships with these animals throughout history.

MG: *Another very interesting aspect of your work is its narrative. I read that you wanted to be a film maker, so the idea of storytelling has probably always been of interest to you. If we look at what happened in the art world in the past twenty years, heavy conceptual thinking has given way to narratives. Is this one of the reasons why your art has become so interesting to the public?*
WF: I guess the first time I noticed it was during my exhibition at the Hamburger Bahnhof.

MG: *I saw this show – it was beautiful.*
WF: Thank you. When Udo Kittelmann, the curator and director, put it together, he was deliberately making a statement. My show was scheduled before a big Bruce Nauman exhibition. Udo said Bruce Nauman was always trying to get everyone pissed off with his work, but we've reached a point where Nauman has become acceptable – almost classical. There was no dispute. So, Udo put up my work because he knew it would upset people, since it wasn't going to fit into the official art discourse. He recently told me that every day, someone comes up – he likes to exaggerate, so it is probably every six months, but nevertheless – to argue with him over that exhibition. They would say that it was illustrative, that it looked like a natural history museum, that it's *not* contemporary.

MG: *How do you react to such comments? You have probably often been told that what you make is illustration and not art.*
WF: I don't pretend my ego is so big that I don't care. Every artist cares, so you come up with a response. I think that a huge part of the history of art is illustration. The entire Renaissance is basically an illustration of Bible stories being retold again and again. Here is an illustration of Adam and Eve, the life of Christ, the life of Mary – it goes on and on and

on. You look at Goya's works, which were illustrations of current events, and you think it's engaged and political – we accept it. The idea that it's wrong to make narrative stories that are, in some form, illustrations is a brand new construct, which we can question. Why is it a bad thing to be called an illustrator?

MG: *A very large part of the history of art is illustration and decoration, although art history doesn't necessarily like this idea. Your art follows a different path, going back to other sources.*
WF: My generation was stuck. Robert Ryman, who is a great artist, said, "If we are going to make an honest painting, it's got to be about paint. How do you make a painting about paint? You can remove the colors so you only have the white paint. You can focus on what kind of white it is – if I used this white out of this tube it's slightly warmer, this white from this tube is colder". These were my teachers.

MG: *So your generation had to liberate itself from the modernistic thinking about the purity of the medium.*
WF: If I were an artist working in the 1950s and 1960s, I would have probably ended up in the same place. It would totally make sense. You keep on looking for the answers to the basic questions of your time and end up with this result. Like in an evolution, it has to happen – somebody's going to paint that white painting. If you go to Robert Ryman's show, it starts to mess with your head because you see the differences between these two white paintings. Suddenly, your eyes start working in a different way – you are truly attuned to your senses and it's a great experience.

MG: *But the idea of pure modernist painting has been quite limiting.*
WF: It is an intellectual exercise. I didn't come to my work by going against it. In a funny way, I love the creative process in all its manifestations. You have John Cage, who says, "I'm not making music, but I am using sound. I'm just going to find the beauty in sound". I really believe that if you're able to follow someone like Robert Ryman or John Cage to the end of their thought process and take it seriously, you do get a result – it's a sharpening of the senses.

MG: *How did you justify the fact that this attitude didn't work for you?*
WF: I've always been interested in the biological processes of evolution. I learned about the 19th century models of evolution, which were progressive – the idea was that every animal is evolving into an improved version of itself and that everything is changing to become more intelligent and more human. But this isn't what evolution is like at all! Evolution is like

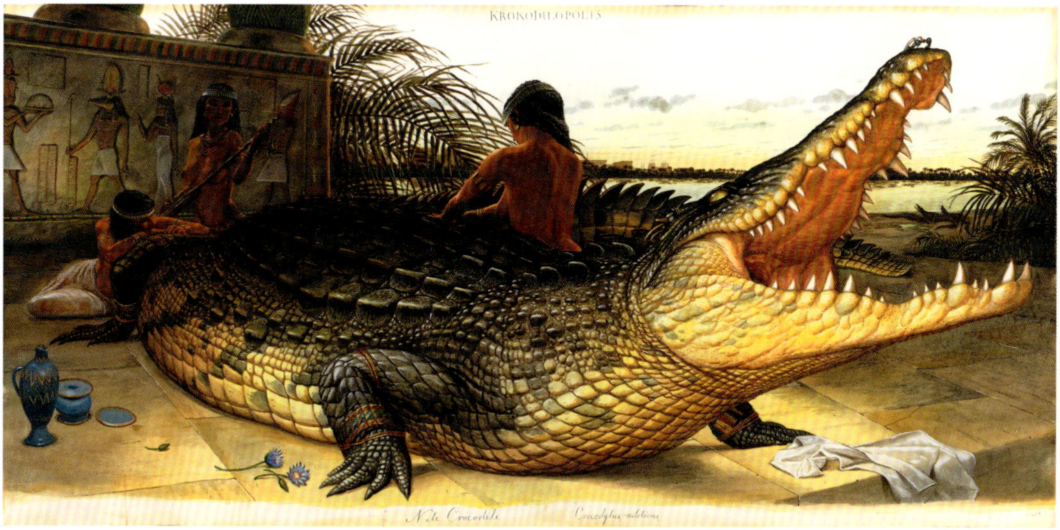

2
Walton Ford
Krokodilopolis, 2010
Watercolor, gouache, ink and pencil on paper, 152.4 × 302.9 cm

this crazy tree that grows in all directions, finding every atom for life without any hierarchy. There isn't something that works better – you are simply finding paths for survival. Our history is like that too.

MG: *No progress and no hierarchies for you.*
WF: Young people today know this too. If you see a musical playlist by a person in their twenties, it's going to have Billie Holiday, some contemporary rap and classical music. It is all over the place because they don't see a hierarchy. When I was young, at my art school people would say, "Punk is cool, disco sucks" or "Forget arena rock – we don't listen to Led Zeppelin anymore, we listen to the Sex Pistols". You had to make a decision. We don't make a decision now.

MG: *Is it not confusing that everything can exist next to each other?*
WF: You start to see that the world is full of interesting things. I think this is progress, actually. But in our history, we're taught to reject the past in favor of the present.

MG: *The art world is one of the last solid bastions trying to keep this hierarchy and old order alive.*
WF: Yes! I find that museums are the most timid in this respect because they have invested the most in a story of progress. I studied in Italy, in my senior year. I was an American kid who had never been out of the country before. I went to Italy and I saw the frescoes, the churches, and the *Giottos*. I realized that the idea of progressive art history was wrong – it implies, if Medieval artists knew how to use perspective, they would have

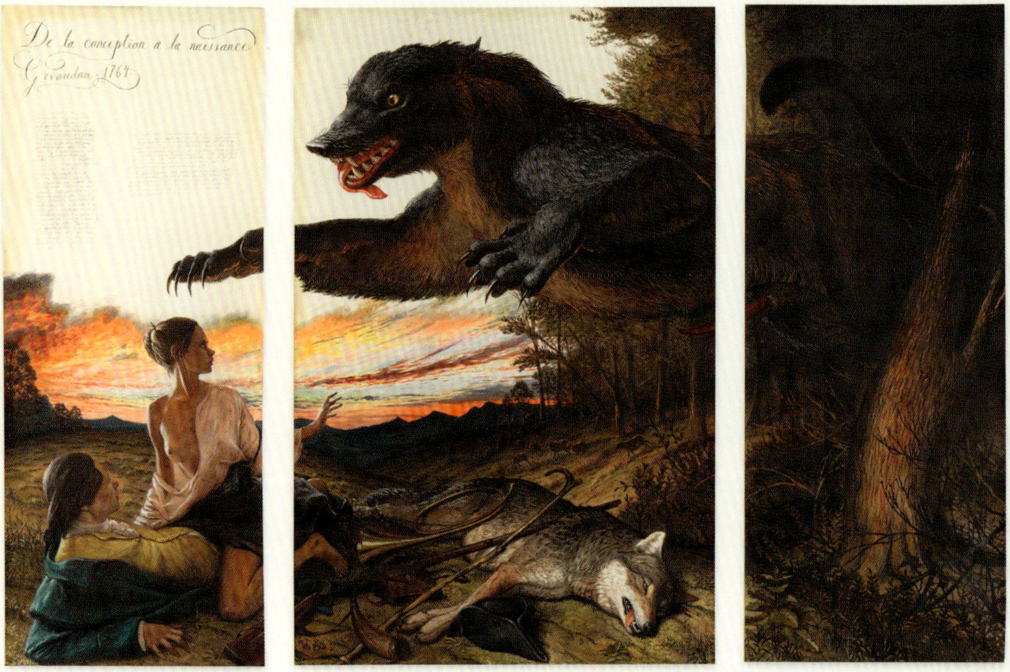

3
Walton Ford
De la conception à la naissance, 2014
Watercolor, gouache and ink on paper, 258 × 166 cm middle panel; 258 × 110 cm each of the side panels; 258 × 386 cm overall

done it. The point is that they didn't have any interest in it. If you were making a Medieval painting, you were trying to create a painting about invisible spiritual enlightenment. You weren't interested in creating a natural world, because you had to grasp an inner world of spirituality. I thought they were perfectly capable of doing whatever they wanted to do, it's just that this is what they chose to do. I never bought into the idea that we don't have choice or agency because we're stuck in this progress story and aren't allowed to be tangential.

MG: *The progress story has had its own agenda. Perspective was a great instrument to give art the status of science and make it more prestigious. Speaking of museums and their agenda, how have institutions treated you? I read that your first museum exhibition was at the Brooklyn Museum in 2006, which was relatively late. I was wondering if anything has changed between 2006 and 2018?*
WF: That it is true, but I do feel that things have changed a lot. The Brooklyn Museum is a very good example. Anne Pasternak, the current Director, is very open and creates a dialogue. She even sent a letter to artists, including me, asking for feedback. She is very good at interacting with artists, rather than just doing all the fundraising and keeping

the narrative going. It's probably best to look at this from institution to institution, to be fair. I have felt a lot more acceptance lately.

MG: *Do you have an explanation for this?*
WF: Sometimes I think if you just stick around and don't give up, they will get used to you. When I was in college, somebody like Cher, who was a joke in the Disco era, started becoming acceptable. Now she's like Mount Rushmore – nobody would say anything about her. You don't go away. Maybe that's all it is.

MG: *Are museums buying your work?*
WF: I have some museums that want my work, but it's still hard to find somebody that will purchase my work and then donate it. If I give the work away, then I run the risk of having it go into storage. Nobody really values something they are given. I just think it takes time. Right now, I can't complain because everything seems to be going well. People are paying attention, looking at the work and liking it. I pretty much have what I could hope for as an artist: an audience and the ability to get up and go to the studio instead of having some job I hate.

MG: *Let's go back to the beginning of your career. You finished at the art academy in the beginning of the '80s and came to New York. The '80s and '90s must have been very difficult times for a young artist in NYC.*
WF: I had nothing going on in the art world back then. I was in the studio every day, but I worked in manual labor jobs as a carpenter and metal worker. I helped build museum exhibits, doing whatever job I could get, and lived in cheap neighborhoods, in Williamsburg. Back then, in 1983, no artists were there. Greenpoint was a Polish neighborhood with a lot of abandoned buildings. In the Italian part of Williamsburg where I lived, there was a very tightly knit community with cappuccino and pizza parlors, and a few low-level mafia members living there. I could keep on working because I kept my head low.

MG: *If we speak about the beginning of the '80s, this was the time of the Picture generation, of Neo-expressionism and also of Basquiat. Who was most appealing to you?*
WF: I wasn't aware of anybody as much as I was aware of Basquiat, who was exactly my age. Picture generation people like Cindy Sherman were a bit older, well-established, and already a big deal.

MG: *Did you speak with anybody about your art?*
WF: Nobody was interested in what I was doing, in East Village or any-

where else. Still, something encouraging would happen every year. I got the Guggenheim Fellowship, and one year Bill Arning, (now Curator at the MIT), or Marcia Tucker, (now Curator at New Museum), would come to the studio and say that my work was amazing. I could live off that for one year. Marcia put me in a group show, as she understood that my pieces were going in a really weird direction. She was kind of a genius, but couldn't really do anything. I had a day job and I used to babysit her kid, who is now all grown up.

MG: *What about your artist peers?*
WF: I was an artists' artist perhaps. Other artists thought I was up to something interesting. Anyways, I knew I was no good at anything else.

MG: *What were you good at? That thing we referred to as illustration and nature?*
WF: I did a lot of paintings about my childhood memories in my twenties, which was a kind of sorting through trauma, but then I saw David Lynch's *Blue Velvet* and thought, "Oh shit, he did it better than I ever could, so I'll leave that alone". Later on, I became interested in the nature and history of the 19th century. Both sides of my family were very old American families from the South. They came over in the 18th century to one of the first settlements. My father's family settled in Tennessee. Before it became a city, Tennessee was a plantation owned by my family. My mother's family settled in North Georgia, way back in the 1750s. My parents were liberal and artistic southerners, so we moved North to get away from the conservative thinking, that they grew up with and didn't like. I was raised in this progressive household, but with southern people, carrying a history of plantation and slave-owning in their past.

MG: *Any feelings of guilt about that in the family?*
WF: I didn't do anything. I wasn't even raised that way. My father would cry every time he saw *To Kill a Mockingbird*, although you could open old family memoirs and scrap books with confederate money in it – really amazing. I could go to the South and talk to relatives who were bigots, and were my flesh and blood. This put even more distance between me and them. I understood that best when I went to Germany – a German that was born in 1960 isn't a Nazi. But I do have to think about it, and I explore it in my paintings.

MG: *There is a lot of cruelty and violence in your paintings.*
WF: For sure. If you have a family who lived in America since the 18th century and was prominent, there is no question that their history was

extremely violent – that there were natives that had to be killed off, tons of wildlife that had to be slaughtered, forests that had to be cleared, slaves that were brought over to do all the work. You can't avoid the horrors of an old family in America. You can't pretend that your own flesh and blood wasn't a part of the violence, so I was interested in exploring that. Although my family was very enlightened, I was raised to have pride in the fact that we were here before anyone else, whatever that's supposed to mean. It still made them a little better than everyone else.

MG: *It sounds like a very complex issue, which might explain the complexity of narratives in your work.*
WF: I didn't want a packed answer – I didn't want to let myself off the hook. I used to hear from bigoted relatives that, as a family, we were kind to slaves. I don't even want to hear that shit.

MG: *So your interest in history and nature are both very personal. Then you came across this famous book by Audubon called* The Birds of America, *which gave you a methodology for how to pursue your interests?*
WF: It wasn't just him that I devoured, but every natural history artist that I could get my hands on. I read books about prehistoric history and would know about artists who were famous for drawing dinosaurs. I became a nerd with science museum art and textbook art. I'd know about artists who illustrated guide books and field guide books, such as Peterson, who was this really important bird guide artist. As a child, I didn't know where it was going to lead, but I knew this was what I was interested in from a very early age. I thought, maybe I'd make guidebooks and illustrate children's books about natural history. Or maybe I'd work in a museum or in a national park. I was trying to imagine a future for myself that allowed me to make paintings about this world. I think I'd be delighted if I could see the life I put together for myself.

MG: *What about the medium you've chosen? You make big artworks on paper and use watercolors, which isn't easy. There aren't many artists who have a career as big as yours from mainly using paper.*
WF: The first time I tried to make my own natural history art as a child, I paraphrased artists. I copied Audubon and Edward Lear, who wrote *Pussycat*, and did beautiful illustrations of birds and things. Generally, natural history artists used watercolors, ink and gouache and worked on paper, partly because they made drawings and notes about animals, discoveries and encounters on expeditions in their journals about the field. They had to use watercolors because oils take a long time to dry, and they are very hard to transport. If you have a little paper journal, you can just make a

sketch of a bird you just shot, put watercolor on it, close it and put it in a waterproof bag, and carry it to the next place.

MG: *You used watercolors on paper because they have traditionally been the medium for natural history artists.*
WF: Exactly. These expedition-watercolors were a big part of my childhood. The language of natural history art starts with Dürer's work *The Rabbit* in the Albertina Museum, which is a watercolor gouache ink on paper. It hasn't changed because it's a very good way to make a study of living or dead things immediately.

MG: *You learned that language quite early on.*
WF: Then I went to art school and forgot all about it. I painted, made films, acted – I did all these various things to figure out different ways of telling stories. Eventually, I came back to what I was doing as a child, just picking up watercolors and making these fake nature studies. Once I started doing that, I decided that I wanted to amplify the scale and take something that would have been in a small journal, but make it a life-sized animal. The first one I did was a tiger – it was 10 ft by 5 ft and very elaborate. I knew I could do it, from a technical standpoint, because it's very close to fresco work, which I studied when I was in Italy. You have to make these preparatory drawings and have to be very careful. When you finally paint you must know what you're going to do. I thought that if you can paint a fresco with life-sized figures, I can paint this watercolor. No big deal, technically, compared to what they did.

MG: *Frescoes were painted very quickly.*
WF: You could find the seams where they'd plaster as much as they could paint in one day, so you don't paint the entire thing overnight. I do the same thing when I'm painting my watercolors. I just give myself what I can handle. Each day I do more, but I don't need to finish the whole thing at once. When you finally see the finished product, it's 9 by 12 ft, and you can't figure out how I did it. That's how I felt when I looked at these frescoes for the first time.

MG: *Do you paint by yourself, without assistants?*
WF: No assistants at all – I don't like that.

MG: *Why not?*
WF: The best part of the art-making job is making the art. I totally admire workshop artists like Damien Hirst or Jeff Koons, but to me they are CEOs of large business corporations that make luxury objects at a very

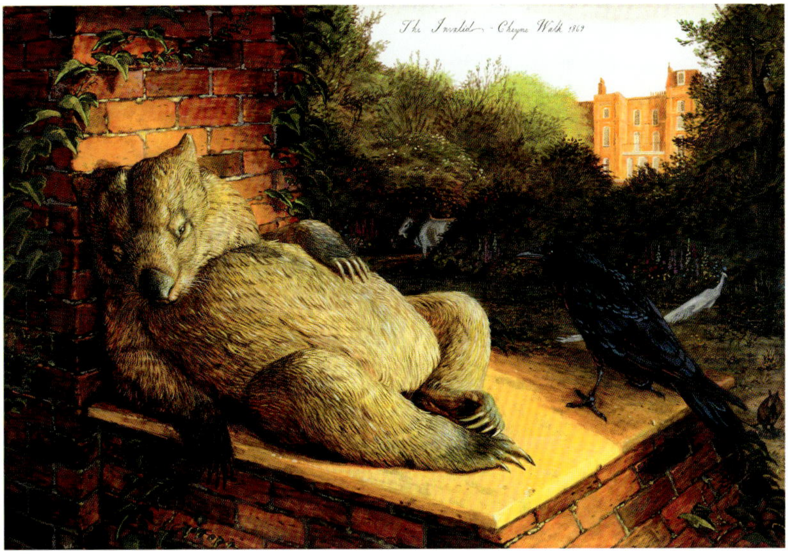

4
Walton Ford
The Invalid - Cheyne Walk 1869, 2017
Watercolor, gouache, and ink on paper, 105.7 × 151.4 cm

high level. For me, this is the worst part of the job. I never set out to run Mercedes Benz – I'm not interested in high-end manufacturing. I want to sit there like a craftsman and make the beautiful object with my own hands and my own skills. I have assistants, but their work is to make sure that I'm able to make the flight or get Skype to work.

MG: *What do you think about the idea of the artist today? You mentioned the the CEO-type of a luxury brand corporation. At the same time, the idea of the artist as a bohemian revolutionary, or as being avant-garde, have become old fashioned. So, what is so special about an artist today?*
WF: When I was in my twenties, it seemed very clear. If you were in New York in the '80s, you knew what was happening there was very special and was not understood by the general population at all. I could go to a concert for $5 and see the *Talking Heads* play. I would see these outfits and these drag queens – I'd go to the Pyramid Club. I'm lucky to be alive, because a lot of people from that time are now dead. We weren't taking care of ourselves in the '80s, in downtown New York or in Brooklyn. I felt like we were all shamans who understood something that other people didn't.

MG: *How did it manifest itself?*
WF: I got clothes from the Salvation Army, like a suit that was thirty years old – it was weird, really out of sync with the rest. If I watched MTV, I saw guys in leather jackets with broad shoulders, who looked ridiculous to me – like Michael Jackson-outfits. We were more like strangers in paradise, walking around in these sort of fedoras and old suits, and we felt like we

were ahead of the curve. We'd look like the guy from Joy Division. I would hitchhike and had my head shaved so people would ask me whether I was in the Marines, but I'd reply with, "No I'm in an art school".

MG: *You were one of the avant-garde trendsetters.*
WF: Except that my art was all fucked up. I was cool when I went to the club, but people didn't quite understand why I was making these old fashioned pictures. Regardless, I felt like I was in the right place at the right time. I was hearing music that no one would hear for years to come. We would always know about things beforehand. This idea of the artist seems over now, and I don't understand where it's going. Today an artist feels very lucky if he gets a corporate gig like a shoot for a fashion magazine. In the '80s, there was an intentional rejection of such actions.

MG: *Were you against corporate structures?*
WF: I don't want to go back in time, but yeah, the feeling was: "fuck the man and the corporate world". When an artist started selling his paintings, he was immediately suspected and had to buy all the drugs immediately, invite everybody to dinner, spend all his money on other people and not live in a better place. You might have lived in a bigger place, but it had to be a shithole on purpose. It was important not to pretend you were like some kind of "Wall Street guy".

MG: *The "Wall Street guy" was the ultimate horror?*
WF: Exactly.

MG: *Today, your works are expensive and you're making money.*
WF: Today, my feeling is that artists should be well-paid. Why should it only be movie stars, sports figures, industrialists or people in the startups making money? It's cool if an artist gets paid for what he does, so I'm all for that. I think the art-making impulse is the best one we've got. The second best is our altruistic forms of behavior. Those are the two things that make us different from bacteria or some horrible virus – we're destroying everything we touch. If I go to the Met today, I look through all this unbelievable stuff they have and I feel good about being a human being. I don't feel bad about being a successful artist because if you're successful, you have a chance for your work to be cared for, due to it being somewhat expensive.

MG: *What do you think about the new generation of artists?*
WF: My girlfriend is younger than me. She's a dancer and she recently brought me to some dance performances, which were really cool. There

is still really interesting stuff around – young choreographers and musicians experimenting. The scene of young artists doesn't feel so different, but I don't think that they feel something's going on in a palpable way.

MG: *Don't you think that the younger generation is more moralistic now?*
WF: Well, the moralistic thing is like a pendulum swinging. The biggest difference between my generation and theirs is their lack of a sense of community. When I came to New York, there was the East Village gallery scene – everybody was in a band and would go home, paint and then go to the same bars and the same restaurants. The rent was cheap, the food was also cheap and shitty and the drugs were expensive. Everybody was doing the same thing, listening to the same music and reading the same books. There was a lot of uniformity in that, but it also created a sense of community. Right now, as it gets more and more expensive to live in inner cities, the beautiful neighborhoods that were available to young artists are no longer affordable, so they live in different places. There isn't one neighborhood that they all gravitate towards. It's not their fault, it's a real estate issue – it's a greed thing.

MG: *What are you working on right now?*
WF: I have a small exhibit in St. Moritz with Vito Schnabel, who took over Bruno Bischofsberger's beautiful, old gallery. I'm making an exhibition about a subject I explored many times, but I'm doing it again because it's perfect for this gallery. There was a female black panther who escaped from the Zurich Zoo in the winter of 1933. For ten weeks, she was in the Swiss countryside and nobody could find her. They could never find her tracks. They had clairvoyants try to find her, and asked the police to search for her. Then, ten weeks later, some peasant found her under a barn, shot her and ate her. He treated it like he shot a deer – he butchered her and cooked her up. So, this story is everything I'm looking for. It was from this book called *Wild Animals in Captivity*; a kind of zookeepers' manual. Since I found the story, I've constantly been making paintings about her. Sometimes, I have her floating above the snow because she didn't leave any tracks and I make her into a sort of magical creature. I have a painting of her with fire in the snow, on the evening when she's walking away in the smoke, and the fire is what she was cooked on. I have a lot of ideas about her all the time. She's a sort of dreamlike animal.

ADRIAN GHENIE

December 2017

Marta Gnyp: *Do you feel at home in Berlin?*
Adrian Ghenie: I'm a Romanian living in Berlin. I still think in Romanian – I never learned German.

MG: *I think you like to keep a distance.*
AG: I do. The idea of integration has been an alien concept to me. Integrate into what? I was never integrated into anything. I've always felt like an outsider. It's a feeling you are born with.

MG: *Do you also feel like an outsider while in Cluj?*
AG: Coming from Berlin makes you different. Being internationally successful isolates you more than anything and more than you'd like, to the point where it becomes very weird.

MG: *Because people treat you like a god?*
AG: It activates a whole spectrum of irrational feelings towards you. Jealousy, love, fantasies and conspiracy theories – people create a distorted image about you.

MG: *Do you try to explain yourself?*
AG: After a certain point, I realized you cannot change anything. No matter how hard you try, it will only add to irrational explanations. They consider everything but honest, altruistic purposes.

MG: *I assume these projections and feelings are not limited to just Romania?*
AG: Depending on the group, they'll project what they need onto you. I read a random article written by a guy named Kenny Schachter, who I don't know, reporting on an auction. He mentioned that I was supposedly calling the auction house to say that they put the starting price on a piece too low. There's a point, after a certain level of notoriety, when people start putting words in your mouth.

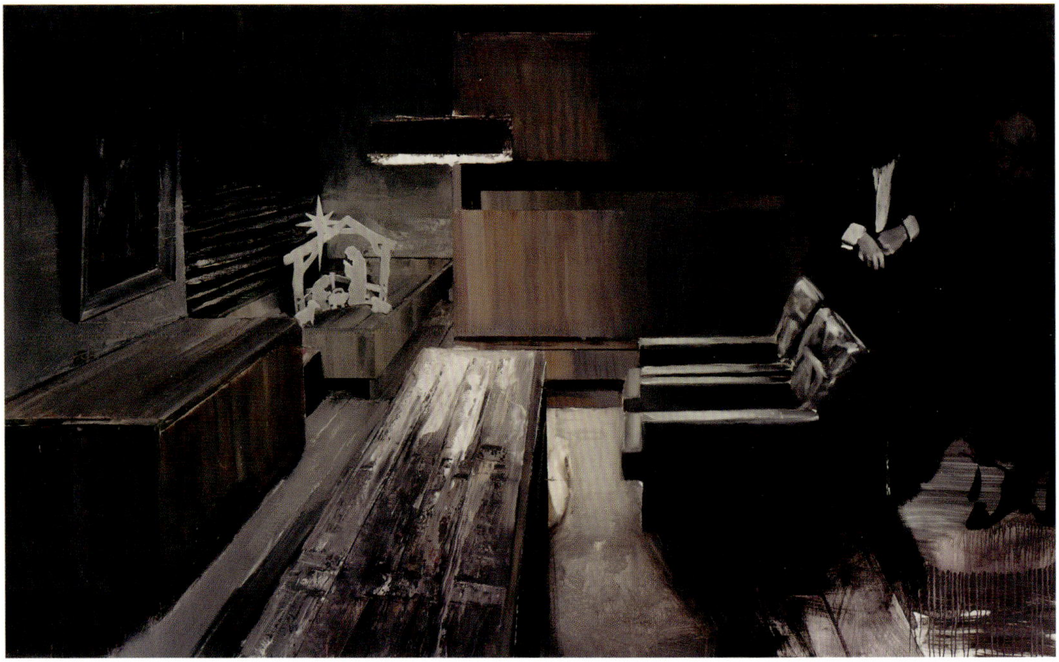

1
Adrian Ghenie
Secret Nativity, 2007
Oil on canvas, 145 × 230 cm

MG: *Does this somehow influence your work? Your work shows the dark side of human beings and of our history.*
AG: My work is more like a Jungian dream, which is not necessarily bad or good – it simply is. I'm not investigating the dark side of history. I'm interested in paradoxes within history. So, I dive into a collective subconscious that already exists and is weird and paradoxical, lacking a clear direction.

MG: *So the viewers have to make sense of it themselves.*
AG: I found a correlation between my own approach and the method of director, David Lynch. When you watch his films for the first time, they are dark and creepy. It's hard to point out exactly what is going on – it's like a dream. The only thing you know is that you want to watch it, which is more important than clarifying whether it's a good or bad movie. With my paintings, I don't really care if people give them a verdict of good or bad. For me, it matters that they are interested in looking at them.

MG: *The image never ends in your paintings.*
AG: One of the artists I was always inspired by was Titian, during the Renaissance in Venice. He painted semi-transparent layers, one on top of another, so each layer functions as a light box for the next. If you want to have a very special red, you'll place a red yellow under it. Or if you

want the red to be cold, you'd use blue. Imagine how abstractly you're required to think! You start a composition that, in the end, has to be a crucifixion, with spots of color being completely different from the final image. This sense of anticipation fascinates me. You work with this painting in an in-between phase for months, and all the layers are created to get to the final one.

MG: *Is this the way you paint?*
AG: The surface of my paintings is also built in layers but differently, and that creates their richness. I hope people will respond to that quality, even in an unconscious way. You look at the image first, but the image is not actually relevant. There are thousands of images of crucifixions from Titian's time, and they're boring. The complexity behind the optic juxtaposition of so many layers gives it its quality in the end.

MG: *Do you start with a clear image in your head?*
AG: Sixty percent of it.

MG: *Did you acquire knowledge about old masters like Titian at the Academy, or did you discover them on your own?*
AG: I applied to art academy in Cluj, but failed. I don't blame them because I was nothing special at the time and the academy was sponsored by the state, with only sixteen places available a year. The competition was vicious. I started thinking about how to get there, and asked an academy teacher to coach me, which was common. They would teach you what to do in order to fulfill the academy's expectations. At the same time, at home, however, I did a lot of copies of Rembrandt and Titian, mostly from books. But I also looked at originals, in a museum in Sibiu, that has a fantastic collection. I read about the technicalities of each period – how to paint on wood and on canvas, how to paint a fresco and also how to prepare the canvasses.

MG: *You were a classical painter when you entered the Academy.*
AG: People imagine that an art academy in Romania is very academic. It's actually the contrary. My teachers were more abstract kind of painters – figuration was out of the question.

MG: *Because they wanted to escape the politics?*
AG: My teachers were of Generation '68, most of whom painted or wanted to paint like the Americans – Rauschenberg or Pollock. The worst thing one could say in this climate was that they wanted to do a copy of Rembrandt, so I kept that to myself.

MG: *Did you learn a lot during the copying process?*
AG: Copying is an attempt to reconstruct, like what police do when they re-enact a crime. In my case, this period got a special unexpected dimension, which is embarrassing right now. During the '90s, my financial situation was dreadful. I was very poor, so I painted a lot of trashy paintings for people and, sometimes, for hotel lobbies.

MG: *Are they now putting them up at auctions?*
AG: Yes. [laughs]

MG: *What did you paint?*
AG: My mother's neighbors would ask me to paint a nice landscape, and would give me 50 DM. Back then, I never expected that the Internet would be invented and all this stuff would appear online. Sometimes I'd make a copy of a Pissarro or a Renoir. Most commissions were based on a religious theme, such as Christ or a crucifixion, which I knew exactly how to paint because I had inexhaustible resources for this type of imagery, such as Velazquez. These works are artistically irrelevant to my CV, but at the same time they played a role in my learning process.

MG: *Did you need to make loads of irrelevant art to find your own voice?*
AG: There's a funny bias in the thinking of gallery owners, curators and critics. They expect you to come out of nowhere and suddenly paint something brilliant. Nobody wants to understand that there is a point in your career where you are making shit. Normally, most of the material from this stage would disappear, but now it all stays online.

MG: *How did you experience your time at the academy during the '90s?*
AG: In the '90s, everybody was poor and everything was cheap. Somehow, we survived with very little. That Pissarro landscape gave me a lot of freedom because with 50 DM, I could go out and have drinks with my friends several times over a period of a few months.

MG: *How did you cope with the absurdities of the system?*
AG: There was a factory in Bucharest supplying paint, brushes and stretches for artists, but only to artists' union stores. I remember, as a sixteen year old, going to a store wanting to buy colors to paint. Since I wasn't a member of the artists' union, the lady in the shop couldn't sell me white, black or red – the only color she could give me was violet because nobody wanted violet.

MG: *Did you ever convince her to sell you the other colors?*

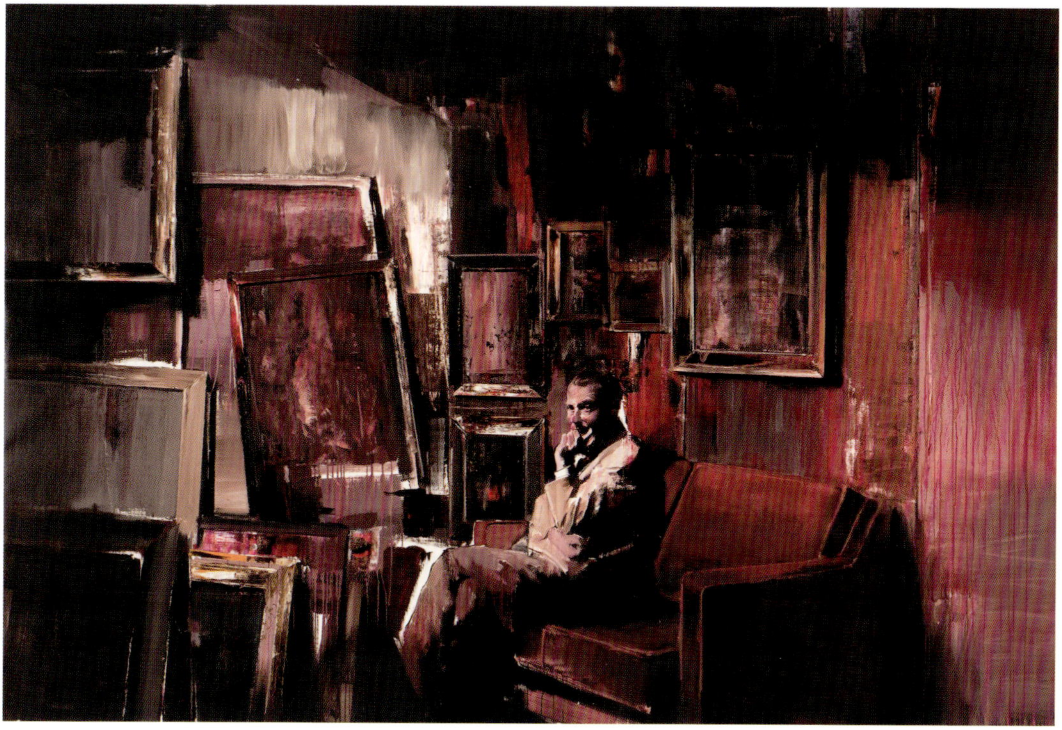

2
Adrian Ghenie
The Collector, 2008
Oil on canvas, 200 × 290 cm

AG: I did. In the end, we became good friends, so she would sell me more material. I never convinced her to sell me white though.

MG: *What about brushes?*
AG: I shaved my cat to make brushes. We made frames using beams from fences.

MG: *What happened when you finished at the Academy and "real life" began?*
AG: I graduated in 2001. At that time, Romania was kind of an outcast from the rest of the world. Only since 2005 has the EU has become more relaxed about Romanians traveling to the West. I managed to travel for a short amount of time to the West because my friend's father sent us invitations and agreed to pay for expenses.

MG: *Were you fascinated by the West?*
AG: Of course.

MG: *Is your art infused with history because you witnessed all of these historical transformations?*

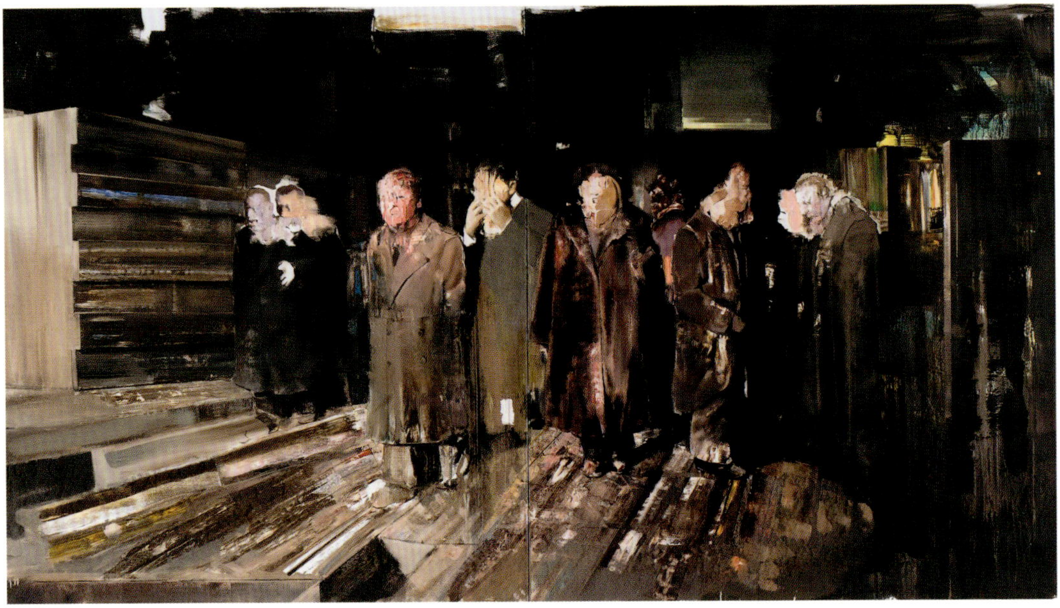

3
Adrian Ghenie
Nickelodeon, 2008
Oil and acrylic on canvas,
230 × 420 cm

AG: My family is more to blame. My grandmother was Tatar Russian – a dramatic case. Born in 1911, she lost eleven brothers, as well as her mother and father during the civil war, in just one winter. My great-grandfathers were rich shepherds who left Romania in the 19th century, heading to the East looking for large areas to feed their herds of livestock. My father was born in 1933, in Crimea. My Russian grandmother, who never really spoke Romanian well, would tell me all the stories. I was fascinated.

MG: *Your early works from around 2008 were called* Basement Feelings. *Was this how you were feeling at the time?*
AG: They were created in relation to my father and his last years of life. I knew my father as a depressed dentist who was too bored to go to work, and who was sick and tired of his patients. My mother and father gradually began to live separate, parallel lives. He withdrew from all his responsibilities and started collecting junk, rubbish and objects that he placed in his garage and the basement next to it. It was like a jungle.

MG: *Did he go mad?*
AG: He was kind of a maniac. He had thousands of empty bottles. He drank half of them by himself. Also, car-wheels, two guns that he owned legally because he was a hunter – all kind of objects. He had this idea that one day he would repair all of these things, and we would need them. He slowly created this amazing atmospheric installation. My mother would tell me to go downstairs to fetch him for lunch, so I'd go there and sometimes

we'd talk a bit, and he would show me something. This environment was unique. Our neighbors had impeccable garages, where they kept their pickles and cars. When my father died, I had to clean the space, which was an incredible journey through the family history.

MG: *Was it magical?*
AG: It was. And it was scary at the same time, because it was so dirty and full of weird objects, that you could barely find your way around.

MG: *So, your first series of paintings was about going deep into yourself.*
AG: Yes. I was thinking about that space in most of those paintings. The space suggests "basement", so you can see a concrete texture, but then there's always an abandoned piece of furniture with the texture of rotting wood.

MG: *Would you consider this series to be the very beginning of what you're doing now?*
AG: It happened beforehand. When I left Romania in 2001, after my graduation, I was confused: I didn't know what to do, so I emigrated to Austria, where I decided to quit painting because I had this idea that I didn't understand anything and that contemporary art was too complicated.

MG: *Why?*
AG: Maybe I was too into classical art. I thought, maybe I should have a normal life. In 2001, having a career in art looked simply impossible. I didn't know where to start. It was like a big mystery to me that completely overwhelmed me.

MG: *But you were aware of your skills?*
AG: Yes, but I thought maybe those skills could be better pushed in a different direction. I thought that I should restore paintings. I didn't feel as if I knew the codes of the art world, so I quit painting and lived in Vienna, like a normal immigrant trying to survive. This ended up being a complete disaster, so I later returned to Romania to live with my mother, which was really depressing. I said to my good friend and then artist, Mihai Pop, "I'm not an artist anymore, but art is the only thing I know a bit about. Maybe we can do something related to art, but which doesn't imply I have to do it". So, we opened the PLAN B gallery with a few other friends who shared similar experiences.

MG: *Did you enjoy being a gallery owner?*
AG: After one year, it became extremely stressful for me. I had to deal with artists and had to deal with collectors, which meant that I had to be

social, pay attention to and listen to them. I don't naturally have these qualities, and it became a burden that was killing me.

MG: *When did you start painting again?*
AG: I remember it very well. I was in my room. There was a TV on my desk, and my mother was in the other room watching a soap opera. I was bored and had no money – it was February and raining outside. I had a beer with friends the day before, so I couldn't go there again. I thought to myself, "What the hell should I do with this evening?" Then it crossed my mind: I still have that box filled with colors from previous years. I saw that the red was still fresh, the blue was fresh, and so was the white – and I squeezed them. It only took a few moments to ignite my desire again. For the first time in my life, I had absolutely no ambitions, and I painted without thinking of showing the results to someone.

MG: *What did you paint?*
AG: A very small, urban scene. I took a few voyeuristic pictures, using a cheap camera from my room on the sixth floor of the building. I had this panoramic view of a big courtyard, at dusk, mostly filled with teenagers, among weird, communist architecture. The couples would hide and kiss. I painted these very humble, naive nocturnal scenes. I did four or five of them and then stopped.

MG: *Why?*
AG: Because I didn't have any sort of pressure on me, so it went on and off. After a few months, I showed them to my friends, who found them very interesting.

MG: *Do you still have these paintings?*
AG: No. When I started having a career, they also entered into the big market machine. [laughs]

MG: *Why did this breakthrough happen in that particular moment?*
AG: Something that's hard to explain is how the best stuff often comes to you when you're doing it without ambitions or expectations.

MG: *Did this moment make you aware of your freedom?*
AG: I became aware of its mechanism. When I looked for a subject, I no longer cared about what other people thought. If you want to be a commercial artist, you never start with a small painting that's 99 percent gray and full of shadows. I realized I could completely ignore what people think, want and say, and just look for something that gives someone the feeling that they are connecting with something inside you.

MG: *Like the basements.*
AG: I started to think about images that were somehow inside me, and until then I wasn't aware they were so important. Don't go to a library and look at *Artforum* or a catalogue of god knows who. Just try to remember an image that is specific to you, and live in that thing until you know exactly what the image's temperature and atmosphere is.

MG: *Did people start appreciating your art all of a sudden?*
AG: I don't think my work would have been noticed if it hadn't coincided with Europe opening up to Eastern countries. I only later understood that the West had a programmatic interest in the East. I came up with this very specific subject, along with this Eastern European atmosphere, that perfectly matched their expectations. They didn't want a secondhand abstract expressionist piece made by an Eastern European guy – they wanted that basement feeling. For them, that was the feeling of Romania and its dictatorship.

MG: *You have gradually used more colors in your work.*
AG: At the Art Academy, I painted almost like a fauve – the monochromatic phase of my early paintings after 2006 was very specific for that time, and never happened before or after that time. When you're confused and you don't know what to do, you tend to reduce your palette. Think of Picasso's blue and pink periods. It's a sign of the economy you impose on yourself, which helps you navigate inside yourself. When you do something that's based on your own archive, investigating what's inside your head, you can't use every color – it would be confusing.

MG: *Did you paint another series in this limited scale of colors?*
AG: I became fascinated by Jungian theories and was investigating dreams. I tried to remember what the color in our dreams is, if any.

MG: *The international art world noticed you quickly. Did this speedy transition intimidate you?*
AG: I don't want to pretend I'm extremely brave, but somehow you play the game and you realize you have to move with it. It's like when a port opens up and you have to go through the port because you don't know when it'll be open again.

MG: *You grabbed your chance.*
AG: I was lucky to get the chance. We'll never be able to tell how big the percentage of luck in our success is. One person, who played a great role in me being noticed, is Jane Neal, a British curator who

was interested in Eastern European culture. She's well connected and associated with the Prague Biennale. I met her at the right time and the chemistry was right.

MG: *Coming back to your manner of painting: I think you're one of the few artists who aren't afraid of painting lavishly and beautifully. Why is that?*
AG: This has to do with the chronological way in which the West sees the history of art. Older art is considered a less valuable resource than art which is closer to us in time. For me, chronology doesn't exist in art. Caravaggio and de Kooning were trying to solve the same problem. Deep inside every painting exists a deep, abstract challenge. If you don't look at art chronologically, every single work of art is a piece of research already done for you – just take it.

MG: *Are you not a big fan of the idea of the avant-garde and the modern celebration of progress?*
AG: Avant-garde was, for me, a liberation and a dictatorship at the same time. Modernity created repulsion towards classical beauty; I don't have repulsion for that beauty. I had this feeling that modernity was exactly like a Bolshevik revolution: there was a promise but, in the end, they created their own kind of dictatorship. The artistic canon became a new religion. But Picasso, Malevich or Mondrian are not my only fathers, but all artists are. Chronology is the disease of the West. Internet and mobile phones have sped this up and made us even more obsessed with chronology.

MG: *Why is it so bad?*
AG: People are blind to how much they can steal from the past. Most of the artists are stealing from the same pool – 1980 onwards – constantly recreating and recycling the same thing. This is why painting is a complete disaster today, in my opinion. Old masters are supposed to be in museums, in a box, and you're not trained to look at them.

MG: *Does the problem have to do with skills? Stealing from Velazquez is probably more difficult than stealing from Pollock.*
AG: After teaching for three months at an art academy, I concluded that I can teach students to paint in a classical way in just a few months, but that it would take me a lifetime to remove the crap and misguided manipulations implanted in their heads at art academies.

MG: *What is the crap you are referring to?*
AG: The art world, today, is a gigantic factory of shortcuts. Wherever you

4
Adrian Ghenie
Lidless Eye, 2015
Oil on canvas, 43 × 30 cm

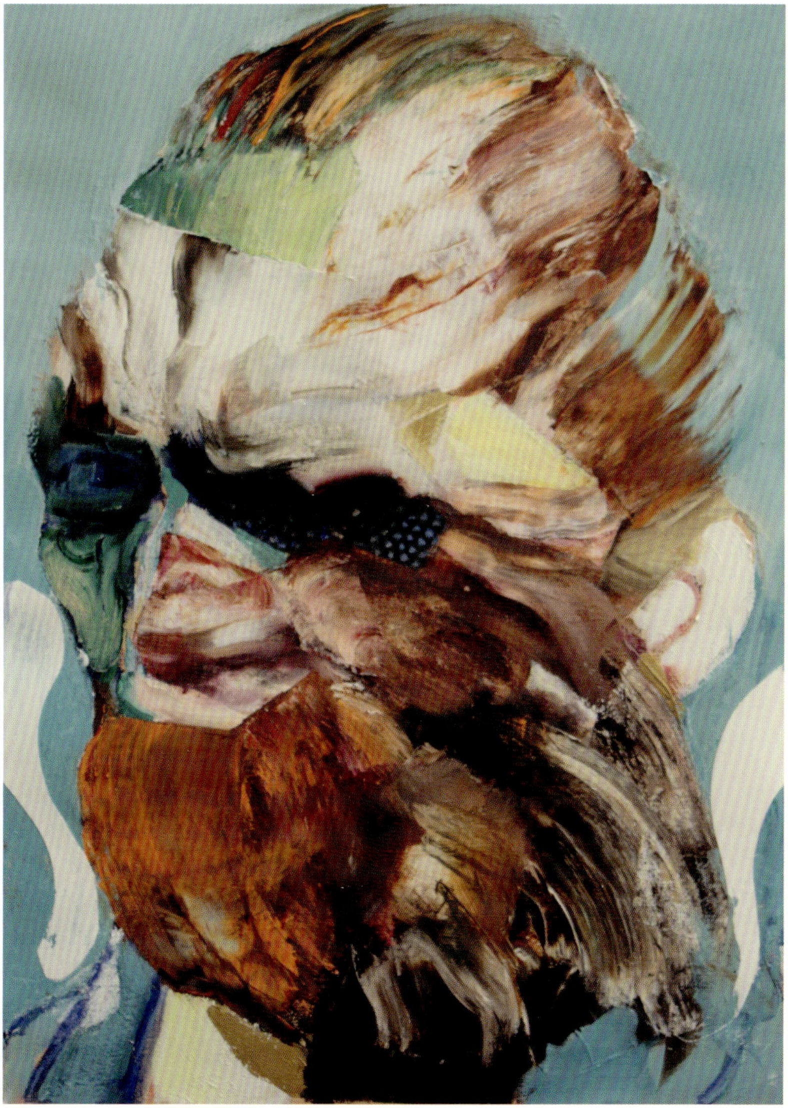

go, art students will just look at catalogues and try to steal a formula and reinterpret it – making a shortcut out of a shortcut. "Maybe I can fool a gallerist and the gallerist can fool a collector". At the same time, I'm not suggesting we kill modernism and go back to Caravaggio.

MG: *Instead, you want us to swim in the entire ocean of* history of *art?*
AG: Rethinking the chronological model should come from art theorists. The "new" is not necessarily clean and sustainable. Picasso already showed us how to do it; he was looking back to primitive art, Velazquez, Romanic sculpture, African masks and the Baroque.

5
Adrian Ghenie
Degenerate Art, 2016
Oil on canvas, 47 × 39 cm

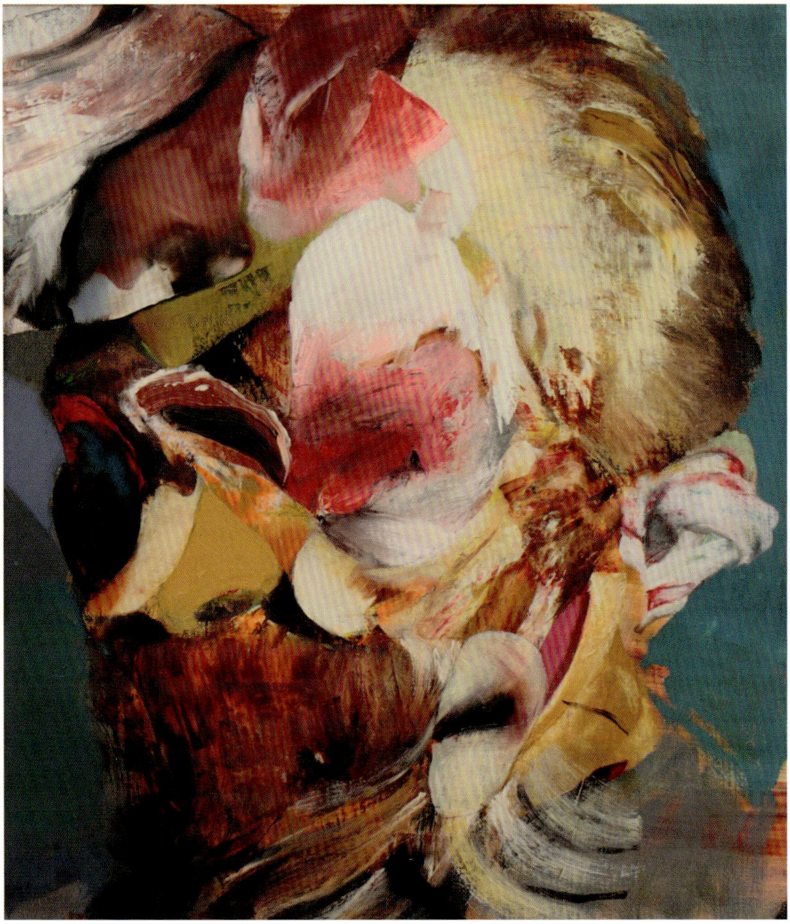

MG: *What are you looking at?*
AG: Everything. I'm stealing from everyone. An incredible place I can always explore is naïve art. Absolutely everything is a gold mine, for me. To imagine having to look at "quality artists" to find good ideas is a catastrophe.

MG: *How do you search?*
AG: You must have a very cold outlook, without judgment. There's a nice anecdote about Francis Bacon looking at Rothko's work. He didn't look at Rothko in awe – he wanted to figure out whether it would fit as background for his silhouettes. Rothko, for him, was a background-provider.

MG: *No hierarchy, no chronology, and a cold eye. What are you working on now?*
AG: In the beginning, when people were asking me what I was doing, I was at least able to offer them a framework, if not an explanation. Now I've

become so blind in regards to my subject matters that I look for people to explain them to me.

MG: *You seem to have become fascinated with van Gogh in recent years. Is this a tribute?*
AG: No. It's a very subjective reaction to him. Years ago, when I was in Paris during my first trip to the West, I went to Musée d'Orsay and saw his self-portrait. I was horrified – I found it unbelievably cold. I bought a reproduction of this work and thought about it for a while: why is it so special? I realized he's not looking out at us, but is looking back at himself through a mirror. Most of the time, when you see yourself in the mirror, in the morning, it is superficial – you see what you want to see, and you rarely have this cold, lucid eye that, in a glimpse of a second, makes you realize that you saw yourself.

MG: *You perceived the painting as cold?*
AG: I remember and classify paintings by temperature. For me, some painters are minus 40, like Van Gogh. Rembrandt is on the other side of the scale – the warmest in art history, in my opinion. Breughel and most of the Italians from the Renaissance are also very warm. I developed this ability as a kid. I was very small when my mother would take me to this museum in Sibiu and I'd be drawn closer to paintings that I experienced as being warm.

MG: *What about the eye of Van Gogh?*
AG: That eye is, for me, one of the coldest places in art history. In most of my Van Gogh heads, the eye is removed and it's a black hole instead.

MG: *Would you like your paintings to be warm or cold?*
AG: Impossible to say. It's like not knowing the smell of your own home. I cannot judge my own paintings in terms of temperature.

MG: *Let's talk about the temperature of the art market.*
AG: In the end, it's not so interesting. At the beginning, the financial results were flattering. It would be dishonest to say that I'm not flattered by success. But then, I started feeling weird, so it's almost like an anomaly.

MG: *Was it influencing your life too much?*
AG: The numbers were not in balance. I was too young for those numbers.

MG: *They enabled you to be taken seriously by a lot of people.*
AG: Do you want to be taken so seriously at the age of forty? I don't.

MG: *Doesn't it give you a feeling of independence? You can do whatever you want.*
AG: I don't want to do all that much. With most of this money, I finance projects that involve other people. My personal life is a very modest one and that hasn't changed. Imagine if you gave millions to Giacometti – do you think he would change his studio or habits? Neither would I.

MG: *Why?*
AG: Being a painter implies, without being a burden, a sort austerity that cannot be abandoned or reformed.

MG: *You go to clubs.*
AG: To preserve my human demeanor.

MG: *Otherwise you'd prefer staying in the studio?*
AG: Painting is a physical process, involving your hands. Your pants are dirty and you eat with hands covered in paint. Studios are messy and humble environments. If you spend hours in this environment, it keeps you grounded. You can't do a painting if you're in a clean room, because that kind of cleanliness completely breaks your relationship with materiality. You need to see the materials in their phases when they are accessible and dirty.

MG: *In this sense, not a lot has changed, if you compare yourself to Rembrandt.*
AG: Exactly. The materials around you are in a stage of decay, ready to be destroyed. You put a tube of red on a palette, and that is essentially pure red. But next second, you mix it with something else, destroying its purity. This is what you do thousands times. It's amazing when you squeeze a full tube of yellow out and it looks so beautiful and clean. And then, the next second, you ruin it.

MG: *Is it exciting to ruin it?*
AG: It gives you a feeling of power, and that's the addiction. I act on this purity and change it into something else. You are in charge of the change. This is the moment that makes someone become addicted to painting. You can't be surrounded by money in this case, because that won't work. Bacon was a millionaire, but he never left his messy studio.

MG: *What do you think about painting in our time?*
AG: Painting is a time-consuming medium, and is dying out because of this. It is a strange death. More paintings are made and more colors and

canvases are bought than ever in history, but the result is very mediocre because it contradicts the speed we live in. Painting is a process based on failure. You learn how to do it by doing it wrong.

MG: *Let's think about something positive for the future: you are supporting a museum in Romania.*
AG: It is contemporary art foundation. I bought an historical building in Cluj and consigned it – for free – to the *PLAN B Foundation*.

MG: *What do you want to achieve with the Foundation?*
AG: Firstly, it's important to map what has happened in post-war art in Romania. We'll do research and publish books. The second task will be to collect and display contemporary Romanian art. Every time I go to Romania, I realize what has happened there is so interesting. But there are many artists and movements that are completely undocumented. The ideal situation would be that, if a visitor came to Cluj in ten years, they would have an idea about what Romanian art has been like over past fifty years, after leaving the gallery and the library.

MG: *Are you giving back to society as a very successful artist? Or are you genuinely interest in the history and what needs to be done?*
AG: Both. It's a kind of detective job. You grow up with the idea that everything was invented in the West and that there was nothing in the place you come from. Then you realize it's not quite like that, so a lot needs to be done.

MARK GROTJAHN

January 2013

Marta Gnyp: *Let's start from the beginning of your career as an artist: you finished your artistic education at Berkeley, then opened a gallery in LA. Why didn't you concentrate on just being an artist?*
Mark Grotjahn: The gallery we opened was not exactly a commercial space. At that time there were only a few galleries in LA that would give a solo show over to a young artist. So, for a young artist, the only possibility would be a big group show. We thought we had a better eye than other galleries and decided to organize straight up solo exhibitions. We have always thought we were artists in the first place, so we created a beautiful space in which the artists could showcase their work and the public could see what artists were capable of doing, not just showing one or two small objects.

MG: *Why did you want to become an artist in the first place?*
MGR: When I was fifteen, my art teacher showed me a book called *Concerning the Spiritual in Art* by Kandinsky, in which I found an answer to what I was doing. It opened my eyes to the fact that the designs and drawings I was making could be considered art. In a way, this is the moment when a certain kind of art education started for me. So, from reading Kandinsky, I moved on to Paul Klee, then to Schnabel and Baselitz.

MG: *Always painters?*
MGR: No, not always painters. I moved on to Richard Prince and Mike Kelley, as well.

MG: *So always a very strong visual appearance.*
MGR: Yes. Although I also really like dry, conceptual pieces like those of Adrian Piper.

MG: *One of your first well-known projects was a conceptual project, the Sign Exchange program, that you started at school in Berkeley and in San Francisco and then continued while running the gallery.*

1
Mark Grotjahn
Untitled (Green Butterfly M. Grotjahn 03), 2003
Oil on linen,
175.3 × 137.2 cm

MGR: I started it as reactionary work. When I was in Berkeley, everybody was doing figurative work; barely any of my colleagues knew who Mike Kelley was. I was really bored with the work I was doing so I decided to give up painting the figure and started looking at people using painting and drawing, but communicating effectively through these forms of media. This drove me to the *Sign Exchange* program: people would paint a hotdog for a restaurant sign, or a picture of a beer or hamburger, because that was what they were selling. So I started copying this work and tried to exchange my replicas with the "original" artworks.

MG: *What was the reason for this exchange?*
MGR: When I started the project, I thought they were better than mine because they were communicating with their audience. I wanted their audience, so I started trading the signs in order to get it.

MG: *Didn't the restaurant owners think you were crazy?*
MGR: In 90 percent of cases, when trying to trade signs, I was successful. Some of them thought I was weird, some of them thought I was funny. They'd sometimes just want to get my sign and get me out of there as quickly as possible. Sometimes the owner would let me go to the back of the store and I'd get to see where they kept their guns and money.

MG: *Then you brought the "real objects" to the gallery and showcased them as objets trouvé, like your artworks.*
MGR: I considered them as my art, although they weren't found-objects, but traded objects.

MG: *Was it a kind of search for what makes art "art"?*
MGR: I intellectually believed that art can be whatever you wanted it to be, but only by doing something does the idea become true. It's one thing to say you know something, mentally, but it's another thing to actually know it, physically. It's one thing to say I believe art can be like this and another thing to do it and know it.

MG: *So you did it.*
MGR: I did. I moved out here, opened the gallery, worked with different artists and took care of my conceptual needs, in terms of working outside of myself, being with other people; like being in a band. Artists love to work and they love to talk about their work. It's great. Those were different kinds of human connections. At a certain moment, I started looking at why I got into art in the first place, why I was interested in art. Then I thought about line and color, and then I started making abstractions.

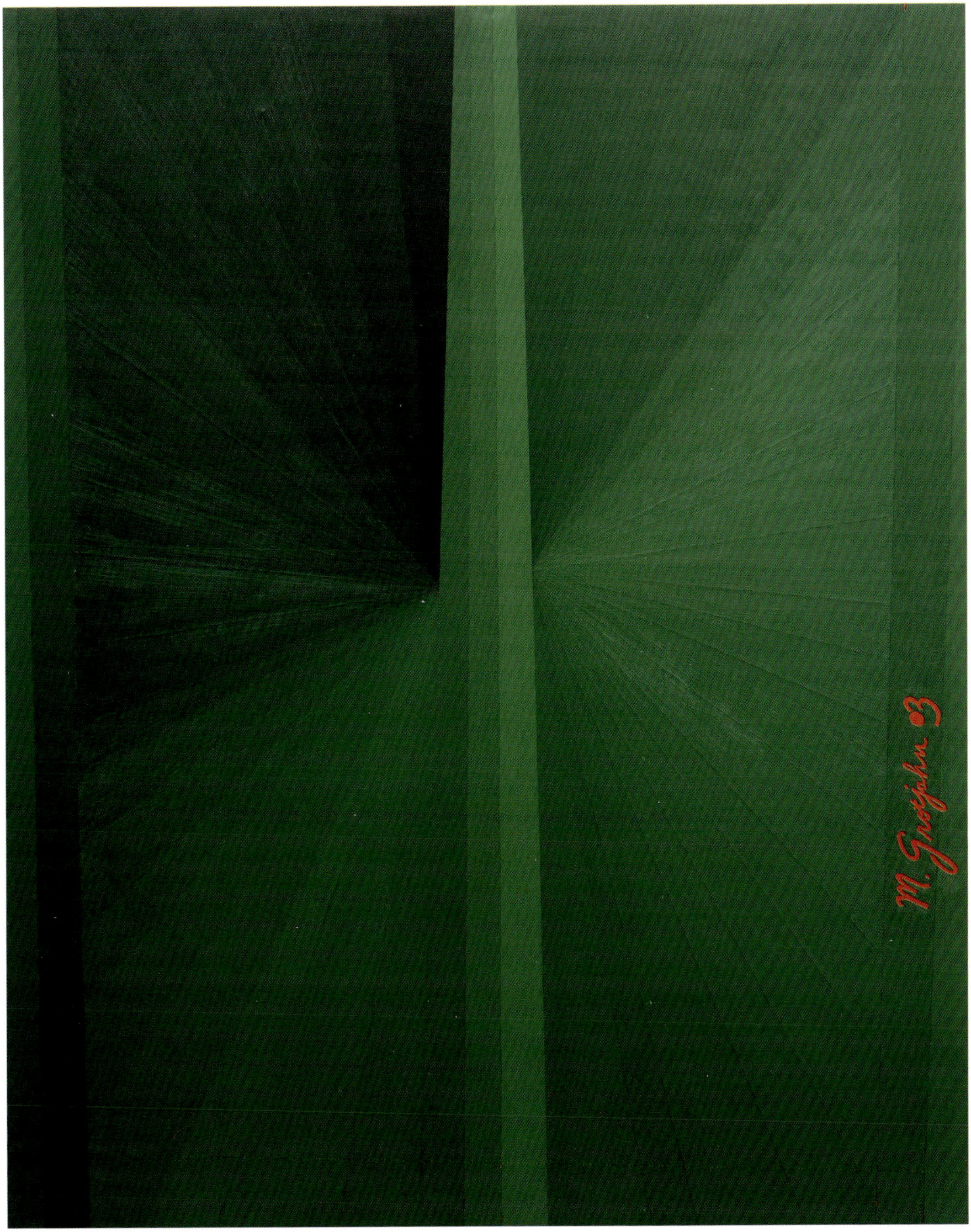
M. Grotjahn 03

MG: *Did you start producing different paintings and drawings?*
MGR: I was actually looking for one or two motifs to exploit. I think, because the *Sign Exchange* was a conceptual work, I was always coming up with different ideas. I wanted to pick one idea and stick with it. See what I could do with one motif.

MG: *So while doing abstract paintings and drawings you were looking for motifs that you could use as a structure.*
MGR: Yes.

MG: *This was the latter half of the '90s, which means an extremely difficult time for painting; there was a clear anti-painting attitude constructed by many art theorists and historians. Painting in this period was not so obvious.*
MGR: That's partially true, especially regarding the handmade works where you could see the artist's hand. At that time, I was also thinking about Gauguin, which was a very romantic notion of the artist. So, again, it was a kind of reaction to what was going on in LA at that time.

MG: *You were playing with the romantic notion of the artist and with the historically-oriented media when you discovered that the mathematical perspective could be an option for forming a structure in your work. Did you realize that by doing this, you would immediately connect your work with art history?*
MGR: While I was making the three-tier perspectives I was thinking of Kandinsky, Mondrian, etc. I thought I was doing non-objective work. I no longer see it like that, in retrospect. I knew that the history of non-representational painting is already more than 100 years old and I knew that I was part of that language. But it's like playing in a rock n' roll band and asking if you're aware that you're part of rock n' roll history.

MG: *Still, using perspective is perhaps more than that, because the introduction of perspective was an extremely important moment in art history, when painting began to be taken seriously since there were scientific methods applied to it.*
MGR: I have never thought about my artworks in this way. I really like to have my cake and eat it too. Yes, I call them perspectives but I never saw them as perspectives; I saw them, really, as non-objective. When I look at them, of course, they do look like roads or landscapes but I never thought of them in these terms when I was making them. That came from other people and I think it makes sense they saw them in those terms, especially considering the fact I *did* call them perspectives. It was naïve of me to not see them in their relationship to the scientific, the Renaissance, etc., but I just didn't.

MG: *What about the multiple vanishing points? Was it to experiment with optical effects?*
MGR: It was strictly a formal device I found interesting. That doesn't mean I didn't find it interesting because of my knowledge of art history; I never specifically thought of it as an idea.

MG: *Did you intend to make your works more controlled and less emotional by using these geometrical and mathematical devices?*
MGR: Mondrian is geometrical and still highly emotional. When I went onto the *Faces*, I used different marks that are, I think, traditionally seen as expressive. The perspectives were very meditative and this is a different kind of emotion. There was a certain kind of peace and a certain kind of beauty that I was going for. I don't think they are less expressive; it is just that the other ones, being the *Faces*, are viewed as more expressive.

MG: *Speaking of contemplative and beautiful, let's move on to the motif of the butterfly, which at some point arrived in your work.*
MGR: The butterfly came about because I tried to make some horizontal three-tier perspectives; the majority of my work is vertically orientated, so I tried to work outside of that and make a painting with horizontal orientation. I made the first two tiers vertical and I pointed the perspectives towards each other. As soon as I did that, and applied color, it became a non-objective painting again. I got out of landscape. It certainly became more of a painting and less so a representation.

MG: *Did you yourself call it a butterfly?*
MGR: I called it a butterfly but it's just a way of categorizing it as a group of works.

MG: *When you read articles about this category, many art critics connect the butterfly motif with nature. Did you also make this connection yourself?*
MGR: It wasn't exactly what I was thinking about. I called some paintings "perspectives" but I'm not interested in perspective; I called some "butterflies" but I don't think they're butterflies; I call my sculptures masks but they are not masks.

MG: *You play with us.*
MGR: I guess I play with words.

MG: *There seems to be plenty of conflict in your works. You just mentioned one: contemplative versus expressive. Could we go further by saying ra-*

2
Mark Grotjahn
Untitled (Face for Greece 843), 2009
Oil on cardboard mounted on linen, 183.5 × 132.1 cm

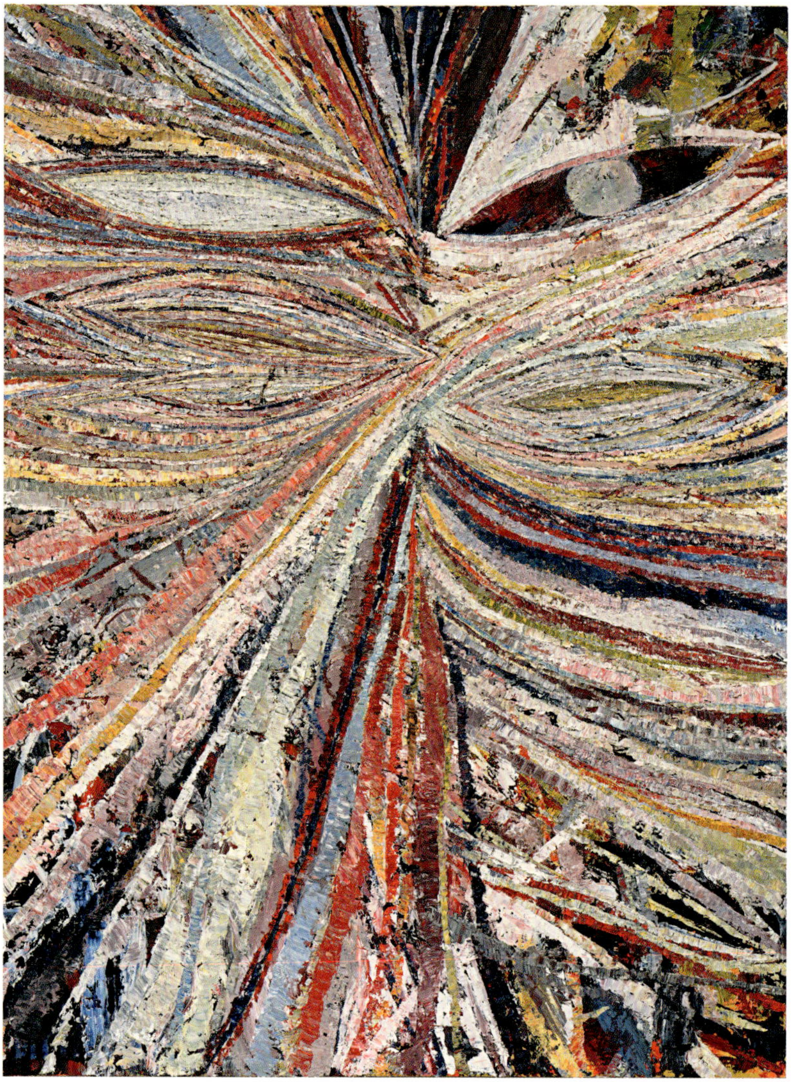

tional versus emotional, chance versus conscious decision, abstract versus figurative? Do you need them?
MGR: I don't know whether I need them. Maybe somehow it's important for me to have structures in order to keep myself interested in making an artwork.

MG: *Do you create this tension yourself?*
MGR: It happens; I don't consciously create it. I see it running through the work. It might be that I need this conflict in my work. I just consciously choose to work in different styles. When I moved here, nobody was signing their pieces because it was the cliché of the artist taking all the

3
Mark Grotjahn
Untitled (Standard Lotus No. I, Bird of Paradise, Japanese Tiger Mouth Face 43.33), 2012
Oil on cardboard mounted on linen, 186.7 × 134.6 cm

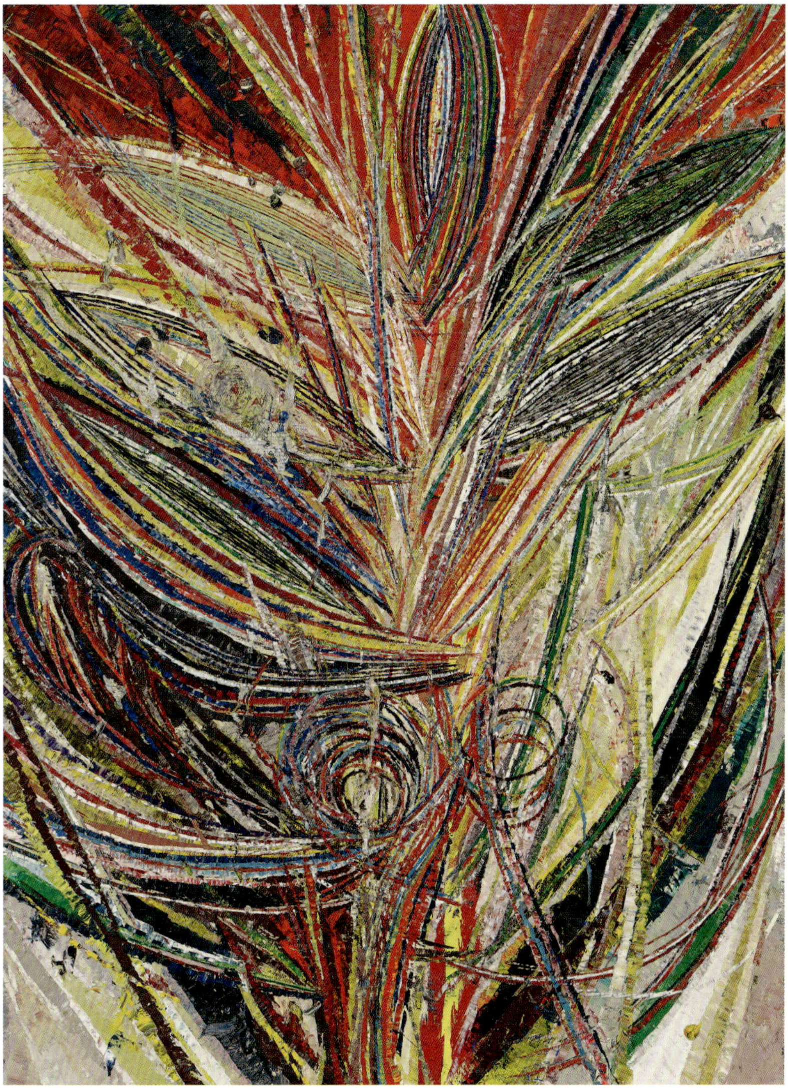

credit for the work, putting their ego first. All of the work that was being shown in the hip, cool galleries of LA was conceptual work and nobody was signing their work. It was another cliché or an unwritten rule that I wanted to challenge.

MG: *This is why you enlarged your signature on the canvas.*
MGR: Yes, I put it in, front and center. I wanted to say: stop thinking that as an artist you don't have an ego and you don't have a signature style. I wanted to challenge that: actually, I am an artist, I have something to say, clearly I have an ego, I have the need to put this work in a gallery and I want it to be seen. I definitely do.

MG: *So you weren't extremely popular among the conceptual artists.*
MGR: No, I'm still not.

MG: *How do you work? How long does it take to finish a painting, for instance a butterfly-painting?*
MGR: About three weeks, working seventeen days straight. I couldn't stop because otherwise the paint would start to change in consistency. But I haven't made one since 2008 – it's been a while.

MG: *I read that you injured your shoulder a couple of years ago and this is the reason you can't make them any longer.*
MGR: While skiing, I hit some ice and I went down. There was no choice in the matter so I went down. I didn't see a doctor for two weeks until my wife told me I should see one. He said there was something wrong and my arm turned out to be broken. I couldn't paint for two hours straight, let alone ten hours straight. I moved on to *Faces*. This is something I could paint, I could look at, and step back from.

MG: *You don't have any assistants?*
MGR: I do have assistants, but my assistants don't touch my paintings once a painting has started.

MG: *Were you sad that you were forced to stop the butterfly-paintings?*
MGR: I don't know whether I was sad. I knew I had to stop for a while and that I might go back to it when my arm recovered. I just never did.

MG: *Your recent exhibitions were with bronze sculptures, which you called* masks *– interesting and provoking works. Again, there were many comments on its dialogue with early modernism or folk art. You had always made them out of cardboard, so it was a special decision to make them in bronze. I also read that you considered them to be very personal, not for public consumption. Why did you decide to display them anyway?*
MGR: I kept them private for thirteen, fourteen years. I gave them away to friends or, occasionally, traded one. At a certain point, I wanted to do a show with them. When you cast them in bronze, they change. In a way, I depersonalized them; they feel less as a diary and are more of an armature for a painting.

MG: *Let's now talk a bit about the place you work and live, Los Angeles. Los Angeles is now considered a very important artistic hub. Is this true for you? Is there a sense of being in an artistic community?*

MGR: There are many galleries and many new spaces that I haven't had the chance to visit yet.

MG: *Are you so extremely busy with your own work that you don't have time to visit other exhibitions?*
MGR: I've been into making my own work and not spending a lot of time looking at other galleries. I work five, six, sometimes seven days a week. You can see in the butterfly work that they are very obsessive. I am a compulsive person. When I'm not making my work, I feel as if I'm wasting my life away.

MG: *What makes you so popular among collectors nowadays? If you speak to American collectors, many of them admire you.*
MGR: It's true. I guess I *am* popular. There are many people who would like to have my work. I don't know what it is that I'm doing. For a long time, I wasn't like this.

MG: *You really don't know why Mark Grotjahn is considered* the *artist?*
MGR: Am I *the* artist? I'd like to be that, sounds good to me.

MG: *You've been part of the Gagosian gallery since 2007. Were you surprised when they asked you to join?*
MGR: No, it was like a two-year process. I had three galleries already – Anton Kern, Blum & Poe and Shane Campbell.

MG: *Many artists complain about the pressure of huge production on the market. Once you are with top galleries you're more or less obliged to produce many artworks for the market. Do you mind?*
MGR: I like being rich. It's easier to be rich than to be poor. One-hundred percent. It's easier to have too many people wanting your work than to have nobody wanting your work. Being an artist is hard, no matter what, but being a poor artist is harder than being a rich artist.

MG: *But don't you mind the pressure of having to always deliver artworks of a very good quality?*
MGR: I don't have to produce a lot. It's up to me. Since all my work is really handmade, I don't really produce that much; I wish I produced more. I wish I was like Jackson Pollock and I could make a few paintings per day. He was a genius. But, unfortunately, I'm not that good so it takes me three to four weeks to make a good piece.

MG: *He had to hurry up – he died very early.*
MGR: He died at forty-four, my age. I'd like to produce a lot, but it's not

4
Mark Grotjahn
Untitled (Call Me Jackson Washed Black Brown Nose Morgan Mask M21.d), 2012
Painted bronze,
85.7 × 74.9 × 81.3 cm

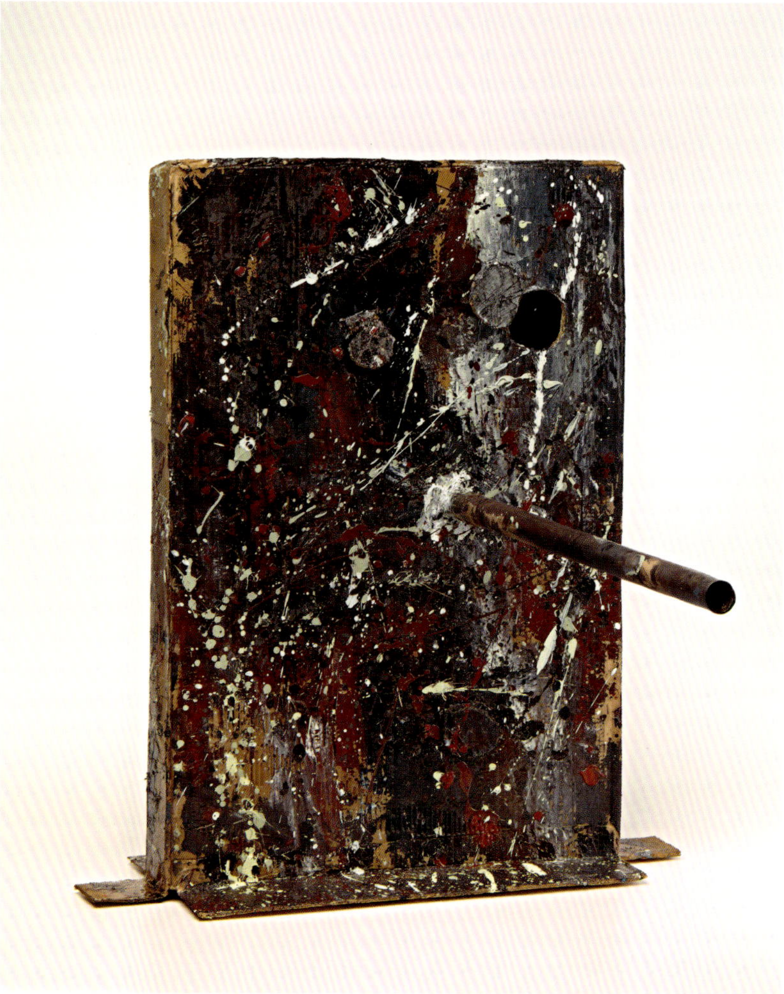

the way I work. I try not to put out paintings that aren't good. Here, in the studio, I sometimes think they're great, but then I try to look at them for at least six months before I release them. I'm pretty good at that.

MG: *How interesting. Do you rework them sometimes?*
MGR: Sometimes, but I just like to keep them around, at least three or four months to know whether they are good enough. In my mind, they might be good but I'm not always the best judge. If my work goes out and it's not good, that's my fault, not the market's fault.

MG: *How many paintings are you producing per year?*
MGR: Ten to fifteen per year. Van Gogh did 800 in the last ten years of his life.

MG: *I can imagine you like the idea that your paintings have become so expensive?*
MGR: Yeah… All my high school girlfriends regret breaking up with me.

MG: *How did it feel when you recently heard that one of your paintings was sold for $4 million at an auction?*
MGR: I watched it live online, and it got me high. I have personally never sold a work for that much. So this guy made more money with one of my paintings than I have ever made from one of my paintings.

MG: *In the end, this auction was also a kind of advertisement for you. Everybody knows that Mark Grotjahn is now worth $4 million.*
MGR: I grew up looking at Picasso books, they seemed like magic to me. I want artists to own buildings; I want them to have financial power.

MG: *Of course, there were great artists, in history, who were rich and very much involved in making money for themselves. What do you think about the role of collectors nowadays? If I got you straight, they shouldn't make more money with your paintings than you do.*
MGR: It's okay. I guess it's what I signed up for. I'm just sometimes disappointed that someone sells my work and he's one of the collectors who used to put an arm around me and say, "I will never sell your work, not even for $5 million, never". And then they don't want me to come over for Christmas because my painting is no longer on the wall, as they sold it without telling me.

MG: *Has it happened to you often?*
MGR: Yes, it's happened to me enough times that it's no longer shocking.

MG: *The idea of money must be comforting when you are making your paintings. When you work, do you sometimes think about the fact that the object you are creating can become so valuable and expensive?*
MGR: I don't let the fact that I sell my paintings get in the way of trying to make the best painting possible. I don't take phone calls from my art dealers when I'm working. I don't want them to get to my head. So I have ways to protect myself against that and from it coming into my studio. But occasionally, I have to talk with my bookkeeper about insuring the artworks.

MG: *It must be interesting. But it's not only about being able to work. It's also about the very nature of the artworks. Your paintings are often con-*

nected with the idea of transcendence and spirituality; you said yourself that art started, for you, after reading Kandinsky's Spirituality in Art.
MGR: When I was a teenager, I believed you could connect to this universal language. I don't believe that any more, I believe that there's a language you learn and that you can understand. Of course, I'd like my paintings to be transformative; I would love my paintings to make someone happy to be alive.

MG: *Do you think that your personality – you know what you want, you are provocative, playful, intelligent – is important in positioning your work in the market?*
MGR: A few years ago, a friend of mine overheard my dealers talking to some collectors, they were telling them that I have narcolepsy, that I like to gamble, that I go to strip clubs, and, of course, they were using that as a marketing tool. They probably still are. The culture of the artist is extremely interesting. I love artists' biographies.

MG: *From what you said about being an artist, I think you like cultivating the romantic idea of the artist, breaking the rules, being an outsider, provoking and challenging assumptions.*
MGR: At the same time, being very traditional. I have two beautiful girls, I have a wife, a house. But I'm am an artist. It's a weird thing to be one. You come to work and you do this. This is a choice, but it is a strange life.

MG: *You chose to take part in a court case against one of your collectors. Did you enjoy it?*
MGR: Enjoy it!? I hated it, it was terrible.

MG: *What you did as an artist was unprecedented.*
MGR: I'm in a position in which I can afford to hire a lawyer to fight someone who doesn't want to pay royalties. I didn't enjoy doing it, but I felt like I had no choice.

MG: *Did you want to set an example on behalf of other artists as well?*
MGR: I did it for myself but I think doing it was important.

MG: *Are you involved in the private life of many collectors?*
MGR: I try not to be anymore. Because once you go skiing with them, all of a sudden, they expect a painting from you for the price of a lift-ticket.

MG: *Do you consider yourself as an American artist?*
MGR: I'm American, although my father was born in Germany; I'm a first-generation American.

MG: *Now I get your name! I thought it was Dutch.*
MGR: All Germans say it's Dutch but it is German; it definitely traces back to Prussian roots. But I have never met any German who would give me the credit of having a German name. The maiden name of my grandmother was Gross, which is definitely German.

MG: *What has happened to you over the last ten years must feel amazing.*
MGR: Yes.

DAMIEN HIRST

March 2018

Marta Gnyp: *Let's start with your most recent project, your exhibition,* Veil Paintings, *currently being shown at Gagosian LA. What struck me when reading the reviews is that even the most basic artistic act, which is an artist painting by himself, by hand, is in your case considered provocative.*
Damien Hirst: Oh yeah, I just find that funny.

MG: *Did you expect this kind of reaction?*
DH: Not really. I've always made art myself and always used other people. Almost as soon as I could walk, I started getting other people to help me make art.

MG: *There is no difference for you, whether you paint a piece yourself or let someone else paint it?*
DH: When I'm doing a series of works, I always paint the first ones. That's what I have to do in order to show the studio what I want. But I don't really see a difference. We live in such a multifaceted world today that using a single approach is very difficult. If you say, "I'm just gonna paint like this and I'm gonna make my work as art that reflects the world" – I don't think that's possible. That's why I end up making paintings, sculptures, installations and videos – *everything* that I possibly can, because we've come to be constantly bombarded by a world that's like that. It's the visual language we live with.

MG: *Your last project in Venice,* Treasures from the Wreck of the Unbelievable, *was more like curating your own ideas and production instead of making it yourself.*
DH: To take a tiny piece of paper and a pencil and make marks on it is exactly the same as what I did in Venice – there's simply no difference. It's just organizing elements, it's always art. It's funny, because for years people have been saying, "he doesn't paint his own paintings". To me, it seems like a silly debate. It's strange to have it for art and not elsewhere; somehow people think it's important, but I don't think it's important.

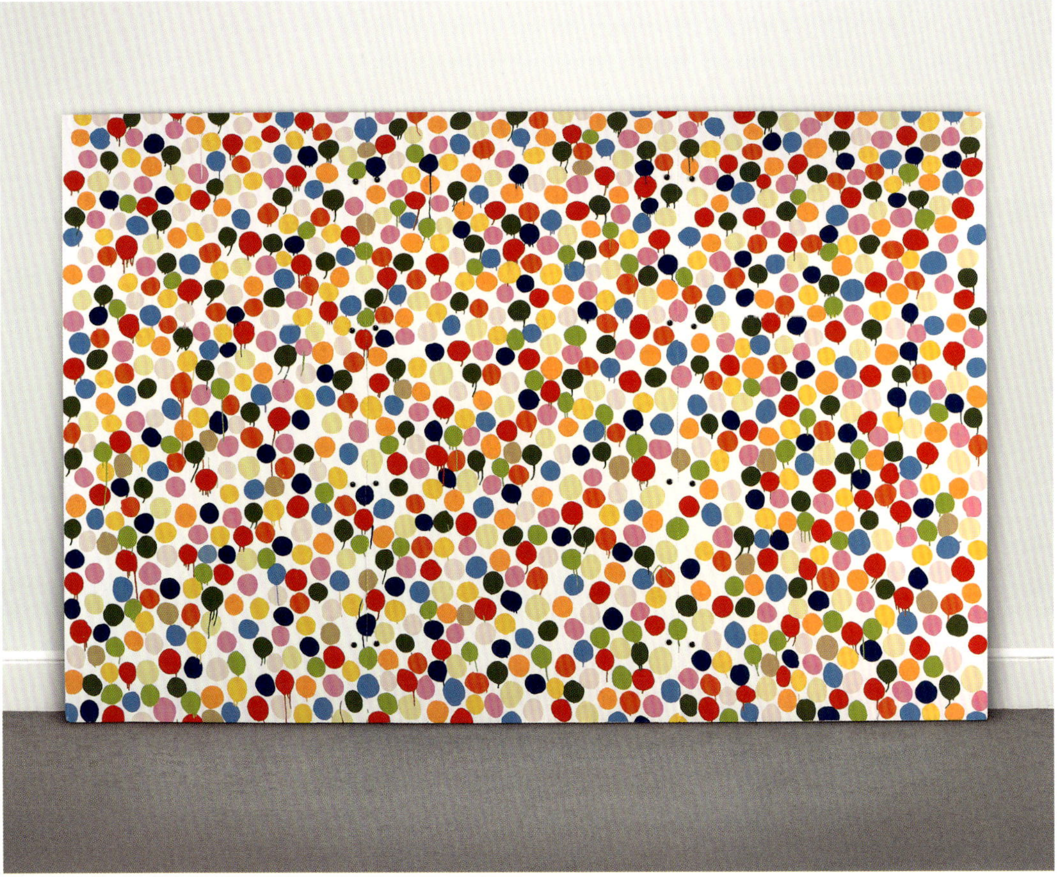

1
Damien Hirst
Spot Painting, 1986
Household gloss on board,
243.8 × 365.8 cm

You would never expect an architect to build his own house. Frank Gehry didn't physically build the Guggenheim, which is very much *his* building – and I think art can work like that.

MG: *If we you go back to the origins of your work, the core of your ideas was formed in just four years. Between 1988 and 1992, you created* Spot Paintings, Spin Paintings, the Natural History series *with animals in formaldehyde,* Medicine Cabinets. *I wonder, were you aware at the time of this gigantic outburst of creativity?*
DH: Yeah, but it wasn't just me, it was also my generation. I had lots of friends who were making a huge amount of art as well. The thing we had most in common was the fact that we had nothing in common – and I think that was sort of acceptable. We all drank in the same bar and we all felt very comfortable with each other because we were all doing very different things. I think that makes sense, whereas maybe for other artists in the past it didn't.

MG: *You embraced difference as a part of the ideology of the group.*
DH: Before I went to Goldsmiths, I was very aware that I had a lot of conflicting ideas and wasn't sure which one to go with. I couldn't really make decisions, so I was becoming inactive. Then, at Goldsmiths, I realized that it didn't matter: I could just pursue them all. You could say that the guy making the formaldehyde artworks doesn't really suit the guy making spin paintings, and it could become a little bit crazy. But I decided I was just going to pursue everything: I was going to make work from every idea that I had, even though the ideas looked conflicting.

MG: *It probably took a lot of time to pursue all the ideas.*
DH: The first painting I sold, I used the money to pay other people to make more paintings for me. I was selling a painting for 500 pounds and I still spent 400 pounds of that to pay other people to make more paintings.

MG: *You must have been very convinced about your ideas.*
DH: Only really when I started at art school. Don't forget, you start painting and drawing when you're very young. I was drawing from when I was around four, five years old. I only started thinking I could make a living doing art when I was at Goldsmiths and I just had to relent.

MG: *From the very beginning of your career at Goldsmiths, you were a kind of entrepreneurial artist, a curator, and a very public person. We have models of this approach in the post-war art world, such as Andy Warhol or Jeff Koons, but your activity as an entrepreneurial artist was special in the European context. Was it a spontaneous decision or a consciously chosen attitude?*
DH: I don't really know. I don't want to give Margaret Thatcher any credit but she was around at the time, pushing for people to do things themselves. There was the Prince's Trust by Prince Charles. There was a big push in England saying, "Do it yourself". There was also a lot of really great art at my art school. I worked for Anthony d'Offay Gallery, so I was looking at work by great artists like Carl Andre and then going back to my art school. I was thinking, the work done in my art school was at least as good and as confident as that of the gallery. When I was still a student in 1988, I organized the *Freeze* exhibition that had seventeen artists in it, but with the art world being the way it was then, there was just no room for something like that. I had to be entrepreneurial, if you want to call it that. It was just a really creative time with lots of exciting art going on and lots of friends all in the right place at the right time. I don't know what caused it. We came out of a time when there was a lot of poverty.

MG: *You just mentioned Anthony d'Offay. Were you an assistant in his gallery?*
DH: I was like a backroom assistant sorting out paintings, hanging works, dealing with artists, moving things around, putting things in trucks – all that sort of stuff. When I moved to London, I didn't have any money, so I got a job at d'Offay for three days a week: Thursdays, Fridays and Saturdays. I was on a full-time course, but managed to squeeze it in. So I was doing both – Goldsmiths and working for Anthony d'Offay at the same time.

MG: *It's quite amazing that you got the job as a student, because at the time Anthony d'Offay was probably the most important gallery in Europe.*
DH: It was the most important gallery in the world. I was being directly influenced there – handling great art and then going to art school and back. I was backwards and forwards between college and Anthony d'Offay. There were always really creative people there, like Sadie Coles, Matthew Marks, Tanya Bonakdar; a lot of great artists like Gilbert and George and Joseph Beuys. I met Warhol there.

MG: *Was this also the place that taught you how the art world functioned?*
DH: It was more about understanding great art, I think. It was the first time that I was in direct contact with really great art: Yves Klein's paintings, Carl Andre's sculptures, Dan Flavin's pieces, great Richters, Bruce Nauman. There was just loads and loads of great art around.

MG: *In this early period, in 1990, you made the work,* A Thousand Years, *an extremely mature work for someone that young. Was it not intimidating for you to make such a profoundly existential work at such a young age?*
DH: I don't know. There were a lot of doubts when I told my friends at college what I was making and they started laughing at me. I like to get into a sort of punk rock position of not caring – you have to say, "I don't care. I'm just going to do this". I thought all great art was about important things. I was struggling with art that was about superficial things. The *Spot Paintings* felt a bit superficial, the *Medicine Cabinets* didn't, but they were sort of my take on Jeff Koons's *Hoover* pieces. For some reason, I just thought I had to make a piece about something really important; it just had to be about life and death and it had to be minimal. I was looking at other artists like Jannis Kounellis, who I loved. There was a great tutor at Goldsmiths who I used to work with called Jon Thompson, who has died now. He was friends with Gilbert and George and with Kounellis. Kounellis really blew my mind with the installation, *Untitled (12 Horses)*, that he did with live horses; the pieces with living animals started getting

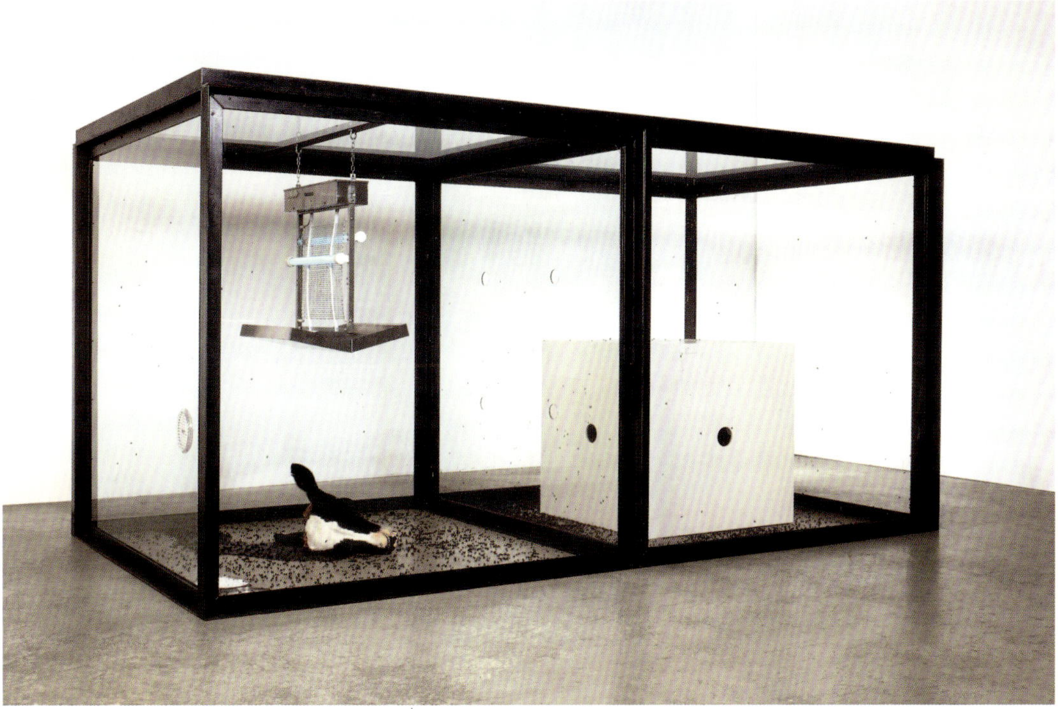

2
Damien Hirst
A Thousand Years, 1990
Glass, steel, silicone rubber, painted MDF, insect-o-cutor, cow's head, blood, flies, maggots, metal dishes, cotton wool, sugar and water, 207.5 × 400 × 215 cm

me really excited. I didn't think it was mature, really, I just thought it had to feel important.

MG: *What about the other person who was also very important for you and the other YBAs, Charles Saatchi? Could you tell me something about the relationship between you two?*
DH: Well, I often say that Charles should have gotten the Turner Prize for his contributions to British art instead of me. He really changed the scale of everything. Before Saatchi, there was Cork Street in London and everything was shown there. The Waddington gallery was probably the biggest, so, you could show medium-sized paintings in there. There were no giant paintings like you got in America, for example Warhol's *Most Wanted Men*. I was thinking of making small collages like those of Kurt Schwitters, which would be nice in those types of galleries, before I went to Goldsmiths. Then, when Saatchi opened his first space at Boundary Road, I remember the first time I walked in I just got snow blindness. It was a kind of shock to me. I've never seen a space that big be dedicated to art – even museums didn't feel that big because of all those fire extinguishers and other stuff – this was just a white space with a gray floor with amazing art in it. After walking in there, all I ever wanted to do was

to make art for that space. It changed what I was doing and it changed the scale of what I would make. I didn't care that it wouldn't fit in any other gallery. I just immediately started making big paintings and then never stopped – and for that reason, Charles was massive. I was one of the few artists lucky enough to show at Saatchi – it was like a dream come true.

MG: *Are you still in touch with him?*
DH: Yeah, I had lunch with him about four or five months ago in London. He was very depressed that I didn't smoke anymore. When he asked me "Come on, let's go out for a cigarette", and I told him that I no longer smoke, he was so sad and dejected, and said, "No! Not you as well!"

MG: *Is he still as feverishly involved in art as before?*
DH: I think he is. He's got huge things going on since Boundary Road, but I have no idea what the future holds. Their *Rolling Stones* exhibition, in 2016, was a massive hit in London. He's not like he was to me then: he was a god-like figure in the beginning. He's more human now.

MG: *Speaking of the Turner Prize – what was more important to you: winning the Turner Prize in 1995 or having this very successful exhibition at Gagosian, in New York, in 1996* "No Sense of Absolute Corruption" *that exposed your work to the American public?*
DH: Definitely the New York exhibition. It's about how you measure success, the show at Gagosian was much more of a real success. I always get worried about prizes, being judged and other people making decisions about you based on who-knows-what. To be an artist you have to measure yourself on your own terms. It can get quite confusing if you start measuring yourself in other people's terms like you do with the Turner Prize. I'm not into prizes.

MG: *What about François Pinault, the other collector who has been very important in your life – how did you meet him?*
DH: He met me. He just came to the studio one day, a long time ago. He's got the biggest collection of my work in the world. He's bought pieces from the beginning, he always buys; he's incredibly supportive and he genuinely loves art. When I started collecting on a bigger scale, it was by watching François, because I thought, "Oh, I should buy a few more expensive things to get inside the minds of my collectors" – and then before I knew it I was a big collector myself.

MG: *Regarding your exhibition,* Treasures from the Wreck of the Unbelievable, *in François Pinault's private museums in Venice last year, did*

you discuss your ideas with him beforehand or did he just give you carte blanche, *so to speak?*
DH: That's what's exciting about Pinault – when he likes it, he likes it. I remember him asking me, "What are you working on next?" And when I showed him, he just got very excited and wanted to get involved. I'd already been working on *Treasures* for years before that. When I did my two auctions with Sotheby's, he obviously got a bit disappointed about that because he's Christie's. I promised him that I would do a big thing with him after I did the auction with Sotheby's. He was just disappointed, but then he bought from the auction anyway.

MG: *Are you planning to do another auction directly with Christie's?*
DH: I think exhibiting *Treasures* at the gallery is big enough.

MG: *What about you as a collector: do you collect what you think is great art or do you buy because you want to support friends?*
DH: There're many reasons, and in a way they all come together. I would definitely support friends, but even if I support friends, I buy things that I like. When I was younger and I was making money and no one else was, there was this big divide between me and friends, which was becoming a bit of problem. When people started asking to borrow money from me I got upset about it. Then a friend just said, "Why don't you buy one of my paintings?", and I thought, "Yeah, why don't I?" – and by buying my friends' work, they could come and drink with me if I was in some expensive place! I did it for that reason, but then, in buying artworks, you really become attached to them and you want more – so the whole thing escalates. I would never buy anything I didn't like – but there are many different reasons to like things.

MG: *Do you have a big collection at the moment?*
DH: Yeah, it gets bigger every five minutes.

MG: *Are you buying post-war and contemporary art or are you also making excursions to other periods?*
DH: I love contemporary art but I collect other things as well. I've got a huge skull collection. I collect Haida art, which is an indigenous tribe from the Pacific Northwest Coast, that I love. I've got quite a big collection of their work. My skull collection contains more than 1,000 different skulls. I collect Chinese scholar stones as well. I collect photographs of atomic bomb explosions.

MG: *The idea is to display them all at your Newport Street Gallery in London?*
DH: Yeah, that's the idea.

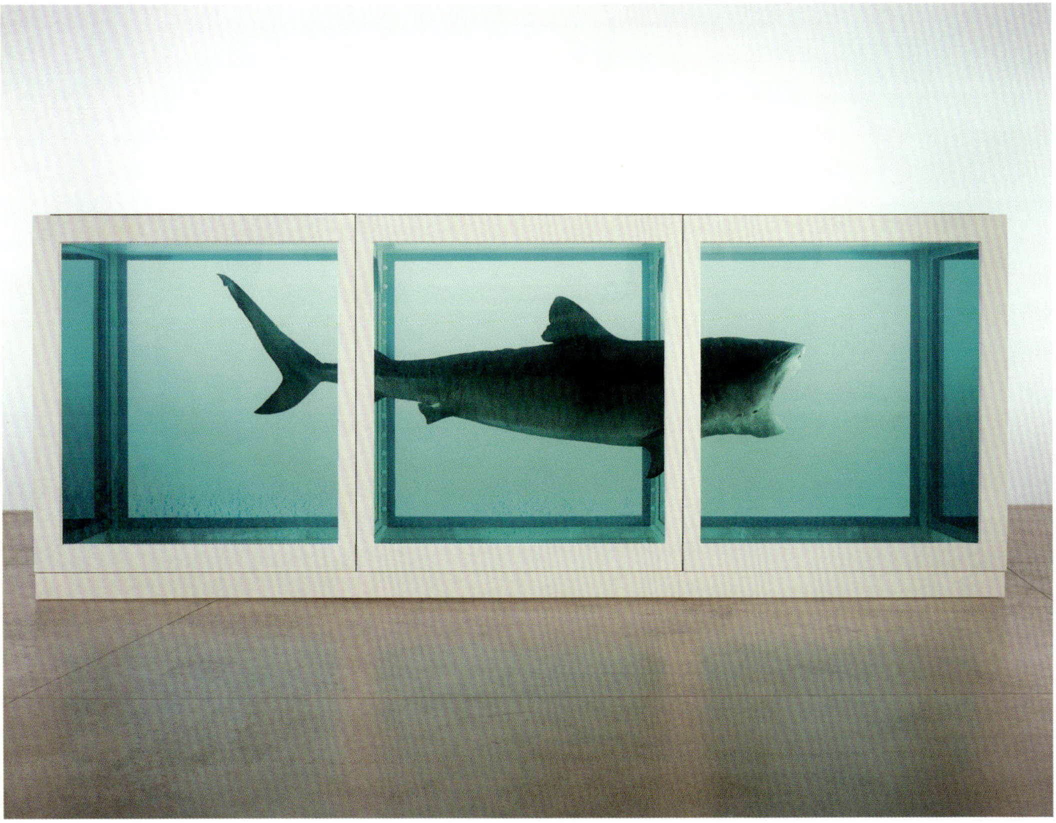

3
Damien Hirst
The Physical Impossibility of Death in the Mind of Someone Living, 1991
(side view)
Glass, painted steel, silicone, monofilament, shark and formaldehyde solution, 217 × 542 × 180 cm

MG: *Do you also think about making exhibitions at Newport that aren't related to your collections?*
DH: Originally, the whole idea of building the Newport Gallery was to showcase my own. I'd been feeling guilty because I had so many boxes full of things that had never been seen by anyone. After doing a few shows and borrowing a few things, I realized it's a kind of egomania to just think you can show your own collection. It's impossible to get every single important piece made by an artist you love. When you do a show, there may be two or five or ten works that you want to borrow to make the show perfect. So I've changed my mind a bit.

MG: *Do you have a lot of your own work?*
DH: I do have a lot. I kept things and I buy things back from other people sometimes – I'm a hoarder. I've also got a huge collection of my own clothes. I was looking in my wardrobe the other day and I thought, "I've got more clothes than I could possibly wear in my lifetime". People keep talking to me about getting rid of things – I find it very difficult. I collect cars as well.

MG: *How many do you have?*
DH: Fifteen, but I can't drive.

MG: *So why do you collect cars?*
DH: Oh, my friends drive them. They drive me around everywhere!

MG: *Do you have a car for every single mood?*
DH: No, I just buy them. My dad used to be a car salesman, so I was into cars, but when he wanted me to learn to drive, I rebelled and refused. So I love cars but I never learned to drive.

MG: *You could still learn to drive if you wanted.*
DH: I've got a provisional license but I also get quite a lot of ideas when I'm being driven around – looking out the window.

MG: *What about your other fascination, the one with death. You once mentioned that you've been thinking about death every day since you were seven.*
DH: I think everybody does but a lot of people try to sweep it under the carpet. I was always told to confront things that can't be avoided – and you definitely can't avoid death. That it's important. I suppose in the Western world we are fucked up, because the way we deal with it seems wrong to me. Somehow art seems to be connected to death. I spoke to my friend, Ashley Bickerton, the other day, when his father had just died, and I said, "Oh, that's terrible, that's never good". And he said, "But you're never gonna die, just your body will". I replied, "I think I'd like to turn it the other way round: I'd rather that the body lives and everything else dies". There are no answers, only questions, and death is a big question.

MG: *Death is connected to art and art is connected to religion. There are a lot of religious and ritualistic elements in your art.*
DH: As an artist, I feel very connected to the past and I think that contemporary art is connected to the past as well. I was brought up Catholic until I was twelve so I was indoctrinated as a child, and it's quite difficult to get rid of the imagery whether you believe it or not – indoctrination works very powerfully against logic.

MG: *Which is sometimes not so bad – in the case of Catholicism, you get a big part of Western art history free of charge.*
DH: I love stories. Every religion has great stories.

MG: *You have always been rebellious towards the art system. Your auction at Sotheby's, which meant a direct sale of your works through an auction*

and you avoiding the gallery, was quite a rare event in the Western art world – why did you do it? It wasn't nice towards your dealers really.
DH: Oh, I don't know – I quite like the idea that it's not nice for the dealers. I suppose I may just enjoy risk too much. I've been lucky that a lot of the things I've done haven't failed. When I look back, it's really risk that is the common thread – I don't know if that's a good thing. A lot of people say, "It's amazing, what you did", but to me, it just looked risky and I feel lucky that it worked out. If the Sotheby's auction had been a few weeks later it might have been a different story. Everything's a celebration of art's possibilities and of what artists can do, really. I remember thinking, around the time of the Sotheby's auction, that even if it fails, what I was attempting to do was exciting in its own right – it's not just about whether you succeed or fail but about what you're trying to do. I remember thinking that artists in the future would believe it was cool even if it failed – I was hoping they would. It was about putting the power back into artists' hands.

MG: *Going back to your show in Venice, which was also quite a risky undertaking, after reading many reviews, you could say that the critical reception was negative but the collectors' reaction was positive. What does this say about the art world, in your opinion?*
DH: I didn't really read it like that. I thought the critical response was very good. There were a few reviews in the beginning that were negative but I felt that, in the end, it leveled out. What I liked at the end were the mixed feelings, with a lot of critics disagreeing – some said, "It's great!" while others called it a flop. The collectors seemed to buy, though obviously not everybody. It felt polarizing across-the-board. A lot of people liked it, a lot of people didn't – critics and collectors alike – and that made me feel like I was on the right track, really. I remember, after reading the first two reviews, which were very negative, I thought, "Oh my god, I really hope this isn't gonna be a negative thing again", because it's quite hard to deal with when it's just all negative. But then, some positive ones flowed back in and the critics started disagreeing with one another. I thought it was gonna be great.

MG: *After all these years, you still haven't gotten used to negative critics?*
DH: Well, I don't think anyone can. We're all humans. You've got to try not to take things personally, but if you put your heart and soul into something and then it gets a universally critical response, you've got to try not to believe them. I try not to enjoy the good reviews, so I can ignore the bad ones. In the end it's about how you measure success. My manager came to me just before *Treasures* opened and asked, "When will

it be a success to you?", and I said, "It already is now". Success is simply to have actually achieved it. Living a life where everyone loves you is a lot easier. "Everybody loves me. The world is a beautiful place". But this can't always be the case.

MG: *Sometimes I think that the real material of your work is not bronze or paint, etc. but actually the art system itself. As much as modernism has always tested the limits of a medium, I think you've also been testing the limits of the art system.*
DH: I think the art system is designed to follow artists, not make artists follow it. Without artists it absolutely couldn't exist, whereas without the system artists could still exist. I love art. I love the art world. As I was saying earlier, you really have to measure your own success in your own terms. It's difficult if you make an artwork that you know is terrible and everyone's telling you it's great, and also if you make an artwork that you know is great and everyone's telling you it's terrible. I've experienced both, so I think you just have to believe in yourself.

MG: *If we speak of the art world of today and you compare it to that of the 1980s and '90s – are we hijacked by moral purists? You mentioned Anthony d'Offay before, with whom Tate has recently cut all links on the basis of mere accusation.*
DH: That's got more to do with the world than the art world, really. It's human nature we're talking about. I can think about my time at Anthony d'Offay's gallery separately to thinking about Anthony d'Offay as a human being. I don't really know the facts of what happened there, but whenever you get people with power, you're gonna get people who are abusive with power, and it's a subset of human nature which has been there forever, though nobody likes it. It's in the press a lot more now but I don't know if that means there's more of it or if it's just being spoken about – whenever it's happened, it's never been a good thing, has it.

MG: *I read in an interview that you're now doing yoga and that you're going to therapy, which sounds like you're cleansing your life.*
DH: I've got children as well.

MG: *How old are they?*
DH: Twenty-two, seventeen, and twelve.

MG: *So they are almost adults.*
DH: Yeah, almost. They live with me. I think they got me to change. I'd been partying for about twenty years and it was really great, we got

drunk and did a lot of celebrating – and after a while it takes its toll. I'm fifty-two now. I remember, when I started, I could drink every night and never get a hangover. I didn't even know what that was. Then, I stopped and a hangover would last me like seven or eight days and they were very painful. The moment I stopped was like, "Aw God, the party's over".

MG: *It's unbelievable that you could be so productive, having such a heavy life of partying.*
DH: I suppose that's through getting other people to make your things for you. You set things up in the studio, then leave. I remember, once I got banned from going into my own studio because I would distract everybody and make them all drink and start partying and they said, "Just stop coming in!"

MG: *You then continued making most of the series you started, for a long time.*
DH: I remember when I was making the *Natural History* works, I wanted to do a zoo of dead animals, I didn't really just want to make one formaldehyde work. I wanted to do an endless series of *Spot* and *Spin Paintings*. I was very much thinking of endless series before I even started.

MG: *Which of your works was in a way the most surprising to you?*
DH: I suppose the fly pieces that we talked about earlier, *A Thousand Years* and *A Hundred Years*. They were quite difficult because I made them without using the studio and they were quite complicated. It meant that I saw the work for the first time when I first exhibited them, so it's like you have five minutes before the show, you let the flies out and it was the first time they came out. They just felt alive in a way that I couldn't control. The moment it went from an idea to reality, I lost control. It felt really strange. My top pieces would be the shark [*The Physical Impossibility of Death in the Mind of Someone Living*], *For the Love of God*, *A Thousand Years*, *The Golden Calf*, and a few more.

MG: *What happened to* For the Love of God*?*
DH: It's in a vault in London. It's been on display in Oslo quite recently at the Astrup Fearnley Museum.

MG: *In retrospect, did you correctly judge the financial risk that you'd taken?*
DH: I think so. I remember being quite worried about it not turning out the way I thought it would, whether the value of the diamonds and the precious metals would always be salvageable. You always have the dia-

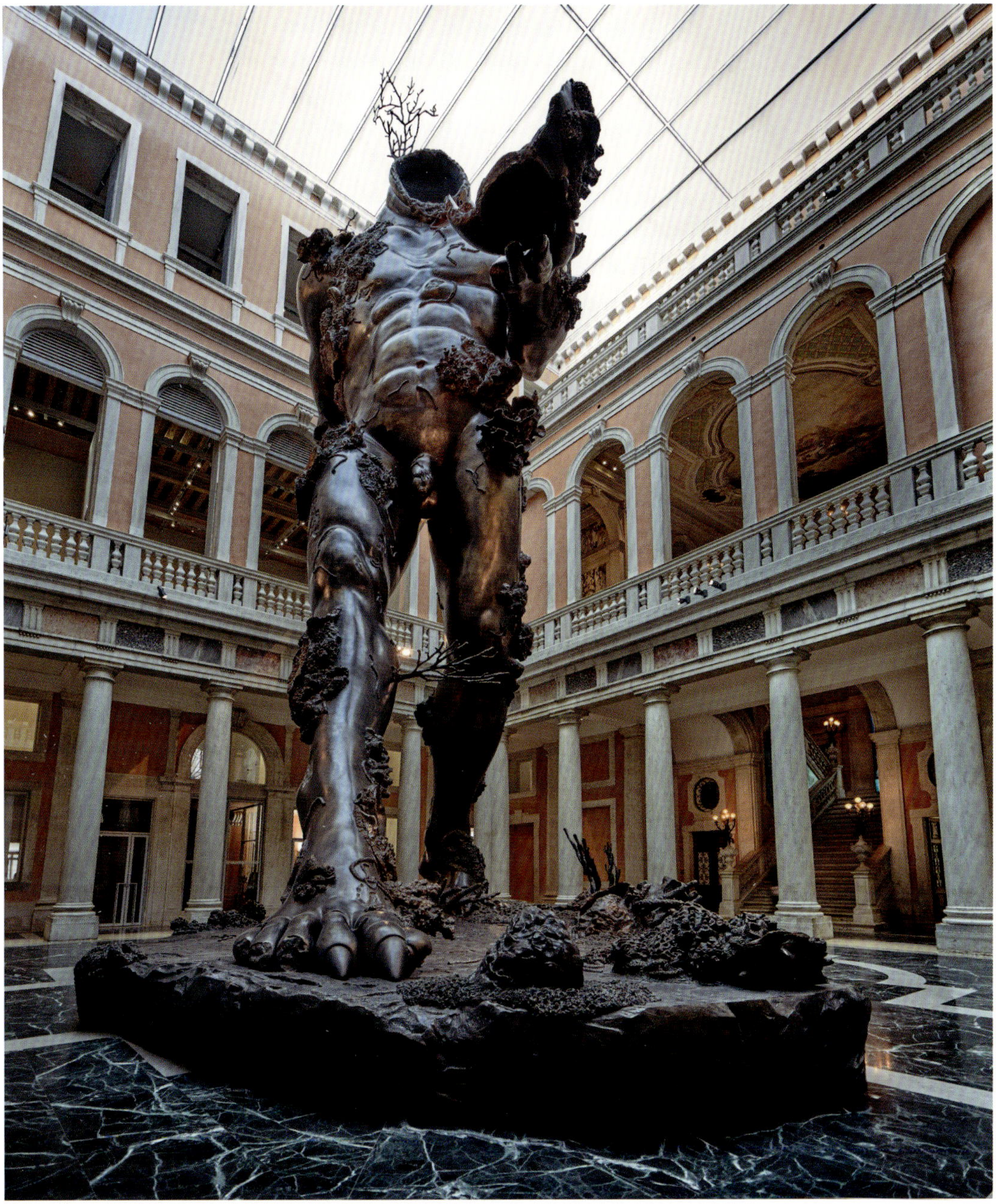

4
Damien Hirst
Demon with Bowl
(exhibition enlargement),
2014
Painted resin,
1822 × 789 × 1144 cm

monds, so, in a way, there's a safety net. But I think it was a lot of money to be spending and, of course, it did get uncomfortable for a while.

MG: *What about your next project?*
DH: Which one? I've always got lots of ideas. The next thing coming up is Houghton Hall with the *Colour Space* paintings – the spot paintings I made recently, which were based on the very first two spot paintings I did. I'm always playing around in the studio, having crazy ideas. I feel quite good, because I've been working for ten years on different ideas, so let's have it out in the world.

MG: *After being a part of the art world for thirty years now, what do you think has changed?*
DH: I don't know. It seems to be more diversified and fragmented. It seems to be lots of small art worlds. In a way, it's gotten Warholian, hasn't it? Everyone in the future is gonna be famous for fifteen minutes. You see a lot more things occurring. Generally, the public seems to be a lot more interested in art than when I started. I think now, with Instagram and things like that, there's so much stuff to see and do and look up. It seems to be changing, but I like the way it seems to be changing.

MG: *You are also active on Instagram – do you like communicating through social media?*
DH: As long as they keep it simple, I like it. It's another way to say what you want to say. I just thought since we have this medium and I'm using it, I should make sure it's good, it's just about me and just about the work. I was quite surprised by how many people have said, "what you're doing is great. I love it. Keep doing it". My son, who's seventeen, said, "I love your Instagram, Dad", and he's got a huge following on Instagram as well.

MG: *You once said that good art is always very simple and should be positive – and I was wondering why art should be positive?*
DH: Because the meaning of art is positive, the actual function of art is positive, the process of art is positive – it doesn't make sense otherwise. If you are truly depressed, you are inactive and you don't make art. I think art is, by its very nature: let's do something, let's create something – a very positive thing. It's hopeful. I think about it in terms of singing songs – you can sing a depressing love song but if a friend calls you up and wants to take you out for dinner to tell you how depressed he is, you don't really wanna go – and that's the difference between art and life. Art by its very nature is positive.

MG: *On the other hand, you also address issues of mortality and death...*
DH: If you look at Picasso's *Guernica*, it doesn't make you want to give up, it makes you want to change the world. You can say that it's about death, destruction, or abuse of power, but the truly negative impact of it is that you don't do anything – there is no art in death.

WILLIAM KENTRIDGE

September 2017

Marta Gnyp: *You were born into a celebrated family of lawyers who were fighting against apartheid in South Africa. Has this helped or obstructed your development as an artist?*
William Kentridge: Coming from a family of lawyers brought to my attention, at a very young age, the unnatural nature of Johannesburg's society – particularly its illogical structure, its evil and its injustice. This was important for developing an understanding myself, as someone born outside the norms of white middle-class society, of which I was learning about in school. In a more fundamental way, with my parents around me, both being strong lawyers with incredible legal skills, I was pressed to find a field which was alien or impervious to the law and legal forms of reasoning. I was interested in meaning and broader ethical questions about society, but needed to approach those issues from a different vantage point than the logical method associated with legal reasoning.

MG: *How did you translate this alternative logic into your artistic work?*
WK: Making drawings with inherent ambiguity or making animated films – in which so much is left unspecified and left for the viewer to complete – is a way of escaping the constrains of the legal world. At the same time, the work is connected to a desire to be closer to the broader goals of South Africa, during the times of apartheid and its opposition.

MG: *Have your personal experiences during the apartheid affected your work?*
WK: I think it would be very difficult to grow up in South Africa during the heyday of apartheid. In the heyday of the anti-apartheid movement, many of us understood that the courtroom we were living in was a very rich subject to work with, as an artist. But it was also a painful place to live in during that time. Obviously, it was much less painful for a privileged, white, South African middle-class man than it was for someone on the other end of the spectrum, suffering under the immediate oppression of the network of laws known as apartheid.

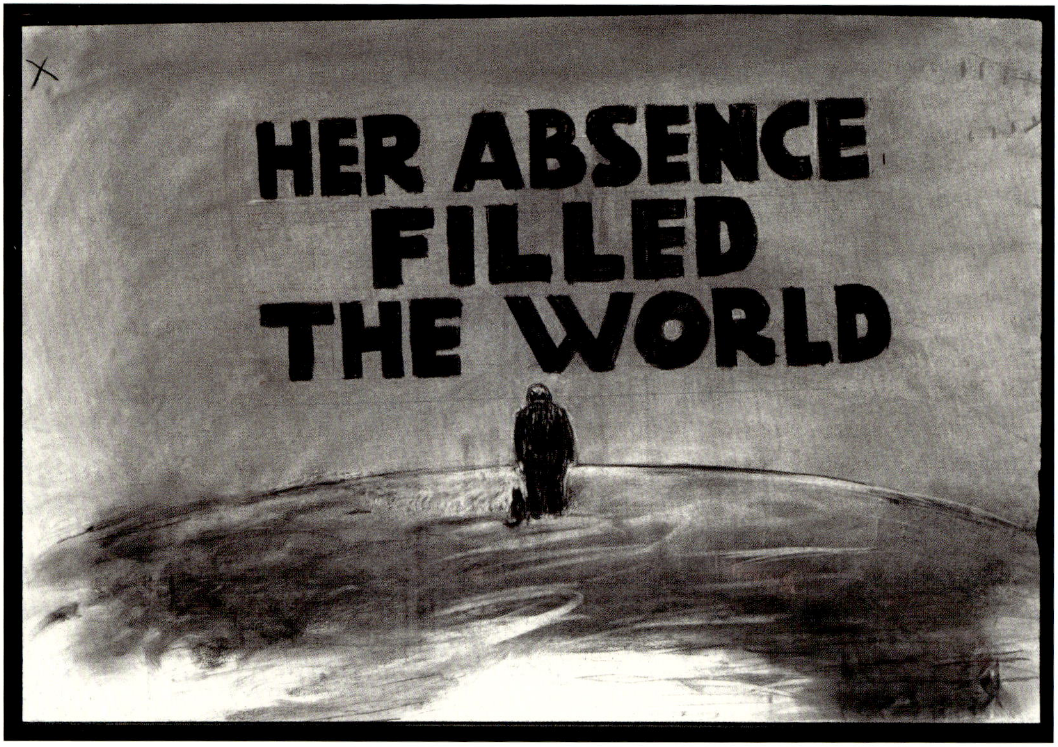

1
William Kentridge
Drawing for the film
Sobriety, Obesity & Growing Old, 1991
Charcoal and pastel on paper, 120 × 150 cm

MG: *How did you find your own artistic language?*
WK: When I started making art, I thought about it linearly – I thought that, in order to know what needed to be done, I just had to think about the images that the world needed. What did the trade union movement or the proletariats need to see in order to make its revolution? After a while, I realized the work I was making, from this perspective, was very inauthentic, because I was thinking on behalf of other people, imaging what they might want. On top of that, I had no idea what they wanted or what was needed, so I had to begin working, in a completely different way, with images and material that interested me, in the hopes that other people would also find a connection to it.

MG: *Which work did you make with this new recipe?*
WK: I made the animated film, *Johannesburg: 2nd Greatest City after Paris*, which wasn't meant to be seen. I worked with the editor, who was also the interlocutor needed in order to make it. I was astonished when the film was shown at some film festivals, and when somebody asked me to show it at an exhibition, I was insulted. I thought, "That's a film – you can't show a film in an art exhibition! Why don't they just display my drawings?" I thought it was ridiculous when it was shown in a museum. I

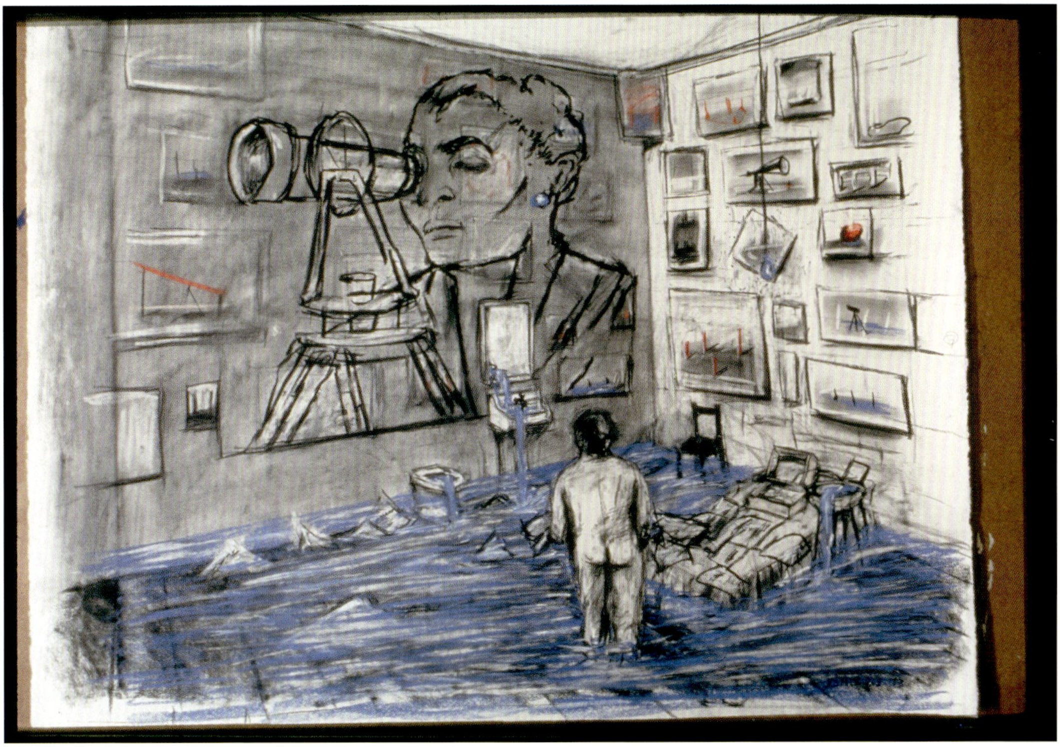

2
William Kentridge
Drawing for the film *Felix in Exile*, 1994
Charcoal and pastel on paper, 120 × 150 cm

had to be dragged off kicking and screaming to understand what it was I had made. So, I certainly mistrust any broad anticipations of how something will work, or who will respond to certain work in a particular way.

MG: Johannesburg: 2nd Greatest City after Paris *is actually a cliché story. The rich businessman, Soho Eckstein, is a bad character, and his wife is cheating on him with her romantic and sensible lover, Felix Teitelbaum. It's your masterly approach towards the medium of drawing, sound and animation that makes the film into a masterpiece. Do you choose which artistic medium to work with, depending on what you want to say?*
WK: Thank you. No, I think the medium chooses me, or I choose the medium and the meaning comes after that. When I create an opera, there has to be a convergence somewhere between the medium or material – ink, charcoal, paper cutouts or transparent projections, for example – and the theme of the opera. This usually means I have to start with a medium to discover what the thematic form of the opera might be. The fragmented drawings I used in *Lulu* led me to understand that this opera is about the fragility of the object of desire. Every object of desire shatters and refutes the position its observer wishes it might have. *Lulu* was never the woman that men wanted her to be, and the men were never the people that *Lulu*

needed them to be. So, I don't choose a medium depending on what I want to say. Rather, I discover what I want to say through the medium.

MG: *You've been using a variety of mediums: drawings, sculptures, tapestries, prints, films, theater and opera, to name a few. Are you bored with limitations?*
WK: I'm not. In the migration of images from one form to another, and in the demands of the different forms that are outside the norms of a particular medium, new images emerge that wouldn't have done so in a less haphazard context. Art at the service of opera has produced drawings that are more interesting than drawings I'd make on their own, if I were only thinking about drawings.

MG: *Stories are very important in your work.*
WK: It would have been impossible for me to maintain distance from the political, in the same way that artists in Europe or North America had, after the war, when they were sick and tired of disruption and change, entering into a formal language of conceptualism and abstraction. It was never possible for me to embrace the Greenbergian idea of thinking about surfaces and edges as a highpoint of artistic creation, which was a norm at art schools when I was a student in the 1970s and the early 1980s.

MG: *Your thinking about art concentrates on the process of making and the studio. Are you fed up with art theory, often overloaded with redundant philosophical messages?*
WK: To keep up with that requires a full-time occupation in reading critical theories and contemporary art criticisms, and I'm just behind on that. I stopped strict critical reading in a serious way when I left university. Now I do it very sporadically, and prefer to see what the experience in the studio can teach us about broader questions, rather than trying to be a good, critical reader of theories I only half-understand.

MG: *If I think about the way you present human beings in your work, a few terms cross my mind: comedy of existence, absurdity, projections and illusions.*
WK: I'm interested in these categories as a kind of naturalism, or as an accurate and immediate description of the world. To try and take the absurd out of this is to enact violence against what is actually happening. By the absurd, I don't mean the joke or the foolish components – I mean the dislocation of logic. The dislocation of logic within apartheid is the antithesis to faulty logic, which gets carried to its last stage of completion.

MG: *Is there any role art can play to make life meaningful?*
WK: I'm not sure art can make life meaningful, but it can show the ways in which we make meaning out of life. So many techniques that are natural in the studio, such as collage, fragmentation or reconstruction, are constructing the world according to the fragments one has laying around them. I would suggest that what the studio shows is a model for how we, out of necessity, operate in the world. Art shows that we don't simply perceive the world as passive receptors, but that we're constantly in a process of constructing the meaning of the world around us, as well as constructing our social-selves.

MG: *If I bring up one of the tools you often use – erasure – what kind of constructions does it bring to mind for you?*
WK: Erasure is one of the techniques that I use that carries certain implicit meanings. Specifically, an imperfect erasure – if we're talking about charcoal drawing and the fibers of the paper – forces you to experience the passage of time, almost making time thick. It makes the idea of time, and its process of transformation, palpable.

MG: *Were you aware of this quality when you started using erasure?*
WK: I discovered it by returning to the technique again and again, and also because it revealed part of the world that is very close to me. Whether it is close to me because of the technique, or whether the technique has led me to something that was boiling up within me, is hard to say. There is obviously a difference between people who have certainty – for whom the world can exist as a series of facts – and people who have uncertainty, in which case the world exists almost provisionally. I could draw a table and the table could simply be a table, or I could draw a table that's in interim states between the forest, the tree, the timber, the table, the fire, the smoke and its ashes.

MG: *Do you find that images have a new meaning because of their omnipresence, brought about by new technical possibilities?*
WK: Sure, in the age of technical reproduction we are bombarded with images, which changes how we read them. Nonetheless, before that, we've always had to construct our lives from an overabundance of fragments and details. This doesn't always translate into seeing 400 pictures of the war in Syria in one day. Nonetheless, I had a dream last night where I was fighting with my brother – did I start the day with that rage? Or did I say no and hold my tongue, trying to manifest a different emotion within myself? I can't imagine that those kinds of questions and options were once never there.

MG: *So, what is the impact of the overabundance of images?*
WK: Their overload is simply a way of magnifying the question and making it more evident, but not fundamentally changing it. Certain images lose their impact because of their ubiquity. It's hard to see archival images in the same way we would have looked at them forty years ago. When you're looking for Italian gas masks or wounded people in World War I, there are 4,000 images confronting you on the Internet, rather than the shock of finding one or two in a book you're looking through at the library.

MG: *Enlightenment is an important subject in your art. Are you somehow longing for the possibility of an enlightened world?*
WK: The benefits of the Enlightenment are becoming more and more fragile. Things that were once taken for granted in the liberal democracies of Europe and North America are extremely fragile and can be undone in a matter of weeks or hours. The promises or possibilities of the Enlightenment seem to be a dream. But on the other hand, we're completely aware of the implications of the Enlightenment in the colonial takeovers, and all the horrors unleashed during that time.

MG: *We're stuck in the Enlightenment project because there's no other option.*
WK: All projects, that see themselves as acting on behalf of others, bring on catastrophes, whether they are trying to beat people into happiness in the Soviet Union, or pursuing undue industrialization to find the purity of peasant life in Cambodia, or enacting the American way of life in Vietnam. We understand these projects as having a kind of Enlightenment-impulse behind them, and they end in disaster because of their perceived certainty. I'm aware of the contradictions and paradoxes of the Enlightenment, but it's certainty the only hope we have.

MG: *What can art do to remedy the toxic political situations in today's world?*
WK: I think that, in its nature – in its deepest structure rather than in its immediate subject matter – it can demonstrate the instability of facts and moments, while also revealing the instability of all statements of authority and certainty. There is obviously a connection between certainty, violence and authority.

MG: *So, art as opposed to the fixed and authoritarian?*
WK: I think art does celebrate a movement, an ambiguity and a disavowal of all things certain. It allows space for the biography of the viewer to be part of the forces shaping the meaning of the work. Statements of

3
William Kentridge
Drawing for the film
Stereoscope, 1999
Charcoal, pastel and colored pencil on paper,
120 × 160 cm

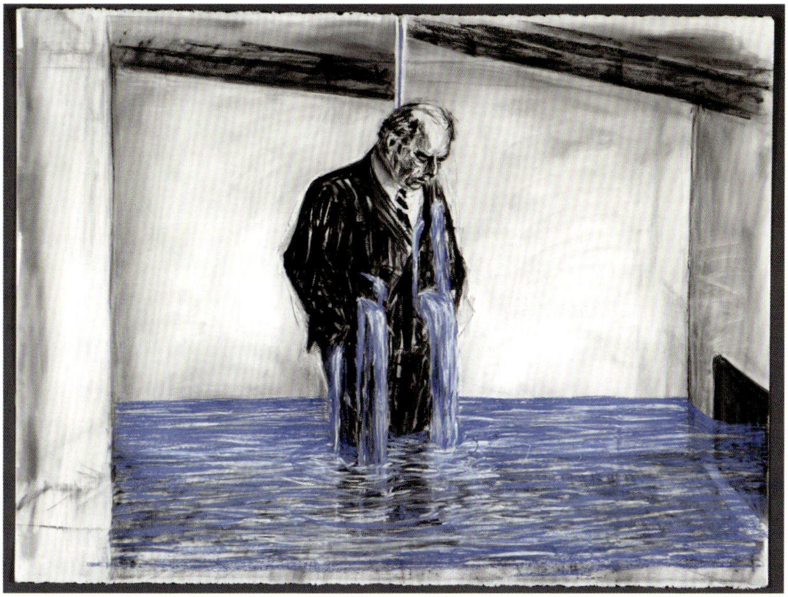

authority take out that biography, but we know from every image we look at that it's always a mixture of what the world brings to you and what we project onto it. The only way we make sense of the world is through this mixture of reception and projection, and projection is always inflected by the particular biography of the viewer.

MG: *Why are you so fascinated by opera?*
WK: When the opera house is looking for new voices and new ways of seeing opera, you can think of an artist working in an opera as a director or designer. But you can also see it in a completely different way: the opera is offering the artist fantastic, enormous canvasses – the proscenium, 17 meters wide, 10 meters high – as a space for projection, where forty or one-hundred performers will do what you instruct them to do, making drawings with their bodies. And not just that – they have the most remarkable voices to sing with. They'll throw in an orchestra of 120 musicians. It's an extraordinarily rich way of working with material, resulting in the creation of a 4D drawing, whose edges are shaped by the libretto and music.

MG: *In addition to directing* Lulu, *you recently directed* Wozzeck *by Alban Berg. How do you choose the operas you want to be involved with?*
WK: So many people said that *Lulu* is one of the greatest operas of the 20th century, and I thought I'd discover this while spending years making it. It certainly is one of the masterpieces of the 20th century, but having

completed it, experiencing the pleasure, joy and intimacy of the *Wozzeck* was a revelation for me.

MG: *How important is music for our understanding of images?*
WK: It's not that you need music to understand them, but listening changes how you look at them, which changes what you hear.

MG: *You seem to like the multiple perspectives provided by vision. Why is this so important to you?*
WK: Consider stereoscopy as an example: one can't help but sense a depth of space when looking at a stereoscopic view, but in reality, they are two flat photographs, combined in our brains to give the illusion of depth. The same happens when we perceive the world around us. Each retina receives a flat image and our brain combines these images to give ourselves a sense of depth, through which we navigate the world. There's a sense of complicity that affects how we look at the world. The devices we use – whether they are orphic mirrors, stereoscopic objects or virtual reality headsets – are about agency and making sense of the world. This quality, as much as the pleasure of working with those particular materials, is what makes them so important.

MG: *What makes an image powerful? I experienced a sense of power when looking at your drawing,* Her Absence Filled the World.
WK: I don't know. *Absence* is an artwork with an empty landscape, with words written in block letters above it. Interestingly, it was shown in several commercial exhibitions, but nobody was interested in buying it, so it stayed in my own collection by default – and now I'm very pleased to have it. There are a lot of people who do respond to the image. I think it's because it floats halfway between reading and looking – you read the text, but it's connected to the simplicity of the horizon and landscape in the drawings. What makes an image powerful is the mixture of what you get from the drawing and what you project onto it. When these meet, it's as though they're saying, "Here's something coming from outside of me, but it seems to correspond with and understand something inside of me as well". That's the consolation of art; showing a connection with other people within ourselves.

MG: *The contemporary discourse of African art is dominated by post-colonial rhetoric. How can the African art of today escape being seen as solely post-colonial?*
WK: When we're talking about art from one continent with such different histories and trajectories, the idea that it should be unified under one

simple umbrella-category or geographical location is ridiculous. In any exhibition of African art, usually a third to half of the artists shown are not artists who are living in Africa at all, but are individuals who used to live there, or whose ancestors used to live there. Diaspora has always dominated Africa. The first Ptolemaic maps were made by explorers from outside the continent, and slave raiders actually defined the outside parameters. The notion of Pan-Africanism came from America. This external image of the continent has been colored by different histories, but the colonial past has been extremely pervasive and important for almost all the countries of the continent.

MG: *What is your relationship to black South African artists? Some of them consider you to be from a different planet, since your set of cultural references is not their own.*
WK: Some of them might see me as coming from a different planet, but there are others who feel camaraderie in what it means to be an artist. If identity politics becomes the language of discourse for artists from Africa, then, of course, it's a strange situation for me, being an African artist with a cultural heritage that comes from Eastern Europe, rather than from many generations of people living in Africa.

MG: *What do you mean by "camaraderie"?*
WK: I was at a conference in Kenya for artists from Africa, and the theme was "blackness", which I felt comfortable about – but I also felt a bit on edge. I was interested what people's feelings were about it. At the end of the day, many artists came up to me and said that in the studio, "blackness" is not a subject they think about. They live in Zambia or they live in Kenya, and they're aware that they are black, but in the studio, they are simply considering other things. That showed me the importance of contact with artists in Africa or anywhere else in the world – it has to do with the camaraderie found in the studio. There are things I can show artists, black and white, and it has to do with the nature of what is possible in the studio, and what debt we owe to our profession.

MG: *What do you think about identity politics hijacking a big part of our current artistic discourse?*
WK: I'm not so interested in identity politics. I'm more interested in other principles and ways of seeing the world. In art, that comes from a broader perspective. Having said that, there is, of course, remarkable work that's been done on the subject of blackness, and on the particularities of identity in society. One needs to start from the particularities of the self – that primary impulse, which in my case is Soho Eckstein and

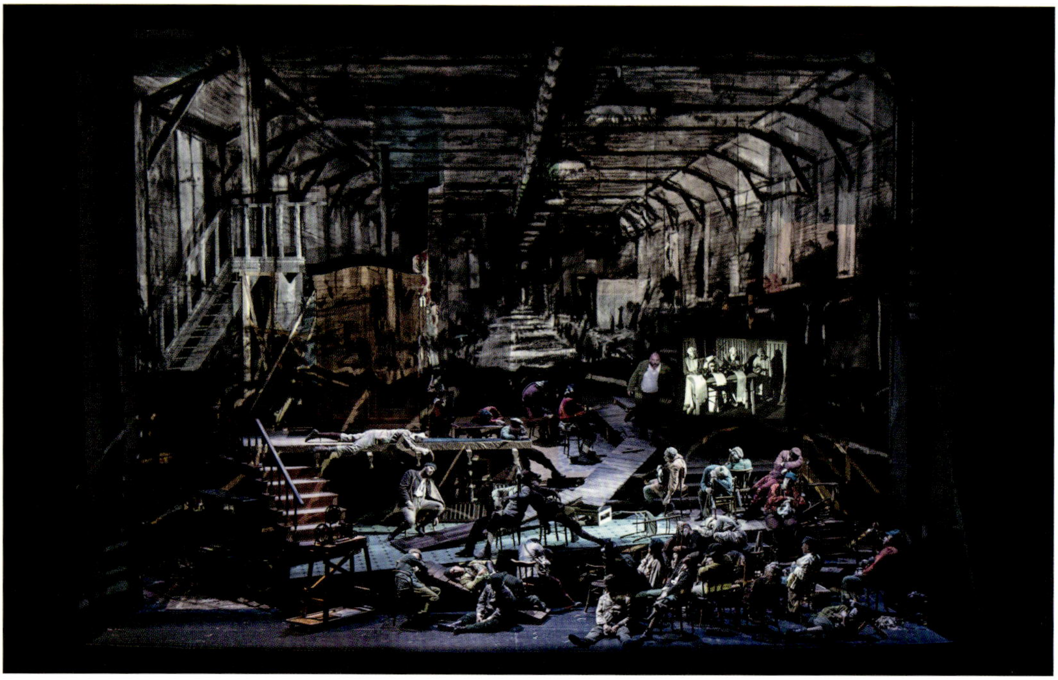

4
William Kentridge
Performance of *Wozzeck*, Salzburg Festival, 2017

Felix Teitelbaum – middle-class, white, South Africans with European heritage.

MG: *What do you think about traditional or tribal art?*
WK: This kind of art was developed out of the opposition to apartheid ideology in South Africa, which required the understanding of black people as "tribal", briefly appearing for short outings to the city while staying stuck in their rural roots. A principal opposition to this restriction placed on black South African lives was demanding the possibility for a cosmopolitan, urbanized African population that listened to the same music – to jazz and to Beethoven – and had an interest in opera. Having done that as a grownup, I understood I'd need to undo this learning and understand that there's a part of African life that is very much connected to different relationships, to ancestors, and to traditional medicine, which it has had to disavow in an ideological way. This means there's a huge gap, not in my understanding, but in connection to this section of South African world.

MG: *Do people copy your work?*
WK: When you're 60, there's a generation that's a lot younger than you around, and people have seen your work – it's very difficult to avoid being contaminated by it in any way. I can see similarities in the use of charcoal

and animation by some artists, which must have come from seeing my work. But in the same way, my work came from seeing pieces made by artists like Dumile Feni. After a while, you either stay stuck in this mode, or you find your own voice, which becomes a different way of working. That doesn't worry me.

MG: *What was the breaking point in your career as artist?*
WK: I managed to work, on a very small scale, as an artist during the period of cultural boycotts in South Africa, but there was a transformation after the release of Mandela and the first democratic election; exposing the world to us. All the curators were so curious about what this closed country was – they came to see my work and accepted it on their own terms. The timing was good. I participated in the first and second Johannesburg Biennale. Then, there was a biennale in Sydney and Documenta in 1997. My work transformed, from a small South African aberration, into a large aberration within the broader world of art. It was a defining moment in my career.

MG: *Did your work quickly receive recognition from the broader public?*
WK: It was never a problem in South Africa. When I first tried to show my work in New York, knocking on gallery doors, showing my portfolio, they waved me away without even opening the doors. That changed around the time of Documenta, in the mid 1990s.

MG: *I read about the raisonné catalogue of your juvenile works.*
WK: It wasn't done with my collaboration or with my approval. I didn't even know it was going to happen until my father received a copy. I know the person who was involved in making it and know that he has a deep interest in tracking down my artistic work. Even though I wasn't keen on the book being made, once it was out, I was quite curious to see old drawings and pictures – most of which look like the incompetent drawings of a child. But a couple of them look so similar to what I'm doing now, so it's shocking to see how little I have evolved throughout all these years.

MG: *What did you learn during your mime classes in Paris?*
WK: I learned an enormous amount. When I teach drawing now, in most classes, I use exercises learned at school in Paris. I learned about the energy and the start of a gesture, and what is sufficient enough to be able to carry the gesture to its correct conclusion. I also learned about the importance of finding out what the essential impulse is to a mark or a gesture – whether on a piece of paper or on stage – and what parts are detail and decoration, superfluous to it. Not that I can always follow the

understanding of it, but the clarity is there. The classes also clarified the act of making art; the fact that art is something performed by the body, rather than by the brain.

MG: *In your opinion, what has changed in the art system, in the past thirty years?*
WK: The integral moment of change, in the art system, happened 100 years ago, in 1916 during the heyday of the Dada movement, when the meaning of being a visual artist fundamentally changed. What was ridiculed and seen as scandalous, during the first Dada performances in Cabaret Voltaire, set the agenda for artists of whom I am certainly reaping the benefits from. It created openness, so an artist can work in theater, in music, or in sound – so they can shift between 2D and 3D, between the permanent and the ephemeral, and can work with texts as a part of their language. I don't think this is a product of the past thirty years, but maybe the benefits of it have been more accessible in the past thirty years.

MG: *Why do you always wear the same white shirt, as if time hasn't passed?*
WK: If I'm working on a project now, where I'm making a drawing or a film of myself, you can compare it with a work I made fifteen years ago. That continuity – a kind of art comedy-character – makes sense. I need the formal connection between having myself live on stage and projecting myself in my work. I do actually own some blue shirts and I recently bought a green shirt, just to show people it could be done. But in truth, those remain unworn in my closet.

ROBERT LONGO

March 2017

Marta Gnyp: *2017 looks like a big year for you. You're due to have an exhibition in May at Metro Pictures in New York, then in September,* Proof: Francisco Goya, Sergei Eisenstein, Robert Longo, *from the GARAGE Museum in Moscow is coming to the Brooklyn Museum, a week later you'll be opening an exhibition at Galerie Thaddaeus Ropac in London, and then an exhibition at the Sara Hildén Art Museum in Finland.*
Robert Longo: I've just been on the phone with New York and felt kind of guilty that I'm here in Berlin with all the work that needs to be done.

MG: *What are you doing in Europe?*
RL: I've been in touch with a few conservators because I'm very interested in X-rays of paintings. I went to see X-rays of Raphael's *Pope Julius II* in London at the National Gallery and I then went to the Courtauld Gallery to see the X-ray of Manet's *A Bar of the Folies-Bergere*. I realize that conservators don't have contact with living artists.

MG: *It's breathtaking, what they can do to art.*
RL: They're almost like scientists, but also like monks. It's clearly a calling. What they do is miraculous; they are saving art. I have great respect for them. When I was young, and didn't quite have the courage to say I wanted to be an artist, because everything I did failed, I thought maybe I'd become an art historian or an art conservator. I even obtained a small scholarship with the Academy in Florence, to study the restoration of paintings.

MG: *How old were you at that time?*
RL: It was 1975, so I was twenty-two. I hated it. I watched these guys doing horrible restorations; until this wonderful woman started the renovation of *The Last Supper* and introduced the new idea of taking the restoration off and showing what's there. The conservators I met recently are pretty amazing.

MG: *What is so special about X-raying paintings?*
RL: Like doctors, they'll make an X-ray only when something is wrong

1
Robert Longo
Untitled (Jules)
from the series *Men in the Cities*, 1979–1983
Charcoal and graphite on paper, 243.8 × 152.4 cm
Collection of Centre Pompidou, Paris

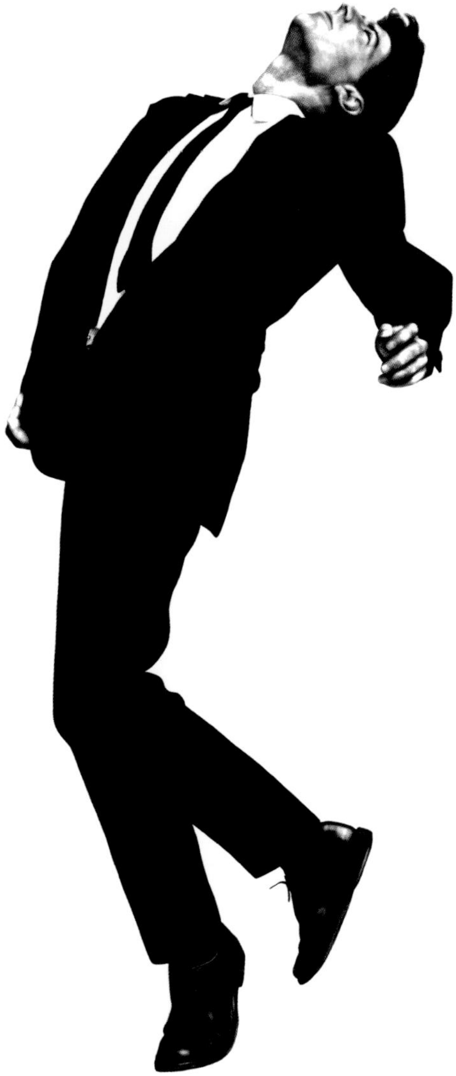

and they expect that they'll need it to take care of the paintings. In his great essay, *Art in the Age of Mechanical Reproduction*, Walter Benjamin talks about the loss of aura. But when you see the X-rays, it is aura! The X-rays show what's invisible. For my first X-ray drawing, I used this really small Rembrandt painting of Jesus, which was based on a Jewish man living in Amsterdam at that time. The underpaintings, which were made visible thanks to X-rays, are quite extraordinary; they are Semitic, while the actual painting looks rather European. The X-rays exposed the walnut's white lines; it looks electric, like a scene from *The Matrix*. The expression on Jesus' face is incredible.

MG: *X-rays also enable you to see the changes in paintings.*
RL: One painting I've always loved is Rembrandt's *Bathsheba at Her Bath*, showing a woman reading a letter with this incredible resignation in her eyes. She has to contend with the king wanting to bed her; meanwhile her husband is away fighting for the king. In the painting underneath, though, the expression on her face is quite different, like she's...

MG: *Curious...*
RL: Thinking, "maybe it's not going to be so bad".

MG: *Will your work for the shows this year be based on the X-rays?*
RL: Not exclusively. My work has always had a political edge buried within it, but, over the past five to six years, it's gotten more aggressive. The drawings in the exhibition at Metro Pictures will be very political, in that they come from a place of rage in regards to our current political state.

MG: *Could you give me some examples?*
RL: There's one drawing based on a telescoped, an infrared photograph, taken at night, of prisoners at Kandahar Airport in Afghanistan. Another one shows the riot police forming a wall of shields in Baltimore, Maryland. I've made a 12×30 ft drawing of refugees lost in a massive sea.

MG: *Do you always use an existing photograph to make your drawings?*
RL: I sometimes use a couple of photos in composite. I remember when I saw photographs of the riot cops in Ferguson, in a newspaper, I was thinking, "where is this? Is this in Ukraine?" Then I saw McDonalds in the background, and I thought, oh my God, this is America! It was outrageous to see these soldiers. Then I wanted to draw the protestors with their hands up. The problem was, I couldn't draw them as they were; it looked as if they were dancing.

MG: *How did you add power to it?*
RL: Do you know that photograph, taken during the Olympics in 1968, of these two black athletes, Tommie Smith and John Carlos, when they raised their fists in the Black Power salute as a form of protest? I came from the tribe of sports; I played football in college, and sports have always been a part of my life. I remembered when the American football

team, the St. Louis Rams, were introduced in the stadium and they came out with their hands up, in solidarity with protestors after the shooting by a police officer of unarmed teenager, Michael Brown. The equipment they were wearing was very similar to the equipment the police were wearing.

MG: *You combined sports and riot photographs.*
RL: I'm more interested in the collision of images, rather than pastiche. Michael Brown, the kid that was shot in the street in Ferguson, was the size of a football player. He wasn't one, but he could've been. So there is complexity in this image.

MG: *How do you make art out of disaster?*
RL: By utilizing beauty to communicate issues that are at hand, almost like disarming the viewer, getting them there because something is interesting to look at and, at the same time, it makes you think of something else.

MG: *Lets speak about "new" and "real". In the '70s and '80s, you and a few artist friends dismissed the idea of the new by responding to post-structural ideas on authenticity and originality. You, the Picture Generation expressed this.*
RL: We didn't know about that; we were a bunch of friends and we were making art. When Cindy Sherman and I moved to New York in 1977, the art world was dead. The most exciting things going on in New York were the punk music scene and movies like *Taxi Driver* and a Fassbinder festival in the city. Emerging art was Schnabel and the trans-avant-garde bullshit. We were involved in a very different kind of art that was all media based. We were taking pictures of pictures. The division was very clear to me. Those guys – Schnabel, Cucchi, Clemente and Chia – were wrong. It was almost like a war. Neo-Expressionism seemed to be about what art was, whereas my friends and I were interested in what art could be.

MG: *Did you feel connected to the Conceptual art movement?*
RL: Absolutely. Conceptual artists broke down so many things. It was like they built this car and my generation got to drive in it. We had the freedom to do whatever we wanted.

MG: *The ideas for your work were informed early on.*
RL: There's a primordial time for an artist, occurring somewhere between the seventh and fourteenth year of your life, when you go from being a boy to a being a man, or from girl to woman. That period of time is when all the seeds are planted. I can track everything I do to that time. For a boy, when you stop playing and start fighting.

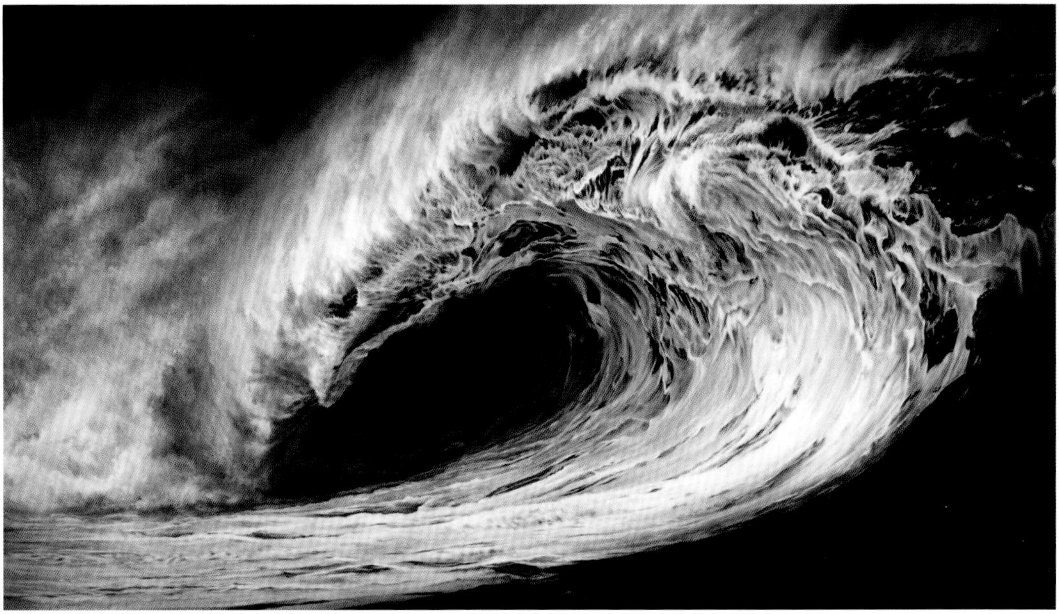

2
Robert Longo
Untitled (Hellion), 2011
Charcoal on mounted paper, 176.2 × 303.2 cm

MG: *Let's go back to New York in the '70s. How did you start?*
RL: There wasn't anybody like Polke or Richter in the US at that time. But we knew about those guys. There was a great bookstore where I saw Richter's work in a book for the first time. The reason I was going to the bookstore was because it was close to a record store. Getting the most recent punk record was far more important than art, at the time. What's interesting is that what used to be avant-garde, the white walled art galleries, became dark shitholes where people played music. There was this really interesting integration of artistic disciplines at that time. I played in a band, like a lot of other artists; people were making films and doing performances. Performances are these transient events that happen in real time, they work with the idea of the public, there is no residual artifact.

MG: *What kind of performance did you do?*
RL: They were more like theater, or a memory of theater.

MG: *Did you play yourself?*
RL: No! I treated them more like objects. The first one I did was *Sound Distance of a Good Man* at this alternative art space called The Kitchen in New York, in 1978. I used a three-tier platform. On the lowest platform, there was an opera singer singing in a white gown. On the middle platform, you could see a grainy black-and-white film about a man arching

his back towards a lion statue, a 16mm film of a still image, so the grain was vibrating. At any moment, the protagonist could move. On the highest level, there was a rotating platform on which black and white men were wrestling in slow motion; it looked like they were having sex. There was no narrative, it was violent, we played with the effects of music and image. It lasted for five minutes. People were crying.

MG: *Was it meant to be a unique performance or did you re-enact this?*
RL: We did it three times. It became quite well known. It's been restaged in later years.

MG: *How did you like playing in a band?*
RL: The problem about playing in a band is that you have to practice. I would rather be in my studio. This period, between 1977 and 1981, was very important. I did this performance in 1978, along with several small shows; it was slowly happening, then it exploded.

MG: *The breakthrough moment for you was the series:* Men in the Cities.
RL: If anything, I'll probably be remembered for that. I did that series for a short period of time.

MG: *Why did you call it* Men in the Cities?
RL: You mean there were women in it? I remember, in elementary school, being told you can say "men" to refer to both men and women. The title actually referred to two things which somehow came together: Wim Wenders's movie *Alice in the Cities* and the record, *In the City*, from this really great punk band called The Jam. The first *Man in the City* was a man trapped with his feet in a fall and trying to escape. It was based on a dream I had. But the whole series is based on high impact moments and violence. As kids, we used to play this very stupid game: "who could best fall to their death?" It was like ballet. Do you know Robert Smithson's idea about entropy? I wanted to do something anti-Robert Smithson, the moment between moments. If I want to stop time, I want to take a split-second of eternity, forever. I also realized that my art history background came back. I really love Michelangelo's slaves at the Academy, caught in the moment before death. I stripped away the background and put my figures in a situation where you're not sure whether they're dying or dancing.

MG: *Why has this series of images become so relevant? They seem to capture the zeitgeist of the '80s.*
RL: You got me. I don't know. I started running away from this work because the images became misunderstood. People kept calling them

"yuppies", although the people I drew were my friends wearing punk clothes from a free shop: skinny ties, pony shoes, narrow pants. But my studio was down by Wall Street so I knew what yuppies looked like. These people were, to me, like collapsing buildings.

MG: *Almost visionary…*
RL: Recently, after the shooting of Turkey's Russian ambassador, people sent me images saying it looked like my work. I got freaked out. Forget about my work, this young guy shot this poor guy and now he's dead. At the same time, I realized the guy was about the age of my models; he could be in one of my drawings.

MG: *Did you dress your friends for the photo shoots?*
RL: There was a very clear delineation of how to get dressed. Men always wore a tie; it was like an urban uniform. Women were in skirts and on high heels. I would take my first models, like Gretchen (Bender), Cindy (Sherman) and Troy (Brauntuch) up on the roof and torture them. I threw tennis balls at them; sometimes I'd put a rope around the entire group and another person would pull them. It was pretty funny.

MG: *Cindy was your partner at the time. Did you exchange ideas about each other's work?*
RL: When Cindy took her first couple of photographs in the studio, I was really excited about them. I thought they were really cool. We had all these film books in the studio with films made by people like Godard; we had all kinds of books. I was watching movies all the time to steal and make my drawings from. For both Cindy and I, we were leaving behind appropriation and, instead, choosing to generate our own images in the spirit of appropriation. The images obtained ghosts of existing images. When she developed her first photographs in her apartment with cold water, they came out really grainy so they looked like film stills. Then she wanted to go out into the world. We had a Volkswagen van so she would change in the back of the van, we'd drive around and I would take the photographs.

MG: *You did.*
RL: Yes, those outside, not in the studio. This was what we were all doing: she was my model, I took her photos. We were helping each other. It's incredible that Cindy became the most famous artist in the post-war period. I think her work is really great. She consistently amazes me.

MG: *You two still have a very good rapport.*
RL: Very good. She's the godmother to my son. When we started to get

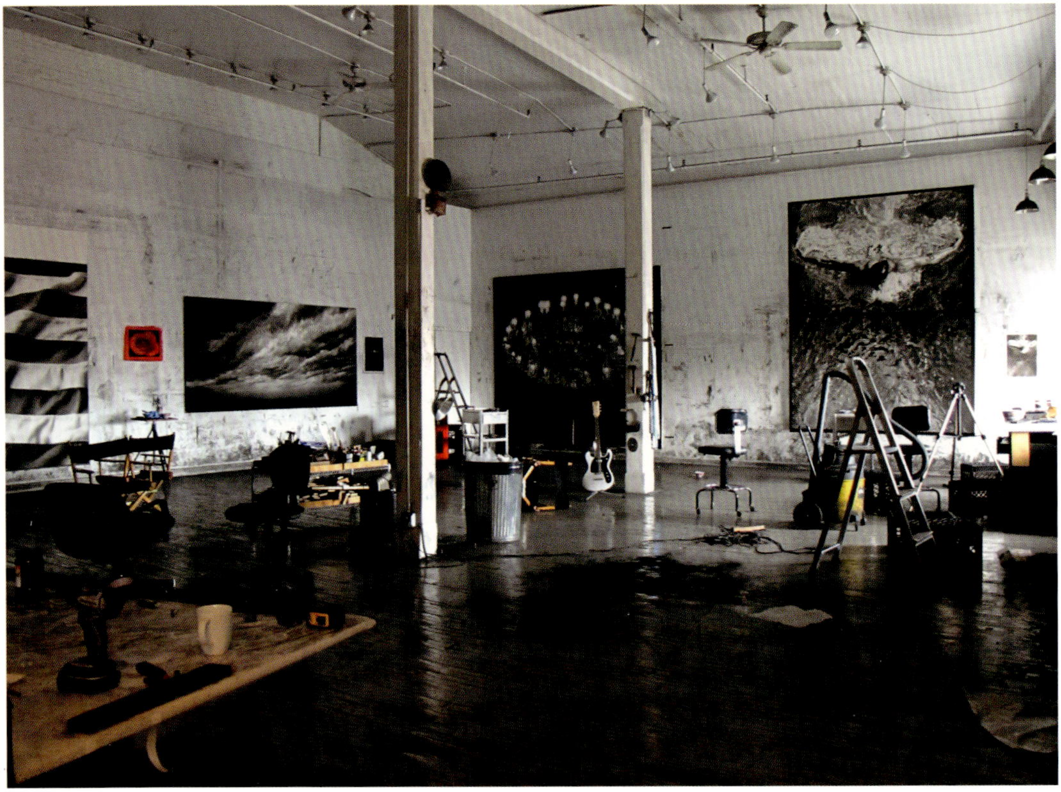

3
Studio view, 2011

successful, we were no longer living together, but we'd call each other on the phone saying, "I bought a TV today! I bought a stereo today! Wow".

MG: *That moment, of experiencing success, must have been fantastic.*
RL: It was really great because I could quit other jobs. Making art as a job was pretty amazing. I haven't done anything except making art since 1979. I'm really lucky. If there is a God, he's the one who gives out luck. When younger artists ask me, "How do I make it?", I always say: you have to create the vibe for luck to have a chance to visit you. It's like making a net, made out of other friends who are artists, people you talk to, writers, musicians, and this net is the thing that catches luck. You have to amplify the possibility of luck happening. If you are at home in your studio all by yourself, there's little chance somebody is going to discover you. But it's not a hassle. A lot of artists think that they need to go to the openings, they schmooze with collectors, they schmooze with art dealers; that's all bullshit. You have to have a community which is the genuine zeitgeist. Artists must pursue truth, not fashion the truth.

MG: *In 1977, you participated in the seminal exhibition:* Pictures. *Did you and your artist friends realize the importance of this show?*

RL: One of the greatest gifts we could get was to have a man like Doug Crimp, the art critic, to look at our work and translate it into words. As an artist, I couldn't articulate the work in the same way Doug could.

MG: *Such an interpretation is not the task of the artist.*
RL: This is why the artist makes art. You make art because words are not enough. All of the people in the *Pictures* exhibition were friends. I was very close to Jack Goldstein and Troy Brauntuch. I knew Sherrie Levine, it was an exciting moment because we thought, "Wow, this is our time!" Then, nobody sold anything from this show, nothing really happened, although the show travelled around the country. Then Doug expanded the essay to include Cindy, Louise Lawler, Richard Prince, and a few other people; the press started covering us. Metro Pictures opened in 1980, and then it all started.

MG: *You were known as the first post-war generation of artists who profited financially from their art.*
RL: When people become critical about the art market, they go back to the first group of artists who started making money. There was this horrible article in 1989 titled *Four Artists of the Apocalypse*, featuring Julian Schnabel, David Salle, Eric Fischl and me. The irony is that the money we made, compared to artists like Koons and others after us, is like pocket money. But we are the guys who perpetrated the original sin of the art market.

MG: *Did this financial success surprise you?*
RL: When we first moved to New York, we never thought we could make money. Never. The plan was, "maybe I'll do a show, maybe I'll sell some art, maybe I'll teach at a college". There were few artists and maybe five small galleries. The idea of money was never on the agenda. I'm glad that people are interested in my work, but the idea has always been to make money in order to make the work.

MG: *Do you remember the feeling when you sold your work for the first time?*
RL: I sold my first piece for $25. It feels like someone is taking your children away from you. Later on, when I signed with the gallery, it became an adoption agency and their job was to find the right parents.

MG: *At a certain moment, the dream ended.*
RL: I remember my exhibition, *Black Flags*, in New York, with bronze castings of American flags. There were reserves on the pieces, like usual;

I thought everything would be fine, and all of the sudden, the art market crashed. I only sold three of them. Then I did something that saved my life: I became involved with a French woman and I just moved to Paris.

MG: *You escaped New York.*
RL: And saved my life by doing it. If I'd stayed in New York I would have become really bitter. No one was buying my work at the time. Europe helped me a lot. I did some big, amazing artworks when I was in Europe. I met my wife, actress Barbara Sukowa, in Europe.

MG: *Why did you go back to New York?*
RL: I remember Robert Wilson told me once, "You have to go back to New York. Don't do what I did. Don't leave and do your work elsewhere. You'll always want to go back". I lived two and half years in Paris and went back in 1992. Slightly later, I got involved in making a movie, which was such a torture. I couldn't make the movie I wanted to make.

MG: *Did you go to Hollywood?*
RL: Hollywood came to me. I met Keanu [Reeves] a few years before and I wanted to make this small, weird, arty sci-fi movie with him. I couldn't raise two million dollars, unfortunately. In the meantime, Keanu got big, so they finally gave us about $26 million dollars instead, but tried to turn the film into an action movie. *Johnny Mnemonic* opened the same day as *Batman* and *Die Hard*. It was number four for many months; it wasn't very successful, initially, but then it actually made a lot of money. Now it's like a cult movie to a lot of people.

MG: *What did you do after this experience?*
RL: I felt lost. I went back to the studio but I didn't know what to do. I had no assistants. My wife said, "Why don't you start drawing again?" And then, the only question was what to draw. My wife, who is European, helped me in seeing things very differently.

MG: *In what way?*
RL: I used to watch two TVs simultaneously, with the stereo on and look at magazines, all at the same time. I became numb to this kind of media assault. She made me aware of this. Having children made me think of the consequences of images. In a weird way, I got back to the beginning, when I was looking at images in the media, and realizing the number of images passing through you every day. You have no idea what they do to you. My youngest son had just been born and I didn't want to travel anymore. I decided to stay in one place and do one drawing a day – an

image that I would pick out of the media or choose because I felt I had to. When you render an image, you take it into yourself and process it on a molecular level; you own that image. It becomes a part of you. I created 366 images, one each day. It was a leap year. I titled the series *Magellan* after a 24-hour film made by a friend. When I showed *Magellan* in 1996/97 at Metro in New York, they covered the whole gallery. I think we sold two of the 366 drawings.

MG: *You didn't consider it as one work?*
RL: I did! But I needed money. So people were saying: "I really like the dog, can we have that dog?" *Magellan* broke up in the beginning, but slowly twenty-five were sold here, fifteen were sold there, then somebody bought a hundred – eventually they were all gone. *Magellan* has become a lexicon for everything that followed.

MG: *Was this the moment when you understood the impact an image could have?*
RL: *Men in the Cities* were works that looked at you as much as you looked at them. It was an image that happened in a split second, so you got it. It's not something that asked you to sit and look at it for a very long time.

MG: *A very quick look.*
RL: Then I started going back to history. I tried to comprehend how things are put together, what makes a good image and its composition. A friend in Paris gave me a book and said, "One day you'll find it interesting". It was a book with photographs of Freud's apartment, taken a few days before he left because of the Nazis. For some reason, the images of his apartment reminded me of my family's doctor's office in the Bronx. It was a really old office my father and I used to go to because of his heart condition. Each time, it felt like waiting for my father to die. To me, Freud's apartment looked similar. Here is Freud, trying to understand the deep, dark secrets of the mind while Nazis are on the street actually acting out that very darkness. I did a series of drawings called *The Freud Cycle*, based on the photographs in his apartment. One of my main goals of this series was to attempt to draw absence.

MG: *Why did you make the wave series?*
RL: I was teaching my middle son to surf. I was sitting in the water pushing him into waves and then looked at the waves closely for the first time. I had studied waves in order to know how to surf them beforehand, but never really looked at them. I became really fascinated by their autonomy and power, and I started the wave drawings. The series was self-propellant.

MG: *What has become the greatest challenge for you?*
RL: Staying relevant. I feel that I'm making the best work I've made in my life, now. I'm very happy about it.

MG: *From a skills point of view?*
RL: To do what I do requires assistants. For many years, I was the assistant of Vito Acconci and Dennis Oppenheim. Hiring assistants is like being a parent; I want to be better than my father, which, in this case, means I want to be better than Vito. I treat my assistants with great respect. I create a situation where they work reasonable hours, they get paid really well and I expect them to do an excellent job.

MG: *Isn't it complicated to work with assistants?*
RL: When I made something all by myself, it was very difficult for me to be self-critical. It was like masturbation. I was so in love with what I made. But, if you have somebody working with you, it's not a big deal to just destroy it, erase it. I am able to detach myself, and have a more critical eye. I have certain assistant who are really good at details, certain guys who are really good at filling in areas. I can work on a couple of drawings simultaneously, and then, ultimately, there's a moment when I have to finish them. That's when I become the person who brings it to life.

MG: *It's a very traditional artist's studio like Rembrandt's.*
RL: When I was doing the show in Russia, last year, I flew my assistants to Moscow as well. A young curator, Vika Dushkina, curated an exhibition with them. So, they came to Moscow, not as assistants, but as artists.

MG: *The focus of your work in the past several years has become drawing.*
RL: Deep inside, I'm a sculptor. The drawing process is more like sculpting than drawing. It's not the academic rendering like Rembrandt. The white that you always see is the untouched surface of the paper. I've worked on this very special paper for the past thirty years. The paper has just enough grain to look like a photograph. I use a lot of different color charcoals. Usually, the last step is the erasing which is the carving. It's all very physical. I want people to look at my work closely enough that they can see the hand, but I don't want the hand to be a part of the work. I love to see the brushstroke, the evidence of expression, but in drawing, it's overly sentimental. There is a precise balance between illustration and photo-realism. I want to make images hyperreal.

MG: *Do you speak to your collectors?*
RL: A few.

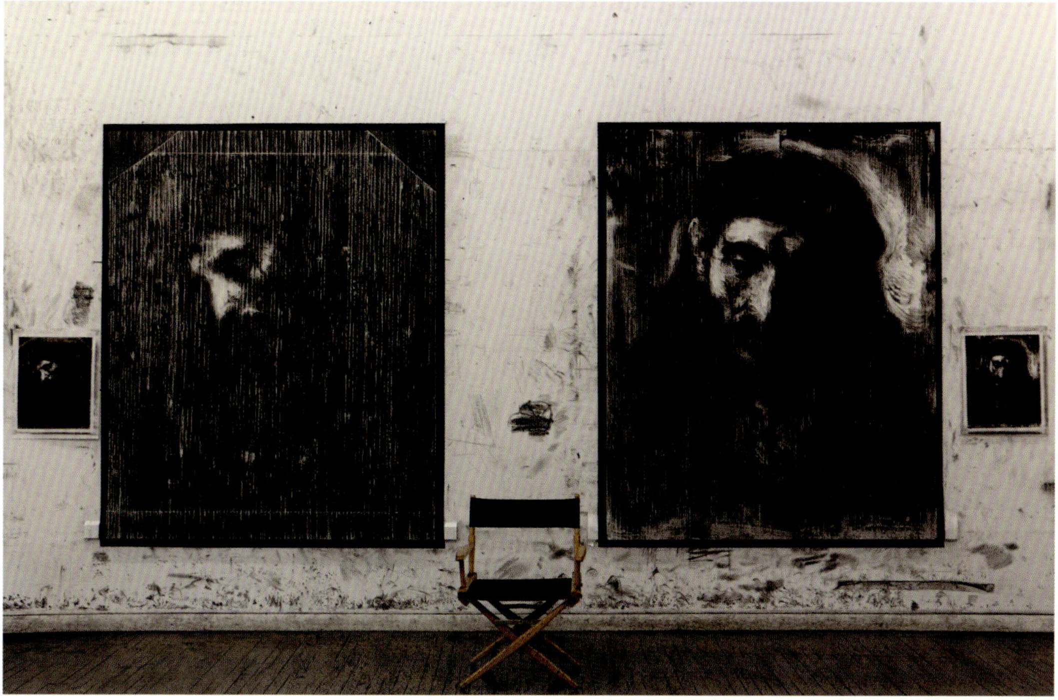

4
Robert Longo
Untitled (X-Ray of Head of Christ, c. 1655, After Rembrandt), 2015 and *Untitled (X-Ray of Head of Christ, c. 1648-1656, After Rembrandt)*, 2015
Charcoal on mounted paper, 224.2 × 177.8 cm

MG: *Do you like it?*
RL: A few, I do. Part of the problem is that I'm not terribly social. I can't go to their houses and schmooze with them; I'm not like that. I always feel, when I go there, as if I'm supposed to steal something. I'm incredibly grateful that people like my work.

MG: *Do you feel uneasy when other people own your work?*
RL: When you buy an artwork, you don't actually own it. You own the right to look at it for as long as you want. The responsibility is much greater; you become a caretaker of this work, which is an interesting privilege. I, myself, have no problem with people who resell work. Collectors take a risk by buying art.

MG: *No soreness towards people who own your work?*
RL: Very rarely, people call me to say the work needs to be fixed. When I investigate it, it's usually something they did. Like somebody has a drawing of mine in their beach house on the wall facing the ocean. What do you want me to do?

MG: *You mentioned how greatly you appreciated Douglas Crimp because of defining what you and your friends were doing. What do you think about current art criticism and theory?*

RL: If someone writes about you critically, it's truly a gift. Hal Foster, who is one of my great friends, has written a lot about my work. Recently the writing of Kate Fowle, the chief curator of The Garage Museum, has been very informative for me.

MG: *Have you noticed a change in art criticism?*
RL: Honestly, I don't read it. Criticism seems to be an objectified art form unto itself. What I have noticed is the enormous wave of curators that now exist. It's changed. There are star curators, where artists function as illustrators to the curators' theories. Crimp and Foster were writing close to the first person perspective. It was not that they were writing about art, but rather, they were using art to talk about the ideas that were in the work. When we did the show in Moscow, Kate Fowle asked me who I wanted to ask to write for the catalogue, other than her. I said Chris Hedges. He's a Pulitzer-prize winning journalist. I thought we'd never get him, but we did. I thought it would be great to have someone with a different, political perspective, a perspective outside of the art world. I am very proud of the *Proof* catalogue.

MG: *What is a recipe for good art?*
RL: You can compare making art to tuning a radio. Do you remember the old radios, when you had to turn a knob? If you go too much in this direction, or too much the other way, you'll lose it. Making art is about this kind of balance between the personal and the socially relevant. I think that balance is really crucial.

SARAH LUCAS

June 2014

Marta Gnyp: *The idea of the book,* Tittipussidad, *which you recently launched together with your friend Julian Simmons, relates somehow to Diego Rivera's house in Mexico.*
Sarah Lucas: Diego built Anahuacalli to house his collection of pre-Hispanic artworks. It's built in an area of volcanic rock, out of that rock, which is dark, almost black. The design was based on Aztec temple-designs. The largest room was intended as his studio. It currently displays some of his huge cartoons. He also intended the building to be his, and Frida's (Kahlo), tomb. As it turned out, the President wanted Diego's remains for the Hall of Great Men. Frida's ashes are in a jar in her own house. Most of the artifacts in the museum are figures or pots – rather than abstracts, as you suggest.

MG: *You wanted to visit this his house and see this collection? How big is it?*
SL: About 60,000 objects, of which probably 20,000 are on display.

MG: *Why were you so fascinated by Rivera?*
SL: For years, Julian and I had had the idea of going to Mexico and responding to its early artifacts, ancient rather than modern. The project in Rivera's museum was a great opportunity to achieve this wish.

MG: *Did you find what you were looking for in Mexico?*
SL: Naturally the Museo National de Antropologia was our first point of call. We also visited Diego's house, Frida's house and Trotsky's house. In this way, they began to tell us their story. I had no particular plan before arriving in Mexico. So, tracking down material was also a part of our engagement with the place. Ordinary things like tights, cigarettes, and cotton. Through the testimony of people I know and books I've read, like Carlos Casteneda, I was attracted to Oaxaca. The city – not the coast. Our whole trip was five weeks, two in Mexico City and three in Oaxaca. It was my first trip to Mexico, although I'd read a lot about the country beforehand. When we got there, everything unfolded very quickly. It was

amazing; we really had a great time, as you can see, such a big book from such a short trip. But actually, we stacked many things in.

MG: *Is it a kind of chronicle of your creative process?*
SL: It's about the whole thing, the making of it, the people who were involved in it. It's a storybook with pictures.

MG: *Why did you choose this title?*
Julian Simmons: We made a Spanish word out of "tittipussy", by adding the Spanish "dad" particle to it.
SL: We loved the "dad" thing; it was a kind of feminine adjustment to it. In English it would be: *Tittipussyity*.

MG: *What did you do with all the artworks? Did you leave them in Mexico?*
SL: Some stayed there, some developed into bronze sculptures. I hadn't made these kind of characters, before Mexico. It was something that suddenly happened there.
The shiny gold-bronze sculptures seem to be directly influenced by the Aztecs.

MG: *How does this new trajectory in Mexico relate to your former artworks? You have often been compared to Louise Bourgeois and Eva Hesse. Do you mind?*
SL: I can see what people are saying. But I'm not looking through books with Louise Bourgeois pictures. It just happens. It's a tactile thing. We share a very "hands on" approach to manipulating materials. But we're from different eras and different lives. In that respect, I think what we are expressing is quite different.

MG: *Speaking about the different angle: in 1996 you made this well-known self-portrait with two fried eggs on your breasts and a cigarette in your mouth, looking very provocatively at the camera. Was this how you saw yourself back then, or how you wanted to be seen?*
SL: I didn't think about it. I was using myself as raw material. Handy at the time, since I was there and I was cheap.

MG: *What about your latest portrait made in Mexico?*
SL: It's me on the toilet. Julian just caught me there.
JS: We were with a lot of friends. I just went to the bathroom, had a camera with me; I saw Sarah and took the picture.

MG: *You look totally happy and even slightly childlike. You must be very self-secure, to let yourself be photographed like this.*

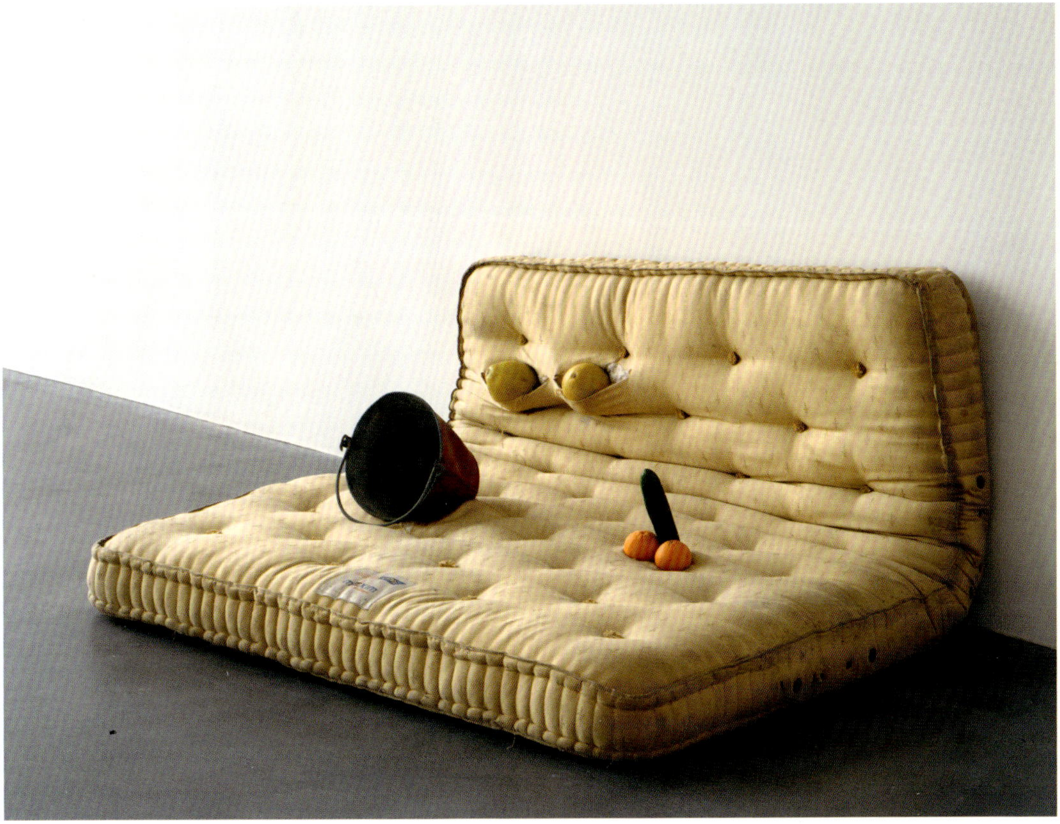

1
Sarah Lucas
Au Naturel, 1994

SL: I'd just pulled my slip down and had a lot of Mescal the moment he came. Nicole, at Contemporary Fine Arts, said there had been a couple of complaints on Twitter. I don't see it as offensive. I decided to put it in the show as it made a link with my first show in Berlin, *Is Suicide Genetic?*

MG: *Let's talk a bit about how it all started. You were one of the main representatives of Young British Artists.*
SL: Not so young anymore, but still childish. [laughs]

MG: *In 1987, you graduated from Goldsmiths College and in 1998 you participated in the* Freeze *exhibition, which turned out to be one of the defining moments of contemporary art. The work you made for* Freeze *was an aluminum object put on the floor, but a couple of years later, you made* Two Fried Eggs and a Kebab, *which seems like a radical change in use of materials and in the conceptual approach to art.*
SL: When I was at college, I didn't really find my voice. It happened only after I left. I was actually quite disillusioned by my work at *Freeze*. You

2
Sarah Lucas
Self-Portrait with Fried Eggs,
1996

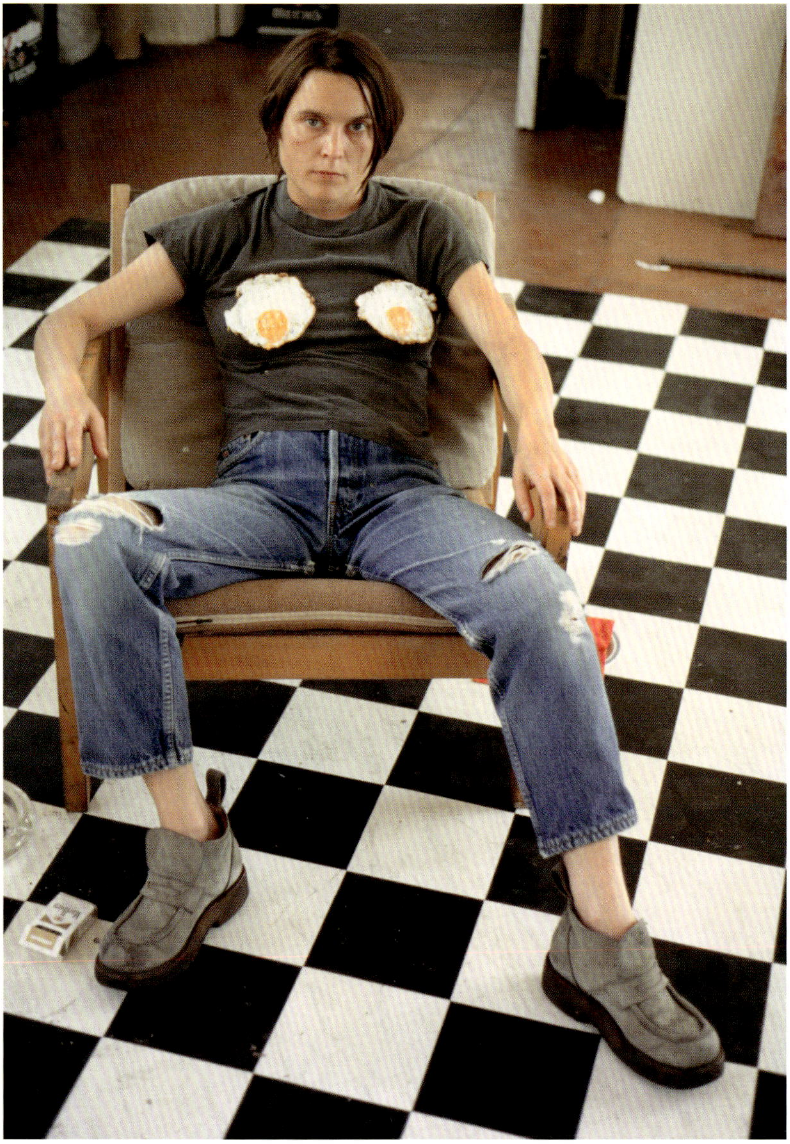

don't think like that at college because you're at college to make art. Therefore, making art is a "given" – no need for the question. Tutors are there to criticize what you do but they don't question the fact that you made something. Out on my own, grappling with huge piles of bricks, plastic or aluminum, and filling up my tiny room with it, I began to wonder why I was doing it – what good is it to me?

MG: *Were you brooding on a concept or did you just start doing things because they interested you?*

SL: I was looking around for something to read. I always read a lot but I'd become bored with Literature. Andrea Dworkin fell into my lap and she was very compelling.

MG: *Was it a conscious decision to take the feminist position as the subject of your work?*
SL: I got very interested in the idea of censorship: whether censorship is a good or a bad thing. I have never found an answer to it. In 1990, I put on the exhibition called *Penis Nailed to a Board*. I took the title from the headline of a newspaper article about a group of men who were playing sex games, which partly involved nailing the penis/foreskin to a board. They were doing it because they liked it. The police snooped on them and they were taken to court and punished. But they were just doing it in private. They were "consenting adults". Still, most of them received a prison sentence. The perversion of the policemen involved wasn't mentioned. That case made me think, what is going on here? Is it a good thing to say you can't do something? If we are surrounded by sex and violence, which we are, especially by violence in the media, it does affect people. All these thoughts made me rethink my angle. And then my artworks began, really.

MG: *You just said that violence affects people. Does your work affect people in the same way?*
SL: As people, our knowledge of ourselves and the world comes completely from what is around us. We exist "in there", not somewhere else; there is nowhere else. So, of course we're affected by images. I'm making what I make self-consciously from inside "there"/"here". And I am self-conscious. I think people perceive the "me" in my work – or at the very least the woman in it, and that affects their reading of it. They also realize this in a gallery space and that makes them self-conscious.

MG: *For your new voice, you also found new materials, everyday objects.*
SL: Yes, but again, before I went to college I was always making objects by hand; that was what I liked. College was the place where you go to learn: to learn about other artists and think about sculpture, which was almost the opposite of what I was previously doing.

MG: *Before you went to college, were you conscious about making art or becoming an artist?*
SL: No. I was just decorating my bedroom with stuff cut out of magazines and making mobiles out of coke cans and suchlike. Creating an environment for me and my friends.

But when I look back, I can see how everything somehow fits together, comes back if relevant.

MG: *So, after college, you found your language and started* The Shop *together with Tracey Emin. Did you have an artistic concept for this or did it just happen?*
SL: We had a shop, rather than a studio. I didn't have my own studio at the time – I was sharing one with Gary (Hume), my boyfriend at that time. Tracey and I just became friends. I thought: I don't want to go to the studio, it's so boring. *The Shop* was not a big concept but we implemented some concepts within it. At the time, nobody had a mobile phone so we didn't know what would happen, really.

MG: *Did you somehow sense this could be a project with big artistic potential?*
SL: We did. Although it was strange, it only lasted six months. During these six months I got to know so many people! They came through the door because we had *The Shop*. And then, we realized how big the scene really was.

MG: *Did it help to create this idea of togetherness, which in turn was important to create the image of YBA?*
SL: Before the '90s, the contemporary art scene was limited to a few galleries. These galleries would take on a new artist once a year or so. They had the authority and they could be quite stuffy with it. In the '90s – and *The Shop* was a part of this – a bunch of artists emerging from colleges began organizing their own exhibitions in abandoned buildings. More and more artists started turning up to see them. Eventually we started getting beer sponsorship, and this helped. It was a buoyant scene, kept up by the enthusiasm of many young people. We were our own audience. From that, new galleries emerged – Sadie Coles, Jay Jopling, many others. It was a revolution.

MG: *At the time, Europe was in a heavy economic crisis, the art market for contemporary art in Europe hardly existed and the network of commercial galleries was missing. Despite this situation, you started, in a very short space of time, to work with both new and established galleries. You joined Barbara Gladstone in New York, Contemporary Fine Arts in Berlin, Sadie Coles when she started in London. Why did the galleries find you so interesting?*
SL: I did a couple of projects at Anthony d'Offay under the auspices of Sadie Coles. I didn't know then that she would one day have her own

gallery. I did a show with Jay Jopling at his original White Cube. Various exhibitions in alternative spaces. I also showcased the work of Gary Hume and Angus Fairhurst in my bedsit and invited our friends along. I suppose I was quite active.

MG: *How come Barbara Gladstone found you?*
SL: Barbara invited Gary to do a project in her summer project space in Rome, in 1990, and we went there for three months. I went along as Gary's girlfriend. And that was when I first met Barbara. Apparently, she was quite impressed by something I said at the table one night.

MG: *What did you say?*
SL: We had dinner: Barbara, Gary, me, and Mario Merz. Mario asked me why I wasn't talking. I said, "When I've got a platform, I'll talk". Barbara liked it.

MG: *Do you think your feminist position has helped you?*
SL: Yes. The galleries that existed at that time – Lisson, Karsten Schubert, Anthony d'Offay – were only taking in men. Suddenly there was a great liberation of women artists: me, Tracey Emin, Gillian Wearing, Anya Gallaccio. We suddenly came out and became visible.

MG: *Has being a woman also helped in the reception of your work? If* Wanking Machine *or a work like* Au Naturel *had been made by a man, they would have been called sexist and macho. In your case, they are a feministic critique.*
SL: Sure. That was very much in my favor. But that was, at the same time, what was so funny about it.

MG: *Your approach to and use of materials has been very exciting. Have you always had this sensibility for materials?*
SL: I believe I have. I remember, as a child, I used to unpick wool. I always liked texture.

MG: *There's also a certain truthfulness to objects and characters in your work. A melon is a melon before it becomes a breast; a cigarette is a cigarette before it signifies death. Is this how you want to treat materials?*
SL: Yes. I've tried to be dishonest sometimes, but I can't live with it. Not because it's dishonest, but because it looks wrong, it has to be natural.

MG: *A very good example of staying true is your urinal artwork that did function as a normal urinal. Was it a kind of competition with Duchamp?*

SL: Not really. You can't say this was the idea, in the same way you can't say it has nothing to do with him. He's there. So it would make a difference for this piece, but it's only one difference. I've made toilets so many times now.

MG: *Why are you so fascinated by toilets?*
SL: I'm not sure. I think that must be something that happened before I was really conscious.

MG: *Is this something British?*
SL: Maybe. I don't really know. But it suddenly struck me. I didn't set out to make autobiographical work. Quite the contrary. Nevertheless, it becomes a biography of sorts – looking back on it. And, looking back, it also seems more personal to me than I imagined it was.

MG: *I read the book about YBA written by Gregor Muir; there was so much drink and drugs all the time, how did you survive it?*
SL: I don't know. Eventually, at a certain point, I moved out from London. Just to calm down a bit. But it was really good fun and I loved it!

MG: *It was like you were rolling from one party into another.*
SL: It was like that.

MG: *When did you find time to make art?*
SL: I've never had a proper studio. Generally, I'm still making work on the hop. I myself am surprised by how much I've made in this way. (I'm) also quite proud of it. Making work in the situation keeps it close to my life. I never wanted it to be a job.

MG: *Is your house then full of all kinds of materials?*
SL: You'd be surprised; there's nothing to see. It is a mystery, but I've always managed to get everything done. A lot of what I make is quite immediate, quite ready. It's always like a thought process, but it can be instant.

MG: *How do you work with bronze?*
SL: That is quite a different thing. I can't do it at home and I work at a foundry.

MG: *Saatchi bought the urinal. Was he important for the development of your career?*
SL: I think he was. The first piece of mine he bought was *Two Fried Eggs and a Kebab*. I had an exhibition in a tiny little shop, where, by the way,

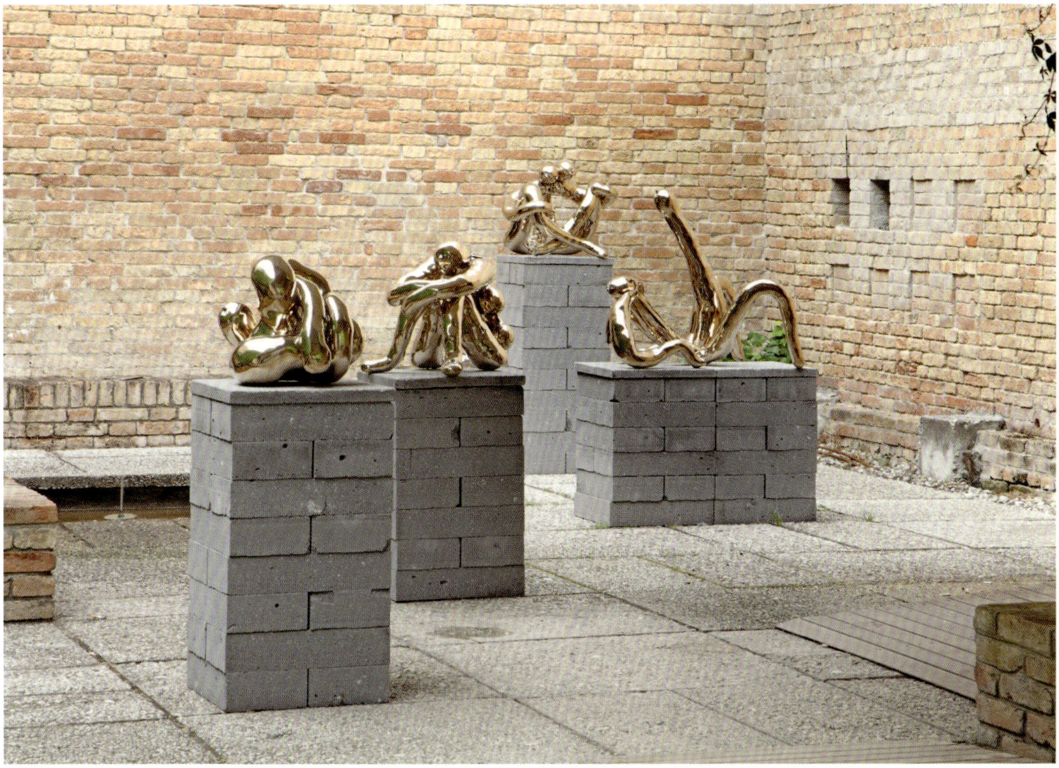

3
Sarah Lucas
Installation view, *Il Palazzo Enciclopedico*, Venice Biennale, 2013

Sadie's gallery now is. He just drove up in his jaguar or something, came in and said, "I'll buy it". I was eating a donut in that moment and jam dropped out of my mouth. [laughs] I wasn't one of the people, though, where he bought everything they did. Fortunately.

MG: *I can imagine that, at the beginning of your career, it wasn't easy to sell your work, with its explicit kind of vulgar sexual connotations.*
SL: True, they aren't something you want to have in your house. But I was also always making easier things. I don't believe I was thinking about selling anyway. Things just happened.

MG: *Did you sense that you and your artist peers were doing something different?*
SL: Sort of. *Two Fried Eggs and a Kebab* was a breakthrough moment. I was simply frying eggs every day, while the exhibition was on. It wasn't difficult. I suppose it became a bit of a performance. Using these materials and actually cooking on site seemed radical at the time. We were definitely doing what was missing. But I don't know whether any one of us expected what would happen.

MG: *You also met Jeff Koons. Was he an inspiration to you?*
SL: When I was in college, Saatchi organized an exhibition, including Koons and some other Americans from New York, which influenced Goldsmith students immensely. He made banality look so yummy.

MG: *Was art history important to you?*
SL: Not massively important. The first artist I liked was probably Eva Hesse, because of the texture of her work and the textiles she used. Then, there was Jeff Koons's stuff and, later on, I got much more interested in British artists like Gilbert and George. More recently, I became good friends with the late Franz West. Influences come and go. I think that a lot of influences are unconscious, anyway.

MG: *Can you imagine what your unconscious influences would be?*
SL: Well, I could speculate about it. Maybe my subconscious is influenced by Louise Bourgeois. I don't know. I'm obviously responding like everybody else to the times I live in and my surroundings. You're made up by them, you can't escape it.
You can't get any distance to it either. I can't get away to have a look at myself.

MG: *Is being British an important part of you?*
SL: I can't take it out of me – any more than being a woman.

MG: *Have you thought about your sense of humor as British?*
SL: It's only since I started doing a lot of travelling that I started to understand what people mean by it. You take so much for granted; you don't have any objectivity towards it. My works are based in real life. Funny, but also sad; very human in a way.

MG: *Did you consider the work,* Au Naturel, *a bit of a joke?*
SL: Yes, I made it in Germany for an exhibition at Portikus, in Frankfurt, curated by Georg Herold, another artist I like very much. Some of the artists were students from the Städelschule, the rest were English and we made what was called "Football Karaoke". The English were driving, in a van, from England to Frankfurt. Some of us brought works with them, I didn't. I went to a secondhand shop and made *Au Naturel* and *Bitch* for that show. A lot of my artworks have been made in quite low-key circumstances. I don't have to be overly self-conscious, or too premeditated. I can just risk it because it's fun, putting on an exhibition and doing it with friends. That sort of working environment suits me very well, which means I don't have to over-think things. What I like about making objects is not having to think too much, but just doing it. Of course, there is a lot you

can think about, some sort of awareness of people and surroundings. But it's quite fluid for me; the thinking comes later.

MG: *It seems you are not afraid of how people look at you.*
SL: I am sometimes. But I stopped bothering about that. I have some very self-conscious moments. I remember, one time, I was invited to Rotterdam to have one of my first museum shows in Museum Boijmans. I was setting up the artworks, all on my own in this empty museum. Suddenly a whole bunch of local pensioners were standing behind me while I was adjusting a couple of breast melons and, then, I thought, you can get me sometimes. I have some moments of embarrassment.

MG: *Do you intend to provoke?*
SL: I think so. It's not so much about other people, but about myself, finding some sort of edge. What people think about me and know about me is much less than I actually do, but it's all people talk about. I can live with that. I'm not trying to be nasty to anybody.

MG: *You are now a famous artist. Has this changed anything for you?*
SL: Got a bigger house . . . I don't know, I sometimes think about it. Change is a good thing. I must have changed but I don't think that I've changed so much either.

MG: *Do you use your popularity? For example, Damien Hirst has been using his public persona as a part of his artistic strategy.*
SL: These days, it seems to matter. For instance, when I did the self-portrait, I had no idea anybody would be interested in it. It was quite a surprise to me that there was something to it. After a while, I stopped doing it because the kind of interest people tend to have in an artist is quite lewd, like a cult personality. And I'm not so interested in that. Sometimes I like it, though, and I think, "this is definitely worth it for me".

MG: *What about your family? Are they startled that you have become such a well-known artist?*
SL: They are pleased and, I supposed, proud, but we don't discuss it.

MG: *Did they support your artistic path?*
SL: They did, although they were not particularly interested in art. I didn't go to galleries when I was young. I only went to museums a couple of times.

MG: *Did they find it strange, when you decided to go to the art school?*

4
Sarah Lucas
Titti Doris, 2017
Installation view

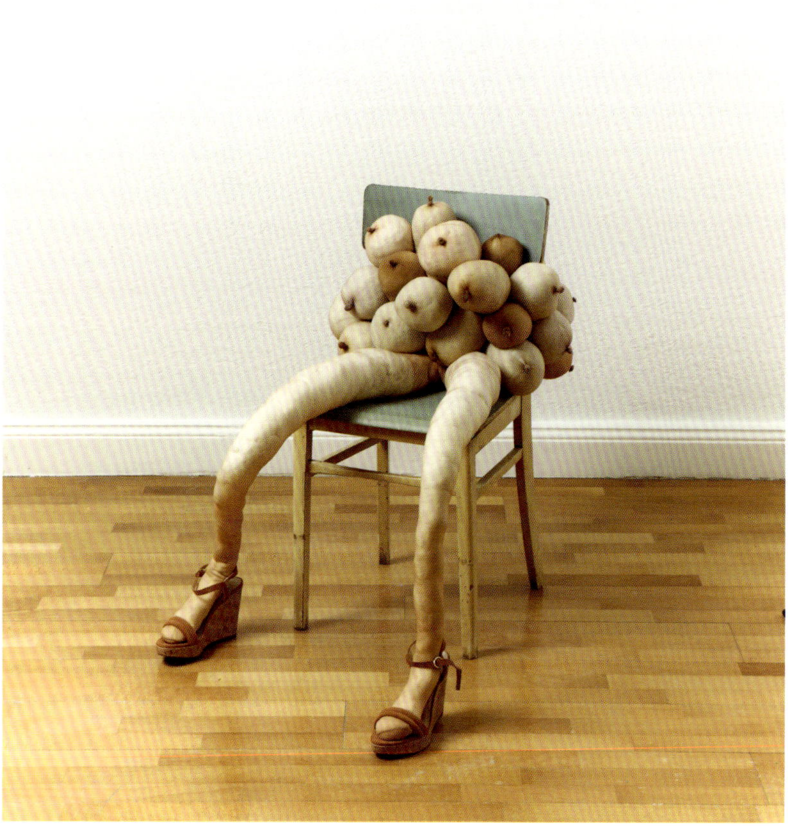

SL: I was always a bit weird, so nothing was strange. For a long time, I was the poor relative in the family: if this is what she likes it's okay, but the price for this is that she's poor. When that changed, it was a weird moment.

MG: *You were born and lived for quite a long time in London.*
SL: I never imagined that I could have a life somewhere else. I still have a house in London but now I live in the countryside, most of the time. It started as a weekend place with Sadie Coles, but then, I stayed there more and more, and we bought a house so I could live there permanently. It helps me get out of the craziness, because London gets really crazy. And I'm sort of addicted to it.

MG: *What about the current nomadic condition of the artist?*
SL: I like travelling for work but I don't travel a lot for pleasure. I like having a reason to be somewhere. It's a different way of engaging, even trying to get materials and stuff. You have to make adjustments; things like toilets are different everywhere. Even blocks – nowhere in the world do you have the same blocks, which is okay; you just have to adapt your ideas, then different things happen. I'm still expanding my use of materials.

MG: *Do you often collaborate with other artists?*
SL: Because Julian and I live together, it's just the way it is between us. We do a lot of things together because we always liked that. I also liked doing projects with Tracey and shows with Damien and Angus. Making art is just a part of my everyday life and everyday friendship-circles. It's a lifestyle.

MG: *So, for you, art is a way of life?*
SL: Yes. That is my alternative to not having a studio: actually, this is just a part of my life.

MG: *Have you ever thought about art as being your profession?*
SL: Never. Back then, when I was doing what I liked without having any money, I thought that's how it would be. I didn't mind.

MG: *Would you mind now?*
SL: I didn't mind then. I couldn't give a shit about money, about having a washing machine or a house. I lived in a squat for three years; I just wanted freedom.

MG: *Do you now experience money as giving you that freedom?*
SL: Yes, I don't have to worry, but, I'm not very big on buying designer products, etc. I spend a lot of money on eating, drinking and stuff like that.

MG: *Do you yourself buy art?*
SL: No, mainly because I can't look after things. My house is like my studio so it's a great risk to put something there. I do have pieces made by my friends, which we exchanged.

MG: *Do you look at art a lot? Do you visit galleries?*
SL: Not so much anymore. I used to do it a lot, throughout the '90s in Germany and New York. I'm not looking for something in the same way that I was looking back then, looking for a clue: what is art, what is good, what do I like. It might start again.

MG: *Is there anything that can give you the excitement of the "new"?*
SL: I don't know, I've always read books. All sorts of books: novels, a bit of philosophy, I like music a lot. Julian makes really nice music. It's about immersing myself in a certain sort of atmosphere.

MG: *You had an extremely well-received retrospective in Whitechapel last year.*
SL: It was quite absurd. I really stuffed a lot in. There are so many minimal exhibitions. I just thought, if you have a retrospective just get it all in there. It was really fun.

MG: *How did having a retrospective feel, for you?*
SL: It was a bit weird and melancholic, seeing all these things together. I treated the technique of hanging pieces as a whole artwork of its own and the hanging was completely fresh.

MG: *Did you discover anything new about yourself, looking back from your perspective today?*
SL: How well all these things work together. There are a lot of different materials, different approaches, but they were all happy together, which is nice. Where does it all come from? Even the radical works, when you look back, they just seem very harmonious and continuous. And this was a surprise. Because you never know what you are doing.

SHIRIN NESHAT

March 2018

Marta Gnyp: *Let's start with your most recent project; your film:* Looking for Oum Kulthum. *Why are you so fascinated by this Egyptian singer?*

Shirin Neshat: Looking back at my career, I find that I've had a long obsession with strong Middle Eastern female artists. In my earlier photographic works, I used the poetry of the well-known Iranian poets, Forough Farrokhzad and Tahereh Saffarzadeh; later I made the film *Women without Men*, based on a novel written by the legendary Iranian novelist Shahrnush Parsipur, and now with this film I pay a tribute to Oum Kulthum, the iconic Egyptian singer. So perhaps, unconsciously, I've been drawn to women who are not only brilliant artists, but also have lived difficult yet interesting lives. Each one of them seem to have challenged the traditional roles of women, and their journey as artists has been unpredictable, fascinating and highly successful.

MG: *What was so specific about Oum Kulthum?*

SN: In her case I was first and foremost drawn to the power of her music. She was an amazing singer; and without a doubt the most important and powerful artist of the twentieth century in the Middle East. Her music moved millions of people. A woman reaching that level of popularity as an artist was unprecedented, especially in that part of the world.

MG: *Is your admiration a form of research into the complexities of artistic success?*

SN: Indeed, there is always that unconscious sense of self-reflection on my behalf. I feel, as an artist, I've been looking at the trajectory of iconic female artists whom I admire, to learn about how they balanced their personal lives with careers; how they faced the challenges of being female artists living and working in male-dominated societies. So, in the end, by studying and incorporating their work into mine, I not only pay tribute to such great artists, but I also confront my own personal issues and dilemmas as another female artist from the Middle East.

MG: *Are you identifying yourself with Oum Kulthum, to a certain extent?*
SN: I wouldn't dare compare myself with her, because she's a legend.

MG: *Still, there must be some similarities between the two of you.*
SN: There are. First of all, like Oum Kulthum, I have devoted my life to my work. Secondly, although she lived in a conservative and religious culture, she lived a truly untraditional life as a woman. She never had children and her marriage was only a marriage of convenience. In my case, I also lived an unusual life. I left my family when I was only seventeen years old, and later, after a short marriage, I raised my son alone as a single mother. So, both of us, like many artists, didn't enjoy a nuclear family structure. There are other parallels, for example, Oum Kulthum was always surrounded by her male collaborators, such as musicians and composers; and in my case, although I seem to make highly feminist work, I work mostly with a team of men.

MG: *Why are you always stressing that you are a female artist and not just an artist?*
SN: If you look at my work carefully, you'll find that all my protagonists and narratives are female. This is partially because I am a woman, therefore I relate more closely to issues of women, particularly those living in oppressive societies. Also, I am immensely inspired by strong women, mainly Iranian women who have been up against a wall for so long yet have remained resilient and defiant.

MG: *It's striking that you see yourself as Iranian, although you've been living in the USA for the past forty years, meaning most of your life. Don't you feel that you are American and that you're not in exile, but at home, in the USA?*
SN: It's true that I'm not just Iranian anymore, and that I've lived outside of my country for a very long time, but this doesn't stop me from remaining Iranian. I would say that I'm American in my lifestyle, education, and certain characteristics, such as my independence. I've lived in New York since 1983, so I feel very much rooted in New York culture. But my emotional and psychological foundations are still deeply Iranian. I'm married to an Iranian, I speak Farsi daily, I'm part of an Iranian community and my family still lives in Iran.
So, my identity is complex. I'm not just an Iranian living in exile. I'm a native New Yorker and an American. Slowly I find my work is moving away from the Iranian subjects; *Looking for Oum Kulthum* is no longer about Iran, but about me as an Iranian looking at an Egyptian artist. My newest project will be about America.

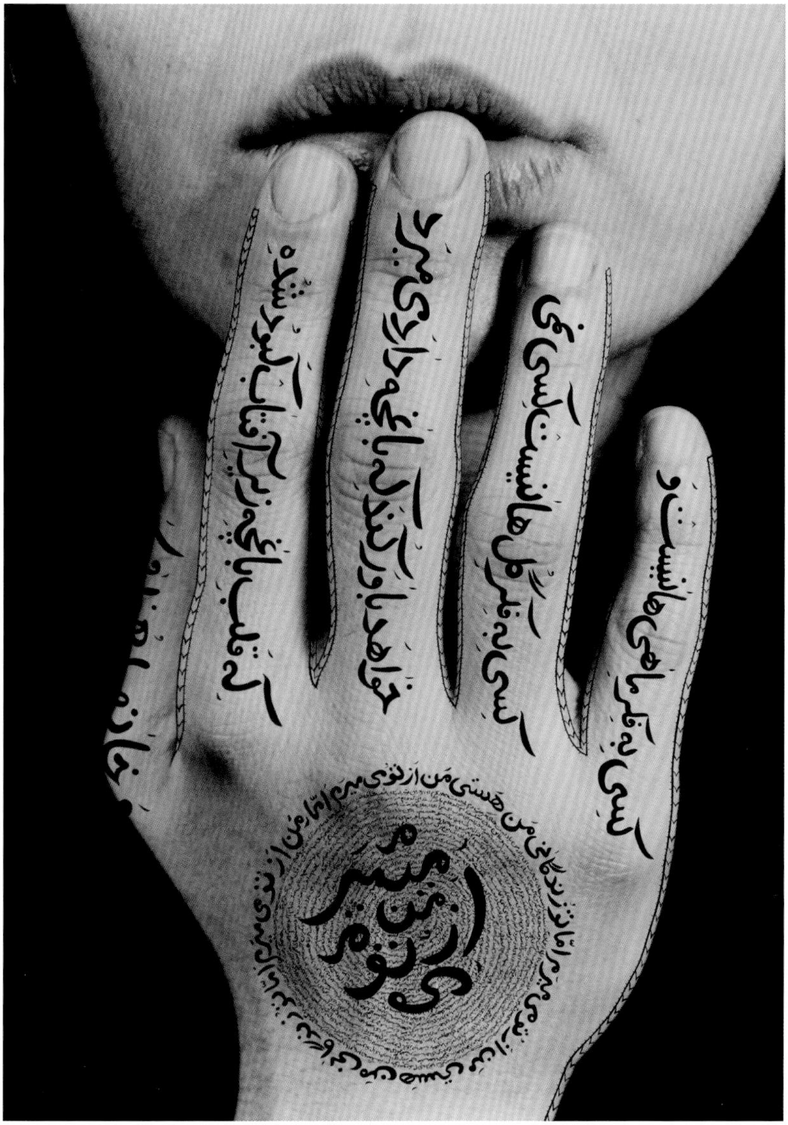

1
Shirin Neshat
Untitled, 1996
RC print & ink,
121.6 × 84.5 cm

MG: *I was wondering whether you celebrate your Iranian roots naturally or deliberately when you operate in the public space: you tend to wear heavy makeup, oriental earrings, etc.*
SN: It's precisely about being both – Iranian and American, two cultures that are in constant conflict; and how I feel emotionally, psychologically, and politically, being constantly divided between the two. And therefore this form of contradiction is reflected in my entire composition, including my style which appears, on the one hand, very modern and minimalistic, yet extremely ancient, Eastern and almost tribal, on the other.

2
Shirin Neshat
Rapture, 1999
Film still

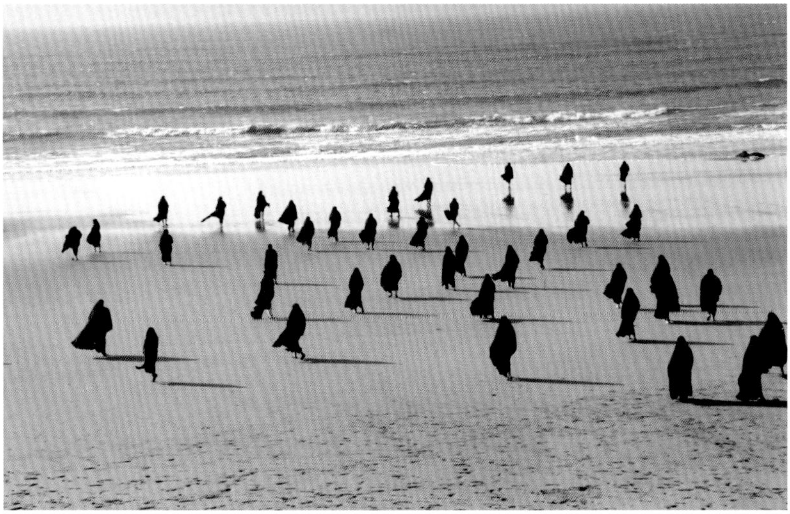

MG: *Let's go back to the moment when you arrived in the USA, in 1975, to study art at Berkeley University in California. Was art a conscious decision or just one of the choices you made?*
SN: When I was a child, I always had this romantic interest in becoming an artist, without understanding what it really meant. I'd never been exposed to art in galleries or museums. All I remember is that, from childhood, I had an instinctive desire to be an artist and everyone at school called me an artist for making some silly drawings. Eventually, when I came to the USA to study at Berkeley, I quickly learnt I didn't have what it took to be an artist. Therefore, that whole romantic idea of being an artist was shattered.

MG: *Were you disappointed?*
SN: The truth is that I was a very mediocre student, I was barely accepted to the graduate school. But, I was smart enough to recognize that. When I came to New York from California, I made no effort to create art for the next ten years.

MG: *You worked at the non-profit organization Storefront for Art and Architecture. Did this time and the conversations about art shape you and give you the confidence that you needed for your work?*
SN: I never related to the education I received at art school; and never believed that artists are born naturally talented. I generally find it hard to accept that students in their early twenties would be capable of producing significant and meaningful work. I believe art stems from one's collective life experiences, struggles, and responses to the world we inhabit. Art

cannot be entirely developed on the basis of one's intuition or simply an elaboration of art history.

MG: *Are you saying that artistic education is redundant?*
SN: I shouldn't generalize, since my opinion is uniquely based on my personal experiences. As a matter of fact, as I've recently been involved in teaching as a guest critic at Yale University's Photography department, I've met several students who are exceptional and brilliant despite their young years. So my whole argument could be wrong.

MG: *What was it that brought you back to art?*
SN: I went to Iran in 1990, years after I left the country and years after the Iranian revolution. I felt a deep connection to the country, so when I came back to New York, I started to make art again but without any specific goals or strategies. It was these few works that some curators found interesting, and so, my career took off. By that time I had found the necessary maturity, a methodology, and, most importantly, a subject matter I was passionate about, which related to the Iranian revolution, so I began articulating my artistic voice and signature.

MG: *You started with a romantic idea of art, abandoned art all together in 1983 and then returned to it twelve years later, when after your emotional experiences in Iran, you started with the series* Women of Allah.
SN: I had been working at Storefront for Art and Architecture for nearly ten years by then, helping program other artists and architects' work; but I reached a point when I felt the urge to build my own artistic identity. This all crystallized when I started travelling to Iran again in 1990, when I got inspired by my discoveries, and my interactions with Iranian people, whom I had lost touch with. Back in New York, I wanted to make sure not to lose this connection with my country again, so art became a form of excuse, a link to keep my relationship to Iran alive, even from a distance. In terms of form, I was thinking about how to develop my own visual language. Painting was totally irrelevant to my subject matter now, and although I had never been a photographer, I realized that photography would be the perfect medium for me because it had the realism I was looking for. I was especially taken by photojournalism. I started collecting images from newspapers and magazines, various references, and then next, I went to a friend who was a photographer and asked him to shoot a few portraits of me. Soon, some people in the art world showed interest in what I was doing. I remember submitting a proposal to a very small non-profit organization in New York called Franklin Furnace, which got accepted. One thing led to another and my career started.

MG: *I'm interested in the relationship to women that you captured in* Women of Allah. *I read articles about this series in the 1990s. In an early one from 1995, I found a quote – that I assume was yours, "Chador as symbol of rebellion against imperialism", while in 2017 you said that women are used as "the battleground for men's ideology". This is quite a change in thinking about the subject. At the beginning of the 1990s, you seemed to be quite fascinated and terrified by what was happening in Iran, while your interpretation now is very clearly negative and rejects political changes in Iran.*
SN: All the works I've done, *Women of Allah* and later, *The Book of Kings*, are about raising questions as opposed to providing answers. It's true that after twelve years of absence, when I first came back to Iran, I experienced some kind of romantic infatuation with the revolution, but that changed very quickly. *Women of Allah* basically explored the mindset of a typical militant woman who was brainwashed and remained faithful to religious fanaticism and the Islamic revolution, which had even institutionalized the concept of "martyrdom". These women believed in the government's rhetoric, that by returning to the idea of "veiling", they would be resisting the Westernization of their country. In many ways, putting the veil on – as imposed by the Islamic regime – or taking it off – as ordered to modernize the country during the regime of the Shah, shows how Iranian women throughout history have become the battleground for men's rulings and ideology.

MG: *Were you criticized because of your ambiguous attitude?*
SN: Oh, yes. Especially by Iranians who were against the regime and thought I made this work to support and endorse fundamentalism and the current government. Really, the work was made to show my understanding and reading of what had transpired in the country during the post-revolutionary era, without making any judgments.

MG: *How do you keep your convictions and beliefs outside your work?*
SN: What's in the work is my curiosity together with the information that I gather through my research. I'm not a religious person and have never been interested in sharing my own personal beliefs and agendas with the public.

MG: *For* Women of Allah *and* The Book of Kings, *you have chosen similar visual solutions – black-and-white photography, texts in Farsi on their bodies – yet a lot has changed. If you look at the two series, you see the change in society.*
SN: Both series are works of fictions. The Islamic Revolution, 1979, and the Green Movement, in 2009, are the two single-most important political

events in modern Iranian history since the *coup d'état* of 1953, which was the period we captured in the movie: *Women without Men*.
I never thought history had such a significance place in my work and thought process. But now, when I look back, the *Women of Allah* series depicted the religious fervor that transformed Iranian society from a monarchy into an Islamic Republic, after the 1979 Islamic revolution, when religion began to dominate and rule Iranian society.
Later, *The Book of Kings* in 2011, depicted a different uprising, the green movement, thirty years after the Islamic Revolution, when we were faced with an altered society. This uprising was led by a new generation of Iranians, who were not religious and were modern, educated and forward-thinking. Furthermore, this generation of activists were not interested in overthrowing the government, but in simply demanding basic democracy and human rights. Therefore, *The Book of Kings* is a very accurate portrait of current Iranian society, where religion is no longer as dominant a factor in the country as it used to be.

MG: *Why have you never been prosecuted by the Iranian government for your work?*
SN: As far as I'm concerned, I'm only a poet. I'm not attacking the government. I don't make polemical artwork. I'm not sure why the government has problems with me and my work, but I don't consider myself a political activist.

MG: *I was thinking about Salman Rushdie, who also writes fiction.*
SN: He touched on something that became sacrilegious. I have never been interested in offending people of religion. I may have been publically vocal against the government, to object against their human rights records, but I've never used my art as a platform to promote my own ideals.

MG: *Let's go back to New York of the 1990s, when you started making your photographic series and were first noticed as an artist. What was the artistic situation in New York like at that time when your career took off? Who did you feel connected to?*
SN: In the mid-1980s, there was a lot of excitement in the East Village; a true bohemian cultural moment. The scene was exploding with graffiti art, rap music, break dancing, and great artists were at the pinnacle of their careers, such Andy Warhol, Keith Haring and Jean Michel Basquiat. I found myself at the center of this underground art scene. I lived in the East Village and became friends with many artists, especially some graffiti artists, and went to many well-known clubs. Eventually I married Kyong Park, who was also very much a part of the underground scene of New

3
Shirin Neshat
Roja, 2012
Ink on LE silver gelatin print, 152.4 × 114.3 cm

York City, and founded the small alternative space called Storefront for Art and Architecture, in 1983. But, unfortunately, in the early 1990s, things changed and that fascinating scene transformed quickly into a more commercial and pretentious art environment.

MG: *Your ex-husband, Kyong Park, opened Storefront, where you worked as well.*
SN: Yes, I spent ten years working with him. And through my work at the Storefront, I got to know and work closely with many great artists and architects such as Kiki Smith, Alfredo Jaar, Vito Acconci, Mel Chin, David Hammons, Steven Holl, Jean Nouvel, Coop Himmelblau and others. The environment was exciting and productive, always about ideas and the process and never about money. I always say that my true education came from my years of working at Storefront and not from my education at art school.

MG: *The work you were making in the '90s was quite different from the work of others. Did you feel part of a group?*
SN: It's true that I was very much on my own, in terms of the subject matter and the way I was exploring the medium of photography. Plus, at that time, I became very intimate with a team of Iranian collaborators, including writers, musicians and cinematographers. We created our own independent community. We were working and travelling together all the time. So, I slowly moved away from the Storefront group and was now surrounded now by my new Iranian colleagues.

MG: *Your personal life was very much connected to the development of your work.*
SN: Very true. Once I decided to be an artist again, my relationship, to both my husband and Storefront, strangely ended. I became romantically involved with Shoja Azari, who was one of my main Iranian collaborators and to this day we continue to work and live together. All of my video-based work, as well as the feature-length films, have been made in collaboration with Shoja.

MG: *Switching to making films must have been quite an enterprise.*
SN: By the end of the '90s, I had made so many photographs that I felt the urge to push beyond my signature work, which by now had become somewhat popular, and to experiment with moving image. So, together with my team, I went to Morocco and began making a number of video installations, which was a huge departure for my work. I was now able to leave the notion of studio work behind and incorporate landscape, music,

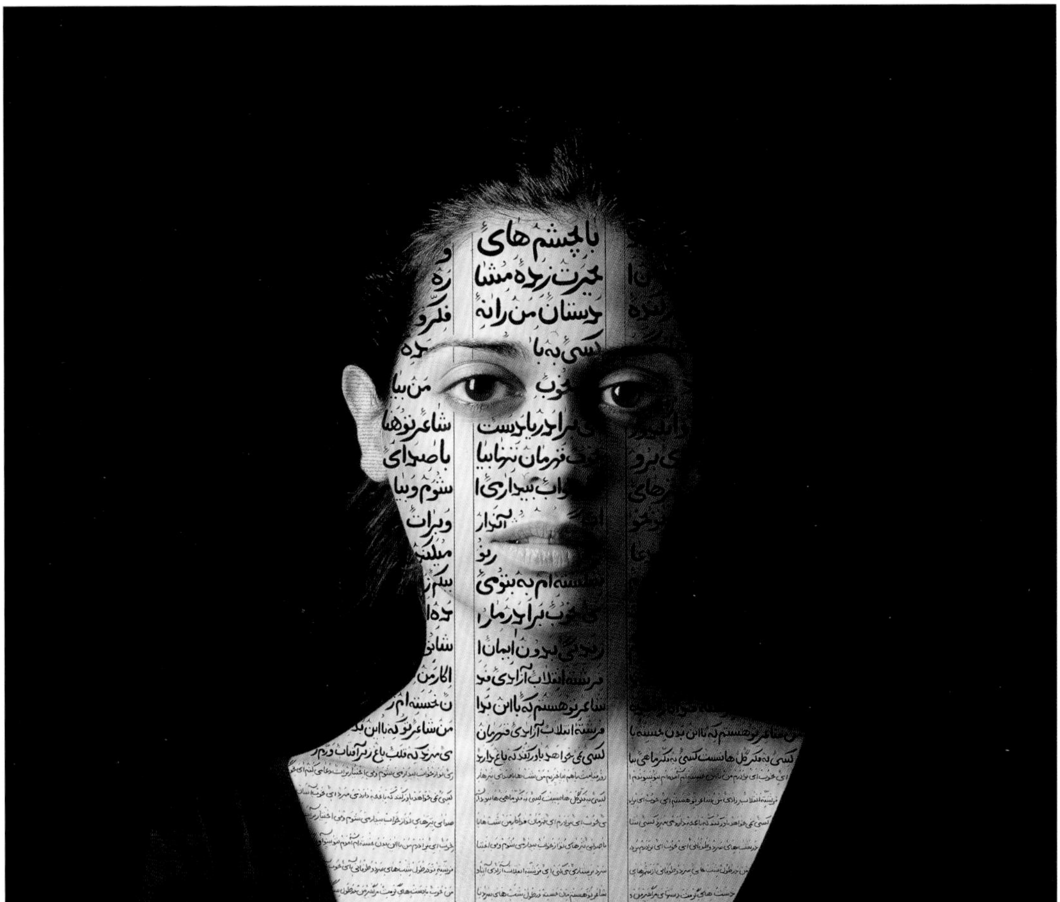

choreography and narrative into my work. Most importantly, I learned to direct films.

MG: Rapture *was your first important video. Did you lean on your photographic knowledge to make it?*
SN: I would say *Turbulent* and *Rapture* were both my first important video projects, which clearly borrowed heavily, aesthetically and compositionally, from my black-and-white still photography. Every frame of *Rapture* is a photograph with the exception that there's always a thread of narrative. For me, these two videos were the opening to a wide range of possibilities in the art of video installation and cinema. So the team and I went on to make a number of other pieces across the world, from Morocco to Turkey and Mexico.

MG: *Is film is your favorite medium at the moment?*
SN: The answer is yes. I think that film is my favorite medium at the moment because I can continue making photographs within the construction of a film. Although the only thing I enjoy in the process of being a still photographer is the solitude of studio work, something that's lacking in filmmaking, since it's such a collaborative medium by nature.

MG: *Was the* Golden Lion, *for your video* Turbulent *at the Venice Biennale in 1999, your artistic breakthrough?*
SN: Absolutely. Receiving that prize was my official entrance into the contemporary world of art, on an international level. Then, later, in 2009, receiving the Silver Lion award for Best Director at the Venice film festival helped my film career immensely.

MG: *Recently, you've even become an important voice in the fight for more women in the film industry? I read a few articles about you desiring more space for women in the industry.*
SN: I wouldn't say that I'm an advocate for women in the film industry. There aren't a lot of women making films in the USA and I was simply asked for my opinion, but the situation seems to be slowly changing. I must say, though, being a Middle Eastern woman filmmaker has helped me get a certain amount of attention and recognition, so I can't personally complain about discrimination.

MG: *What are you working on now?*
SN: I'm working on a new feature film which I hope to shoot in the United States in late 2018. I'm also preparing a major exhibition, opening at the Faurschou Foundation in Denmark, on March 16. It's about the process of making the film: *Looking for Oum Kulthum.*

MG: *What approach did you choose to tell the story of Oum Kulthum?*
SN: It's a film inside a film. It's a story about the challenges of an Iranian female artist/filmmaker making a film about the legendary Arabic singer, Oum Kulthum.

MG: *Which means this exhibition will be about making a film that is actually a film about making a film. Was it difficult for you to make the film since Oum Kulthum was Egyptian and you are Iranian?*
SN: There were multiple challenges in making this film. First of all, it was extremely courageous as a non-Arab, to dare to make a film about the biggest icon of the Arab world in the twentieth century, especially without speaking any Arabic. Secondly, the style of the film became an interesting challenge of interweaving the many different layers of narratives; the biopic/period part of the story of Oum Kullthum; the production and the director's personal story; together with dreams sequences and edited archival footage. Of course, I knew Oum Kulthum since childhood, as she was well-known across the Middle East, but I spent nearly six years in research, development and the final execution of the film.

MG: *How do you explain her popularity?*
SN: First of all, she was blessed with a tremendous voice and technical vocal training that, to this day, no one else has been able to master. And, although she was not beautiful and even rather masculine, she was able to reach deep into the heart of her audience. She sang very emotional love songs that threw people into a state of ecstasy. She was known for being loved by men, women, poor, rich, secular, non-secular, Muslims and Jews. Her popularity, by the end of her life, reached the point where four million people poured into the streets of Cairo to mourn her death. I must also mention that, towards the second part of her career, she became very patriotic and helped her country through economic hardship and political crisis. So, the Egyptians worship her and have a rare affection for her beyond her musical gifts.

MG: *Her music is full of repetition.*
SN: Her style of singing connects to a more mystical history of music in the Islamic world. Described as "Tarab", it's a commonly known terminology for describing Oum Kulthum's music and how she repeats lyrics to the point where her audience reaches a form of orgasmic experience, losing all sense of time and place.

MG: *Why did you decide to make this exhibition about the making of?*
SN: The exhibition came as unusual invitation by the Faurschou Founda-

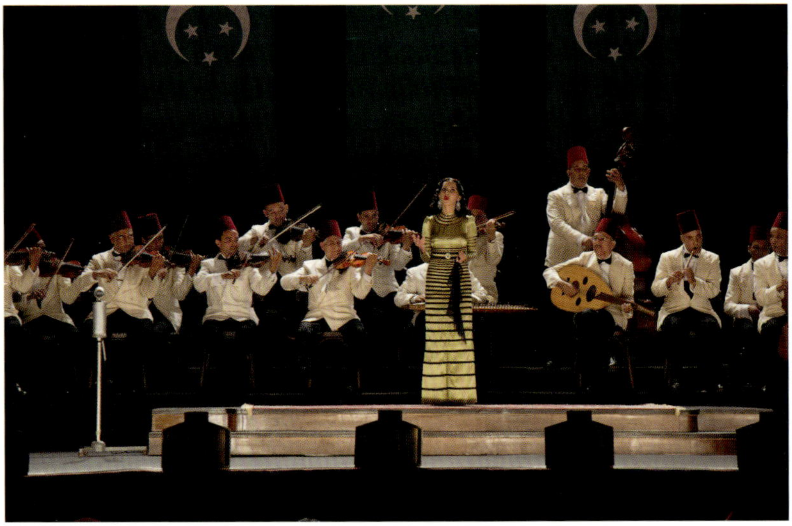

4
Shirin Neshat
Looking for Oum Kulthum,
2017
Film still

tion. I actually found it interesting to find ways of sharing my process of making a film with the public. In the end, the exhibition focuses on how a visual artist might approach making a complex film, such as *Looking for Oum Kulthum*. Therefore, the exhibition becomes about the portraits of two artists: one a contemporary living artist, i.e. me, and the other the historical legendary artist Oum Kulthum.

MG: *Did you go to Egypt yourself?*
SN: Yes, I went a few times with my Egyptian colleagues and collaborators. We met and interviewed Oum Kulthum's family, her adopted son, and many other experts. Today, I think, after six years of research, I must have one of the largest archives on Oum Kulthum. Sadly, in the end, we didn't shoot the film in Egypt, due to political reasons. We shot it in Casablanca, Morocco.

MG: *How did you finance it?*
SN: I had to raise some of the money by selling my own artwork. Otherwise, the main support came from Middle Eastern private and government sources, as well funds from European countries such as Germany, Austria, France and Italy.

MG: *The production of the film took six years, comparable to* Women without Men. *How do you divide your time during such a period of time?*
SN: Normally, through such long production periods for movies, I keep busy with other activities as well. For example, in 2017, while editing *Looking for Oum Kulthum*, I also directed a major opera, *Aida*, held at

an exhibition at the Venice Biennale and had a solo gallery show in New York and Istanbul.

MG: *You have given music a very powerful role in your other films as well.*
SN: Music has played a major role in my film-based work. I strongly feel that music is a rare art form that transcends cultural differences and affects people on the deepest level without the need for translation. Also, music has helped me to emphasize the emotional nature of my work and, to some degree, neutralize some of the sociopolitical themes.

MG: *Last year, you directed the opera,* Aida, *at the Festspiele in Salzburg. How was it for you to make an opera?*
SN: Fantastic! Although an entirely new experience working with a new art language; in many ways, it was not unlike making a long video installation where one works with the fusion of image and music. Although, I was rather terrified at the beginning being given such a responsibility. I tried to trust my own artistic logic and aesthetics and gave it my best.

MG: *With your Iranian background, you could give another interpretation to the story of* Aida.
SN: *Aida* is a very controversial opera; heavily criticized and regarded as "orientalist" by many Middle Eastern intellectuals. Its depiction of ancient Egyptians and Ethiopians is quite barbaric and racist. Yet the main story revolves around an enslaved Ethiopian princess living in exile in Egypt and in love with the military's commander-in-chief who invades her country. The classic, *Aida,* has been heavily criticized for its *cliché* representations of Arabs and Africans, yet has been hugely popular with the public. So I had the difficult task of making a reinterpretation of *Aida* that addressed all its critics, yet was still enjoyable and had the same level of grandeur as the original.

MG: *I've seen photos of the set: you used a very simple cube and projected videos onto it.*
SN: I took a very minimal approach. The stage was very sculptural and transformed every time it turned.

MG: *Could you tell me about your next project?*
SN: It will be a film about an Iranian woman living and working in Midwest America, in a mostly white, poor and Republican town. The film is inspired by my own experiences and interactions with the part of America that is removed from major cities and Americans whose relationship to foreigners, such as Muslims, are reduced to the information they gather

from the media. I find the cultural clash between someone like myself and the Americans living in such areas so vast, complicated and interesting that I finally decided to make a film about it.

MG: *A film about the clash of cultures...*
SN: ...Yes, culture clashes... Yet, a shared sense of humanity and good values, prevailing underneath our differences.

MG: *Who are you making this film for? Not for these people?*
SN: I'm not sure. I don't usually think about that question when I'm making my films, but I certainly hope a diverse group of people will see this film, which will be in English for a change; and I do think the subject matter is rather timely and relevant today.

DEMETRIO PAPARONI

April 2018

Marta Gnyp: *You are an art historian. What motivated you to study art history?*
Demetrio Paparoni: I've never studied history of art in a systematic way. I am self-taught. I quit my studies in pharmacy before graduating because I was strongly drawn to art. Mine was a journey backwards; I was first interested in contemporary art and, only thereafter, in the history of art.

MG: *Why did you choose to be involved specifically in contemporary art?*
DP: In the '70s, I used to travel to rock concerts during the summer, but I also took the opportunity to see some exhibitions. I was in my element; I was excited by the explosion of thoughts and emotions that art was able to trigger. The initial impact I felt was largely emotional. Later, when I was trying to understand what I saw, I noticed that works are like a hypertext, where every detail forces you to study it, to learn things that you didn't know or on which you have only focused on superficially.

MG: *Every artist forced you to study different contexts.*
DP: The work of each artist is rooted in the history of where he or she comes from, as well as being influenced by his or her own experiences, studies and encounters. Trying to understand Joseph Beuys, Gerhard Richter, Georg Baselitz or Anselm Kiefer forces you to explore the history of Germany. Attempting to understand Richter means you also have to learn about the tragedy of German families during the Nazi period, about the disturbing effects on children and grandchildren of knowing how their loved ones acted during the rise of Nazism. Studying Kiefer involves realising what it means to live on the boundaries between things. Studying Kapoor means you have to enter the boundary between spirituality and science... There is much more to it, of course; I am oversimplifying. This also applies to those artists who have made their work as a radical exploration of language, who force us to engage with philosophy or sociology, such as Joseph Kosuth or Lawrence Weiner.

MG: *Forty years ago, many art history departments didn't include contemporary art in their curricula. Art history was about the history of art, not*

1
Wang Guangyi
Mao Zedong – Red Square
N. 1, 1988
Oil on canvas, 150 × 130 cm

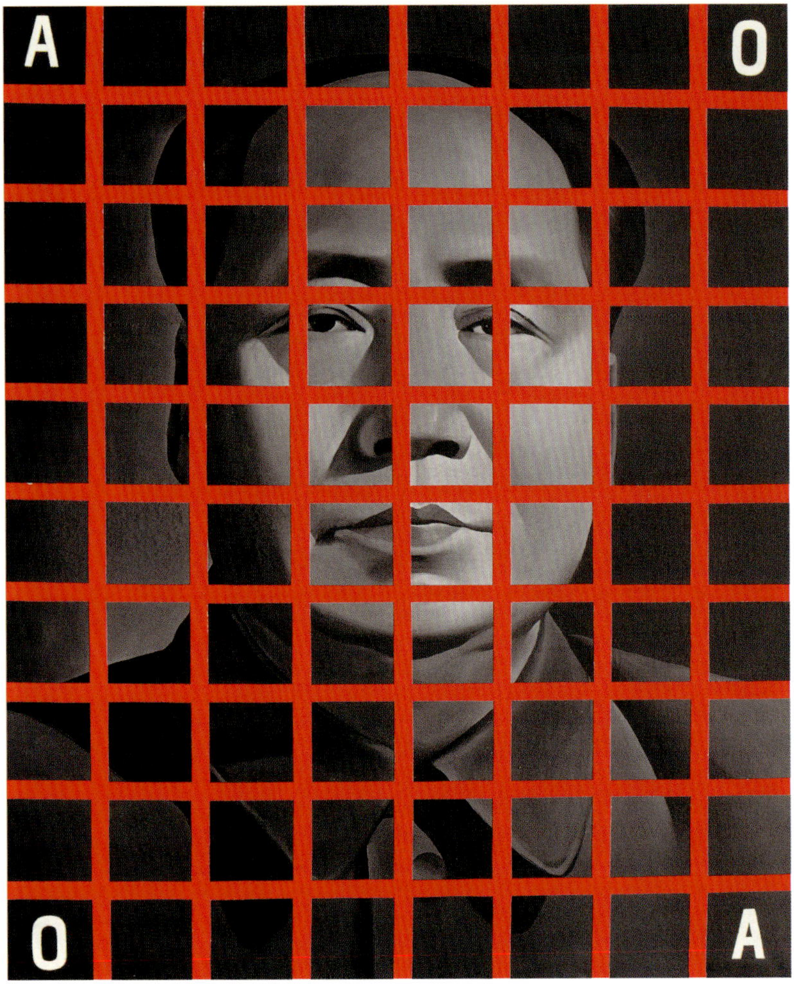

analysing the phenomena and art of the present. It has changed but the question remains: are we able to comment about art from our own time in an appropriate way?

DP: I am convinced that we have to, even if it is difficult. However, I am not convinced that teaching approaches are always correct. A view that is too close-up does not allow for the consideration of complex phenomena that refer to increasingly complex scenarios. One cannot speak of contemporary art without engaging in criticism. We're witnessing the revaluation of artists who were formerly ignored or considered minor, and it would be oversimplifying to say that this is only due to market demand. The fact remains that the market benefits from revaluations and, for this reason, in many cases, we see critical acclaim being used for purposes of manipulation.

MG: *How do you approach the process of valuation or interpretation of art?*
DP: Commenting on the present implies emotional involvement so it is difficult to keep distance to the various phenomena we are considering. Nowadays there are many publications on contemporary art. In addition to texts written by critics, we are helped by those written by the artists themselves, or interviews that they've given. Starting with what the artists say and the motivations they give for their works, it's possible to construct a reasonably correct matrix of interpretation. But to do this, it is first necessary to focus on artists who have a real cultural impact. While the history of art is already well established; something that has been analysed and therefore something you can teach simply by referring to reputable texts, the same is not true for the art of the last fifty years, which is subject to interpretation, reappraisal, debate.

MG: *There is, more or less, a consensus about the meaning of art from previous historical periods versus the fluidity of judgments of contemporary art.*
DP: This doesn't mean that art of the past is immune to revision, that there can be no discoveries or studies leading to the re-evaluation of well-established theories, but the overall system of interpretation is essentially uncontested. Art is living matter; by its nature it tends to question established values and cannot be constrained. To put it another way: although it has not lost its spiritual potential, although it provides information and aesthetic, as well as intellectual enjoyment and can help us understand the art of the present, the art we see in museums cannot help us understand the present itself. Works of art, whether created yesterday or today, always contain secrets that, once decrypted, thwart their innovative potential. I see it this way: the art of the past helps us read the art of the present, the art of the present helps us read the present.

MG: *Do you think we're still in the postmodern period, in terms of aesthetics and theory?*
DP: More so today than we were yesterday. The '80s were transitional years and the '90s confirmed we were entering a new era that is still in existence today. It's been said that postmodernism was born with the ending of ideological contrasts, which are known as the great narratives. I have to take a step back to explain this. During the Second World War, many European artists went to live in New York and made their presence felt on the American art scene, which, since the Armory Show of 1913, had shown signs of restlessness regarding the dominance of European art. A breakthrough was needed, one that would make their autonomy explicit, and then assert the supremacy of American over European art,

which at the time was still spearheaded by Surrealism, with narrative and symbol at the centre of its aesthetic.

MG: *You refer to the New York School and the critic Clement Greenberg.*
DP: In defining the modern and innovative character of the work of artists such as Jackson Pollock or Willem de Kooning, Clement Greenberg focused alongside the subjectivity of the artist first and foremost on the absence of narration, and on the literary and symbolic dimensions of the painting. Greenberg had anticipated this vision of art in his early essay *Towards a Newer Laocoön*, published in *Partisan Review* in 1940, in which he theorized that narrative and symbol belonged more to literature than to the modern visual arts. He thus turned the narrative dimension into the boundary that visual artists could not cross if they were intending to operate in the context of modernity. Around 1947, these principles were elaborated to support abstract expressionism and, later, in the first half of the sixties, to support post-painterly abstraction. In this sense, they constituted a point of reference for the criticism to come, both American and European. It was from these ideological assumptions that the idea of the superiority of American art emerged. The transition to postmodernism re-established the parameters used by American art to denote what was current and what wasn't, and therefore brought into play the role of narrative and symbolism in art. The art of the '80s had a certain restlessness as it went through this change. On the one hand, there were artists who, although figurative, remained anchored to Greenberg's principles of modernism, but on the other hand there were artists, including abstract and post-conceptual artists, who wanted to go beyond formalism. Neither group envisaged the possibility of new approaches at the level of form or aesthetics. At the same time, the shift from the "presentation" of the object to its representation has ceased to be considered a retrograde step.

MG: *So, did postmodernism provide artists with total freedom, in your opinion?*
DP: Outside of any ideological system, the artist has enormous freedom: there are no codes that have to be complied with in order to be considered "current". In the context of postmodernism, this turning point, nowadays, affords us an alternative perspective on artists who were previously not given proper attention. Decades later, it's curious to observe that there're artists who were considered *progressive* at the time, because they avoided any involvement in narration and symbolism, yet appear *conservative* today; while others, who would've been considered traditionalists because they thought the opposite way, do not appear as such nowadays. It's by considering the role of narration that this turning point can be under-

stood. Works like the *Cremaster Cycle* by Matthew Barney would have been unthinkable in the '80s.

MG: *Artists have also given up the idea of avant-garde.*
DP: It was clear to young people who appeared on the art scene in the '90s that planning for the future, in the way that the avant-gardes thought and had done from the early 20th century up to the seventies '70s, was no longer a given. So, art took care of the here and now. To do this, it could only look for the causes of present-day problems in the folds of history. It had to give more weight to the story. Hence the obvious interest of art in historical themes and subjects, in bringing them back into play, often through works full of familiar details, juxtaposed in such a way as to give life to a yet to be published whole.

MG: *You wrote a book about contemporary art and its methods. What are the methods?*
DP: Artists have always tried to apply methods in order to arrive at their desired result. The method adopted reflects the spirit of the era and goes hand in hand with the advances of science and developments in philosophy. In the modernist era, the work of the impressionists developed in parallel with the evolution of the photographic medium, which would later go on to have a deep impact on the work of other artists, not only in terms of form, but also by indicating a way forward. For example, it allowed for performances or temporary installations to be documented. The way to de-contextualise or juxtapose the images and the automatism of the surrealists owes much to psychoanalysis and to the discovery of the unconscious; Pop art adopted the methods of mechanical printing and poster design used in advertising; minimalism adopted mathematical and geometrical designs, and so on. Underlying every work of art, there's a point of reference prompting the artist to find a way to construct his or her work by following a method.

MG: *Could you give me an example of a contemporary artist?*
DP: Chuck Close, a super-figurative artist, constructs his work from a grid, enabling him to reproduce a photographic image on canvas. The fact that, in the '60s and '70s, Close concentrated his focus on the face of the subject in such a way as to eliminate all narrative and symbolism is inseparable from his conception of art. Certainly the use of the grid is not a novelty in art, but this doesn't mean that it always leads to the same conclusions. Now we all know how old the use of the grid is; it's the way in which artists use it, making it a personal method that changes the meaning of the work. The method determines the spirit of the times.

MG: *Do you refer to the modernistic reading of the grid?*

DP: Not only. In the past, the grid was used to achieve as faithful a replica of the image as possible; now that a photograph is preferred for this purpose, the use of the grid leads to a more hand-crafted and uncertain image. The same method therefore takes on a different meaning depending on the times in which it is used. It would therefore be overly simplistic to say there's nothing new under the sun. The Chinese artist, Wang Guangyi, another example, twenty years after Close's first "heads", created portraits of Mao using a grid. Unlike Close, however, who, after all, conceals the grid, Wang Guangyi brings it to the forefront to reveal the trick behind the transformation of a political leader into a charismatic figure. In this case, the highlighted grid has the task of desacrilizing the depicted subject, which is thus part of a story. Aniconic painters, such as Frank Stella, Robert Ryman, Sol LeWitt, Sean Scully, Gunter Förg, Peter Halley, Jonathan Lasker, Ding Yi, Liu Wei, Sarah Morris, Bernard Frize and many others, have also used the grid, but have given it a completely different significance.

MG: *So the same method can be applied for different reasons.*

DP: We must be careful not to confuse the method with the means: the method is the strategy that enables the artist to arrive at a form, results in which he recognises himself. Being aware of the method used by the artist is useful to the critic because it allows him or her to not only understand the artist's approach to art, but also his or her attitudes. The method, for instance, helps you understand whether the artist has an objective or subjective vision, an instinctive or scientific approach. It matters less whether the image was obtained by using a grid, a photographic projection, a tracing on a light table or by computer generation. What matters is that the form is the result of the process of its construction, so the method becomes a strong element in the evaluation of the artwork. If you go to a piece by Anish Kapoor, you cannot help but ask yourself which method he used in order to give life to his anti-forms; when observing a photo of Thomas Demand, displaying places that seem real, but which are actually made from three-dimensional models in paper or cardboard, you have to ask yourself why he chose this method to represent reality; the drawings of Cai Guo-Qiang created by micro-explosions of gunpowder refer to the tradition of fireworks in China, thus denoting the weight that the artist gives to the culture of belonging; the oil paintings of Nicola Samorì, flayed with his bare hands or with a scalpel, a burin or a chisel, or forced by the pressure of one half of the painting on the other, show us wounds in the canvas of the painting where the method reveals how for this artist, painting imitates a biological process that, in time, leads

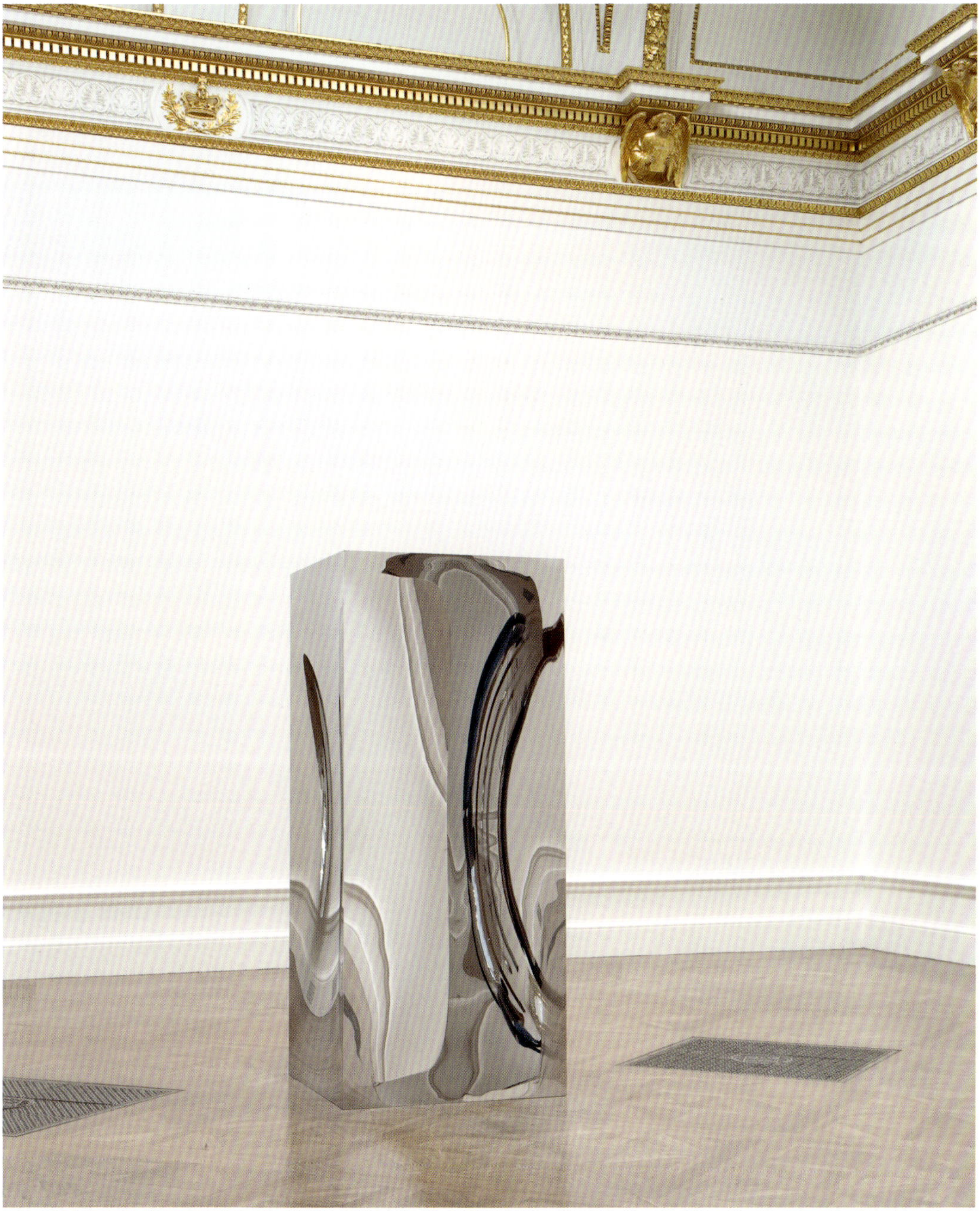

2
Anish Kapoor
Non Object Door, 2008
Stainless steel,
281 × 118 × 118 cm

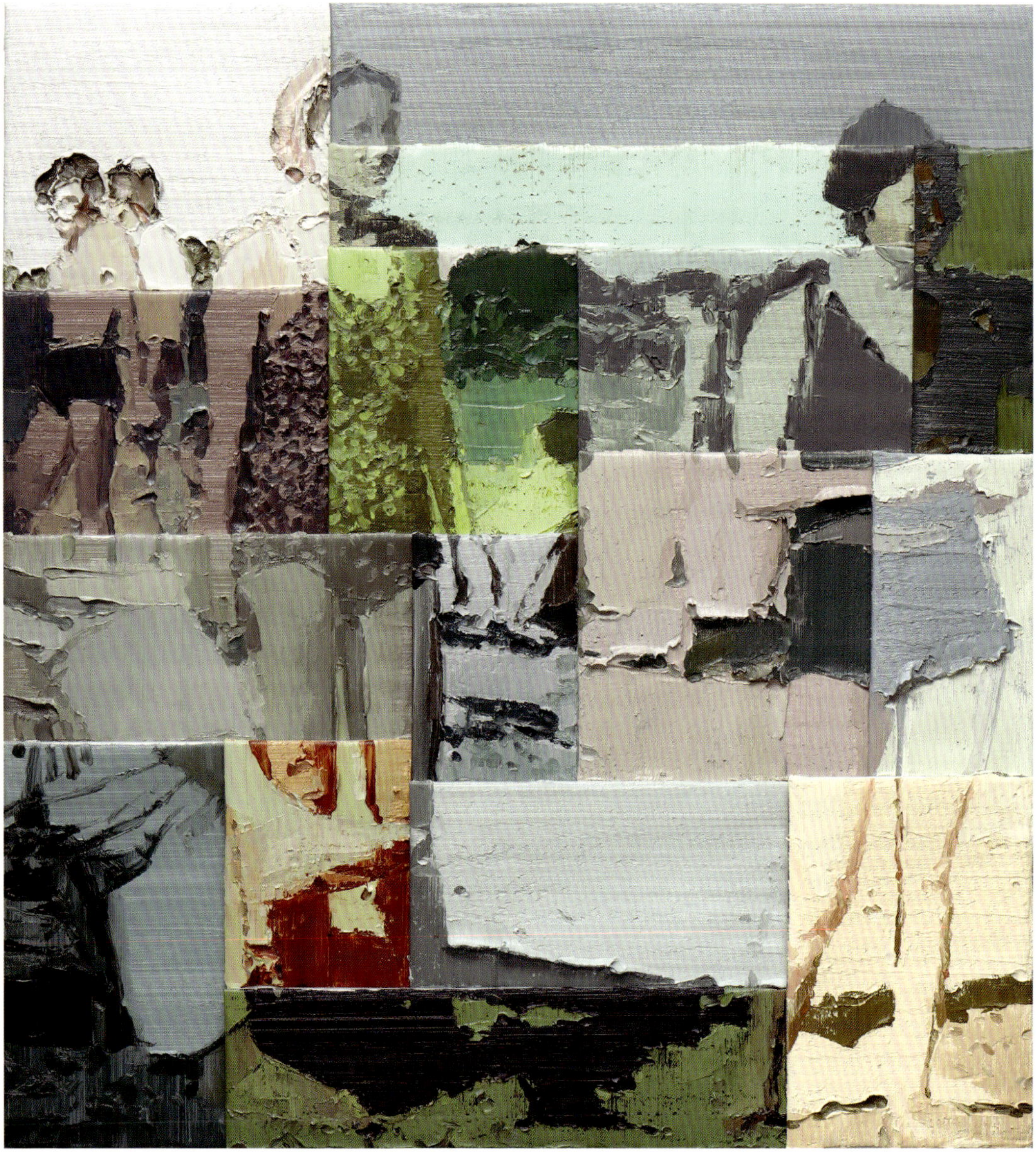

3
Li Songsong
Big Girls, 2013
Oil on aluminum panel,
280 × 250 cm

it to age and die as living beings do. Let's stick with painting: one of the methods used by Li Songsong is to start with a well-known image, taken from the media, and to reconstruct it as a painting, fragment by fragment, using highly mixed media, focusing on one area at a time in random order. It's only when he has finished painting the last piece that the image will take shape, revealing itself to the artist in its entirety. The method used by Li Songsong refers to the difficulty of interpreting reality through the information that comes from the media. The method is, in short, the touchstone that allows the critic to access the artist's personal universe.

MG: *Do you think that, one day, we might abandon the categorization of mediums or categorization of abstract or figurative art?*
DP: The contrast between abstract art and figurative art was radicalized by the formalism of Greenberg. As we've already said, a new wave began in the '80s and its identity was defined in the '90s, however, when artists definitively clarified that art would not be playing its game on the opposition's home ground. In the 1990s, Jonathan Lasker told me that, whenever a painter bisects a pictorial surface with a horizontal stroke, he is depicting the horizon. This indicates how bland the distinction between abstraction and figuration can be.
We assume the intentions of the artist are to define the nature of the work, this also means we can read an abstract work figuratively, and vice versa. Peter Halley's abstract geometric paintings have a figurative narrative that has sociological implications typical of realist painting. This is why I actually believe that these two visions, the abstract and the figurative, can coincide completely with each other. The fact that many artists have rejected the idea of a world regulated by contrasts indicates a turning point.

MG: *What do you think about the opening up of the art world? As an art historian, are you happy about outsider artists and self-taught artists entering the art field?*
DP: Those who approach art are always interested in knowing the individual artist's history, his or her training, even if this has an extremely limited impact on the judgement of the artwork. Contamination is increasingly frequent and accepted in the arts; any contribution to the debate is considered a resource. As an artist, you accept anyone who's capable of adding to what has already been said, even giving weight to a small segment of a sentence, if this opens up new possibilities.

MG: *Do you think, as an artist, you need to have an awareness of art history? Can everybody be an artist?*

DP: Personally, I don't know a single artist who isn't interested in the history of art. After World War II, artists were already looking at the experiences of the historical avant-gardes as history of art. And today, we consider the experiences of the late 20th century to be history of art. Despite this, there are artists today who, without knowing it, repeat experiences that were widely consumed in the '60s and '70s; this is confirmation of the need to know what happened. Today, the artist and the critic are faced with a problem that's not so inconsiderable: the art scene has expanded dramatically, artists who live in countries once excluded from our field of vision have come into play. The internet has amplified the amount of information we can access and, since there's too much information, there's too much we don't know. This makes the contemporary scene particularly complex, much more complex than it was a few decades ago. In relation to the history of art, each artist confronts his or her own limits. The more you focus on something and study it in depth, the less you know how far it is from that perimeter; the more you enlarge the area you survey, the less you go into detail.

MG: *Defining the quality of contemporary art is one of the biggest issues of our time. We don't have any fixed characteristics of what or how art should be. Do you believe in "objective" quality? Or is quality simply declared by those who have the greatest authority and power?*
DP: We recognize the value of art on the basis of what our culture allows us to appreciate, as such. This means that judgements of merit are somehow manipulated through a system of information that directs our evaluation. In the '50s, there were some critics that went out of their way to show that Hopper was a minor artist. Now, there is no doubt that Pollock won because he invented a language never seen before, but it's a big leap from that to stigmatizing artists like Hopper, or the American regionalists who came before him, as something lesser. Today, we know it's not like that. For example, today, American criticism honors regionalists by rediscovering them through the work of John Currin. History is living matter.

MG: *What do you think about the theory of art being present in the works of many artists? Do you think artists should be educated in art theory?*
DP: It seems unlikely that a good artist would not be able to justify what he or she was doing by integrating it into the theoretical debate of our day. It might be that he or she refuses to verbalize it, but it wouldn't be the case that the artist didn't know what he or she was doing and why.

MG: *You've been in the art world for more than 30 years. What has been the biggest change during this period, in your opinion?*

DP: In terms of language, the most substantial changes for artists have arisen from the possibility of using the tools of scientific technology within their own work.

MG: *You are very much involved in curating and writing about Asian artists. Is their understating of art and art history different from the Western one?*
DP: Chinese artists know the history of Western art better than you can imagine. In the first half of the '80s, artists were still required to respect the rules of Maoist realism. The limitations on freedom of movement, the lack of circulation of books and the consequent lack of information was not comparable with other artistic experiences. In the second half of the '80s, the Chinese translation of Gombrich's *History of Art* aroused great interest in the Chinese art world. In the meantime it's become easier to cross borders. All this has led to a greater knowledge of Western art, both from the past and the present; knowledge that has given rise to comparison. It's no coincidence that we also find iconographic themes of the Christian art from the Old Continent in the works of artists such as Yue Minjun, Wang Guangyi, Zhang Huan, Zeng Fanzhi and many others.

MG: *What is so specific about Chinese contemporary art?*
DP: Within the artistic field in China, over a period of about twenty years, artists have entered postmodernism, rapidly consuming the experiences of modernism. This explains why Chinese artists have often simultaneously used very differing language to express themselves. A Westerner, who had been going around galleries in Beijing or Shanghai for the last thirty years, could have confused a personal exhibition with a collective exhibition. At the same time, if, on the one hand, Chinese artists have used our own language, on the other, they have never lost the connection with their artistic tradition, from landscape painting to calligraphy, from the manufacture of porcelain to woodwork, through to Maoist realism. If you talk to Chinese artists, many of them tell you, with a certain pride, that they were influenced by traditional Chinese art and, in particular, by artists of the Song, Yuan and Ming dynasties. A pre-modern artist who has influenced and continues to influence the training of contemporary artists is Qi Baishi, who died in 1957. It's necessary to look at the contemporary scenario from the point of view of an Asian to understand the full extent of the great artistic revolution experienced by China. Suffice it to say that, although not repudiating their culture, they face languages and iconographic themes that were once alien to them.

MG: *Do you think we can have anything like a global history of art?*
DP: To think that a global history of art can exist is to believe there can

4
Nicola Samorì
Emanto, 2016
Oil on linen, 200 × 150 cm

be single models of reference for all; I don't think that's possible. On the other hand, it *is* possible to have a history of art that tackles the art of different geographical areas in different chapters, analysing the points of contact and the differences. The interests revolving around art make it very difficult to write a global history of art, because we're still in an American-centric system. Damien Hirst explained it very well when he said that, if English art continues being important, in a few decades we'll consider Hamilton and not Warhol to be the father of Pop art. Think how different a chapter on Pop art could be if it were written by an English person, rather than an American.

I don't think we'll ever be able to conceive a global history of art, because if there is one thing that indicates a difference between populations, it's the arts. Let's ask ourselves some questions: when visiting big international exhibitions, do we always recognise the area the individual artists originate from? Of course not. At the level of form, at the level of language, in many cases we have doubts. But if we explore the individual works in depth, the differences emerge easily because the sense of belonging is a feeling rooted in each individual. The sense of belonging affects both the method and the content, which in turn affect the language. I don't think this will cease to be the case in the future.

MG: *I saw a photo of you and Arthur Danto. He declared the death of art because art needed philosophy in order to be understood. Do you agree with this statement in our time?*

DP: Arthur Danto and I have been friends for a long time. For about fifteen years, he collaborated with the magazine of which I was editor, *Tema Celeste*, with writings and conversations that we regularly published. It's also thanks to him that the art of the '80s and '90s has partially freed itself from formalist theses. Danto's attention was focused on what allowed one to recognize something as a work of art, in a particular historical moment, something that previously would not have been considered as such. He was also interested in the way and the extent to which the historical context affects the nature of art and its definition. The fact that these questions were pertinent then and remain so today, demonstrates that a painting from the past remains recognizable as a work of art, even if seen in a photographic reproduction. This is not so with Warhol's *Brillo Boxes*, the central object of Danto's investigation, or with many current works. Inevitably, thoughts run to Duchamp and his readymades, especially those from 1915 through to 1917. Danto has focused his attention on the *Brillo Boxes* because they don't presuppose a manipulation of the object, they're silk-screened, wooden boxes that faithfully reproduce Brillo cardboard boxes. In a supermarket, no one would've taken Warhol's copies for works

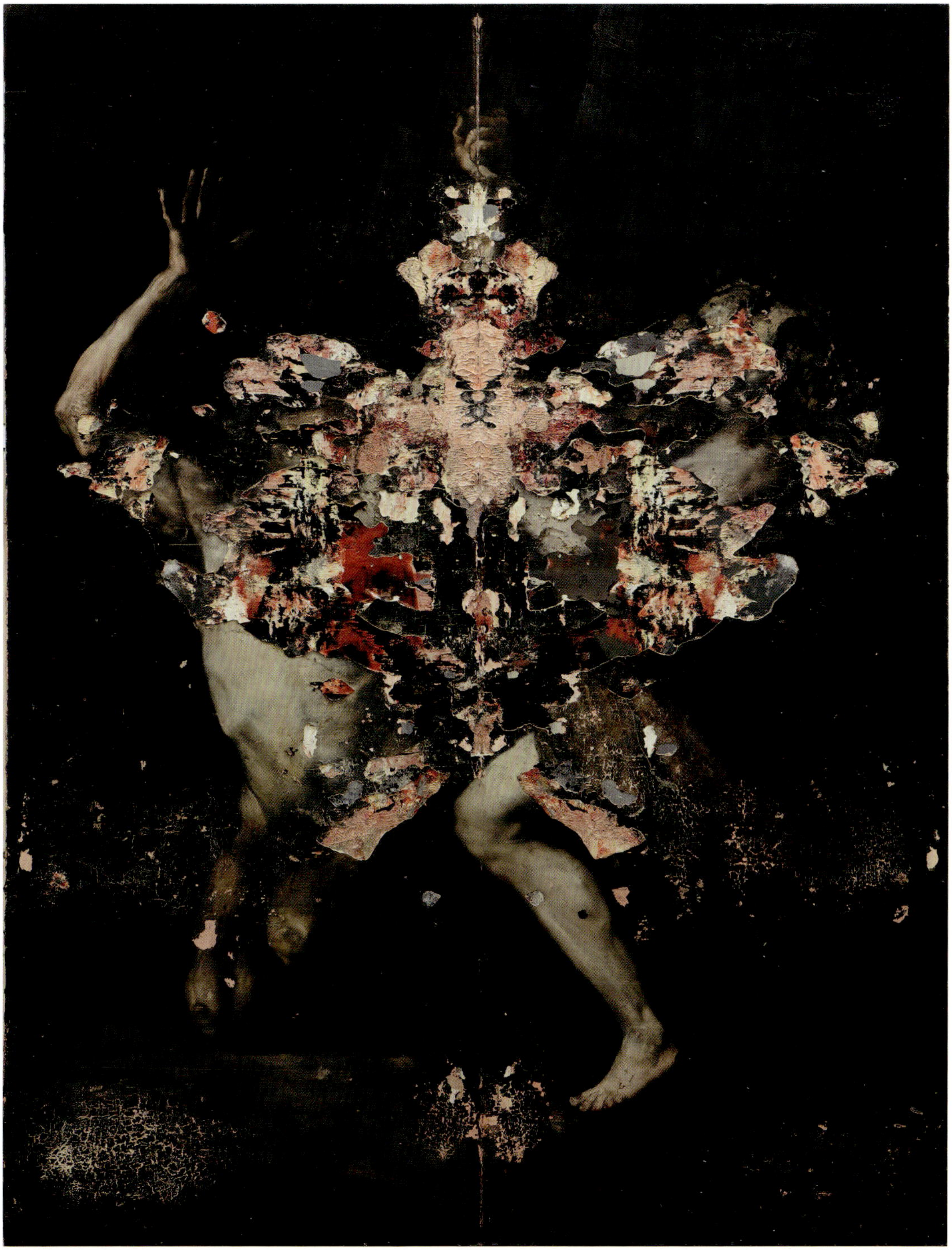

of art. This is a leap towards Duchamp's readymades, whose content lies in their conceptual manipulation. Duchamp doesn't exhibit a urinal for what it is, but turns it into something other than what it is. Danto believes that Warhol, not Duchamp, was the first to witness Hegel's predicted death of art and this is because Duchamp's objects are aesthetically uninteresting but not trivial, while those of Warhol, explains Danto, are just banal. The difference between Duchamp and Warhol, according to Danto, is the fact that Warhol's *Brillo Box* work has a purely philosophical justification.

MG: *You operate as an art critic and curator. Which role do you prefer?*
DP: Curating an exhibition is fun; writing is much less so. It's very tiring. I'm more gratified by the idea of having written a good book than to have curated a good exhibition.

MG: *In your opinion, why is art criticism having such a difficult?*
DP: The art scene has become much larger and everything changes quickly. Being informed about everything that happens is very demanding, not to mention that gaining a prominent place in the art world also involves a commitment to public relations. Making sense of everything that's been seen, then transforming it into writing, requires attention, time and concentration. Besides, compared with previous decades, much has changed in the way artists are approached. Today, the relationship with the artist is increasingly mediated by galleries or by those who represent them and the logic regulating the work isn't always linked to cultural dynamics.

MG: *Can this cause problems for you as a critic?*
DP: I'll give you an example: in 2017 I published a book on the representation of the devil in the art of yesterday and today. I wanted to include some pictures by Basquiat and Mapplethorpe in the book, but the persons responsible for the artists' estates wouldn't allow it. Which is strange, considering that the book has a very rigorous context. Aside from the numbers, it's absurd, in my opinion, that you have to ask for permission to publish an image; what is incomprehensible is the fact that I regularly published works by these artists when they were alive. Now, with the understanding that copyright is an inalienable value, with the understanding that it's normal for a business to be created around the work of artists in order to keep the foundations of their work alive, the fact that the *estate* may or may not grant you the right to publish is a limitation on the freedom of criticism, which can create conditioning. Nobody is interested in going against those who, in the future, might not grant you access to a loan for an exhibition or an image for a publication. Personally, I think that, once an artwork enters the world, even more than

in the past when it's been historicized, it no longer belongs to the artist but becomes a common good. But, I also understand that artists have every right to not accept being placed in a context in which they don't recognise themselves. Decisions made by artists are dictated by cultural interests, those made by people who represent them are not necessarily respectful of the artist's thoughts.

MG: *Do you think that art has become more popular recently or is this an illusion?*
DP: Art has become more popular thanks to the digital revolution, which has greatly amplified its catchment area. But before the '90s, Warhol and Pop art were already marking a transitional moment of this nature. In the '60s, in a student's home, you could find a poster reproducing a newly created piece of Pop art. A moderately wealthy collector could have a high-circulation signed screen-print. Certainly, there is a big difference between a reproduction and an original, but it's a fact that a penniless student and a rich collector could look at the same images. It was a phenomenon that was previously unpublished. It's since then, and particularly since Warhol, that artists have aspired to be perceived as rock stars. Today it's not surprising that artists dream of long queues of visitors wanting to get in to their exhibitions, the same queues as those at the gates of a popular rock band's concert. It was the artists themselves who favored the idea that art should be for everyone.

MG: *Don't you think that art's always been elitist and this is one of the inherent characteristics of art?*
DP: Art has always been elitist due to the simple fact that the possession of an important and costly work helps define the status of its owner.

MG: *What role do you think public museums should play?*
DP: A museum's mission is to conserve and protect the best art and make it accessible to all. What museums preserve are the foundations from which successive interpretations, of artist-generations to come, will follow. This means the relationship between historicity and contemporaneity is necessary. In this sense, a museum is the crucible in which, just as in a chemical reaction, different elements, and in many cases opposites, interact, giving life to new compounds. A museum isn't a cemetery of illustrious works; it should be seen as a place that continues generating vitality.

MG: *Which have been the most interesting exhibitions you've organized, and why?*

DP: I've dealt, on several occasions, with the theme of the impact of the telematic revolution on art, as a theme. The *Timer* exhibition (2007) at the Triennale di Milano and the *Surreal versus Surrealism* exhibition at the IVAM in Valencia (2011) highlighted how society has become increasingly abstract and surreal. *Timer* highlighted the impact on our imagination of live television broadcasts during the Second Gulf War and live television coverage of the attack on the World Trade Center. In the '90s, I worked for a long time on abstraction, but, in 2018, I curated an exhibition of figurative painting at the Stelline Foundation in Milan, because it amazes me that, in big international exhibitions, this expressive form is too often given the role of servant in relation to contemporary art.

MG: *Who do you consider to be the most relevant artists of the last 40 years?*
DP: Gerhard Richter, Chuck Close, Anish Kapoor, Damien Hirst, Matthew Barney, Jeff Koons, Maurizio Cattelan, Olafur Eliasson, Takashi Murakami, John Currin. These artists have had a contagious effect on the West. The situation in China is very different, where there are extraordinary artists who, regardless of having paved the way for change, have not had a real, formal influence on the work of young artists. It should be considered that the development of contemporary art in China has gone hand in hand with its enormous social changes; changes that've allowed artists to create works of art that they couldn't have prevously imagined. Those same protagonists of the new scene, who would have had to give formal direction to the younger ones, have themselves changed their language several times, reflecting the continuous evolution of Chinese society. An example for everyone is Wang Guangyi. When talking about this a while ago with Li Songsong, one of the most significant artists of his generation – born in 1973 – Songsong told me that, according to him on a conceptual but not formal level, Ai Weiwei will exert a strong influence on future generations. He added, "at least this is my hope". It's symbolic to remark how distant the work of Li Songsong is from that of Ai Weiwei. This makes it clear how much Chinese artists feel the need for art to play a role in the country's political evolution. In any case, when it comes to ideas in China, artists who have been actively involved in the 85 movement, particularly Huang Yong Ping and Xu Bing, as well as Zhang Xiaogang and Liu Xiaodong, have been influential on subsequent generations. In Russia, I honestly couldn't tell you. Obviously, the list of artistic giants could be much longer. There are artists who have no impact on other artists, but this doesn't detract from their work.

MG: *You wrote a book on Chuck Close. What do you think about the recent reactions of museums towards his work in the context of the #Metoo*

movement? Do you think that art should be looked at through the prism of morality? Is there any connection between aesthetics and ethics?
DP: When I learned the news, I wrote a post on my Facebook page: "The Washington National Gallery canceled the show of a giant of the second half of the 20th century, on grounds that have nothing to do with art. This is an attack on art and on its capacity to have a higher existence than the life of its artists. Will paintings be sent to the stake soon? Will Gauguin and Schiele disappear from museums? What about Caravaggio and Bernini? Those who took this decision at the National Gallery aren't mad, they are lucid enemies of culture". There is not much to add, except that these gestures of extreme puritanism conceal an extreme hypocrisy, so much so that those same people who have censored Close for yet to be proven events unrelated to his art would nonetheless be careful not to get rid of his work.

MG: *You have written mostly about male artists. Is there any reason for that?*
DP: When I curate an exhibition, I choose the artists according to the project. Should I do a count to see if the balance is politically correct? Should I also pay particular attention to ensuring that all social and ethnic balances are respected? If that's what you think, it's ok by me if you think of me as a politically incorrect critic. In the recent exhibition, *The New Frontiers of Painting*, that I curated in Milan, only seven out of 34 artists were women. You're right: that's not many. I am surely a victim of a culture that leads me to look at work in one way, rather than another. Things will be different for the younger generations, (I hope).

MG: *Where do we go from here?*
DP: The most significant innovations, if they can be considered as such, are coming from science, which offers tools and techniques that allow you to create extraordinarily interesting exhibitions, both in visual and conceptual terms. I'm thinking of Eliasson, for example, or Frederic de Wilde. On the one hand, science has radicalized the idea that one can use the language one wants, in the freest way possible; on the other, the task of designing the future is now entrusted to science. Artists will certainly not stop working or trying new paths, but I think no one today can predict the direction they'll take.

FRANÇOIS PINAULT

May 2015

Marta Gnyp: *Mr Pinault, I brought you two examples of the artist editions that the newspaper Die Welt issues once a year. Each special edition is filled exclusively with images made or designed by one selected artist.*
François Pinault: That's a very good idea.

MG: *I brought you the latest edition, which was made by Cindy Sherman and also the one made by Georg Baselitz. I heard some rumors, so I thought you might enjoy it.*
FP: (laughs) Have you visited the Venice Biennale? Did you see the Baselitz installation there?

MG: *I did. I know who bought it.*
FP: (laughs) It's a very good piece. I bought it on the first day of the Biennale.

MG: *Some critical voices complain about how institutional exhibitions, such as biennales, have become great sales opportunities for galleries.*
FP: It's very difficult to avoid this, since you need to promote artists. There are exhibitions going on in galleries, museum exhibitions, not to mention art fairs, all around the world, punctuated by institutional exhibitions such as the Venice Biennale. At the same time, there are more and more art-lovers who wish to own artworks. The only risk is that, in this context, some people might be tempted by speculation, which is very difficult to fight. Fortunately, it concerns very few artists, not all of them.

MG: *Why has art become so important in your life? Is it a passion or an obsession, or both?*
FP: As a matter of fact, it's art that captured me. I come from a humble background and a tough region, Brittany, where art wasn't part of our daily lives. But, somehow, the Breton forests, its coastline, its granite landscape have sharpened my sensitivity to things beyond the ordinary. The passion for art itself came to me later in life, but in the meantime,

more than forty years ago, the development of my businesses gave me the opportunity to travel more often and visit museums, as well as art centers, more frequently. Visiting exhibitions made me realize that I wanted to develop a more personal and intimate relationship with art; a relationship that over time became a real passion. Is this an obsession? It depends on your definition of obsession. If you take the word in its literal meaning, then the answer is "No". Having said that, fascination for art permanently sustains itself, grows, virtually never stops. So, yes, I am passionate about art or, if you prefer, an art obsessed with a constructive approach. I would say I'm a committed man, in the true sense of the word.

MG: *When was the first time you felt attracted to an artwork?*
FP: At the beginning of the seventies – I was visiting an art gallery when I saw a painting by Paul Sérusier that moved me. It shows a farmyard and the main figure reminded me of my grandmother. At first, I thought my attraction was due to this anecdotal dimension, but then, there was something else. The more I looked at it, the more I discovered. In a way, this painting by Sérusier acted as a catalyst. This acquisition opened my eyes.

MG: *What happened between the 1970s and 1991, when you bought the most expensive Mondrian painting ever, for $8.8 million*
FP: I've always visited museums, galleries, and other art institutions. Gradually I've learnt to look at artworks properly. My eyes had become trained, so, I could see the quality of this masterpiece by Mondrian.

MG: *Why was this Mondrian so appealing to you?*
FP: Actually, I was in New York to see a sculpture by Henry Moore when I came across this work by Mondrian that took my breath away. It's difficult to express, with words, how you feel inside in front of a masterpiece. I was literally struck. It's a well-known fact: passion is priceless. Even though it took me two hours to make a decision. From that moment, I realized I could dream of a collection with very high standards.

MG: *How did you start to actualize this idea of creating an extraordinary collection?*
FP: When I purchased the *Tableau Losangique* by Mondrian, I had this feeling of an epiphany, only to quickly realize it was just the beginning of a big, new adventure. I became aware of the fact that creativity was not done for, that art still exists nowadays, and that artists, worldwide, produce enthralling work. Each discovery led me to explore new territories. I developed an interest in post-war American artists and that took me towards the art of my time and contemporary creative practices. I've

1
François Pinault

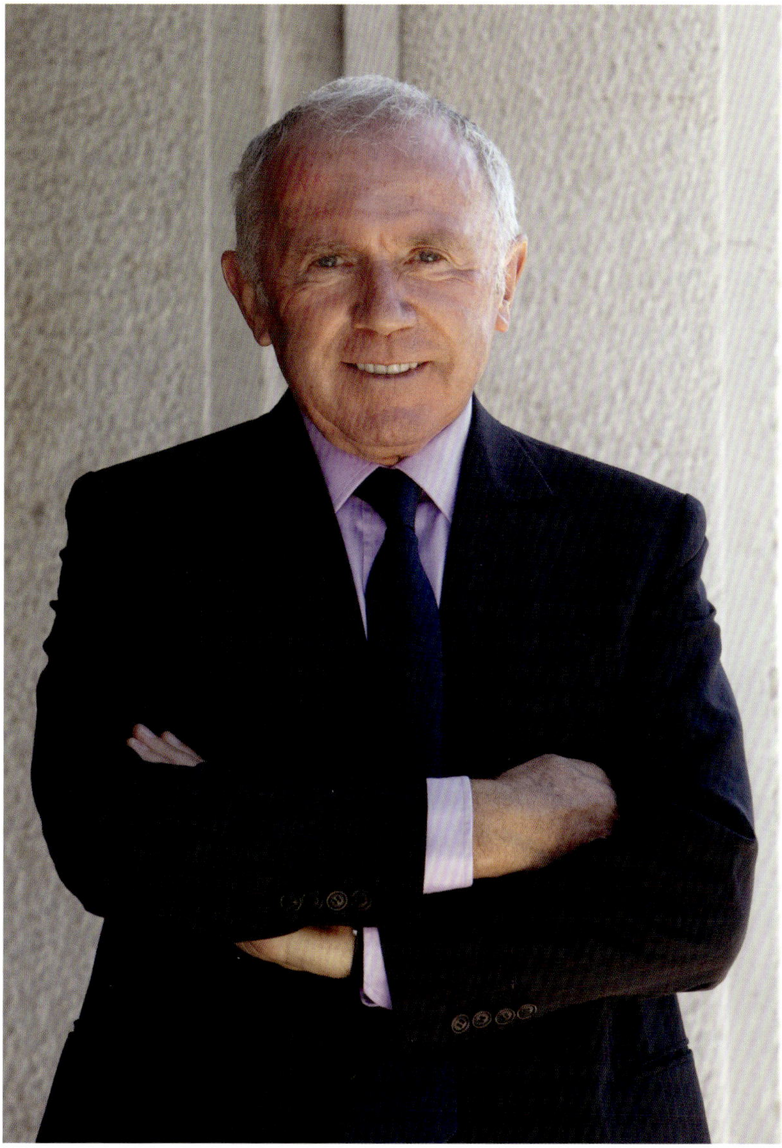

combined paintings, sculptures, videos, photographs, and also installations deriving from different tendencies and cultures.

MG: *In 1980, you were at an auction for the first time; in 1998 you bought Christie's. Was it only a business decision, or were you emotionally attracted to an auction house and auctions?*
FP: I live two parallel lives. My job as an entrepreneur and my job as a collector are two separate ones that never cross paths with one another. The acquisition of Christie's comes from the entrepreneurial side. In

the art field, emotion is vital, whereas in business, it's usually seen as a suspicious feeling.

MG: *Are you an auction buyer? Do you like gambling?*
FP: When it comes to art, I visit galleries, as well as auction houses, and not just Christie's. In the same way, I check Christie's catalogues and those of other auction houses, but not only for contemporary art. Nobody can possibly believe that auctions are a form of gambling only because some "staged" public auctions use the spectacle, the suspense and the emotion. There isn't much room for hazard.

MG: *An auction is a place to create a price. Have you ever influenced the price of an artist's work through deliberately paying a higher price?*
FP: I don't think auctions create prices. They are the proof, the photograph of the value agreed on by the market's art dealers at a certain time and based on a complex set of criteria.

MG: *Many collectors follow what you do and what you buy. Do you see it as a responsibility?*
FP: I don't want to impose my own choices on others. My purpose is to share my passion for art with as many people as possible. A true art lover makes decisions freely; he has to go beyond ordinary feelings determined by a special aesthetic to express his own aesthetic sensitivity. Wanting to convert someone to an aesthetic order doesn't make sense. However, if you can contribute towards arousing people's interest in contemporary art, you've already achieved something. It's my one and only responsibility.

MG: *You have carved out one of the most amazing careers in post-war Europe, building your corporate empire from scratch. What was and is the key to your success?*
FP: Firstly, I don't like the term: "success". It's just an illusion and doesn't mean anything. I come from a rather humble background. I went to boarding school; a religious high school, attended mainly by bourgeois children who despised the peasant's son I was, back then. On top of that, I wasn't into studying. So I left school early. I wanted to take revenge on all these people who had bullied me at school. I came back home very determined, resolute to do something with my life. And that's how I started my own business in the timber trade. I worked very hard.

MG: *Did you ever take revenge on a person?*
FP: Not really. I don't care about it anymore. With the experience of my life and career, I want to do everything positively and not as a reaction.

MG: *You don't like to think about the past?*
FP: I feel in perfect harmony with my time. I believe one must keep up with the times. We can't live by looking back on the past with nostalgia. The past is the past and doesn't let you take any risks. The present and the future mean creation, boldness, and adventure. Of course, I still doubt a lot. Because nothing can ever be taken for granted.

MG: *How would you define the Zeitgeist of now?*
FP: Uncertain, interesting, in motion. I'm very happy to live now. No nostalgia. Past is not better than today. Even the insecurity and uncertainty of our time is, for me, very challenging and exciting.

MG: *Is this the secret behind why you're so strong and full of energy?*
FP: There are so many things to be done, so many territories to explore, so many opportunities to seize... If your objective in life is to be a bourgeois and have a comfortable life, of course you might find it difficult now.

MG: *You've been playing with the idea of a private museum for a long time. First with Île Seguin, near Paris, then with museums in Venice. Why is having a private museum so important to you?*
FP: Living with works of art led me to question myself even more; it prompted me to break with the comfort of a routine, to reassess myself, to become more attentive to the world's developments. I'm fascinated by this conception of art and I'm willing to share it with those who want it.

MG: *We are now facing a surge of private museums worldwide. Why do you think private museums have become so popular?*
FP: I can't really answer for other people. As far as I am concerned, I quickly felt this desire to share the pieces of art, that I loved and collected, with the public. This project could be actualized in Venice, in two prestigious locations: Palazzo Grassi and Punta della Dogana, completed recently by the Teatrino. They have been wonderfully restored and converted by Tadao Ando to suit contemporary art. It's not a static collection. On the contrary, it's a collection that tends to capture the living realities of this world, turned upside down at an increasingly fast pace.

MG: *Is visibility a very important factor for the importance of an artist and a collector?*
FP: Obviously, visibility is important for artists, especially in Venice. But certainly not for an art collector. Every collector dreams of hiding behind the artworks.

MG: *Your financial position is much better than the position many public museums are in. You can buy better works, you can act more quickly and more efficiently; you are not dependent on low budgets and the slow administration of public institutions. Do you compete with public museums?*
FP: In my mind, there is no competition between a private museum and a public one. Quite the opposite, actually. I think there is a lot of mutual benefit in the coexistence of both public and private museums. As you know, there is currently an exhibition dedicated to Martial Raysse at Palazzo Grassi. This exhibition comes after one that was held at Centre Pompidou and to which I lent many works. The two exhibitions offer a journey and a perspective that complement each other.

MG: *The general opinion, which I also share, about the Venice exhibitions this year was that your show* Slip of the Tongue *at Punta della Dogana was better than the official Biennale exhibition. Is this not a kind of competition?*
FP: That is your opinion, which I presume is valid for one year… I would say that we complete each other. The Biennale is very inspiring and challenging for artists, curators, galleries… For all of us.

MG: *Do you think a private collector like you can write a different art history than a public museum?*
FP: No one can claim a monopoly in the creative field. As you said, public institutions have to deal with many requirements, financial obstacles and also legal and regulatory procedures. The choice of works and their presentation in public museums are subject to a complexity of balance, but also a concern of impartiality and geographic interests. That's not the case at a private institution, anyway not at Palazzo Grassi, Punta della Dogana, Teatrino. My choices reflect my eyes, my interests, my commitments and the risks I'm taking. There isn't any specific rule to apply, except to own a work I love. I'm interested in young artists, while still supporting the ones I've been following for a long time, like Thomas Schütte, for example.

MG: *Why did you choose the artist Danh Vo to curate your exhibition?*
FP: From Marcel Duchamp, with the 1936 surrealist exhibition, to Andy Warhol or Mike Kelley, or recently, Maurizio Cattelan; many artists have acted as curators of exhibitions. Asking an artist seemed to me an interesting way to bring in a new point of view on the collection. Regarding Danh Vo, besides the fact that I own many of his works, I was very impressed by the way he had curated the *Felix Gonzalez Torres Exhibition* in Brussels, in 2010. I found his knowledge of space, his sensitivity, his ability to empathize with the work of other artists, extremely fascinating. I have to say, the result is beyond my hopes. He took hold of the space and the pieces to build a true work of art.

Punta della Dogana, 2015

MG: *Public museums complain that they need to attract visitors and, therefore, adjust their programs accordingly. Is the number of visitors also a consideration for you?*

FP: I think, even more important than the number of visitors, is the quality of the exhibitions and the cultural program on offer; also the relationship with the public: the reception, the educational and informational support, the cultural development, and the access for people unfamiliar with art or kept away for geographic, social, economic or health-related reasons. It's our duty to maintain high standards. Nowadays, a museum must take all these factors into consideration.

MG: *You live in many places around the world, however, your activities concentrate mostly in two countries: Italy, where you have your museums, and France, where the core of your business activities is based. What is your relationship to these countries?*

FP: We live in a globalized world. With regard to art, I'm not sure that thinking in terms of country is most relevant, a European label would be more appropriate. Whether one is in Italy, France or Germany, we all belong to the same European cultural space. For example, look at Venice. Venice is not only an Italian city, it's also one of the biggest international platforms for art, one of the main places for meetings and exchanges, for a discovery of an art world which, nowadays, is more open than ever. What I especially like in Europe is its creativity and its ability to constantly reinvent itself.

MG: *What about your artist friends? You are friendly with artists like Rudolf Stingel and Jeff Koons. Can you be on equal footing with an artist when you're a patron/buyer and they are artists?*

FP: Intense or not, the relationship between the artist and the collector is not a balanced one. The artist is the creator, the collector is a *regardeur*, to quote the term used by Duchamp. An active one, indeed a useful one, even a necessary one but that's it and it's fine that way. Even during the Renaissance, when artists were living on commissions and under the protection of their patrons, the most famous among them could still express their own vision in complete freedom. In my opinion, assisting artists in their creative process doesn't mean telling them which way to follow. Actually, it's the opposite, it is ensuring that their own personal artistic expression can thrive. A real collector has never or almost never been the source of artistic inspiration. An artist has something to say or not. That's what makes the difference between a genius and another artist. For me, personally, I'd say I have a sort of companionship with artists. By that, I mean a relationship made up of friendship, complicity, personal respect, and admiration – obviously at various levels according to the circumstances and the personalities – but essentially and most importantly, a relationship built to last in the long term. This notion of loyalty, support, duration remains essential to me, more than proximity, especially in this age too often dazzled by the short-lived, the immediate, the sensational.

MG: *You seem to like visiting artists' studios. Do you prefer talking with an artist before you make an acquisition?*
FP: I really like visiting artists' studios and I do it all year round in Europe, in America, in Asia. I enjoy meeting artists and speaking to them. Although, my first interest will always be the work of art, the emotion it provokes in me and the way it questions me. If there's also an affinity with the artist, then I am doubly satisfied.

MG: *As a collector, do you look for masterpieces?*
FP: Collecting is primarily observing, engaging and making decisions freely. Of course, every collector has been inspired by precedents set by Shchukin and Morozov, whose discoveries now fill the rooms of the Hermitage Museum, as masterpieces from the beginning of the twentieth century. But history will have the last word. These are artists who created masterpieces. The role of the collector is to provide the means for these artists to create in complete freedom.

MG: *You've been working with art advisors, Marc Blondeau and Philippe Ségalot. How important was their taste and advice in the forming of your collection?*
FP: When you collect, you're always surrounded by advisors, if only to let you know about a particular exhibition or a work. Nevertheless, since I started collecting art, I've never purchased a work without having seen it with my own eyes. From very early on, I relied exclusively on my eyes. A private collector can afford this luxury and freedom. However, when organizing exhibitions based on my collection, I bring in curators or even artists themselves, who, by following their own path, help me discover new aspects of my collection. For instance, this is the case with the *Slip of the Tongue* exhibition, curated by Danh Vo at the Punta della Dogana.

MG: *Your wife used to be an antique dealer; I understand you have a great collection of 18th century furniture. Is she involved in your contemporary collection?*

FP: My wife is passionate about decorative arts, especially from the 18th century. We enjoy comparing our choices and findings in our respective fields.

MG: *You once said that you are all about instinct. Do you use instinct when buying art?*
FP: Instinct is my capital. A work either makes a strong impact on you or leaves you feeling indifferently. It's a first impression that is naturally based on your knowledge of the history of art and which then asserts itself through your comprehension of the work-history, the view of the artist and his inspiration. An artist is full of ideas, forms, images. All that generates excitement, amazement, surprise and sometimes rejection. Contemporary artists constantly challenge the artistic canon; hence the interrogations requiring an additional perspective. This applies to all masterpieces. A work of art can't be reduced to its aesthetic elements. It must arouse a critical mind.

MG: *I'm still interested to know more about the way your instinct works.*
FP: Like for everybody, the instinct is the arm to fight for survival. I love or I don't love something or somebody. Rationality is for business.

MG: *Is art not part of the business?*
FP: If you think about the art market, of course, but if you forget the art market and concentrate on the work of art, then your instinct is essential. When you see a painting, you know what it does to you. It is also true that if I happen to appreciate a work too rapidly, I sometimes feel sometimes the danger, because art can be very seductive.

MG: *Are you sometimes seduced by pictures of art on the Internet?*
FP: I don't buy from the Internet, really. I've done some little purchases. It's better to see the works of art in a gallery or in the artist's studio. I'm not buying from mail-order companies. [laughs]

MG: *Do you think that new media changed the art world and made it more global?*
FP: The term "globalization" is overused. It often implies standardization. I prefer the concept of multi-centrality, which makes the period we live in exciting. The world of art doesn't revolve around a single location or a few places anymore – like it was with Paris and New York in the 20th century – but around many centers, interconnected art scenes. The new forms of media have accelerated this phenomenon.

MG: *Do you believe in the distinction between good art and commercially successful art?*

FP: The power of a work of art is the result of an expression, free from the obligation of being useful. The art-lover decides freely and acts regardless of the tyranny of the moment, even if sometimes choices and desires for some people are influenced by the market. This has always been the case. From painters' guilds through Academy juries and now the art market, there have always been some official bodies of recognition. But their judgments have rarely made the history of art. The artistic merit of masterpieces, which today form the core of museums, was hardly acknowledged by official bodies at the time of their creation. The same could be said about prices. The quality of the work remains essential; its commercial success is contingent.

MG: *Do you sometimes sell works from your collection?*
FP: Yes, of course, it happens. As I've said, my collection is in constant evolution; it follows new trajectories, while leaving behind others of a lower priority, which leads me to sometimes part with a work. Unlike public museums, which can't sell their collections, at least in France and most of Europe, (and that's fine this way). This capacity, to always question oneself, is a characteristic and, if it's done with accuracy, is an asset to private collections.

MG: *Would you agree that collectors are among the winners of the recent transformations in the art world because they have become very powerful? Is collecting art about power?*
FP: If it were the case, it'd be extremely sad and uninteresting. Collecting is a complicated passion, fuelled by feelings and various desires, "dosed" differently, depending on each personality: aesthetic pleasure, intellectual curiosity, the desire to live fully with his time, the wish to be part of the creative process by supporting artists. We could, of course, also add economic and social satisfaction, but it would be a parody if only these two mattered.

MG: *What do you think about the often-heard categorization that a good collector is interested in art, while a bad one is interested in money?*
FP: This doesn't make sense. Morality in the art world is a complicated matter. The only thing I can say is that collectors are no saints.

MG: *During the time that you've been the owner of Christie's, the auction house has become very powerful. Christie's, nowadays, is not only about auctions; it organizes curated exhibitions with very high-quality works, such as the portrait show that's on in London now. Christie's makes private deals, which used to be the specialty of galleries and dealers. What do you think about such a concentration of power in one single organization?*

FP: With regard to the curated exhibitions, it's a good initiative. More generally, it's not about the concentration of power. A company must constantly evolve to adapt to the world in which it operates. Otherwise it will disappear.

MG: *Even if an exhibition is not for sale, it allows the auction house to engage in a different way with collectors and to strengthen their position by displaying the high quality of their works. Does this strong position disadvantage galleries and dealers?*
FP: For good galleries, this is not a problem. You have to be the best. We don't know what the future will bring us; maybe the Chinese will take over everything...

MG: *Do you think there should be certain limits to art? What do you think about the expansion of the museum Louvre to Abu Dhabi, where a big part of art history will be excluded because of prohibition of nudity?*
FP: It's a pity, of course. Art must be approached in its entirety. However, it takes time to get used to it. You cannot expect the same degree of comprehension from everybody. Therefore, I think we shouldn't be radically judgmental.

MG: *Should we have moral rules that are applicable to art? Is art allowed to offend people?*
FP: Artists don't produce works to offend people; this would be ridiculous. I love freedom and consider it to be the most important aspect of my life. At the same time, you have to respect others' beliefs and faith of others. Artists whose works shock for the sake of shocking are not interesting. Provocation is only interesting when it serves a purpose, when it's part of a bigger picture...

MG: *You dropped out of school when you were fifteen and served as a soldier in Algeria; did these experiences somehow influence you?*
FP: They taught me the virtue of perseverance, the price of life and the power of solidarity between human beings.

MG: *Did you ever consider going into politics?*
FP: Never. A political career requires expert knowledge of the art of compromise. This is incompatible with my uncompromising character. If I had made such a choice, I would likely have been a mediocre politician.

MG: *If you think about your life – you left your village to join a small city, then you left your region to come to Paris, you've built a business empire – how much have you changed as a person over the years?*

FP: Do we really change? What I do know is that I still have the same drive and the same desire to do something.

MG: *You have rented Punta della Dogana for thirty years. What is going to happen afterwards?*
FP: That's obviously a very important matter. I suggest we talk about it when the time is right, like in thirty years!

SEAN SCULLY

March 2018

Marta Gnyp: *You were born in Dublin, raised in London and you are now living in New York. How do you cope with all these different national identities?*
Sean Scully: When you say the word, "identity", in this context, you only mean the identity of your passport and to me that's just a technicality I somehow circumvent. I'm against nationalism.

MG: *I'm curious to know what made you get your American citizenship in 1983.*
SS: Well, I took it because I'd lived in America for eleven years by then. It seemed a little strange to me to be camping out in somebody else's country and always using a foreign passport.

MG: *Being Irish or being American is not only a matter of passport, obviously. There are a lot of cultural elements that you're blessed or poisoned with, coming from one country or the other...*
SS: Yeah, of course, Irish-American is probably *the* classic combination. When I came into this world, we lived on the street; we didn't have a house. I really am a gypsy by breeding. So, for me, the change from one house to another is normal; it's like putting my donkey in front of my caravan and saying, "come on!" – and off we go again. That's how I started my life. By the time I was eight, I'd lived in about eight different houses. My family had a lot of singers and storytellers in it; nobody was formally educated like me, nobody went to university. They were all travelers, really, and that's what they call them in Ireland: "travelers", "gitano". We all constantly went back and forth between Ireland and England. Ireland and England are very mixed up. Most of the great Irish artists like Francis Bacon, Samuel Beckett, and James Joyce are what you would call Anglo-Irish, which is also a very interesting mixture because you've got both fire and discipline.

MG: *Fire is Irish and discipline is English, I assume?*
SS: Yes, and that's basically what you have in my work.

MG: *I read some tragic stories about your grandfather, who committed suicide in jail, where he landed after participating in an uprising in 1916, which, by the way, paved the way for the independence of Ireland.*
SS: My illegitimate grandfather committed suicide because he was sentenced to be shot – and he refused to be shot. He killed himself as an act of defiance, so I consider him a great hero – and a model for me. My father was also a deserter from the war, which I'm very proud of because I don't think war is any good at all, for anybody. That's one of the things I detest about America – that America is so militarized. It's a detestable aspect of American culture.

MG: *Maybe because they've had much fewer wars in America than we've had in Europe.*
SS: Yeah, so they're still stupid.

MG: *Speaking of differences between countries, do you see a different reaction towards your work in America and in Europe?*
SS: I do. It's taken a very, very long time for me to become really big in America. It happened faster in Europe. I think Europe is more interesting for art now, anyway.

MG: *Why?*
SS: Because it's a unified landmass with incredible sophistication. It has people like you in it, who are asking questions all the time. America is much more of a capitalist, product-oriented society, whereas Europe goes into reasons for things. That suits me perfectly because I'm a very philosophical artist. What I used to say was that I always had a problem north of the equator. [both laugh] My work was very much appreciated in Spain, Italy, and southern Germany.

MG: *In the Catholic parts of Europe.*
SS: Yes, that's where it's really embraced. I always had a problem in the Netherlands and Sweden because my work is too dirty.

MG: *Your work tends to be – I wouldn't dare say religious, but kind of transcendental, which is problematic in these Protestant countries.*
SS: It's problematic, because they don't trust it. I had the same problem in England because they don't trust that profound, metaphysical emotion, whereas in America it's accepted.

MG: *Don't you think that one of the weaknesses of Europe is exactly this constant self-reflection and self-criticism? They don't have it that much in America.*

1
Sean Scully
The Bather, 1983
Oil on linen,
243.8 × 304.8 cm

SS: No, they don't, which is part of the reason for my attraction to America, because I'm a very action-oriented person. I'm a maker. I don't mess around much when I make things. I go in the studio and make a painting. I'm not a person who's inhibited by doubt. In America they used to describe Joseph Beuys as "European bullshit", which means "you'll never get to the point". There's something to be said for that criticism, but, on the other hand, the problem with America is that you have a George W. Bush, who invades Iraq first, as an action, and thinks about it afterwards. I would say it's better to think about it first before you do something like that – and not do it and say stupid things like, "We're gonna smoke 'em out", after killing hundreds of thousands of people and creating three million refugees. I believe the doubt that Europe has is a doubt that's been earned, and it can be very humanizing because, in Europe, we've learned to put the value of human life before all else. Sure, it makes us seem indecisive, but so what? It's not a competition to see who will be the first to reach a conclusion. I think people who jump to conclusions or have hardened opinions are, really, mostly loud-mouths. They appear strong but it's actually backed up by emptiness, which is the counter-argument.

MG: *Well said. Clearly, you're a fervent pacifist. I read, though, that in your youth you were part of a street gang and that you excelled at karate. Was this a way of preparing yourself for the worst-case scenario?*

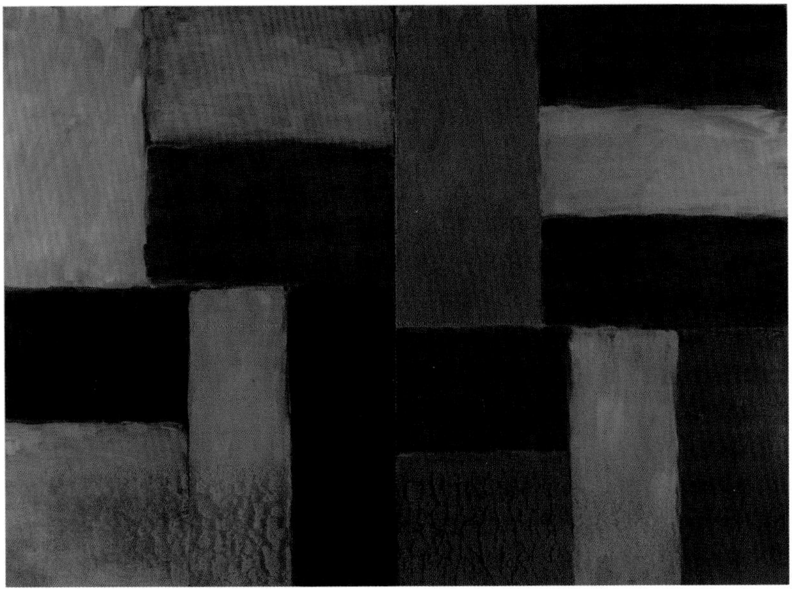

2
Sean Scully
Wall of Light Last Day, 2009
Oil on linen, 275 × 366.4 cm

SS: Joining a gang is environmental. You basically had to be in a gang for survival, and it was exciting. I was in a big street gang. We got into a lot of fights that were basically wars over territory, but that was something I rebelled against. Karate is, of course, violent when you fight, and I had a lot of fights, but at the same time it's noble, and disciplined – you're a knight. That's very attractive to me, because I'm full of all these myths from the past.

MG: *Do you still practice?*
SS: I practice a little bit on my own, but I'm too much of an individual to be in a cult for very long. I'll break with it because they ask you to give up your individuality, which I think is a crime.

MG: *Let's talk about your work, which is full of individuality. You've been making abstract paintings for a very long time. What drew you towards abstraction?*
SS: I wanted to make art that was unifying. I want to stitch the world together and break down differences. I see myself as an emissary of peace and understanding – and abstraction is part of that because it's a language, particularly the way I use it, with these basic structures common to all people.

MG: *Everybody can project whatever they want onto your work.*
SS: Everybody can project whatever they want onto everything, including my work. [both chuckle] My work has structure, it's got integrity, it's seri-

ous and profound, and it essentially comes from Northern Romanticism, mixed in with primitive structures that come from Africa or South America. I wouldn't say that you could project, onto my work, that pedophilia is a good thing, so I don't think it's true to say that you can project anything onto my work. It stands for certain humanistic values. There's an element of classicism in it. The titles are strong indications of the meaning of the work. You can project what you want but the work also has an opinion. It's not entirely neutral – it's humanistic.

MG: *You give hints about how to interpret them?*
SS: Yeah. My work is a way of emotionalizing, individualizing or humanizing the structures that actually dominate us. That's, really, the agenda in the work. We are living in a world made up of walls and grids, a world of geometry and hyper-structures. My work is a way of dealing with that and making it poetic, deep and profound, and, in a way, overcoming its tyranny – because order without pause is dangerous and leads to fascism. Fascists love geometry, but they like it nice and clean. They don't like dirty geometry like mine or geometry that's got incorrect things in it. My geometry is more like Paul Klee's; a little errant.

MG: *You mentioned the grid, which is a charged term in recent art history. Do you connect your work with the modernistic Greenbergian idea of painting?*
SS: No, I'm misusing all that sense of order. For instance, I made a painting called *Falling Wrong*, and people have been very bemused by this title. In relation to the Greenbergian idea, it's a mistake because that idea is all about harmony, taste, and perfection – and my work has nothing to do with perfection. When things are wrong they're right, and when they are right they're wrong. I'm constantly questioning authority and order.

MG: *When you started painting in the 1960s, painting was declared dead, which probably meant there was no interest in your paintings whatsoever.*
SS: That's right.

MG: *How did you survive this? It must have been very frustrating to hear: "painting is over and done with and obsolete".*
SS: That's their business – not mine. I'm hyper-individualistic and I've always pictured myself in highly rebellious terms. I stand for things that could be threatened. Anytime something is being destroyed, I'll always try and save it. It's an instinctive response.

MG: *That sounds fantastic, as an idea, but I can also imagine what it's like when you're a young artist, starting your career and then find there's*

no interest in your work. How did you cope with this?
SS: Well, I don't mind being in a minority.

MG: *But how did you survive, from a practical point of view?*
SS: I survived with my spirit because my spirit is very strong. I'm not really destructible. I've worked since I was thirteen and I've done every kind of job you can imagine and didn't mind making my paintings when I got home. I never expected to make money. I never expected my life to be like it is now. That's not why I went into painting. I thought it was a very profound, existential, heroic position in culture that was necessary, so that sustained me.

MG: *Did your art school give you any problems, in terms of choosing painting?*
SS: When I went to Newcastle University, in 1968, it was *entirely* conceptual. There wasn't a single person making paintings. There was a huge corridor where students were allowed to hang their paintings, but the students thought it would be very clever to not hang their paintings as an act of, you know, "Fuck off!" So I started making my paintings and hanging them on this wall. The students, first of all, thought I was an idiot or thought that this was a joke. But as time went by, they got jealous and then started making paintings and putting them up on the wall – that's how human beings are. It only takes one person to change the world.

MG: *That's a very nice story with a double message. Firstly, that we need strong individuals to change but also that people are extremely inclined to sheepish behavior. I'm curious about what happened after your studies, when you went to Morocco, turning you towards abstraction.*
SS: It wasn't that it turned me towards abstraction because, at that time, I was already making abstract paintings like woven baskets. I've always been very interested in weaving – already as a boy I was weaving, knitting, and making mats for the table, which is traditionally considered to be a female activity. When I went to Morocco, I saw a different geometry. The geometry I had seen and studied before was that of Joseph Itten, Bauhaus, and Suprematism, which was geometry of order. Whereas in Morocco, I saw a geometry of emotion, movement, and spirituality. Something opened up in me through this, so when I came back I started making striped paintings that were very repetitive and very rhythmical. This trip to Morocco transformed me. I ended up wearing a *djellaba* and sleeping in it on the ground. I was so in love with it that I had difficulty coming back.

MG: *It sounds like a very spiritual experience.*
SS: Yeah. It was absolutely transformative.

MG: *Then you found your visual language, which you've pursued until today, more or less.*
SS: Yeah. The basic unit of what I'm doing, instead of the figure as it would be (let's say) in Lucian Freud, is the stripe. I put the stripe in place of the figure because I used to be a figurative painter – a good one, too. People loved me in England for this and were so upset and angry with me when I decided to make abstract paintings.

MG: *Have you never been tempted to go back to figuration after that?*
SS: I just made twenty-two paintings of my son on the beach. My son has really transformed my life – made me into a different person. If you had talked to me fifteen years ago, you would've been dealing with a more truculent, troubled, moody person. The arrival of my son lit up my life. I wanted to make paintings showing him on the beach where we go every year. The only thing I could do to really immortalize this was paint it. So I made twenty-two large, figurative paintings.

MG: *Will you keep them for yourself?*
SS: I keep them for us but I like to show them. I think that Olga [Tsviblova] is going to show them in Moscow, [at the upcoming exhibition].

MG: *What role does religion play in your paintings? You also recently donated a lot of paintings to the Montserrat monastery in Spain. A very meaningful gesture connected to eternity, but also the eternity connected to religion.*
SS: Well, I never said that I don't believe – I'm a believer. And someone once told me that I was a Hindu because I love all religions. I'm a fusionist, in the end. I talked about this once in a lecture in New York, and there was a lady in the audience who was driving me crazy, and she kept saying, "what do you mean by all this 'fusion'?" In the end I said, "Interracial fucking". And then she said, "Ah, okay!" [both laugh] I suppose I'm a Catholic with a very strong Zen-underpinning. I'm very tolerant of all religions and think that religion is a higher place we want to go to, that we'll ultimately and hopefully get to. I think, hopefully, we'll evolve into more unified, kinder, spiritual beings and my work is part of this struggle.

MG: *Your work is done by you – by hand.*
SS: All of it.

MG: *You don't have any assistants that paint for you?*
SS: I don't have slaves like Jeff Koons does.

MG: *He pays them, though.*
SS: My admiration flows over.

MG: *Is it important to you that the work is done by your hand, that it's connected with your mind and heart?*
SS: Yeah. It's the unified action. That's the highest form of intelligence, according to Socrates.

MG: *It means you're productive, but also limited in your output. I read that you've made something like 1,400 paintings. It's now probably like 1,500.*
SS: Maybe.

MG: *Do you keep part of them for yourself?*
SS: I've got a big collection. This is something I like having. It makes exhibitions very easy, because I go up to the mirror and ask myself if I could borrow this painting, and then I look back at myself and I say, "Alright".

MG: *Did you take this into consideration from the very beginning and keep paintings from the early stages of your career?*
SS: Early on, it was easy to keep them because nobody wanted to buy them. It was in the early '70s, in England, when I realized I was in the wrong place at the wrong time because nobody was really interested in what I was doing. That precipitated the move to America where people became very interested. In the '80s, I got very famous in New York and had a huge waiting list for my work. You could say that I was the acceptable face of abstraction in the '80s.

MG: *Who was your gallery owner at that time in New York?*
SS: David McKee. He also represented Philip Guston. As people made a lot of connections between the way I paint and the way Philip painted, it opened museum doors for me in America. Then, it was harder for me to keep my work because everybody had a story about why they should have a painting. Like, somebody says his wife's birthday is next month, and he wants this painting – what are you gonna say? You can't really say no.

MG: *Who were more important for your career: institutions or private collectors?*
SS: I've always been in favor of institutions. I want my paintings to be in museums because I think they are for the people.

MG: *Museums don't have so much money nowadays.*
SS: No, you have to help them. When you write the numbers out, you have

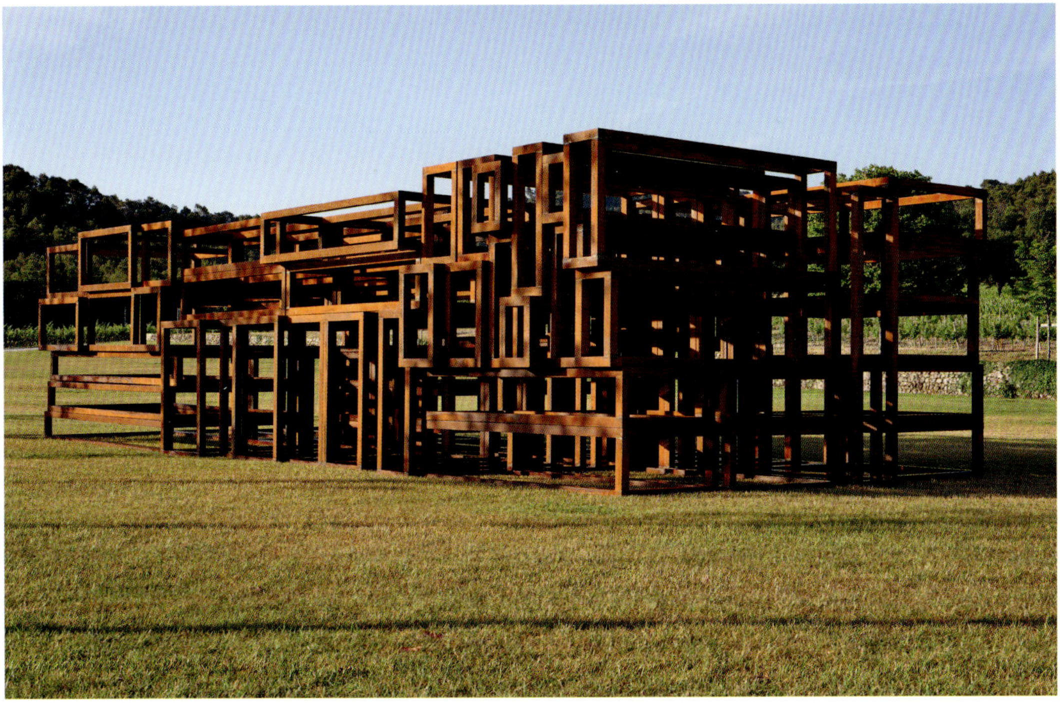

3
Sean Scully
Boxes Full of Air, 2015
Corten steel,
3.66 × 6.10 × 15.24 m

to knock the zeros off until the faces of the curators get kind of optimistic and lighter. As you take the zeros away, it becomes more possible.

MG: *Are you taking the zeros off for the important collectors?*
SS: No, because they can afford what they want.

MG: *What about your fascination for China? You've recently had five exhibitions in China.*
SS: China, in particular, is a country whose people could be affected very positively. They've come out of a terrible past, partially precipitated by colonialism and exploitation, and they came out of abject poverty. Now they have to handle this sense of freedom, that the people want, in a way that doesn't cause catastrophes. I'm interested in this process and in contributing to it. I'm bringing something positive from outside that's not critical of that, but wants to assist in this process, because beating somebody up from the outside is rubbish. It causes isolation.

MG: *You're an outsider who can act because you're not involved in politics over there.*
SS: What's really interesting about China, in relation to abstraction, is that abstraction was *banned* in China. This shows the power of abstrac-

4
Sean Scully
Permanent installation, Church of Santa Cecília de Montserrat, Barcelona, Spain, 2015

tion, because they were right to be afraid of it. All fascists are afraid of abstraction because abstraction provokes free thinking. This is exactly what they don't want. Furthermore, you can't edit abstraction, because if you look at one of my paintings, which part are you going to leave out? None of it, or all of it? If you take out one of the stripes, it won't change the intention of the painting. They were afraid of it, because they couldn't edit it. Since it provokes subversive thinking – and it *is* subversive.

MG: *It's a kind of Trojan horse because it looks so harmless.*
SS: That's exactly right. It's a Trojan horse and it's filled with naughty thoughts. [both chuckle]

MG: *What about your student, Ai Weiwei, who has a completely different approach to China? Was he angry with you for collaborating with China?*
SS: No, he loves me. He came up to my opening the other day in Mexico City, in Luis Barragán. Ai Weiwei invited himself and his family. His son played with my son and he kept pouring me huge glasses of whisky. It was terrible but funny. I don't drink hard liquor but he kept coming over with glasses of whisky. [laughs]

MG: *Do you like teaching?*
SS: Well, I like affecting things – and teaching is part of it. And all great people, including Mahatma Gandhi, have once been teachers because they want to affect change.

MG: *It doesn't distract you from your own work?*
SS: No, it doesn't stop me at all. It's another activity. It's like writing or talking to you. I'm talking to you now and I'm not painting, isn't it awful? [chuckles]

MG: *You've been in the art world for longer than forty years now. What, in your opinion, has been the biggest change, if you look at it from this perspective of time?*
SS: The change seen in my lifetime has been massive. I'm pre-electric, when I was a child, we had gaslight. When I thought of being an artist, I thought that I'd make my paintings and I would maybe have one retrospective. In the meantime, I had about twenty. What's happened in the art world is that art has become powerful because art has, in a sense, replaced religion. Art has become hugely powerful as a great force for good. I was talking with Bono about rock 'n' roll once, and he said that rock 'n' roll was invented to change the world. He was really talking about himself, but I think that art is now changing the world because its power gives

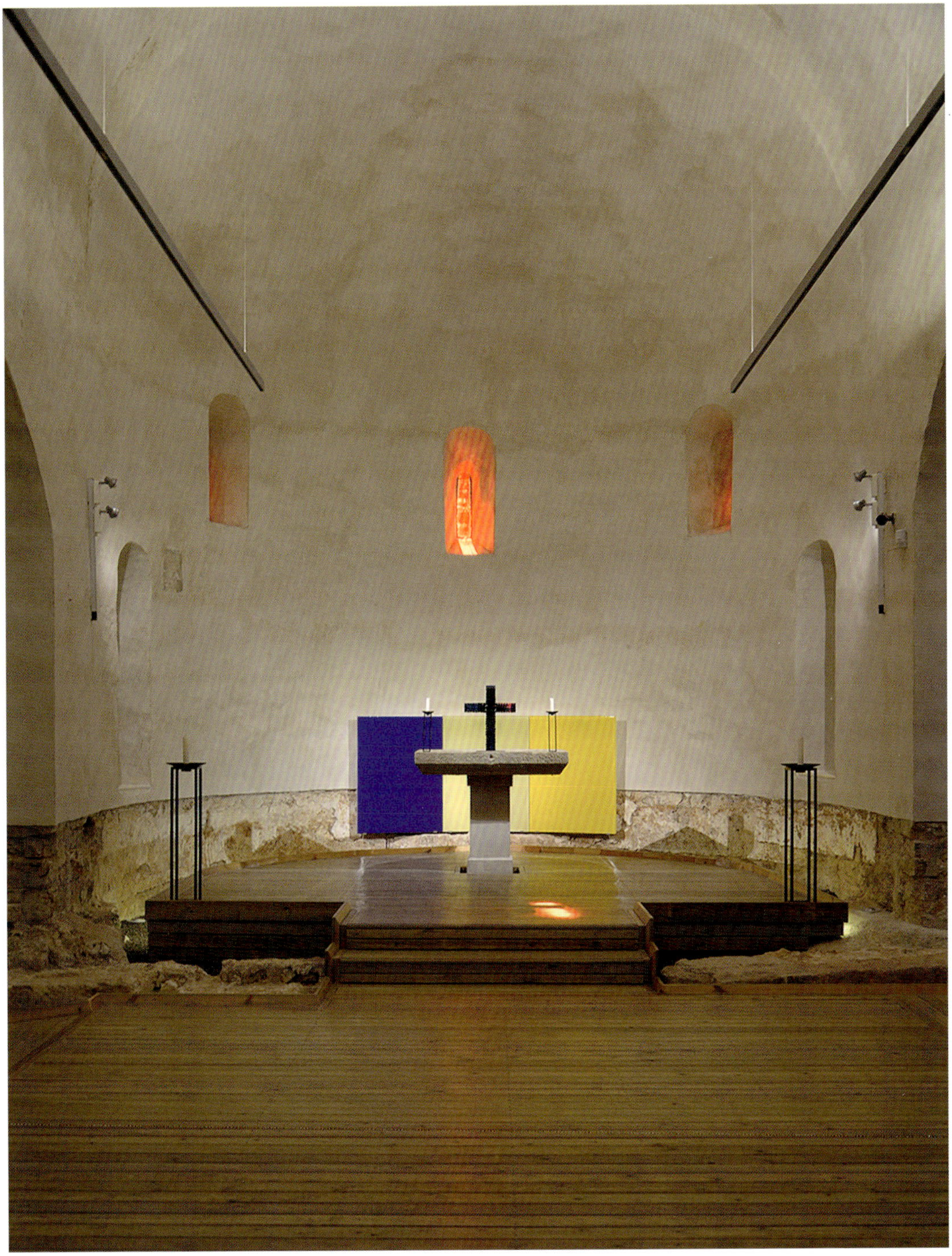

it enormous influence, which it lacked thirty years ago. It's become an industry as powerful as the music industry, and all because technology, images, opinions, thoughts, and ideas are transmitted without barriers. You can jump over borders, which is exactly what I want to do, as I want to knock them down. [chuckles] And art has become like rock 'n' roll.

MG: *You are absolutely right that art has become very popular, but the question is: Are people really interested in art or are people interested in a kind of entertainment related to art, which is not bad, by the way? Art has always been very elitist, which isn't bad either.*
SS: I know. I was listening to somebody talking, last night, about a moving image on a wall in a lobby – that it was more engaging to people than a static image because the static image was easier to ignore. This guy was talking about the destruction of painting by technology, basically. But then a woman said, "Yeah, it's only constantly distracting because it doesn't have any art in it. It's just something that you look at as you walk by. It doesn't mean anything". And she was right. There are going to be different levels of experience – and art *is* elitist. The conversation we're having now is very elitist, dense and profound. It's about history and culture, and where we're going as a people. Of course, people are not interested in that all the time, but some of that, a residue of that, is moving into the culture.

MG: *What exactly do you mean when you compare what happened to music with what is happening now with contemporary art?*
SS: As art becomes more popular, it has become in a sense more like rock 'n' roll. OK, most of rock 'n' roll is like bubblegum music: "I love you, I love you, please don't go! You're making me feel so upset", and on and on and on. But it has attitude, and that attitude has affected culture and made it more liberal and more open. I think the same thing is happening with art. In the music business, for example, there are still people who make serious stuff, like, Agnes Obel, who we recently discovered. It's been a force for good. If you listen to Bob Dylan or The Beatles, and then you listen to Frank Sinatra, he's like bowls of treacle – *Strangers in the Night*. *All You Need Is Love* is a message.

MG: *Do you think new technologies, like online images, have also been important for your art? Do you also notice this availability of images online as being good for you?*
SS: Yes, it's made art powerful. You can go to my church on the top of Montserrat, but there, you get fourteen people a day who can see it as firsthand experience. However, the images of it are also very powerful and

have an influence. I've never been to Machu Picchu but I certainly can feel it in some way, when I see the images. I can feel its spiritual power, and that's important. I think it serves me particularly well because my work is quite repetitive, like LEGO; it fits in the computer world, and it fits in the romantic world, which is, of course, exactly what I want.

MG: *If we think about the changes in the art world, what do you think about the position of the artist? Before, artists were avant-garde, bohemian, romantic, revolutionary, but nowadays artists are quite different, you mentioned Jeff Koons before. What do you think is the position of artists today?*
SS: Of course, artists are different, like lots of other things. When I talk now, I've noticed that the audiences are bigger. For instance, I had a show in Moscow and there were something like 350,000 visitors; mostly very young people. Not that I think that younger people are better than older people – it's very interesting that there's a huge hunger, and it was wildly successful. Nowadays an artist is no longer a kind of traveling gypsy or an existential figure in an attic – that's over. Now, we are more like Rubens, who was the ambassador to London and a powerful figure. And I think art is more like that now. I can't think of another age when art was as powerful as it is today, because it's completely out of control – it's totally free. If you stop it this way, it'll go that way – it's like water. That's my sign, by the way: water. It's unstoppable. [chuckles]

PAT STEIR

Summer 2017

Marta Gnyp: *You were studying art during the '60s, when the age of abstract expressionism in the USA had come to its end; Conceptual and Minimal art were taking shape, simultaneously with Pop art.*
Pat Steir: Painting was problematic but this didn't mean anything to me. On the contrary, it got more interesting because it was less accepted.

MG: *Was it difficult to survive in the art world then, when painting was out of fashion?*
PS: So what? I've lived on my works since 1975, which means people have always liked paintings. Many conceptual artists were my friends. I've always liked minimalists; they were my friends too. They were actually more popular in Europe than in the USA. In America, painting has never lost its audience.

MG: *Did you have fights with other artists about the direction of art?*
PS: (laughs) I was living with the inventor of Conceptual art, Sol LeWitt. It couldn't bother me at all. He was very supportive of painting, by the way.

MG: *The term, "Conceptual art" is misleading because it implicates that the other art is not conceptual.*
PS: Exactly. I wanted to do it all by myself. I was interested in ideas, not the limitations imposed from outside. A lot of my earlier works are Conceptual art if, for example, you take the line as the concept. I think there's a misunderstanding as to what Conceptual art was, especially in the second and third generation.

MG: *There were two artists that you mentioned as having been essential for formulating your artistic thinking; one was John Cage, the other Agnes Martin.*
PS: Yes, both in different ways. John Cage used the notion of chaos to make his work. Duchamp said anything could be art. John said everything is art. I thought I'd use gravity as a very simple element to direct my work.

1
Pat Steir
Elephant Waterfall, 1990
Oil on canvas,
346.7 × 288.3 cm
Private collection

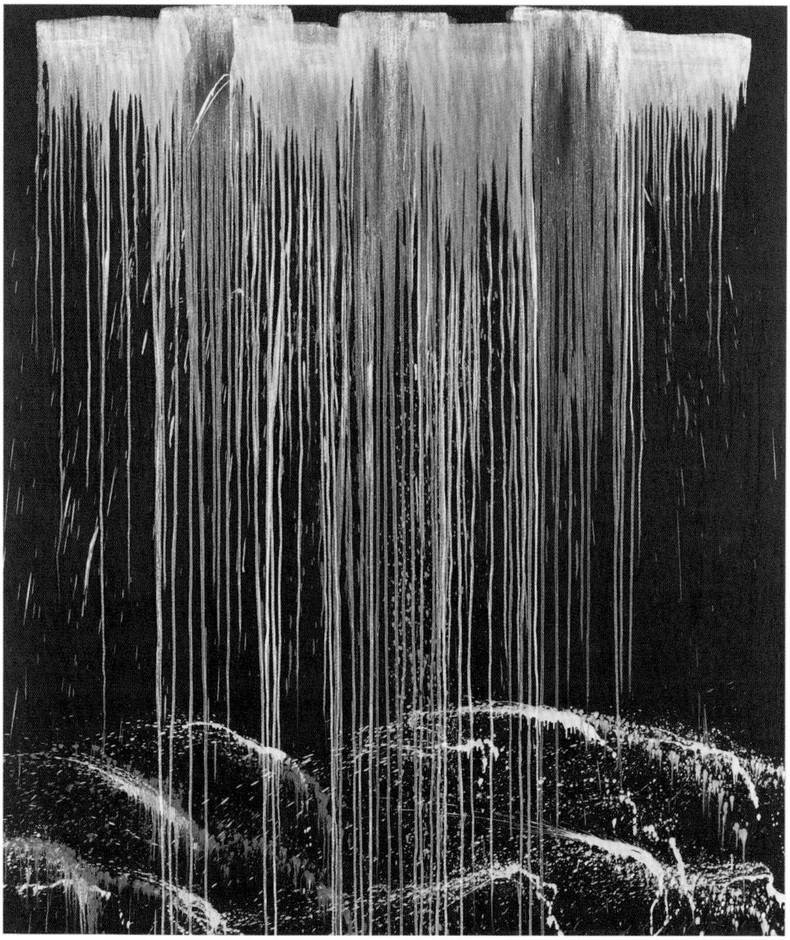

What matters is not only the concept, but also the intention. I was making the concept as simple as possible.

MG: *If everything is art, how do you see yourself as an artist?*
PS: I was impressed by the ideas of John. They were very meaningful to me.

MG: *The other person that was important for your artistic thinking was Agnes Martin. What was so interesting between the two of you?*
PS: Everything. She was such a good artist. She had to make art and she made art every day until she died, with the exception of the last few months of her life. She made very simple, deep works. I admired her desire to make art and the way she did it.

MG: *How did you meet?*
PS: My friend Douglas Crimp (the curator and art critic) curated a Martin

exhibition and invited me to join him in visiting Agnes. He knew Agnes because he did the show with her when her work was not well-known. I think it was in 1971; since then, I visited her every year.

MG: *She was much older than you were.*
PS: Much older. She became my teacher, in a way. She didn't teach me how to make work, but she did teach me how to make art from the heart. She was very special.

MG: *You also knew Louise Bourgeois well – was she someone you could talk to about your art?*
PS: I didn't understand her work. I interviewed her three times, until I wrote about the parallels between her life and her work. We both loved the last interview. She had a caretaker reading it to her every night, again and again. At last, I understood what she did. It didn't attract me though; it turned me away. I can't say she was my favorite artist in the world, but it has meaning.

MG: *Who, then, is your favorite artist?*
PS: Back to Agnes Martin. I can't say exactly why. The work is so incredibly moving. There is something about hesitation and freedom.

MG: *Emotions and freedom are values that are very hard to talk about nowadays, without being cheesy.*
PS: We are living in difficult times. Things always change; this will change too. It's better not to change yourself to fit in. Now I don't know what the values are. I live in America; Trump makes me feel sick. What are our values among artists and art? The audience's value, the critical value, the personal value – somehow they don't fit together at all.

MG: *You seem to like the concept of beauty, which is not so popular at the moment, either.*
PS: I don't do works that are popular and I don't care. Yes, it's important to me that the work is beautiful. It's beautiful because I make it natural. I've never had the idea of wanting to create beauty, not even now. I'm not manipulating the paint; when I'm painting, gravity comes into action and, sometimes, they become beautiful. I allow nature to paint the painting.

MG: *Would you agree with the opinion that your works relate to nature?*
PS: My works do relate to nature, but to the grand nature, not small nature. When I paint waterfalls, the waterfall actually paints itself due to gravity. I have more interest in a large, extensive nature.

2
Pat Steir
Valentine, 2009–2011
Oil on canvas,
322.6 × 277.5 cm
Private collection

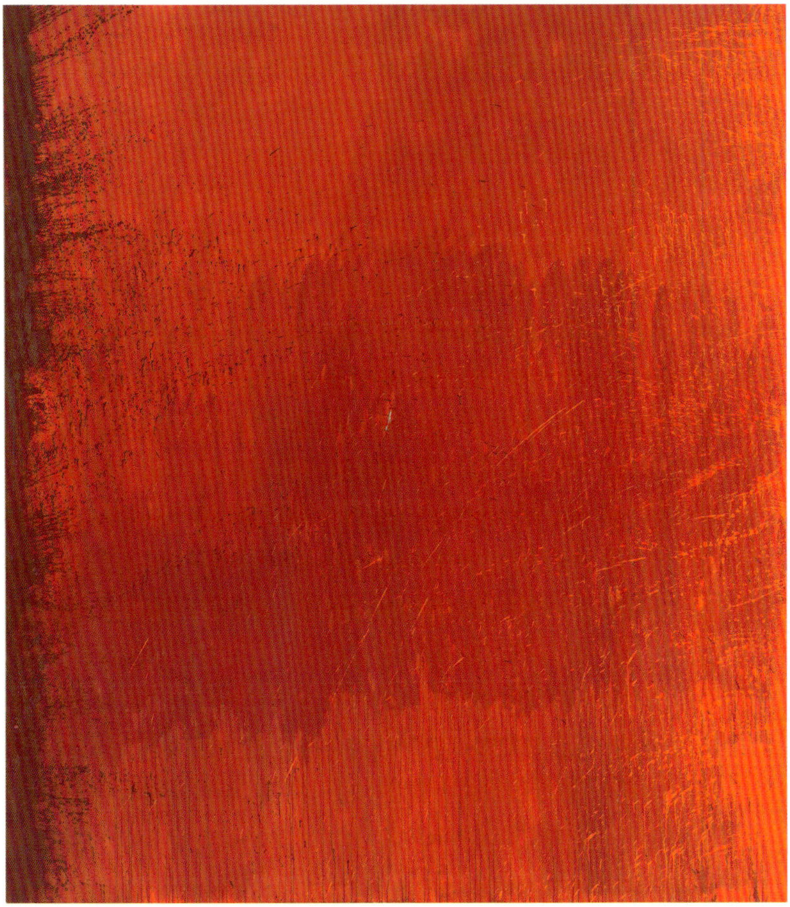

MG: *Did you start out with this concept or did it come later, as an explanation of what you were doing?*
PS: I started with this idea. I wanted the paintings to paint themselves. By the way, I'm not interested in abstraction, but in a painting that's making an image on its own.

MG: *Do you create a situation in which the painting can happen?*
PS: I make it happen. Firstly, I'm creating it using my hands. Secondly, people feel my love there. I can't explain that. I know this is very romantic and romantics are not very much in style. But who cares what's in style? You have to make your own style.

MG: *Could you tell me something about the process of painting?*
PS: The waterfalls were very fast because everything 'till 2002 had one layer. Now the process is very slow because the paintings have many layers. They are oil painted; they dry slowly.

MG: *Lets speak about your first dripping paintings.*
PS: I don't call them drippings; I call them falls. I started to paint them, somewhere around 1989. The first one I did is hanging in the Metropolitan Museum, right now.

MG: *Was it a revelation for you, when you started painting the falls; when you found out your very specific language?*
PS: It seemed that way. But I stress the word, "seem". I'm not the kind of artist that tries to represent myself. I just make art.

MG: *But you developed your own signature.*
PS: I became an artist to be free. I didn't make any effort to fit in because I don't care about that. I don't care about being something according to the rules of art-society. I was searching for something that was relevant to me in painting, which I cannot describe with words. This is why I'm an artist.

MG: *Do you consider yourself as a part of a bigger painting tradition? You mentioned, for example, romanticism; sometimes your work is also placed in the context of abstract expressionism.*
PS: I don't like the term, "expressionism" because I don't want to express anything. I let things be themselves. If you want to express yourself, you should see a therapist. "Postmodern art" fits my work the best, except that I don't think there is any art that is postmodern.

MG: *Do you consider your art spiritual then?*
PS: That sounds more familiar. If you call meditation a spiritual practice, then yes.

MG: *What about your work's connection to Asia. Is it true that you implement Zen Buddhism ideas in your work?*
PS: I saw Chinese landscape paintings with monks on the ground, as if they were trying to make the audience for my own paintings. I've worked several times in China and Japan. I've seen a lot of calligraphy in person, viewed many Chinese paintings. I made woodcuts in China and Japan.

MG: *If you look at your artistic work from the '60s up to today, you've worked through so many different trends, movements and fashions. How did you react to all these changes?*
PS: I like Cindy Sherman's work, Sherrie Levine's work, Lawrence Weiner's work. Jo Baer's work, Robert Ryman's work; many others too. When I like their work, it doesn't mean I have to adopt their philosophy.

3
Pat Steir
Morning Moon, 2016–2017
Oil on canvas,
274.3 × 274.3 cm
Private collection

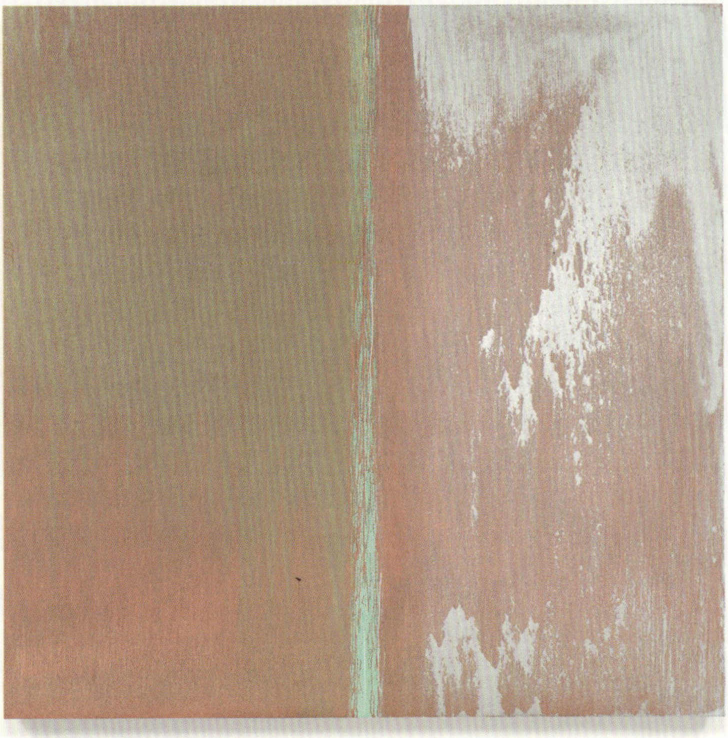

MG: *Has the artistic community changed?*
PS: In the '70s, there was more like one community; there were not so many artists and people exchanged with each other. Nobody disliked anybody, really, but that was it. In the '80s, it began to change, but still, whatever the other artists' identity was, we were also friends. I'm friends with Sherrie and Cindy. I admire their work and I'm sure they accept my work too. I'm very close friends with Lawrence Weiner, who has been very supportive of my work.

MG: *The situation has changed for you. You're getting a lot of attention nowadays. Do you enjoy it?*
PS: Of course (laughs). I love my new gallery. They are fantastic; they're interested in a very broad range of art and they're wonderful supporters of my paintings. The visibility of the works blossoms under their care.

MG: *It must be a great feeling for you, to see recognition for your work that is also expressed in the prices.*
PS: It is, it means people who are buying it are not going to trade it. They

4
Pat Steir
Angel, 2016–2017
Oil on canvas,
335.3 × 287 cm
Private collection

are using it for themselves. When people pay more, they're going to keep it rather than selling it.

MG: *If you look at the forty years your* oeuvre *spans, what is the biggest change in the art world?*
PS: It changes every eight to ten years. What I see, in this moment, is that younger artists are puzzled. Art is a reflection of the society we live in, whatever you make. Today, we live in what seems to be chaos. I see that youngest artists don't know where to turn. They think you're a successful artist because you're selling works.

MG: *You were also a teacher?*
PS: I taught art at CAL arts; several artists I taught later became world famous.

MG: *Why is art important to make?*
PS: Making art is important because art is what we leave behind to tell our story.

KAARI UPSON

July 2013

Marta Gnyp: *Lets start with the* Larry *project, since it seems to have been an essential part of your artistic practice, so far. In an abandoned house in your parents' neighborhood, which you could watch a child as a secret place of sex parties and quasi-criminal activities, you found documents and journals of the owner, whom you gave a fictive name, Larry. The house burned down, you lost one of his journals and then your fantasy began to work. Since 2005, you've been creating a whole body of works including objects, installations, videos and performances that were constructed around the absent Larry and yourself. Why did you invent Larry?*
Kaari Upson: I was still a student at Cal Arts in LA. I was painting and very seriously trying to understand what I could do with painting and how to do it critically. My works were super photorealistic; I was taking pictures of any crime scene with beds, that were generally the places of crimes of passion. So, once I found beds in Larry's house. I went in, got snapshots of the beds and I painted it. I was using these grids to try thinking about minimalism and engage in this high-low debate, but it wasn't going anywhere.

MG: *What other projects did you do at that time?*
KU: I was trying to create an emotional map of Los Angeles. I would search where something had happened, I would go there with a camera, or anything, and try to represent the sense of this place and catch the significant or insignificant memories that were somehow embedded in the space.

MG: *So a lot of the aspects of the Larry-project were already there, the emotional absence, the hidden psychology of relations and memory of the space. What did you find in Larry's house?*
KU: Every room in Larry's house, other than bathroom and the kitchen, had a mattress. I photographed the rooms before the house burned down. There were beds everywhere, as if somebody left them very quickly, as if somebody was squatting in the space. Then I rebuilt different parts of the house, entire rooms became kind of sculptures, which could

be constantly transformed. I was doing it based on a photograph and my own memory. There would be blind spots in it that I'd have to fill, but pretty much everything was reassembled, so this mattress came back, a real mattress that we cast in latex. So that started the process of making this, and that was three-dimensional, because it had a front, sides and a back.

MG: *Why are you so fascinated with the mattress?*
KU: There is this large aesthetic history of artists using beds like a starting point. I like engaging in this discussion in a new way. I did focus on the idea of it having four sides and a face; through experimenting we realized that we could use silicones instead of the original latex because it's transparent. Now they're completely different and are more like paintings. They don't have a fleshy or bodily feeling to them. The gestures are all imbedded in the material now, in a way that I have to work blindly.

MG: *So you have no control over the final result.*
KU: If you do something long enough, you can even master chaos to a certain degree. In my *Kiss Paintings*, I was aggressively putting two oil paintings together as if they were kissing each other, not knowing what would happen. But after working for a while, I could even start understanding how the temperature of the day was going to affect their "kiss". And then, as soon as I understood this, I stopped making them.

MG: *Are you now investigating how silicon works?*
KU: It's about a very active space involving several people at once. One person can't make these. The material has to stay fluid but tactile. You have to start and finish the pieces in one go and they can never be put on hold. They must stay at a certain stage or they frieze up. It's just the materiality of silicon, which gives it such a dynamic way of working because it's a team effort and, besides, it is very physical.

MG: *How would you describe the process?*
KU: It's a messy, very physical act, moving these things around, keeping them wet. It feels like a sport. Things go wrong constantly so you can compare it to athletics; the response has to be really quick. It's very frustrating, because none of the pieces turn out as I expect, so there is no planning. Even the colors change.

MG: *Do you leave them like they appear?*
KU: Yes. When you have time to go back to it, like in traditional painting, it's different. Even my kiss-paintings, I could remake them over and over

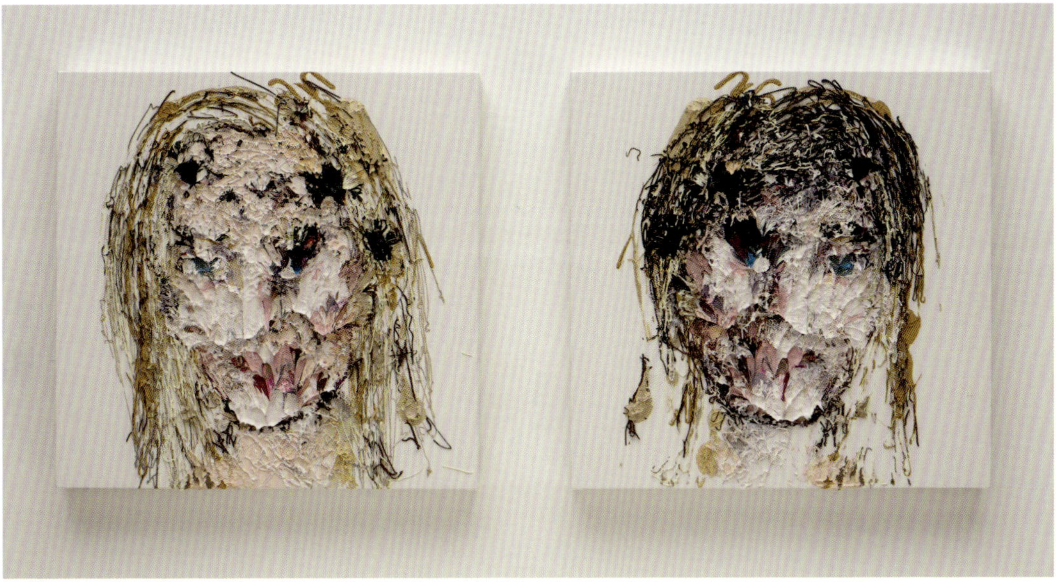

1
Kaari Upson
Kiss #9, 2008
Oil on panel, two panels,
50.8 × 50.8 cm each

again, I could pull them apart and put them back together. In the case of silicone, reworking is not possible.

MG: *Do your artworks function differently outside your studio?*
KU: I recently saw some of my charcoal pieces on their own in a beautiful room. In my studio they were dusty, black pieces that were surrounded by many other objects and actions. If you isolate things, they will acquire meaning on their own. I realize that there's something going on there, they could breath outside the warehouse which normally dominates them. This studio is very different to any other exhibition space. Sometimes, curators tell me, "we want this to look like your studio". But it never looks like it: once you move your studio, it's always this slightly cleaned up version.

MG: *You built a grotto, that referred to the Playboy Mansion of Heffner, in which you performed, engaging with Jungian and sex therapies. You invented characters, like Crissy and Kerry. What was your and their relationship to Larry?*
KU: It's very hard to tell this story so that it makes sense. Yes, when I worked in the grotto, I followed a Jungian therapy with therapists that I could get on a speakerphone. They didn't know the sessions were recorded; it was really high quality speakerphone. The woman on the phone asked me about a dream I had had, a very Jungian approach, and in that moment I decided to give her a real dream. I said, "I had a dream about a person I

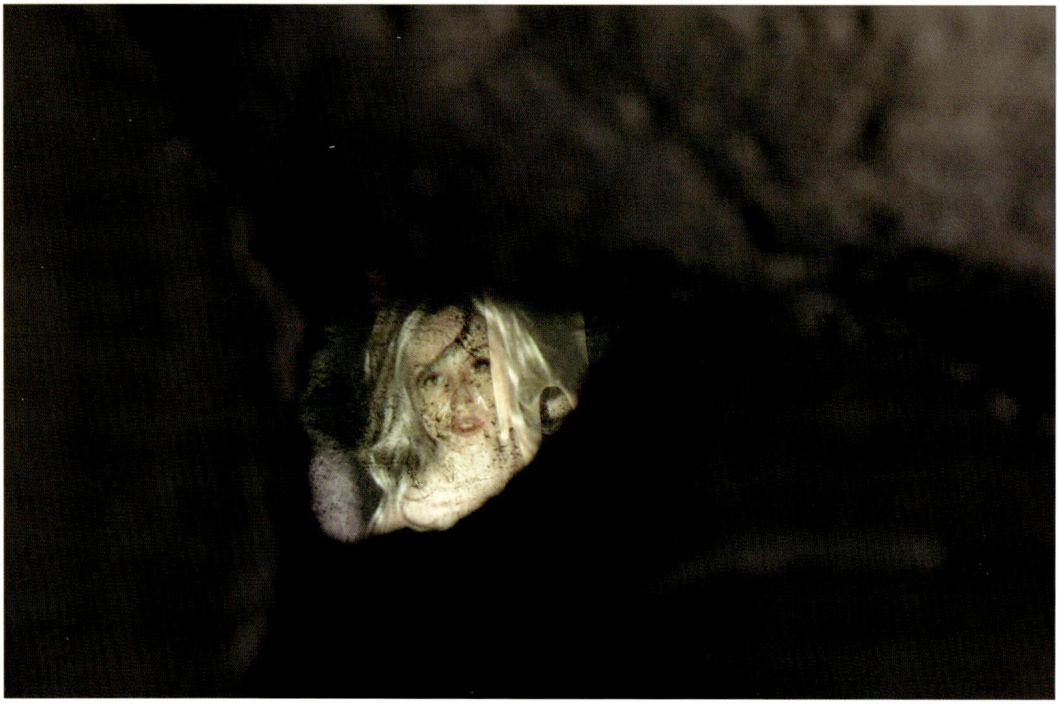

2
Kaari Upson
The Grotto, 2008/2009
(detail)
Mixed media and five videos
(color, sound), dimensions
variable

know from high school. Her name was Crissy. In this dream, I killed her in a very particular way: I ripped out her lymph gland from her neck and then went hiding. I was discovered as the killer while sitting in front of a TV set, looking at my mom's face watching the TV and then realizing my mom knows I killed Crissy. I'm watching her watch the TV. In this way, the starting point could be seen as personal. I don't believe that dreams are the gateway to any imagination; I think it comes from the world we live in.

MG: *What did you do with the idea of Crissy?*
KU: I was in the grotto, dressed with fake breasts and a fake vagina, with a doll that hasn't even become female yet. This woman said, "she is your shadow, Crissy is you". I couldn't get it out of my head because this poor girl really exists. I found her on Facebook and I actually saw a photo of her as an adult. The therapist kept telling me I had to work through Crissy, to confront my fears. So I had to constantly tell her what Christie was like, to do this Jungian shadow work. But then I moved to the drawing and started a dialogue with things that happened in the video: some of them I would forget, some of it would misremember, and some of them would merger.

MG: *Did you discover why Crissy was important to you?*
KU: After three months the grotto has become a place of a narcissistic

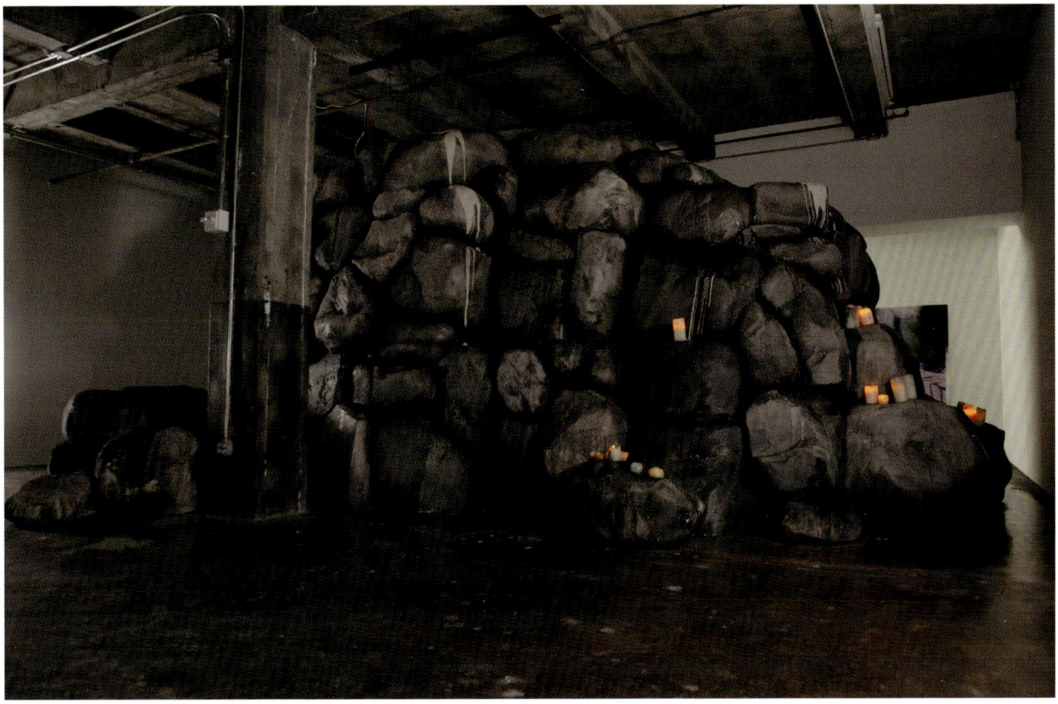

3
Kaari Upson
The Grotto, 2008/2009
(installation view)
Mixed media and five videos
(color, sound), dimensions
variable

self-exploration and I started thinking about my shadow and myself as a perfect double. As Larry was obsessed with Hugh Hefner, his grotto was the starting point for my grotto. Hefner once said that every man's deepest sexual desire is to have sex with identical twins. So here I had my twin, the doll, my perfect double. I recast my face in perfect dimension, my eyes were set in a perfect ration, my nose was cleaned up, my lips were pumped up and we made a silicon mask, becoming my perfect self. Crissy could then be projected into her, so I made phone calls to random sex therapists, making them play with my twins.

MG: *How does a sex therapy on the phone work?*
KU: It's not real sex therapy; it's just phone-sex workers who say they could help you through all kinds of problems. The women on the other side are paid to give a sexual scenario mostly towards men. So, I think it's just for men to have sex for $3 a minute. I called in several times and spoke as Crissy or Kerry, (they kept calling me Kerry even my name is Kaari). I recorded my sessions and found something strange going on in them that I can't quite identify.

MG: *What was so strange in this experience?*
KU: I spoke with a woman once who obviously didn't know her voice was

being videotaped and heard inside the grotto, and this conversation was very confusing. We were both faking, so we were in this weird zone where you don't have a climax to go to and you keep turning it into itself. She was probably really confused that I wasn't getting off, so then, of all of a sudden, the scenario would get dirtier, then something would decompress it and she would have to build it back up again. She kept trying to make it dirtier and dirtier, but the dirtiness was so normal that both our imaginations couldn't go further than what was available, which was porn.

MG: *How were your performances and videos received?*
KU: When the works were firstly exhibited in the Hammer Museum in LA, some people were highly offended. One man said that the silicon breasts and silicon vagina were against God, because the body that God gave us was beautiful and perfect and I was altering it. The grotesqueness and the prosthetics bothered people a lot. But I was just following what was already there: i.e. the model of Playboy's first photo-shopped vagina. It just naturally evolved into this grotesque monster, but it was naturally dirty.

MG: *I'm under the impression that you changed in your approach to this project, from more personal to setting a clear distance between you and your work, as an artistic project.*
KU: When I started this project, I was advised then that I should talk about it in third person as though it's not even me. I don't know why, but it's very important for people to know I keep a critical distance from it.

MG: *This is maybe the idea of being profound and sincere versus being a manipulator.*
KU: That's interesting. People, who know me very well, would probably say I'm on the sincere side.

MG: *Maybe you can be both at the same time.*
KU: It's very frustrating when people feel as though the work is really about you. It's both irritating and slightly enjoyable that people need to decide if I'm crazy or not. In a videotaped lecture, I saw somebody in the audience who said, "she's crazy", because I was cutting a doll's head off in a video. It actually hurt my feelings for a moment, as I'm not crazy.

MG: *What kind of doll was it?*
KU: It was a homemade doll. It was based on Oskar Kokoschka's *Alma Mahler doll*, that he built because she left him. He made this doll and then had a party in which everybody tore her apart. I didn't think he was crazy for doing anything like that, it just totally made sense.

4
Kaari Upson
Paul Allen, 2013
Silicone, fiberglass
and paint,
203.2 × 152.4 × 17.78 cm

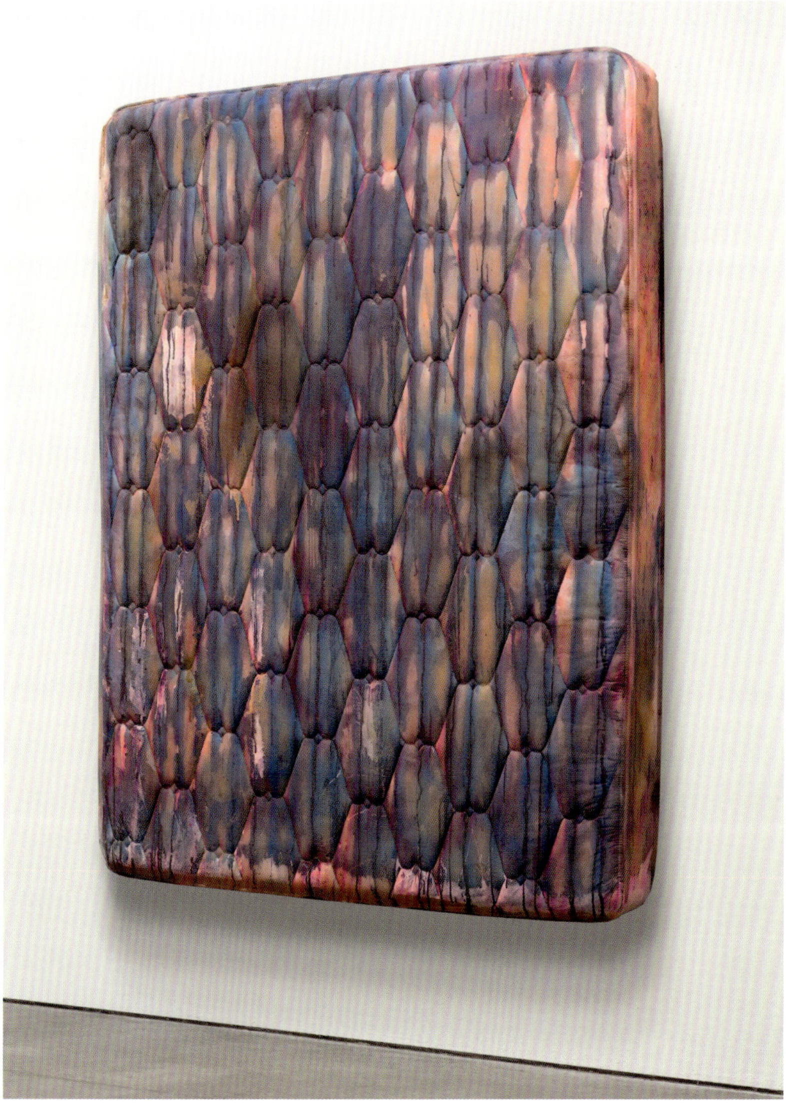

MG: *How did you construct the notion of Larry?*
KU: In the *Larry* project the male is absent; there is actually almost no male at all. The fact is, Larry wasn't there and I used the giant gap of his absence to shove whatever I wanted into that space. It's hard to explain, but it's a very psychological space. He was just absent in the centre of it. I used any sort information, based on a likeness of my father or on Hefner, if it was based on images from his real life. All of my work, at some level, is pointing to some sort of absence. I am very interested in gaps between things, the boundaries between them, and, sometimes, almost obsessively and neurotically filling it.

MG: *Did Larry ever approach you?*
KU: No he doesn't know I exist, otherwise he would sue me. I shouldn't say that, because it's super speculative, but he's not somebody who would shun away from that. It'd be very interesting to have him walk into a room full of him, of this version of him and see where he identifies with it and where he doesn't.

MG: *But he knows everything about his house. You said he was put in jail.*
KU: He went to the house once, after it was burned down. My parents told me that. That was all I heard of him and then, through the Internet, I found out where he lives and even went there once, but will not do it again, because my lawyer told me that, if I went twice, it would be stalking. This legal side is unexpected, since I was simply interested in what that house represented, being across the street from where I grew up. So, I didn't know it was going to be a project until it unraveled itself and I realized it was such a weird way to know somebody.

MG: *Where does your interest in the psychology of relations come from?*
KU: I don't think I have a full understanding of what I'm doing, exactly. I am going after that absence again. I took very influential classes at Cal Arts, with a teacher who was an expert on Lacan's mirror-phase. She made this beautiful diagram on the chalkboard of this triangle, with the father, the mother, the child and the eyes. She was making these very strange diagrams, which got stuck in my head, so I was searching for a situation I could enter in the same way.

MG: *What would your new project be?*
KU: There's this man named Gordon Bell, a computer scientist. He is one of the founders of Microsoft, who was trying to find memory in a computer where we can scan every bit of our life, paperless. He's been doing this for thirty years: he has this weird identifier around his neck that takes a picture every minute of his life and it even has an emotional sensor to it. In interviews, he was constantly saying there were gaps everywhere and that, no matter how much he scanned, no matter how much he put into the computer, his life wasn't there.
He is donating his archive to many different computer research centers. I would be honored to be the person to acquire it for my purposes, from an artistic point of view. I was interested in these gaps, then playing with fantasy, fiction, research and filling these gaps. And, obviously, that's going to be a method that's sort of a constant reflection, mirroring back on me. But the only concern I had was that he was just another middle-aged white man, similar to Larry. So rather than put myself in a relationship

5
Kaari Upson
Resuscitated Crib, 2016
Silicone, pigment, hair and fiberglass,
135.9 × 73.7 × 14 cm

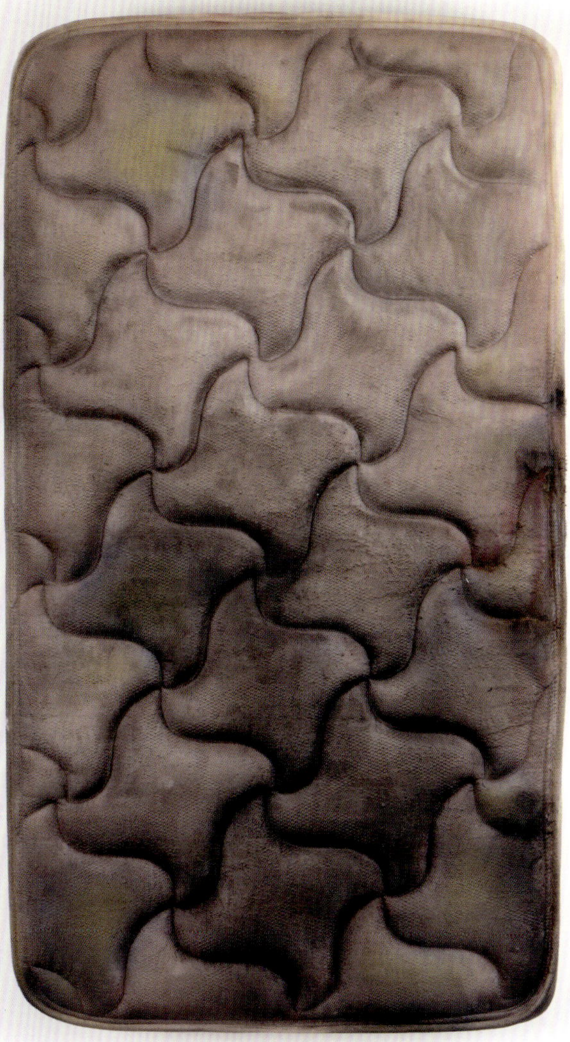

with this Gordon guy, I decided to utilize the apparatus he uses. I thought it would be two strangers running parallel lives, mirroring onto me.

MG: *What do you want to achieve with this mirroring onto yourself? What is the point?*
KU: I don't know what the point is. Being in the now. Trying to make works in the now. There was this weird moment when I heard that these images would come in every minute of my life. My artwork deals so much

with the past, with reflection and projection, that I am never living the present moment. Maybe this work, this physical work with mattresses, is the most present I have ever been.

MG: *So being in the now has become a very essential part of your work?*
KU: I had personal reasons too. I was very bedridden last year, I had breast cancer, but I'm fine now. My doctor said, "all kinds of women get this, don't think it's your negative, psychologically dirty project". But the bed took on its own meaning, without a doubt. I was forced to a restful space and I wanted to turn the bed into something that was playful and super-energetic. I couldn't ignore being a part of it.

MG: *You said the Larry project was intended as an on-going project. Could it stop at a certain moment in time?*
KU: When I was in art school and had just started the project, this great curator in LA asked me what my exit-strategy was. It must be important, I never got it out of my head. It became a drawing: "what is my exit strategy". And for a while it has become a source of debate with a few people, because somebody I was working with asked me when is this project over. Collectors are asking me that because they want to figure out whether I'm a one hit wonder or not. It's a very market-driven question, from one point of view.

MG: *Then what is your idea about the end of the project?*
KU: One curator said that I had to work on this for the rest of my life for it to be valid. Can you imagine? So I'm taking the middle road. I personally had this break where I got sick and I just physically just couldn't do my performances, which had been a source of many ideas. I liked the idea of secretly working on it, like where nobody gets to see it. I won't go back to making smoke-paintings or kiss-paintings, or silicon mattresses. They're done. But I did bury a few things on the side when I made this giant dirt-sculpture, which would be a nice thing to dig up in ten years. But not necessarily.

MG: *You were still in school ten years ago. What did you do before art academy?*
KU: I dropped out at so many art schools. I had a troublesome boyfriend and I was very motivated by my heart. I would move to New York and, all of a sudden, he would move to Indiana and I had to give up and take off. So it was very hard to hold a degree in this situation. I was working restaurants all the time, everywhere I moved to, and I was painting six days a week.

I painted constantly, so when I lived in Williamsburg, where all these great artists worked, I didn't know any of them. Finally, a good friend of mine graduated from Cal Arts and convinced me to get a degree there. Coincidently, I fell in love with somebody and moved to LA, so I was suddenly back. I applied to Cal Arts and they let me in as an undergraduate, which was embarrassing. I felt I was extremely knowledgeable but I didn't have any credits to be able to go higher. I was there for five years and I loved it. It made a huge difference for me, I knew exactly where my works was about.

MG: *How does it feel to be quite successful now, to have galleries and be visible in the institutional field?*
KU: I feel constantly blessed that I can make money doing my art. It's been hard work too. But success is not always fun. You have to have people helping you; otherwise you can't keep up with this market.

MG: *Do you have to produce more?*
KU: Absolutely. I like to touch everything so I need to micromanage these great, younger artists that work with me. It gets a little out of hand, because it starts to feel like a business. This year was the first time I had to ask myself the question, "what is it, what kind of studio do you want?" Yesterday I was here by myself and I loved it, but I couldn't move around my own sculptures. So I feel very privileged and I also feel the stress. It's a really interesting balancing act. I would like to keep things small.

DANH VO

May 2013

Marta Gnyp: *I'd like to start by discussing your artistic position through your work,* 02.02.1861, *since it contains many aspects of your* oeuvre. *It's a letter in French that the missionary, Théophane Vénard, wrote to his father from his prison cell in 1861, just before he was decapitated in Vietnam. Your own father, who apparently doesn't understand French, copies this letter in his beautiful handwriting every time a collector of your work orders it through your gallery. So, in a way, it is a limited edition that's only available up until the death of your father. We are confronted here with a creation of a historical myth – a culturally sophisticated French missionary who is prepared to die for true religion, being pitted against ruthless Asians who don't understand the culture that's been brought to them. A lot of your work explores these symbolic and cultural hierarchies, would you agree?*
Danh Vo: Well, I also see my work in a different way. Of course, these themes are always there, especially in art, where these possible relationships are visible, but for me it's such an important piece because it broke many rules.

MG: *Which rules?*
DV: I think it's successful because I collaborate with my father, who has nothing to do with the language of art; he engaged without understanding what or how he's communicating. It really functioned well because it managed to connect people through their differences.

MG: *The relationship between you and your father forms one of the very intriguing aspects of this work. On the one side, you often mention that you admire your father because of his courage. (Danh Vo and his family, along with 100 other Vietnamese, fled Vietnam in 1979 through a plan organized by his father. The boat was intercepted by a Danish tanker that brought the Vietnamese to Denmark, where Danh Vo grew up.) In one of your interviews, you even said that you regret that you lack his radicalism. On the other side though, you let the whole art world know that your father doesn't know what he writes, which is a kind of ignorance.*
DV: No, he just never learned French. I never learned French either.

1
Danh Vo
Good Life, 2007
12 vitrines, 12 black & white photographs, 2 color photographs, 1 photo camera, 1 letter, documents, installation detail, *Cultural boys*, 46 × 30 × 20 cm

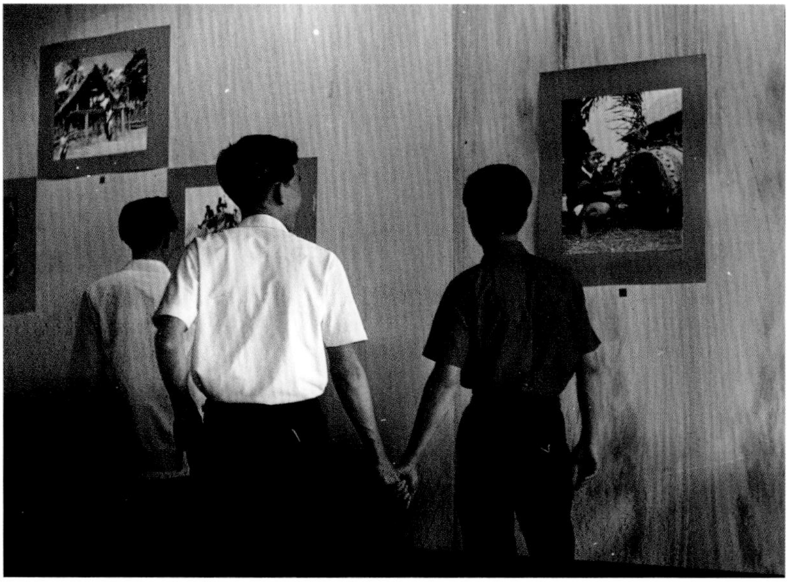

MG: *Don't you present him as an ignorant immigrant?*
DV: I wouldn't put it that way. There is more to it because I have a profound respect for my father. But like in everyone's relationship with one's father or parents, there is a love and hate relationship. They want us to do something with our lives and have a vision for us. My father never liked that I was becoming an artist. He wanted me to be an engineer. So, there is all this complexity in it and I think that's what makes the work compelling.

MG: *Is there a kind of personal revenge in the sense that you, as an artist, create work for him despite never having become an engineer?*
DV: Yeah, I never wanted to be an engineer.

MG: *What made you engage with your father for this project?*
DV: I always knew about my father's beautiful handwriting. What I was interested in, since my father never learned any kind of foreign language aside from Danish, is how the skill of writing that he learned in one place became a handicap in another place. Or put more precisely, it became a de-qualified skill. I've always thought these are very interesting elements of our society: what is it that decides what's valuable and what's not?

MG: *How did your father use his skills in the new place?*
DV: I saw all these examples of his writing when he had his burger shop. He loved writing the menus, like burgers and fries. More than this, my father cheated his taxes. He earned like 200 a day so he would come

home and rewrite the daily receipts. This was easy because he only made €200. When he retired, my sister got a sandwich shop where she would earn like twenty times more than he ever did. One day, he asked her, "Phuong, do you want me to do your daily receipts?" So he started rewriting her receipts, but since she earned twenty times more than he did when he worked, it took him a whole day to rewrite them. It became this totally crazy family business because he wanted my brother to take all the original receipts to his country house to burn them but my brother didn't want to participate. I wasn't living in Copenhagen at that time, so when I came back and discovered this situation, I had a fight with my brother because I didn't think it was about taxes; it was about our father having something he could do, that he was good at doing for over twenty-five years. My father managed to remain active with his skills. The work, *02.02.1861*, is related to that issue. It's about doing something that you're good at. That's what creates the identification and anticipation in any sort of social intervention.

MG: *This story of your father writing and rewriting the receipts makes the piece,* 02.02.1861, *even more personal.*
DV: Maybe it's personal but it's also about what you observe through your daily life. The piece wouldn't exist if I hadn't seen my father rewriting the receipts.

MG: *You then chose this letter by Vénard.*
DV: I don't think I searched actively for this letter. When I found the letter, everything made sense.

MG: *How did you discover it?*
DV: I found it while researching in the Foreign Mission Society. When I saw this letter, I was immediately convinced I could create this work.

MG: *It just happened to you.*
DV: Exactly. You discover something because you can see the potential in it.

MG: *Is this also a way in which you became an artist?*
DV: I don't think I decided that. I went to art school without a conscious conviction.

MG: *But before you went to art school, you decided you wanted to go to art school. So you felt that you did have a special capacity for making art.*
DV: A high school teacher said I had a good sense of color and form. When

you're fifteen years old and you're not so good at many other things, then somebody tells you that you're good at something, you go for it. I was making shitty paintings. I entered an art school and thought, "what am I doing here?" The first conscious choice was that I'm not going to live as an artist because I thought that was about painting colors and form. But, unconsciously, that was probably the first decision that made me an artist. Because you have to deal with all these crafts that are imposed on you, like whether it's form or color or something else.

MG: *I was under the impression that you had a very clear vision of what you wanted from your art, from the very beginning.*
DV: That isn't true. I have no clear idea of where to go. But that's the beauty of it. I think that must be the most boring thing: to know where you are heading.

MG: *When you finished at the academy, you started making work that had nothing to do with what you call "shitty paintings", but which somehow connected you to the world through objects and symbols, using your own life as a point of departure.*
DV: That comes from the idea that whatever you do, it should make sense to you, it should have a purpose for you; that is the first thing you have to trust.

MG: *How was art making sense to you? Was it a kind of personal investigation of your identity as a son of immigrants and as a gay man?*
DV: It was about things that had meaning for me. I've never had the idea that my art has to make sense to society. That is also the beauty of art – that you do what you think is important to you and that someone else might catch that; somebody that you don't know, somebody that has no relation to you but still connects to it. I think that's really beautiful.

MG: *It seems, from the very beginning of your artistic career, you chose projects that made you visible, like the marriage project, (since 2003, Danh Vo has been marrying and divorcing his friends and keeping his partner's official name as his own), to mention an example. This is something that has given you visibility as an artist.*
DV: I must say, I never really thought about it. Maybe I don't remember well enough, but I don't think I ever thought about it. There was a certain degree of provocation in my works but I never thought people would see the work and understand it.

MG: *Is there a work of art you produced which has been especially important to you as an artist?*

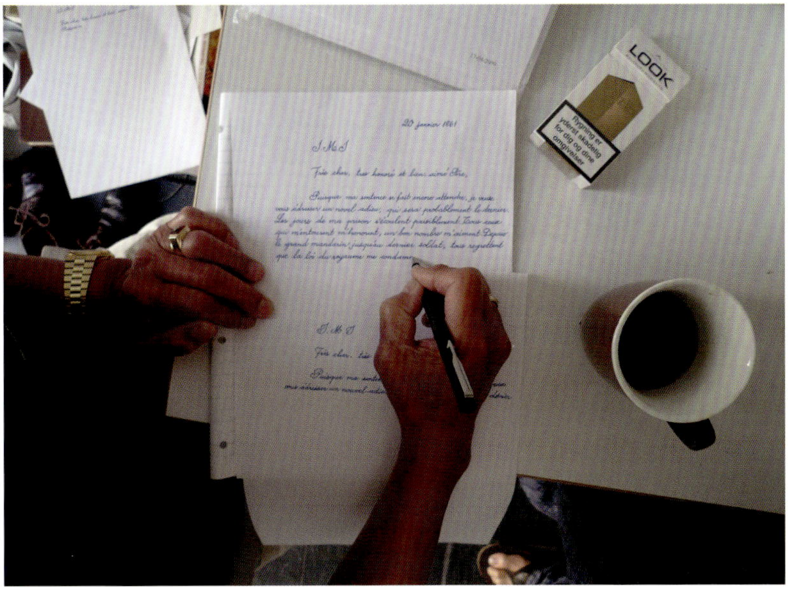

2
Danh Vo
2.2.1861, 2009
Ink on A4 paper,
29.7 × 21 cm

DV: If I had to mention a work that really changed my perception of things, it would probably be my grandmother's refrigerator, TV, and crucifix, (*Oma Totem*), because I never anticipated that people would be able to relate to such a thing. It was just a fridge and a crucifix. Objects that all of us are related to personally, but also objects that have the possibility of meaning something else. But meaning something else was something I couldn't fully understand. The objects were coming from my grandmother, who I obviously know, but the life she had lived is so estranged to me. I can observe it and see it from a distance, but to really understand such a life is impossible.

MG: *But, on the other hand, it functions perfectly on the symbolic level as something universal.*
DV: We could all connect to it, but at the same time, I think there are also profound differences that lie in each individual. That's something that was important to my thinking.

MG: *What about the project,* We the People, *you later made, or your new show,* Mother Tongue, *in New York which presented objects once owned by the US Secretary of Defense, Robert S. McNamara, that you bought at an auction? Are they based on the same logic?*
DV: I think *We the People* was triggered by other motivations. I was labeled as an artist who works with personal issues, which I personally have never thought of that much; there were some works that referred to my private

3
Danh Vo
Oma Totem, 2009
Phillips television set, Gorenje washing machine, Bomann refrigerator, wooden crucifix and personal casino entrance card, 220 × 60 × 60 cm

sphere but I think most of the objects I'm using are familiar to anybody. Still, I wanted to make work that has nothing to do with my private life.

MG: *For* We the People, *you remade, in fragments, one of the most important western symbols – the Statue of Liberty. You used copper, a very expensive material, and you employed Chinese workers to make it. This is really a serious undertaking. Are you ever afraid of failure?*
DV: Of course, this project was nerve-racking.

MG: *Why do you think this project was so successful among collectors? Everyone wants to have a piece of your* Statue of Liberty.
DV: That's difficult for me to answer. I did that project because it was a way of not referring to myself. There were many references to my work, involved with marginalized groups, and I hate being put in a box. I always tried to work against things. It's important for any production that we work with contradictions. So, I wanted to do something that was "too much' and too big. And I did it. It's only from previous experiences that you know what you want. So I still see it as a very conceptual idea and an empirical process.

MG: *Do you make anything yourself with your hands? Creating the idea is essential, but, do you physically produce anything yourself?*
DV: No. I should do what I'm good at. I don't think it's so important whether I produce it myself or not. If I were good at it, I'd love to do it myself.

MG: *Would you agree that having the commercial success that you now have has always been a part of your work?*
DV: I think it should be. It is very easy to sit in the corner complaining because you don't participate in it. I have seen too many of these people. I could sit there and say that I'm not interested in commercial success, but how should we know unless we participate in this situation? We need to achieve different positions in order to understand what we really want with our lives.

MG: *Would you love to be a very rich artist?*
DV: I would like to try it for sure.

MG: *Do you have a special relationship with collectors? I'm under the impression that, through your work, you give them the idea or the feeling that they can understand something about the complexity of the post-colonial geopolitical situation and maybe about the personal and social complexity*

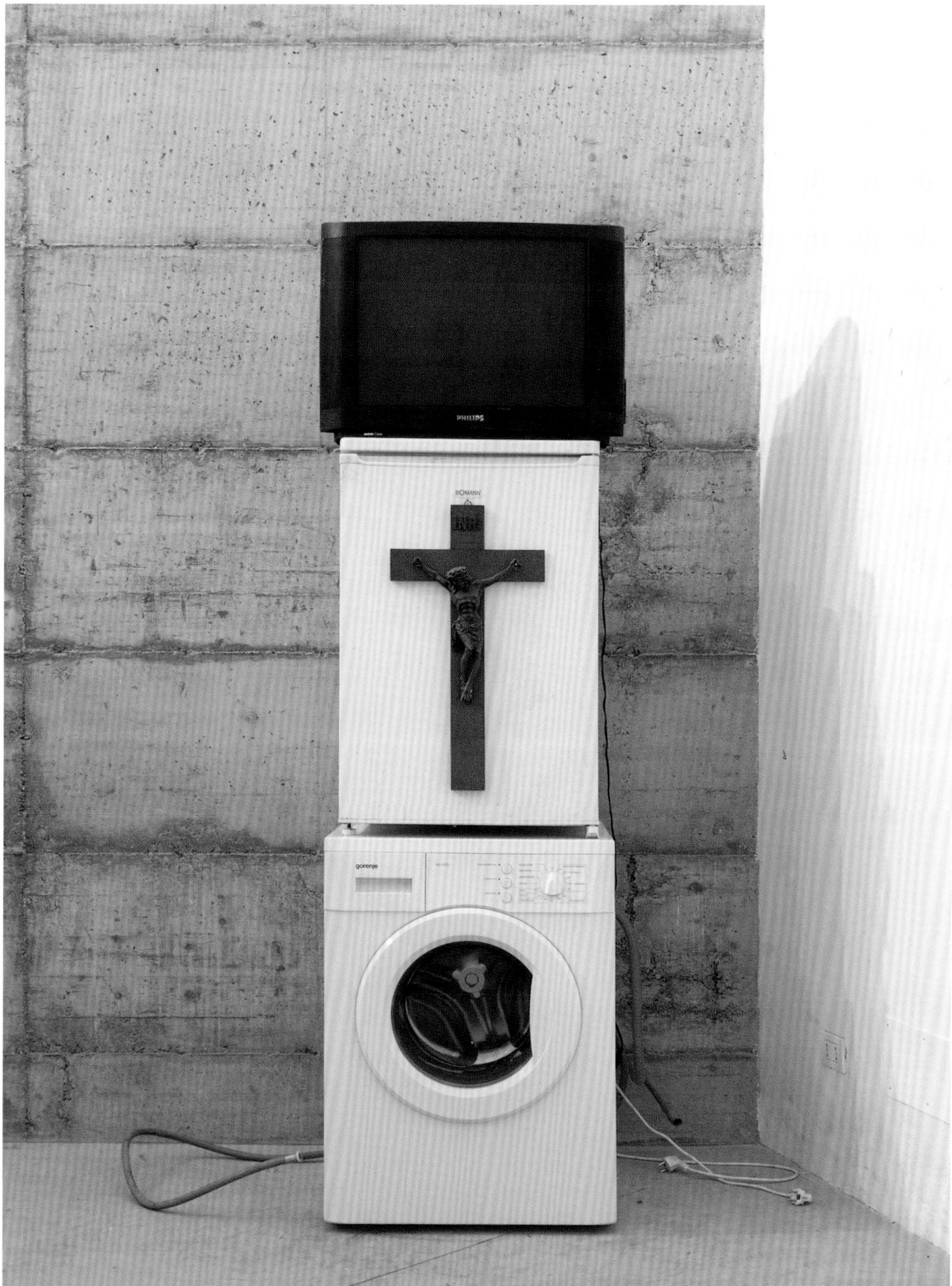
PHILIPS
BOMANN
gorenje

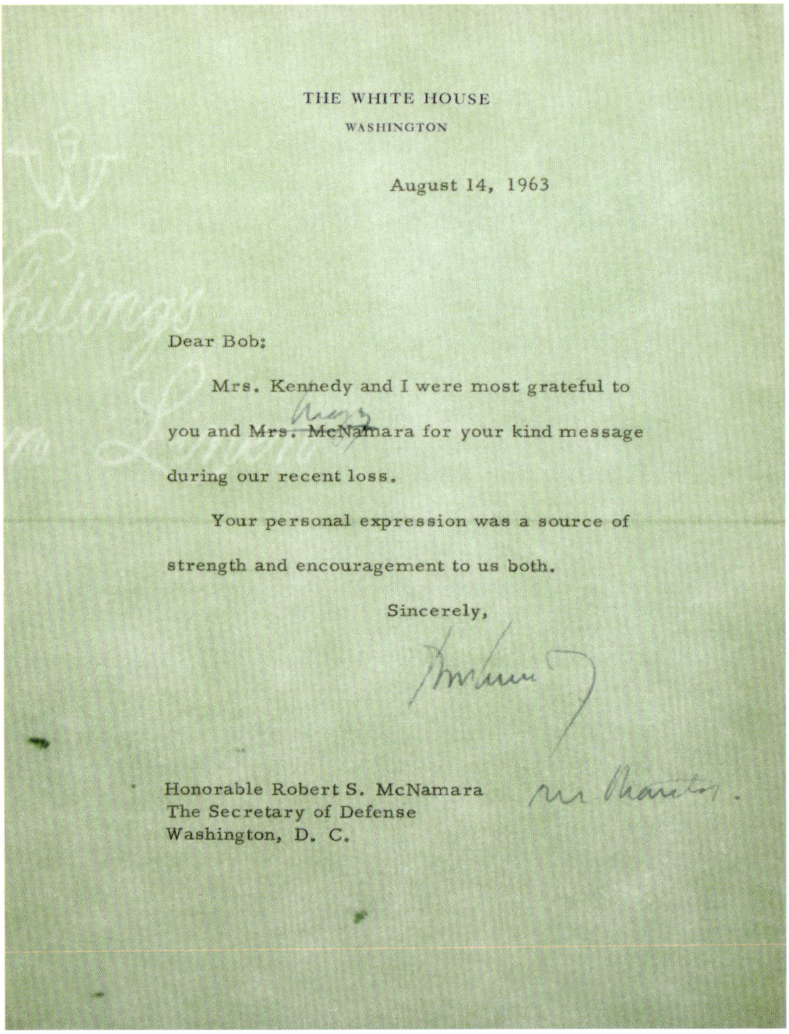

THE WHITE HOUSE
WASHINGTON

August 14, 1963

Dear Bob:

Mrs. Kennedy and I were most grateful to you and Mrs. McNamara for your kind message during our recent loss.

Your personal expression was a source of strength and encouragement to us both.

Sincerely,

Honorable Robert S. McNamara
The Secretary of Defense
Washington, D. C.

4
Danh Vo
Lot 17. Kennedy, John F., as Thirty-fifth President, 2013
Ink on paper,
22.54 × 17.15 cm

of immigrants and minor groups. You maybe even manipulate the viewers by offering them the illusion of an understanding of complex social issues.
DV: I don't believe artists should be a kind of Salvation Army. I don't want to change peoples' lives. I think it's beautiful if people engage in a dialogue and whatever I'm doing is an attempt to engage people in a dialogue. Whether it's students, colleagues, anyone who comes in to take a picture or collectors, there are amazing, intelligent people; there are also stupid ones. I just don't see the world as a uniform thing. There are so many perspectives with which you engage one way or the other.

MG: *I saw the images of your last show,* Mother Tongue, *in New York. What is your native language?*

DV: It's Danish. My first mother tongue was Vietnamese, until I was four. But then, I started kindergarten and started speaking Danish, so, my Vietnamese stayed at the level of a four-year old.

MG: *So what do you speak with your father and your family?*
DV: I speak a little Vietnamese. If I speak it regularly I can do it. I don't speak with my parents that often. It just gets worse and worse.

MG: *Going back to your* Mother Tongue *exhibition, I was amazed how you managed to beautifully fetishize the historical objects of McNamara and J.F.K.; your interventions worked really well on the formal level, but also on the level of providing meaning. The objects, which you dismembered, like the chairs, looked extraordinary on the wall. Would you say you have a feeling for beauty?*
DV: Chippendale chairs are the most unsexy chairs you could imagine. You just have to do something with them.

MG: *How did this idea cross your mind?*
DV: Things happen that you just couldn't imagine. Like the fact that those objects owned by McNamara went into the auction. It's a coincidence that they escaped the presidential library unlike most of his other belongings. These things fall into your lap and then you have to grab your chance and engage with them. If the auction happened five years ago, I wouldn't have had the financial capacity to buy them. There were always these elements in my life that made works possible – something you cannot foresee. The same happened with black-and-white photos of Joe Carier. He took pictures of men holding hands while he was working in Vietnam, between 1962 and 1973. He was gay and he himself was a part of the gay scene there. I met him when I was resident in the US. He was clearly flirting with me. He's like eighty-something, and if I had been five years younger at that time, I would've thought it was disgusting; I would've been offended by it. But, at the time it happened, I thought it was really interesting that he was flirting with me while he was talking about his work in Vietnam during the whole war period. I didn't construct the idea that, for my work, I'd need an American soldier who worked in Vietnam for all these years and have all these stories. It happened.

MG: *You were extremely lucky.*
DV: I think so. I also think that, because I have an open eye for these kinds of things, I give them a possibility of happening. He asked me if I wanted to come to Vietnam with him, if I wanted to see Vietnam again. And I said, why not? So we traveled to Vietnam together. It was only in

Vietnam that I found out he had these photos, because in Vietnam, we saw those guys holding hands and he would say, when he saw that for the first time in 1962, he was so shocked that he couldn't help taking photos of them. I asked, what do you mean? Did you take paparazzi photos during the war? And he said, "yeah, they're all in my basement somewhere". So I traveled back to the US and we then cleaned out his basement and found all these photographs.

MG: *Hard to believe...*
DV: Yes. Life has all these amazing things. One should observe these things. Make use of them when they're there.

MG: *Well, on the one hand, you observe, on the other you are doing a lot yourself. For example, your marriage project – you really started doing it, not just observing. And maybe, one thing led to another thing. By the way, speaking about this marriage project, are you still doing it?*
DV: No, I stopped it. It was an important project because you had all these different bureaucratic institutions attempting to define you through papers. It helped me very much to not take these kind of papers very seriously.

MG: *What about your future projects? Do you have another big venture in mind?*
DV: With *We the People*, I got a sense of what it means to make it and it was good to test myself out. I'm not making a project of this scale anymore; it was a good experience, but it was not the way I want to live my life.

Photo credits
p. 28: courtesy Paula Cooper Gallery. Art © Andre/SIAE, 2018
pp. 33, 36, 29, 43: photo Peter Cox. Courtesy Zeno X Gallery, Antwerp
pp. 46, 47, 51, 52, 55: © Mark Bradford. Courtesy the artist and Hauser & Wirth. Photo Joshua White
pp. 58, 61: photo Glenn Brown Studio
p. 63: photo Mike Bruce
p. 67: photo Lucy Dawkins
pp. 72, 75: © Mary Corse
pp. 73, 76: © Mary Corse. Photo Flying Studio
pp. 80, 85, 88: © Tate, London 2018
pp. 93, 94, 97, 101: courtesy Magdalena Shummer-Fangor
pp. 106, 109, 110: courtesy the Walton Ford and Paul Kasmin Gallery
p. 115: courtesy Walton Ford and Paul Kasmin Gallery. Photo Christopher Stach
pp.120, 123, 124, 129, 130: courtesy Adrian Ghenie
p. 137: © Mark Grotjahn. Courtesy the artist. Photo Joshua White
pp. 140, 141, 144: © Mark Grotjahn. Courtesy the artist. Photo Douglas M. Parker Studio
pp. 150, 156, 161: photo Prudence Cuming Associates Ltd
p. 153: photo Roger Wooldridge
pp. 166, 167, 171: courtesy William Kentridge
p. 174: photo Ruth Walz, Salzburg
pp. 178, 181 and cover: courtesy Robert Longo and Metro Pictures, New York
pp. 184, 189: courtesy Robert Longo
pp. 193, 194, 199, 202: © Sarah Lucas. Courtesy Sadie Coles HQ, London
pp. 207, 208, 213, 216: photo Larry Barns. © Shirin Neshat. Courtesy the artist and Gladstone Gallery, New York and Brussels
p. 220: courtesy Wang Guangyi
p. 225: © Anish Kapoor. All Rights Reserved, DACS 2018. Photo Dave Morgan
p. 226: courtesy Pace Gallery, Beijing
p. 231: courtesy EIGEN+ART, Berlin/Leipzig
p. 239: © Matteo De Fina
pp. 251, 252, 257, 259: courtesy Sean Scully
pp. 264, 266, 268, 269: courtesy the artist and Levy Gorvy Gallery
pp. 273, 274, 275: © Kaari Upson. Courtesy the artist and Sprüth Magers
p. 277: © Kaari Upson. Courtesy the artist and Sprüth Magers. Photo KITMIN Lee
p. 279: © Kaari Upson. Courtesy the artist and Sprüth Magers. Photo Joshua White
pp. 284, 290: courtesy Dahn Vo
p. 287: courtesy Dahn Vo. Photo Danh Vo
p. 289: courtesy Dahn Vo. Photo Jacopo Menzani